The Meanings of things

THE MEANINGS OF THINGS

TITLES OF RELATED INTEREST

Animals into art
H. Morphy (ed.)

Archaeological approaches to cultural identity
S. J. Shennan (ed.)

Archaeological heritage management in the modern world
H. F. Cleere (ed.)

Centre and periphery: comparative studies in archaeology
T. C. Champion (ed.)

Chalcolithic, Bronze and Iron Age cultures in South Asia
M. Lal (ed.)

Conflict in the archaeology of living traditions
R. Layton (ed.)

Domination and resistance
D. Miller *et al.* (eds)

The excluded past: archaeology in education
P. Stone & R. MacKenzie (eds)

Food, metals and towns in African history: African adaptations in subsistence and technology
T. Shaw *et al.* (eds)

Foraging and farming: the evolution of plant exploitation
D. Harris & G. Hillman (eds)

From the Baltic to the Black Sea: studies in medieval archaeology
L. Alcock & D. Austin (eds)

Global record: semi-arid regions
C. Gamble & O. Soffer (eds)

Global record: temperate latitudes
O. Soffer & C. Gamble (eds)

Hominid evolution, behaviour and dispersal
M. H. Day *et al.* (eds)

Hunters of the recent past
L. Davis & B. Reeves (eds)

Pleistocene perspective: innovation, adaptation and human survival
A. M. ApSimon & S. Joyce (eds)

The politics of the past
P. Gathercole & D. Lowenthal (eds)

Signifying animals: human meaning in the natural world
R. Willis (ed.)

State and society: the emergence and development of social hierarchy and political centralization
J. Gledhill *et al.* (eds)

The walking larder: patterns of domestication, pastoralism, and predation
J. Clutton-Brock (ed.)

What is an animal?
T. Ingold (ed.)

What's new? A closer look at the process of innovation
S. Van der Leeuw & R. Torrence (eds)

Who needs the past? Indigenous values and archaeology
R. Layton (ed.)

THE MEANINGS OF THINGS

Material culture and symbolic expression

Edited by Ian Hodder

Department of Archaeology, University of Cambridge

London
UNWIN HYMAN
Boston Sydney Wellington

Published by the Academic Division of
Unwin Hyman Ltd
15/17 Broadwick Street, London W1V 1FP, UK

Unwin Hyman Inc.,
8 Winchester Place, Winchester, Mass. 01890, USA

Allen & Unwin (Australia) Ltd,
8 Napier Street, North Sydney, NSW 2060, Australia

Allen & Unwin (New Zealand) Ltd in association with the
Port Nicholson Press Ltd, 60 Cambridge Terrace, Wellington,
New Zealand

First published in 1989

British Library Cataloguing in Publication Data
The meanings of things: material culture
and symbolic expression. — (One world
archaeology, v. 6).
1. Archaeology
I. Hodder, Ian II. Series
930.1

ISBN 0-04-445017-6

Library of Congress Cataloging in Publication Data
The Meanings of things: material culture and symbolic
expression
edited by Ian Hodder.
p. cm. — (One world archaeology; 6)
Discussions from the World Archaeological Congress
held in Southampton, England, Sept. 1986.
Bibliography: p.
Includes index.
ISBN 0-04-445017-6
1. Social archaeology—Congresses. 2. Ethnoarchaeology—
Congresses. 3. Material culture—Congresses. 4. Symbolism—
Congresses. I. Hodder, Ian. II. World Archaeological Congress
(1986: Southampton, England) III. Series.
CC72.4.M43 1988
930.1—dc19 88-17663 CIP

Typeset in 10 on 11 point Bembo by
BookEns, Saffron Walden, Essex
and printed in Great Britain at the
University Press, Cambridge

List of contributors

D. K. Bhattacharya, Department of Anthropology, University of Delhi, India.
Cristina Biaggi, Independent Researcher, New York, USA.
Lucy Jayne Botscharow, Department of Anthropology, Northeastern Illinois University, USA.
Felipe Criado, Departamento de Historia, Facultad de Geografia e Historia, Santiago, Spain.
Whitney Davis, Department of Art History, Northwestern University, Evanston, Illinois, USA.
Roland Fletcher, Department of Anthropology, University of Sydney, NSW, Australia.
Robert L. Hall, Department of Anthropology, University of Illinois at Chicago, USA.
Ian R. Hodder, Department of Archaeology, University of Cambridge, UK.
L. Carless Hulin, Institute of Archaeology, University College London, UK.
Aneesa Kassam, Department of Literature, University of Nairobi, Kenya.
Else Johansen Kleppe, Arkeologisk Museum i Stavanger, Bergen, Norway.
Zbigniew Kobyliński, Instytut Historii Kultury Materialnei PAN, Warsaw, Poland.
Gerhard Kubik, Institute of Ethnology, University of Vienna, Austria.
Robert Layton, Department of Anthropology, University of Durham, UK.
Pierre Lemonnier, Centre National de la Recherche Scientifique, Paris, France.
Ana Maria Llamazares, Consejo Nacional de Investigaciones Cientificas y Tecnologicas, Buenos Aires, Argentina.
Theodore Mawe, Prehistory Department, National Museum, Port Moresby, Papua New Guinea.
Gemetchu Megersa, Department of Anthropology, United States International University, Nairobi, Kenya.
E. M. Melas, Department of Archaeology, University of Thessaloniki, Greece.
Angeliki Pilali-Paspasteriou, Department of Archaeology, University of Thessaloniki, Greece.
Miles Richardson, Department of Geography and Anthropology, Louisiana State University, Baton Rouge, USA.
Clinton R. Sanders, The Department of Sociology, University of Connecticut, Storrs, USA.
K. Teague, Horniman Museum & Library, London, UK.
Christopher Tilley, Trinity Hall, University of Cambridge, UK.
Polly Wiessner, Max-Planck Institute, Seewiesen, West Germany.
Timothy Yates, Department of Archaeology, University of Cambridge, UK.

Foreword

This book is one of a major series of more than 20 volumes resulting from the World Archaeological Congress held in Southampton, England, in September 1986. The series reflects the enormous academic impact of the Congress, which was attended by 850 people from more than 70 countries, and attracted many additional contributions from others who were unable to attend in person.

The *One World Archaeology* series is the result of a determined and highly successful attempt to bring together for the first time not only archaeologists and anthropologists from many different parts of the world, as well as academics from a host of contingent disciplines, but also non-academics from a wide range of cultural backgrounds, who could lend their own expertise to the discussions at the Congress. Many of the latter, accustomed to being treated as the 'subjects' of archaeological and anthropological observation, had never before been admitted as equal participants in the discussion of their own (cultural) past or present, with their own particularly vital contribution to make towards global, cross-cultural understanding.

The Congress therefore really addressed world archaeology in its widest sense. Central to a world archaeological approach is the investigation not only of how people lived in the past but also of how, and why, changes took place resulting in the forms of society and culture which exist today. Contrary to popular belief, and the archaeology of some 20 years ago, world archaeology is much more than the mere recording of specific historical events, embracing as it does the study of social and cultural change in its entirety. All the books in the *One World Archaeology* series are the result of meetings and discussions which took place within a context that encouraged a feeling of self-criticism and humility in the participants about their own interpretations and concepts of the past. Many participants experienced a new self-awareness, as well as a degree of awe about past and present human endeavours, all of which is reflected in this unique series.

The Congress was organized around major themes. Several of these themes were based on the discussion of full-length papers which had been circulated some months previously to all who had indicated a special interest in them. Other sessions, including some dealing with areas of specialization defined by period or geographical region, were based on oral addresses, or a combination of precirculated papers and lectures. In all cases, the entire sessions were recorded on cassette, and all contributors were presented with the recordings of the discussion of their papers. A major part of the thinking behind the Congress was that a meeting of many hundreds of participants that did not leave behind a published record of its academic discussions would be little more than an exercise in tourism.

Thus, from the very beginning of the detailed planning for the World Archaeological Congress, in 1982, the intention was to produce post-Congress books containing a selection only of the contributions, revised in the light of discussions during the sessions themselves as well as during subsequent consultations with the academic editors appointed for each book. From the outset, contributors to the Congress knew that if their papers were selected for publication, they would have only a few months to revise them according to editorial specifications, and that they would become authors in an important academic volume scheduled to appear within a reasonable period following the Southampton meeting.

The publication of the series reflects the intense planning which took place before the Congress. Not only were all contributors aware of the subsequent production schedules, but also session organizers were already planning their books before and during the Congress. The editors were entitled to commission additional chapters for their books when they felt that there were significant gaps in the coverage of a topic during the Congress, or where discussion at the Congress indicated a need for additional contributions.

One of the main themes of the Congress was devoted to 'Archaeological "Objectivity" in Interpretation', where consideration of the precirculated full-length papers on this theme extended over four and a half days of academic discussion. The particular sessions on 'Archaeological "Objectivity" in Interpretation' were under my overall control, the main aim being to focus attention on the way that evidence of the past – including archaeological evidence – has been used and viewed by particular groups (whether local, regional or national) at different times. Essential to this aim was the exploration of the reasons why particular interpretations might have been chosen, or favoured, by individual societies and traditions at specific points in their development, or at certain stages in their activities. The whole theme atttempted, therefore, a unique mix of critical assessment of the basis of archaeological methodology with critical awareness of the social contexts of the use (and possible manipulation) of the evidence of the past.

Central to this re-evaluation of the strengths and weaknesses of archaeological approaches to the interpretation, and indeed 'display', of the past – whether through academic articles or by means of formal or informal curricula, or through museums or site presentation – is an assessment of the methodologies and approaches to the significance of material culture. This has long been a core issue in archaeological discussion, but it badly needed re-examination. Throughout the history of archaeology as a discipline material culture, or at least the repetitive association of distinctive material culture objects, has been taken to reflect activities of specific social groups or 'societies' whose physical movements across a geographic stage have often been postulated on the basis of the distribution patterns of such objects, and whose supposed physical or ethnic identity (see also *State and society*, edited by J. Gledhill, B. Bender & M. T. Larsen) has often been assumed to correlate with such artefactual groupings. More recently archaeologists have been forced to recognize, often through lessons gained from ethnography, that a distinctive material culture complex may represent the activities of a vast variety of social groupings and subgroups, and that archaeological classification may often serve to camouflage the more subtle messages of style and technique (see also *Animals into art*, edited by H. Morphy, and *Domination and resistance*, edited by D. Miller, M. J. Rowlands & C. Tilley) which probably symbolize complex patterns of behaviour, as well as individual aspirations – within any society.

If the very basis of the equation between a material culture complex and a social grouping is ambiguous, then much of archaeological interpretation must remain subjective, even at this fundamental level of its operations. Whenever the archaeological data of material culture is presented in museums, on sites, in literature, in schools or in textbooks, as the evidence for the activities of 'races', 'peoples', 'tribes', 'linguistic groups' or other socially derived ethnic amalgamations, there should be at least scepticism if not downright suspicion. In a large number of such cases, what we are witnessing is the none-too-subtle ascription of racial/cultural stereotypes to static material culture items.

The overall theme therefore took as its starting point the proposition that archaeological interpretation is a subjective matter. It also assumed that to regard archaeology as somehow constituting the only legitimate 'scientific' approach to the past needed re-examination and possibly even rejection. A narrow parochial approach to the past which simply assumes that a linear chronology based on a 'verifiable' set of 'meaningful' 'absolute' dates is the only way to tackle the recording of, and the only way to comprehend, the past completely ignores the complexity of many literate and of many non-literate 'civilizations' and cultures. However, a world archaeological approach to a concept such as 'the past' focuses attention on precisely those features of archaeological enquiry and method which archaeologists all too often take for granted, without questioning the related assumptions.

Discussions on this theme during the Congress were grouped around seven headings, and have led to the publication of five books. The first subtheme, organised by Stephen Shennan, Department of Archaeology, University of Southampton, which lasted for almost a day, was concerned with 'Multiculturalism and Ethnicity in Archaeological Interpretation' and the second, under the control of Ian Hodder, Department of Archaeology, University of Cambridge, which occupied more than a day, was on 'Material Culture and Symbolic Expression'. The fourth subtheme, 'The Politics of the Past: Museums, Media, and other Presentations of Archaeology', was organized by Peter Gathercole of Darwin College, Cambridge, and also lasted for more than a day. Each of these subthemes has led to a separate book: *Archaeological approaches to cultural identity* (edited by S. J. Shennan), this book, and *The politics of the past* (edited by P. Gathercole & D. Lowenthal, of the Department of Geography, University College London). The fifth subtheme, on 'The Past in Education' was organized by Robert MacKenzie, of the Central Training Department, National Association of Citizens Advice Bureaux, and discussion of this topic (which lasted formally for half a day at the Congress and informally throughout the week by means of displays and educational events) has been expanded into the book *The excluded past*, under the editorship of Peter Stone (of English

Heritage) and R. Mackenzie. David Bellos of the Department of French, University of Manchester, was responsible for a short discussion session on the sixth subtheme 'Mediations of the Past in Modern Europe', and contributions from this subtheme have been combined either with those from the third on 'Contemporary Claims about Stonehenge' (a short discussion session organised by Christopher Chippindale, of the Department of Archaeology, University of Cambridge), or with those from the seventh subtheme on 'Indigenous Perceptions of the Past' which lasted for almost a day. Robert Layton of the Department of Anthropology, University of Durham, was in charge of this seventh topic and has also edited the two resulting books, *Who needs the past?* and *Conflict in the archaeology of living traditions*. The latter also incorporates several contributions from a one-day discussion on 'Material Culture and the Making of the Modern United States: Views from Native America', which had been organized by Russell Handsman of the American Indian Archaeological Institute, Washington, and Randall McGuire of the Department of Anthropology of the State University of New York at Binghamton.

The whole of the 'Archaeological "Objectivity" in Interpretation' theme had been planned as the progressive development of an idea and the dividing of it into subthemes was undertaken in the full knowledge that there would be considerable overlap between them. It was accepted that it would, in many ways, be impossible, and even counter-productive, to split for example, education from site presentation, or literary presentations of the past from indigenous history. In the event, each of the books resulting from this overall theme has its own coherence, they also share a concern to make explicit the responsibility of recognizing the various ways of interpreting humanly created artefacts. In addition they recognize the social responsibility of archaeological interpretation, and the way that this may be used, consciously or unconsciously, by others for their own ends. The contributions in these books, directly or indirectly, explicitly or implicitly, epitomise the view that modern archaeology must recognize and confront its new role, which is to address the wider community. It must do this with a sophisticated awareness of the strengths and the weaknesses of its own methodologies and practices.

A world archaeological approach to archaeology as a 'discipline' reveals how subjective archaeological interpretation has always been. It also demonstrates the importance that all rulers and leaders (politicians) have placed on the legitimization of their positions through the 'evidence' of the past. Objectivity is strikingly absent from most archaeological exercises in interpretation. In some cases there has been conscious manipulation of the past for national political ends (as in the case of Ian Smith's Rhodesian regime over Great Zimbabwe, or that of the Nazis with their racist use of archaeology). But, apart from this, archaeologists themselves have been influenced in their interpretation by the received wisdom of their times, both in the sort of classificatory schemes which they consider appropriate to their subject, and in the way that their dating of materials is affected by their assumptions about the capabilities of the humans concerned. Nowhere is archaeological explanation immune to changes in interpretative fashion. This is as true of Britain as of anywhere else – Stonehenge especially has been subjected to the most bizarre collection of interpretations over the years, including all sorts of references to it having been constructed by Mycenaeans and Phoenicians. Although, at first sight, it is tempting to assume that such contentions are different from attempts by politicians to claim that the extraordinary site of Great Zimbabwe was constructed by Phoenicians using black slaves, the difference is not very easy to sustain.

Realization of the flexibility and variety of past human endeavour all over the world directs attention back to those questions that are at the very basis of archaeological interpretation. How can static material culture objects be equated with dynamic human cultures? How can we define and recognize the 'styles' of human activity, as well as their possible implications? In some contexts these questions assume immense political importance. For example, the archaeological 'evidence' of cultural continuity, as opposed to discontinuity, may make all the difference to an indigenous land claim, the right of access to a site/region, or the disposal of a human skeleton to a museum, as against its reburial.

All these factors lead in turn to a new consideration of how different societies choose to display their museum collections and conserve their sites. As the debates about who should be allowed to use Stonehenge, and how it should be displayed, make clear, objects or places may be considered important at one time and 'not worth bothering about' at others. Who makes these decisions and in what contexts? Who is responsible, and why, for what is taught about the past in schools or in adult education? Is such education based on a narrow local/regional/national framework of archaeology and history, or is it oriented towards multiculturalism and the variety of human cultural experiences in a world-wide context? What should the implications be for the future of archaeology?

In this book Ian Hodder and his contributors concentrate on one aspect of these questions, the varying roles and functions which material culture may play within a particular culture or cultures. The central concepts involved in these questions were reflected in the titles of the discussion sessions at the Congress. The first, on 'The Meaning, Structure and Transmission of Style', drew attention to one of the core assumptions of much modern archaeology, namely that the 'style' of an object (or work of art) is itself an expressive device which – whether consciously or unconsciously – gives off messages to its users or beholders (and see *Animals into art*, edited by H. Morphy). The second, 'Social Dimensions of Symbolic Meanings', emphasized the culture-specific 'meaning' of much of the symbolism employed by a particular society and also examined the way in which certain areas of social behaviour are especially well suited to the use of expressive symbolism. This was particularly evident in the third discussion session, 'Ritual and Burial', where emotion, the transmission of social messages, and the changing of social status are often intermingled in complex symbolic expressions. The last discussion session, on 'Spatial Meanings' demonstrated that patterning occurs not only in the manufacture and design of material culture objects and works of art, but also in such human activities as the laying out of a town or village, or in the use of space within a compound or dwelling place.

The meanings of things contains 25 chapters by authors from Africa, Australia and Papua New Guinea, India, South America, the USA, and from both Eastern and Western Europe. This variety of views and experience has produced a unique and fascinating account of the ways that material cultures can be, and have likely been in the past, incorporated into almost all aspects of the social fabric. Several of the authors focus on essential points of principle and methodology which must be carefully considered before any particular approach to material culture can be adopted.

One of the many fundamental questions which are posed in this book is whether or not all material culture, from whatever culture, can be assumed to be 'documents' of a kind which can be read or decoded by the outside observer. If so, what is the nature of any such 'messages' and 'meanings' which are conveyed in such 'documents'? Another fascinating question concerns the extent to which acceptance, and subsequent diffusion, of a religious belief or symbol may be qualified by the status of the individuals concerned in the transmission of the innovation, as well as by the social stratification of the society concerned (and see *What's new?*, edited by S. Van der Leeuw & R. Torrence). Not surprisingly, in view of the nature of material culture and the ongoing debates about 'style', several authors are concerned with what we call works of art, and the most effective means of reaching an understanding of their past significance (and see *Animals into art*, edited by H. Morphy, and *Archaeological approaches to cultural identity*, edited by S. J. Shennan). In several of the contributions, from different parts of the world, it is semiotics which is seen to be the most appropriate technique to apply to the decoding of the assumed rules and grammars of material culture expression. The variety of examples in this book makes it clear that there is no single dimension to such cultural expression. Material culture may convey its 'meaning(s)' in a wide diversity of ways, and these 'meanings' are culture-specific at least to the extent that they depend on the particular historic developments of the culture concerned. It is clear that it would be as over-simplistic to merely assume a clear correlation between a material culture 'style' and ethnicity (and see *Archaeological approaches to cultural identity*, edited by S. J. Shennan) as it would be to assume that the very similar art styles of the Dali and Tikari of the Cameroon reflected similar histories (and see Nwana in Ch. 15 of *Who needs the past?*, edited by R. Layton). It is clear, however, that for individuals within a particular society, one important function of variations in material culture in the society concerned is as a (conscious or unconscious) means of differentiating themselves from others of different age or sex or status or subgroup; or as a (conscious or unconscious) means of identifying themselves with those of the same age, sex, status or group. Whatever the details of any particular example, *The meanings of things* seems to bear out one of my main conclusions (Ucko 1969, p. 30), that the successful analysis of the material culture, of whatever date, must be undertaken at various different levels to correspond both to the intentional use of objects for specific ends, and to the level of whatever reality it is which is incorporated in morphological continuities and discontinuities. Many of the chapters of this book add considerable depth to the nature of the archaeological debate about how best the evidence of material culture can, and should, be tackled. The book also does much more for, as the Editor says (in Ch. 1, p. 64), it demonstrates clearly that 'however much we think that we understand a past culture, that understanding always has its own context in the present', a present context which, it is claimed, is bound to be in some sense political.

One of the main aims of the World Archaeological Congress had been to provide a forum in which both archaeologists from any part of the world, and non-professionals from all kinds of backgrounds with a genuine interest in the past, would be able to come together *as equals* to discuss themes of general interest (and see Ucko 1987). In *The meanings of things* Ian Hodder has chosen to develop this aim in a striking way. In adopting a 'random' approach to the ordering of chapters he is aware that he risks the accusation of editorial neglect, and of a resulting lack of coherence in the book. As Series Editor, I have considered these possible criticisms and dismissed them. Despite the fact that I personally much prefer the Editor's alternative book scheme, as proposed in Chapter 1 (p. 76) to the random one that he has in practice adopted here, despite the fact that I personally believe that the 'Material Culture and Symbolic Expression' sessions of the Congress had much more coherence to them than Hodder apparently does, and despite the fact that I personally agree with Tilley who writes in this book (Ch. 14, p. 185) that 'post-structuralism is characteristically a term not amenable to any rigid definition. . . It is simply a term applied to work without any unitary core that is temporarily removed from a structuralist position', I have nevertheless accepted the form of *The meanings of things* as appropriate for the *One World Archaeology* series. I have four main reasons for having done so: (a) I have found great joy in reading this book in the 'random' order presented by Hodder, gaining real pleasure from the riches which almost all chapters contain, and making my own continuing and retrospective discoveries and connections between them. In this respect, Hodder has succeeded, though this success may to some extent be the result of the exercise of his editorial 'power' base in the exclusion of some of the original contributions, and by the inclusion of some new ones. I have also gained pleasure in comparing my male, western, academic reactions to the chapters with Hodder's own (also male and western) academic scheme (in Ch. 1, p. 76). (b) In September 1987 I received a letter (printed in full in the *World Archaeological Bulletin 2*) from Dr Jawaharlal Handoo of the Folklore Unit, Central Institute of Indian Languages, Mysore, India, which made the point that although the 'World Archaeological Congress has played a wonderful role in bringing the experts in cultural studies of the Third World together so that the "dirty linen" of the archaeological sciences could be washed and a new direction given to these sciences, the publication programme as announced by you does not seem to be guided by the same outlook. The choice of the scholarly editorial team is wonderful, but it does not represent the Third World concerns; nor does it reflect the ideologies pursued so far by the World Archaeological Congress. One wonders what could have stopped the organizers or the publishers from inviting scholars from Asia, Africa and other continents to serve on the editorial teams. I had expected each volume to have at least two editors – one from the UK or Europe or America and the other from a Third World country. . . If the World Archaeological Congress believes that excellent scholarship or the editorial excellence exists only in the UK or Europe, then I am sorry to say that this line of thinking will defeat the very purpose the World Archaeological Congress stands for.' Despite my attempt to answer Handoo's points (scc *World Archaeological Bulletin* **2**), and despite the fact that I consider it more or less inevitable that the editors of post-Congress books, if the books are to appear as quickly as possible, will always have to be primarily produced by people local to the host country of the Congress and publisher concerned, I do find Hodder's response to his position as editor of *The meanings of things* an intelligible and credible one in the context of the overall aim of the World Archaeological Congress. (c) C. E. Okezie, a botanist at The University of Nigeria at Nsukka, said of his experience of the World Archaeological Congress, 'This Congress has taught me a lot. My impression has always been that the archaeologist is somebody who goes digging . . . but I've got to see now that archaeologists delve into serious scientific studies. . . I attended all the sessions on my own subject and as many as I could on other subjects . . . it has been extremely beneficial, and I have talked to a lot of people, and got out a lot of information regarding archaeology in general and my speciality in particular.' Such reactions by those involved in the study of the past by members of the so-called Third and Fourth Worlds were not exceptional. If Hodder's 'post-structural' editing experiment – as presented here – has somehow (and even if not for the very same reasons that he himself advances) captured, or even maintained, some of the remarkable spirit and force which united so many people from so many diverse backgrounds during the World Archaeological Congress, then I can do no more than welcome and support it. (d) I have tried to describe on several occasions (e.g. Ucko 1983a, Ucko 1983b, Ucko 1985) how 'control' of cultural activities, and especially control of the past by any group is potentially a devastatingly powerful weapon in the hands of those who are 'in power', to be used for or against those whose cultures or pasts they claim to understand or interpret. The symbolism of an editorial chapter hidden away in the body of this book – as opposed to it dominating the beginning of the book as well as the subsequent structure of all the contributions which follow – seems to me to be both powerful and appropriate.

P. J. Ucko
Southampton

References

Ucko, P. J. 1969. Penis sheaths: a comparative study. *Proceedings of the Royal Anthropological Institute* **2**, 27–67.

Ucko, P. J. 1983a. The politics of the indigenous minority. *J. Biosoc. Sci., Suppl.* **8**, 25–40.

Ucko, P. J. 1983b. Australian academic archaeology: Aboriginal transformation of its aims and practices. *Australian Archaeology* **16**, 11–26.

Ucko, P. J. 1985. Australian Aborigines and academic social anthropology. *Cultural Survival Inc.* **18**, The future of former foragers in Australia and Southern Africa, 63–75.

*Contents**

* For a conventional contents list, *see* pp. 76–7

Preface

Apart from the chapters by Criado (Ch. 22, pp. 79–89), Yates (Ch. 20, pp. 249–61) and Melas (Ch. 17, pp. 137–55), all of the contributions in this book were initially presented at the Southampton World Archaeological Congress in September 1986, in the sesssion entitled 'Material Culture and Symbolic Expression'. Participants from more than 70 countries took part in the Congress, and I have attempted to retain some of that world diversity in this book. Not all of the session participants could be included here, but the enormous breadth and diversity of interest in the topic can still be discerned in the contributions that have been included, many having been significantly revised for publication. Although Davis (Ch. 16, pp. 202–9), Hall (Ch. 12, pp. 178–84), Lemonnier (Ch. 7, pp. 156–72) and Richardson (Ch. 15, pp. 172–7) were not able to attend the Congress, their contributions were discussed, and have been included in this book.

As editor, what should I do with these diversities of approach, interest, method, theory and data? The traditional answer is clear. I must select, edit, ask for rewrites, rewrite parts of contributions myself and organize the chapters into subthemes, until a coherence has been produced. The book is then understandable, an entity with a beginning and an end, internally consistent and ready for scholarly evaluation. I myself would thus have achieved the double aim of defining an independent zone of research and associating myself with that zone. At stake is the position of 'world authority' on symbolic archaeology!

I have been forced by the 'objective conditions' of book production and marketing to go some way in this direction. For example, there simply was not space to include all of the Congress contributions in the book. I had to leave many potential papers out, and my criteria of choice were the extent to which a contribution was made to a general understanding of symbolism, and to the variety of approaches in the book. This was an arbitrary and personal decision, but a necessary one. I could have chosen the contributions at random (a procedure used in the ordering of the chapters in the volume – see below), but I doubt if I could have persuaded the publishers to produce the book without being able to argue for a common relevance of the contributions. During the editing period I came across additional works (by Criado, by Yates and by Melas) which added to the overall themes in significant ways. I included these because I thought they were interesting in relation to the themes and therefore added to the viability of the volume.

In attempting to provide a coherent and finished product, I had begun to impose my own image on a blurred and internally contradictory encounter. I was beginning to make my own 'reading' of symbolic archaeology appear as a universal 'reading'. The meanings I wished to give to symbolic archaeology in general, and to the Southampton meetings in particular, began to infiltrate the very fabric of the book itself. In editing the book, I would need to set out a logical sequence, from beginning to end, which demonstrated the validity of my thoughts. Stated at the beginning, the ideas would return, confirmed at the end. The ordering of the chapters, and what was selected and what discarded, could all be made to build up towards an impressive edifice.

The text itself, this book, would thus become invisible. Long-accepted devices could be employed, such as the ordering of the contributions into introduction, applications and conclusions, or the separation of theory, method and data. My own subjective readings of a set of events would become objectified in a text which concentrated the reader's attention on the content of the message, rather than on the medium in which the message was given. The message would thus appear set, fixed in black and white, enshrined in the printed word. My own perceptions would have become a world text. If successful I would have established an authority through the text.

To control meaning is to have power. As a Western white participant in a world congress in a post-colonial world, that realization of power through the text is particularly disturbing. However, the authority of the text is present in most writing. The meanings become objectified, fixed, but distant from any reality. Rather, the text creates a new reality. It is itself a 'performance' with strategic intent. However, it is not seen as a contextual, subjective performance – only as an objective thing divorced from context.

So I wanted to draw attention to this book as a performance. I wanted to show that the diverse contributions to this volume can be 'read' in many different ways. I have provided some ideas for one such reading in my 'introduction', but my introduction is not at the beginning of the book. In fact, the ordering of the chapters has been chosen at random. Each chapter, including my own, was given a number according to my interpretation of the book's meaning, and was then selected using a table of random numbers. The chapters were then re-ordered in their random sequence. (For a further rationalization of this procedure, see Ch. 1, pp. 64–78.)

Barthes makes the distinction between 'readerly' texts which can be absorbed passively, with less effort, and 'writerly' texts which require more creative energy in making sense of the text. One can argue that 'readerly' texts appear to have a pre-existing meaning which the reader simply *re*-discovers, whereas a 'writerly' text allows multiple meanings to be *dis*covered. In the former case meaning is fixed and more easily linked to power strategies – texts written in the science of archaeology are normally of this type. In the latter case meaning is ambiguous and requires critical participation by the reader and writer. The first type of text is represented by my 'introduction' (Ch. 1, pp. 64–78) and the resultant numbering of the chapters. The second type of text is represented by the printed random ordering.

So I want people to say 'this is a weird book', 'this is a bad book because disorganized and disparate' or 'what a gimmick!'. I want to draw attention to the book as a text – produced as a concrete product with certain ends in mind. In other words, I want to focus attention on the book as a performance which is simultaneously subjective (it is a strategic act by the author or editor and it has to be interpreted by the reader) and objective (it exists 'out there', disembodied, independent and 'real'). Also, I want to draw attention to the confusion between these two aspects of the book – a confusion which appears to give the author's or editor's subjectivities an authority.

Finally, I return to a more traditional function for an editor, which is to express my gratitude to those who took the Chair during the World Archaeological Congress: Bade Ajuwon, Robert Layton, Abi Derefeka and Roland Fletcher.

Ian Hodder
Cambridge

18 *The political use of Australian Aboriginal body painting and its archaeological implications*

ROBERT LAYTON

Archaeology and anthropology can offer complementary analytical perspectives on a cultural tradition. In Australia anthropologists studying contemporary Aboriginal art have described rich systems of visual communication and shown that to a very great extent these systems are incomprehensible without the informed guidance of members of the culture within which the art is produced. Motifs are often not transparently representational, and in a good number of cases seem to have no figurative, or iconic, content (Maynard 1977, pp. 396–7). Further, the same motif may signify different mental constructs in different contexts. The full significance of the subject matter of a painting is often only known to the initiated and, indeed, different interpretations of mythological themes may be proposed by different participants (Clunies-Ross & Hiatt 1977, pp. 138–9, Morphy 1984, pp. 87–96, 124–9).

Faced with this array of data, some Australian archaeologists have turned their backs upon earlier attempts to penetrate the 'meaning' of prehistoric art. The proper approach was previously held to be the identification of motifs as species of kangaroo, totemic heroes, sun discs, etc., and deductions as to their religious significance (for example, McCarthy 1962, Wright 1968). However, Clegg prefaces his tentative identifications with an exclamation mark, 'a typographic convention to denote that an object is named for what it resembles, with no implication that in any sense it really is what it resembles'; hence !track, !trident, and so forth (Clegg 1985, p. 35, see also Clegg 1979). Clegg demonstrates that both the ancient rock art of Panaramitee, in which !animal footprints predominate, and the more recent (but still prehistoric) rock art of the Sydney area depicting !human and !animal silhouettes can be interpreted as the product of a totemic religion. However, in each case the evidence is meagre (Clegg 1985, pp. 19–34), and such a conclusion would overlook much more interesting questions concerning marked differences of style which distinguish the two traditions (*ibid.*, p. 47). Maynard has asserted that as the great bulk of Australian rock art is prehistoric in the sense of being executed beyond living memory in a non-literate culture (Maynard 1979, p. 83, but see Ucko 1983), what modern Aborigines have to say about it can hardly ever correspond with the artist's original intentions (Maynard 1979, p. 86). She therefore disregards anthropological data in favour of 'archaeological questions' such as typology, dating, distribution and the search for correlations with other aspects of culture and environment. The bulk of her 1979 paper presents a unilinear typology of style change in Aboriginal rock art, which is said to pass through three phases: the footprints and simple geometric forms of the Panaramitee style, simple figurative silhouettes and complex figurative forms. It is this approach which I wish to criticize.

Hodder has emphasized that cultures vary in their cognitive structures, and has shown how cognition mediates between environmental constraints and the adaptive patterning of material culture (Hodder 1982, pp. 73, 188, 210). Confronted with a common set of physical or interactional constraints, different cultures organize themselves in diverse forms. The processes by which these adaptations have been achieved are of interest to both anthropology and archaeology.

Australian Aboriginal territorial structure is apparently unique among recent hunter–gatherers. Unlike cultures such as the San and Inuit, descent groups (clans) form an important component in the social system. However, clans do not defend access to foraging resources in the manner reported for the North-West Coast Indians of North America. Rather, they are responsible for localized *sacred sites*, to which unauthorized access is forbidden. Specified senior men must visit sites regularly to ensure that no trespass or damage has occurred, and to perform rituals. Sites consist of trees, caves, springs, stone arrangements or other culturally significant features of the landscape and contain the creative power of the ancestral heroes. Although it is reported that traditionally people would not readily travel beyond their regional community (for example, Dixon 1979, p. 214, Flood 1980, pp. 113–14), relative freedom of foraging movement exists within regional communities. The Alawa, for instance, occupy an area of about 13 200 km^2 in the Gulf country of the Northern Territory (Sharpe 1971) and consist of about 12 clans (see Fig. 18.1). All Alawa can, in principle, forage throughout Alawa country. It seems likely that the need to care for sacred sites has a practical spacing function, periodically drawing people back to the sites for which they are responsible, and thus tending to ensure the community is distributed relatively evenly across its land (Peterson 1972, p. 27, Cashdan 1983, pp. 49–51, Layton 1986). Each clan's sacred sites form one or more geographically distinct cluster, mapping out an area which Stanner (1965) termed the clan's *estate*, although by no means all Aboriginal languages have a generic term for such areas. At collective male ceremonies clansmen wear body paintings which denote their clan membership and territorial allegiance, before a regional audience.

Rock art is associated with such territorial systems in several central and north Australian cultures. In such cases its form and distribution are likely to be explicable, to some extent, in terms of its cultural functions.

In many parts of northern and central Australia the body paintings use simple motifs made up of arcs, circles, straight and wavy lines, and human or animal footprints. To distinguish such styles from those which depict human, animal and plant forms as bodily silhouettes, the simple styles can be termed 'geometric'.

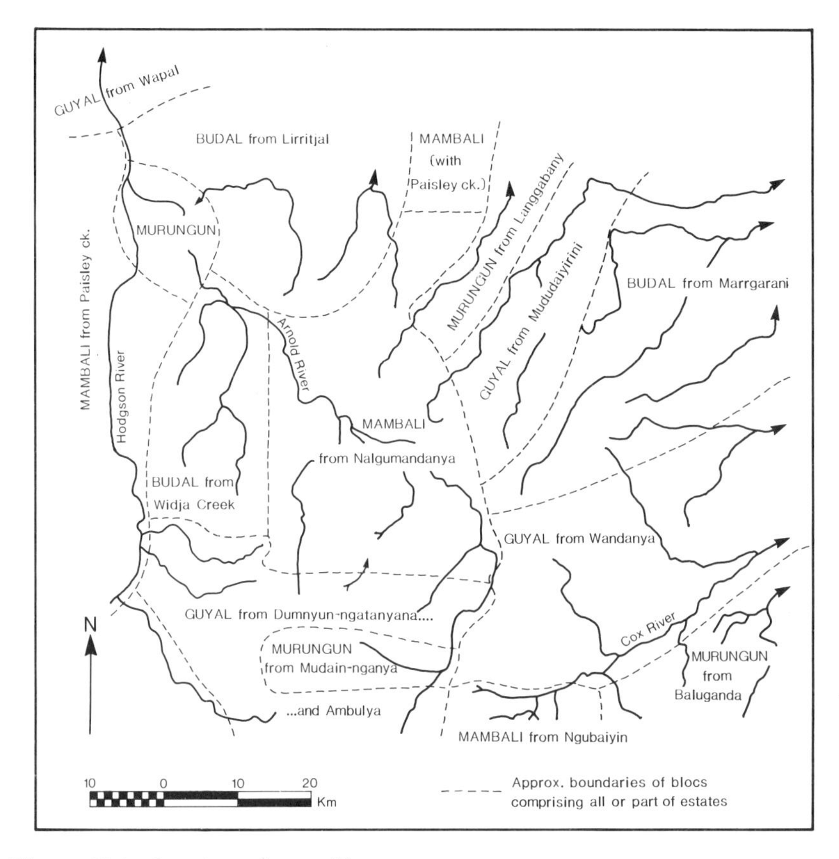

Figure 18.1 Location of some Alawa estates.

Alawa body paintings are in this sense geometric and appear to have affinities with Maynard's early, Panaramitee, style.

A transect from the interior to the north coast of Australia shows that the size of clan estates varies with the quantity of rainfall (see Fig. 18.2). The distribution of estates is also influenced by available water; Pitjantjatjara estates are focused on semi-permanent waterholes (Layton 1983), Alawa estates on rivers which contract in the dry season to chains of waterholes (see Fig. 18.1). This phenomenon has been discussed by several authors (Birdsell 1958, Stanner 1965, Peterson 1972).

According to Aboriginal religion the world acquired its present form in a creation period, when heroic beings with both human and animal attributes laid down the laws of social behaviour, left their mark on the landscape by creating sacred sites, and established the rituals which today re-enact the heroes' travels. The simple, geometric art style records these legendary events in a distinctive fashion (Munn 1973, Layton 1985): a single painting may simultaneously represent the bodily form of an ancestor as human and animal and constitute a map

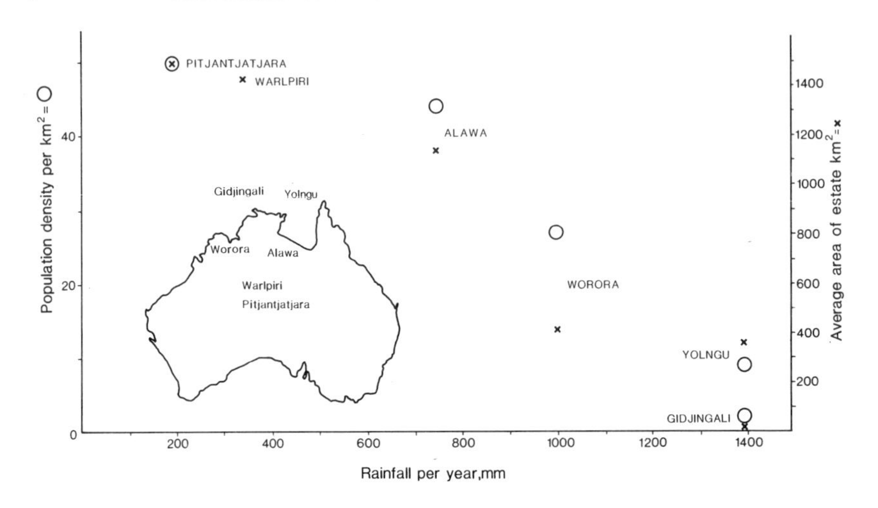

Figure 18.2 Relationship between annual rainfall and (×) average area of clan estates and (O) population density. Inset: location of groups shown on graph.

of sacred sites associated with him. Knowledge about the full significance of a painting is part of the exclusive religious property, controlled by older men and displayed in ritual, on which men's political power largely rests (Bern 1979). Young men are initiated by admission to these ceremonies. Their public appearance painted with a particular design announces their clan affiliation. Their introduction to sacred sites is a context for revelation of religious knowledge.

There are two dimensions to the political use of body paintings. One depends on the progressive revelation of knowledge controlled by men, which establishes (among other things) links between paintings, sites and legends (see Layton 1985, p. 438 for examples, and Bern 1979 for a general discussion of Aboriginal men's knowledge and power). The second dimension also concerns man–land relations. Sometimes two clans whose estates lie on a single dreaming track form a ceremonial alliance. Such an alliance links the clans Budal from Lirritjal and Budal from Marrgarani (Fig. 18.1). Both are large and prestigious groups, but one (Lirritjal) is Alawa, the other (Marrgarani) Mara, belonging to the community lying between the Alawa and the coast. This alliance is demonstrated through the right given to the men of each clan to wear the other's body painting in ritual.

If the male line in a clan fails, young men chosen from neighbouring estates will be trained to take over the ceremonial roles of the threatened group. Their appearance in ceremony wearing the clan's painting is a public statement of their acceptance as members.

Where a clan's estate consists of two distinct blocks of land, the clan's body painting(s) may be interpreted in a way that asserts the spiritual unity of the estate. In one instance two blocks of land belonging to a single estate lie on the route of a single hero. When I observed the paintings, they were worn by two men related to each other as father's brother's sons (E and F in Fig. 18.3). The paintings were visually similar but not identical. However, they were publicly asserted to be 'the same' (i.e. variation between the two designs was deemed not pertinent to their meaning). It seems plausible that if the clan increased in size it might undergo fission, in which case those holding the right to wear the two paintings would no longer claim them to be the same. In fact, demographic accident had resulted in E's branch of this descent group having no children whereas the other had many, and through the agency of two key women's second marriages it was in the process of fusing with another clan (see Fig. 18.3). Presumably either the entire group will hold rights over all three estates or fission will occur.

A major part of the political use of body painting thus seems to be arranging the even distribution of people between estates (this is discussed in more detail in Bern & Layton 1984, pp. 73–5). It is possible to envisage that the corpus of motifs in such a tradition might expand or shrink to suit current political exigencies, but each clan design is usually a simple composition, drawing on a smaller and more enduring body of elementary motifs. Change may be expected primarily in the corpus of compositions, rather than in their elements.

Countering the segmentary tendency of men's totemic ceremonies is a women's cult expressing a concern for the country as a whole (Bern & Layton 1984, pp. 78–9). This recalls Hodder's account of Baringo women's calabash design 'silently disrupting social control' (*ibid.*, p. 75). However, in the Alawa case the women organize a cult which is collectively celebrated and is in more open opposition to male activities, since women attempt to prevent male access to its secret knowledge (cf. Moore 1985, Ch. 9).

Archaeological implications of the Alawa case study

It may be helpful, in assessing how likely such a ritual and artistic system is to be identifiable in the archaeological record, to distinguish between *egocentric* and *sociocentric* status. Egocentric status is exemplified by kinship: I am father to certain others, son to another, cousin to yet others, my kinship status varies according to that other person with whom I am interacting. Sociocentric status is exemplified by membership of corporate groups (groups with defined membership criteria and assumed perpetuity): if I am a member of the kangaroo clan, then I stand in this status toward everyone. Other sociocentric statuses may be based on age and gender: warrior grade, married women, etc. Egocentric status may be signalled through rituals such as greetings between friends, avoidance (in Aboriginal Australia) between mother-in-law and son-in-law, but such rituals are likely to be ephemeral because they are contingent on specific contexts. However, sociocentric statuses are more likely to be signalled in durable forms such as ornaments, artefacts and monuments.

The tradition of Alawa body decoration outlined here denotes sociocentric status, and body designs do in fact also appear in caves, as markers of the site's

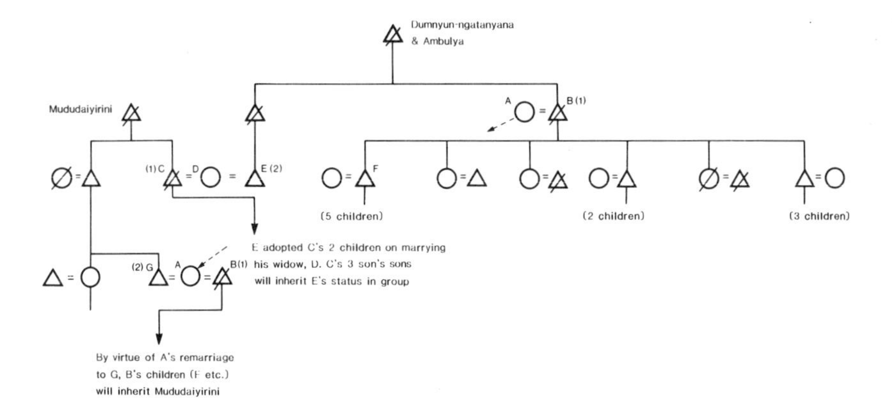

Figure 18.3 Guyal from Dumnyun-ngatanyana and Ambulya/Guyal from Madudaiyirini. Fusion of patrilines.

totemic affiliation. The one decorated cave I was able to visit in Alawa country was largely painted with secular figures such as food animals and hand stencils. It also contained paintings derived from men's ceremonies, and in a small side-shelter a series of depictions of the site's totemic motif. Alawa reported analogous motifs in other shelters, and McLaughlin (pers. comm.) observed an Aboriginal man from a neighbouring community painting ritual designs appropriate to his status at the site, in a cave in the Borroloola area (east of Alawa country).

The visibility of a cultural system in the archaeological record will also depend to some degree on its stability through time. Hodder makes this point with regard to the Deetz–Longacre hypothesis: even if, in the short term, certain residential arrangements generate less diversity of pottery design within households, continual shifting and re-occupation of dwellings will diminish the quantity of information surviving in the structure of the archaeological record (Hodder 1982, p. 122). Since Aboriginal religion ties totemic designs to sites on the land, and since estates are not distributed randomly but according to drainage patterns, the system may well be sufficiently stable to be preserved archaeologically.

For the tradition to be detected, however, the archaeologist would also need to recognize the units of signification, i.e. the clan designs. Aboriginal geometric motifs are so simple and limited in number that, without informants, the pattern might be invisible. Nor may this difficulty always be overcome in other stylistic traditions. It is often a lot more difficult than we like to imagine to identify what rock art motifs represent (Macintosh 1977, Ucko in press). However, in the case of animal silhouettes there is a one-to-one correspondence between each motif and a category of depicted object. There is also often a sufficient quantity of visual information to identify what, in general terms, this category is. (The assumption that this is possible is implicit in Maynard's distinction between simple and complex figurative styles, based on the degree of 'naturalism' that they display.) A tradition in which clans' totemic species are depicted in rock shelters as animal silhouettes is more likely to be archaeologically visible (see Peterson 1972, pp. 18–19 on Arnhem Land, and Layton 1985, pp. 441–6 on the Kimberleys, Western Australia). Elsewhere, I have compared Australian Aboriginal and San rock art with the distribution pattern of the European Palaeolithic decorated caves, and have suggested that the European Palaeolithic data conform better to a shamanistic model derived from the San than to a totemic model derived from the Kimberleys or a secular model derived from X-ray art in the Oenpelli area east of Darwin (Layton 1987).

Antiquity of Aboriginal rock art

Anthropology is best suited to unravelling the complexities of the operation of a cultural system at one point in time, whereas archaeology offers the best evidence (in non-literate cultures) for the development of that system over time, through its partial record.

What may loosely be termed 'geometric' motifs (in the sense of simple forms such as lines, circles and arcs) have a long history in Australia. Even the earliest 'art' at Koonalda, dated to *c*. 20 000 years BP, contains a few forms which have been interpreted as deliberately composed 'herringbone' and circular patterns. More convincing as a tradition containing an identifiable vocabulary of geometric motifs is the art of the Early Man and other shelters in the Laura district of North Queensland (Rosenfeld 1981, pp. 53–4). Rosenfeld distinguishes two phases in the art's development. The earlier phase, dating from *c*. 13 000 years BP, contains 'tridents', 'rectilinear mazes', rings, discs and 'stars'. A later phase, dating from *c*. 5000 years BP (*ibid*., pp. 85–8) includes new motifs such as macropod (kangaroo and wallaby) footprints, identifiably human silhouettes and perhaps other silhouettes. Flood (1983, p. 81) believes that, in another shelter in the Laura region, at least three phases of engraving can be identified. At Ingaladdi, in the Northern Territory, 'bird track', human footprint and circular motifs were found, some on sandstone fragments buried in deposits dated to between 5000 and 7000 years BP (Mulvaney 1969, pp. 176, 269).

At Panaramitee, in western New South Wales, numerous geometric figures are engraved on rocks under a coating of silica known as 'desert varnish'. It has been assumed that the figures must date from the late Pleistocene in order to have allowed the overlying 'varnish' to accumulate (Flood 1983, pp. 121–2, but see Rosenfeld's 1981, p. 51 critical comments on such dating). Calcrete deposits at the Panaramitee style site of Sturt's Meadow have been dated to *c*. 5000 years BP (Dragovitch 1984, Rosenfeld 1986, p. 4). Panaramitee motifs include concentric circles, macropod and bird tracks, arcs, human footprints and clusters of small circles sometimes construed as 'eggs'. There are occasional motifs which may be simple silhouettes.

To demonstrate the existence, over a long period, of a vocabulary of geometric motifs is not to prove that they were always used to perform the particular totemic functions found among contemporary Aranda, Alawa and other communities. Although Maynard concedes an obvious overlap in motifs between recent central Australian art and the prehistoric Panaramitee tradition, she does not accept one to be a continuation of the other. Why she will not accept recent central Australian art as belonging to the Panaramitee tradition is not immediately clear. Her stated reason is that 'technique and form are totally different' (Maynard 1979, p. 102). Panaramitee work was produced by 'pecking', whereas recent rock art is painted or pounded on to the rock surface. Form, in Maynard's typology, denotes the way in which motifs are delineated (solid, outline, etc.; see Maynard 1977, p. 393), but she does not explain how form differentiates Panaramitee from recent art in central Australia. Her third argument is that the relative proportions of motifs differ between Panaramitee and recent cave art: in the latter footprints no longer predominate. Notwithstanding this, she is prepared to class both outline engravings from Sydney and recent solid painted figures from Laura as instances of the simple figurative style, and to assimilate the earlier Laura engravings to the Panaramitee style despite differences in the shape and frequency of motifs.

The underlying reason appears to be that Maynard's chronological sequence is a unilineal one which develops towards the single goal of 'naturalism'. The Panaramitee style – largely non-figurative – comes first. It then dies out, so that any contemporary Aboriginal interest is the result of such art occurring by chance at what are now sacred sites (Maynard 1979, p. 93). In many areas the Panaramitee style is supplanted by the simple figurative style, which 'conforms to a crude naturalism'. This is in turn supplanted in certain areas by complex figurative styles. What distinguishes these from simple figurative styles 'is that they are, in some respect, more sophisticated' (*ibid.*, p. 100). If there *is* continuity in the use of motifs between Panaramitee artists and modern Warlpiri, Aranda, etc., it is only because central Australian religion is extremely conservative (*ibid.*, p. 103).

Maynard's refusal to examine the cultural context of recent Aboriginal rock art has blinded her to the fact that styles tend to have functional correlates: Munn (1973) showed that the simple forms of modern Warlpiri art serve two alternative functions. In secular story-telling they aid the rapid sketching of a sand picture to accompany the story. In religious contexts they enable a single motif to encode several transformations of the same ancestral figure (see above). In the Kimberleys the coexistence of different styles is explicable in functional terms. Wandjina paintings depicting totemic heroes in a complex figurative style coexist with trickster or sorcery figures in a simple figurative style whose purpose is to subvert the ancestral order (Layton 1985, cf. discussion in Layton 1977). Morphy (1977, p. 242) showed that in Northeast Arnhem Land, simple geometric motifs used in sacred paintings are, in secular contexts, replaced with figurative motifs *in order to eliminate* multivalency. Thus, although art styles might be expected to diversify over time, there is no reason to expect unilineal progression toward a single goal, or to attribute the persistence of a style to blind conservatism.

Can the archaeologist, then, predict cultural context from style alone? Unfortunately, this does not seem to be the case. Totemic heroes are depicted in simple geometric motifs in central Australia, in complex figurative motifs in the Kimberleys. However, I do believe that other aspects of recent rock art provide further clues to past cultural contexts.

Munn showed that among the Warlpiri the same style is used both in secular story-telling and in ritual. This is also the case among the Pitjantjatjara. However, as far as rock art is concerned, there is a difference between Warlpiri and Pitjantjatjara. The former, like the Aranda (Spencer & Gillen 1899, pp. 171, 195, 201), possess major painted shelters in which large, elaborate paintings are the focus of ritual, retouched because they contain the power of the ancestors. Among Pitjantjatjara decorated shelters that I visited, I was told that paintings were *illustrative* of ritual rather than part of the ritual action. Although shelters were often themselves sacred sites, the accumulation of relatively inconspicuous, unretouched and sometimes superimposed paintings were interpreted as illustrations of, for instance, ritual motifs, objects or dancers. Information about them was restricted, not because the paintings themselves were the object of ritual, but because they *alluded* to secret rituals.

The shapes of Panaramitee motifs resemble modern geometric art much more closely than do the early Laura forms. Moreover, Rosenfeld (1981, p. 54) analyses the way in which simple trident motifs at Laura were apparently combined to produce more-complex forms, but in the organization of motifs Panaramitee again exhibits closer parallels with recent art; the pairing of arcs in the form which today denotes boomerang clapsticks (and, by inference, men singing at ceremony), the framing of footprints and clusters of circles within a larger circle, the alignment of footprints to suggest an animal or human walking (cf. Rosenfeld 1986, p. 5). Rosenfeld points out that, at some desert sites such as Walga Rock in Western Australia, extensive superpositioning of motifs can be seen. Many of these motifs have the 'design characteristics' of the Panaramitee style, yet are often integrated into patterns of greater formal complexity than the classic Panaramitee engravings. Rosenfeld concludes that there may indeed have been cultural continuity between Panaramitee and contemporary desert styles, but that 'the greater structural elaboration of the recent art and the painted rock art sites reflect an increase in the degree of stylistic manifestation within the same lexical tradition' (Rosenfeld 1986, p. 11). We may be witnessing the record of increasingly complex and highly structured uses of an ancient artistic vocabulary.

Whether the Panaramitee artists were depicting secular tales and everyday records of foraging, or whether the motifs originally had a deeper religious resonance cannot be deduced. The scattering of juxtaposed motifs over wide areas implies (in my view) that no close parallel should be drawn with the function of modern Warlpiri or Alawa rock art. Here, as in the Kimberleys, major rock art sites are focal points on estates. It seems more likely that the complex and varied cultural contexts of modern Aboriginal geometric art which anthropology studies are the product of a long process of cultural change which archaeology can help to unravel. In doing so, quantitative studies of the vocabulary of motifs, of stylistic convention, patterns of composition and the regional distribution of sites are all likely to yield useful information, particularly where anthropology can provide case studies of such artistic systems in use.

References

Bern, J. 1979. Ideology and domination: towards a reconstitution of Australian Aboriginal social formation. *Oceania* **50**, 118–32.

Bern, J. & R. Layton 1984. The local descent group and the division of labour in the Cox River land claim. In *Aboriginal landowners*, L. R. Hiatt (ed.), *Oceania Monograph* **27**, 67–83.

Birdsell, J. B. 1958. On population structure in generalized hunting and gathering populations. *Evolution* **12**, 189–205.

Cashdan, E. 1983. Territoriality among human foragers: ecological models and an application to four bushman groups. *Current Anthropology* **24**, 47–66.

Clegg, J. 1979. Science, theory and Australian prehistoric art. *Mankind* **12**, 42–50.

Clegg, J. 1985. Prehistoric pictures as evidence of religion. Paper presented to the 80th Congress of the International Association for the History of Religions, Sydney.

Clunies-Ross, M. & L. R. Hiatt 1977. Sand sculptures at a Gidjingali burial site. In *Form in indigenous art*, P. J. Ucko (ed.), 131–46. Canberra: Australian Institute of Aboriginal Studies.

Dixon, R. M. W. 1979. Tribes, languages and other boundaries in northeast Queensland. In *Tribes and boundaries in Australia*, N. Peterson (ed.), 207–38. Canberra: Australian Institute of Aboriginal Studies.

Dragovitch, D. 1984. Minimum age for desert varnish in the Broken Hill area, N.S.W., a preliminary estimation. *Search* **15**, 3–4.

Flood, J. 1980. *The moth hunters*. Canberra: Australian Institute of Aboriginal Studies.

Flood, J. 1983. *Archaeology of the dreamtime*. London: Collins.

Hodder, I. 1982. *Symbols in action*. Cambridge: Cambridge University Press.

Layton, R. 1977. Naturalism and cultural relativity in art. In *Form in indigenous art*, P. J. Ucko (ed.), 33–43. Canberra: Australian Institute of Aboriginal Studies.

Layton, R. 1983. Ambilineal descent and traditional Pitjantjatjara rights to land. In *Aborigines, land and land rights*, N. Peterson & M. Langton (eds), 15–32. Canberra: Australian Institute of Aboriginal Studies.

Layton, R. 1985. The cultural context of hunter–gatherer rock art. *Man (New Series)* **20**, 434–53.

Layton, R. 1986. Political and territorial structures among hunter–gatherers. *Man (New Series)* **21**, 18–33.

Layton, R. 1987. The use of ethnographic parallels in the analysis of Palaeolithic art. In *Comparative anthropology*, L. Holy (ed.). Oxford: Blackwell.

McCarthy, F. 1962. The rock engravings at Port Hedland, north-west Australia. *Kroeber Anthropological Society Papers* **26**, 1–74.

Macintosh, N. W. G. 1977. Beswick Creek two decades later: a reappraisal. In *Form in indigenous art*, P. J. Ucko (ed.), 191–7. Canberra: Australian Institute of Aboriginal Studies.

Maynard, L. 1977. Classification and terminology in Australian rock art. In *Form in indigenous art*, P. J. Ucko (ed.), 387–402. Canberra: Australian Institute of Aboriginal Studies.

Maynard, L. 1979. The archaeology of Australian Aboriginal art. In *Exploring the visual art of Oceania*, S. M. Mead (ed.), 83–110. Honolulu: University of Hawaii Press.

Moore, H. 1985. *Space, text and gender*. Cambridge: Cambridge University Press.

Morphy, H. 1977. Too many meanings. Unpublished PhD thesis, Australian National University, Canberra.

Morphy, H. 1984. *Journey to the crocodile's nest*. Canberra: Australian Institute of Aboriginal Studies.

Mulvaney, D. J. 1969. *The prehistory of Australia*. London: Thames & Hudson.
Munn, N. D. 1973. *Warpiri iconography*. Ithaca: Cornell University Press.
Peterson, N. 1972. Totemism yesterday: sentiment and local organization among the Australian Aborigines. *Man (New Series)* **7**, 12–32.
Rosenfeld, A. 1981. Rock engravings in the Laura area. In *Early man in North Queensland*, A. Rosenfeld, D. Horton & J. Winter (eds.) Vol. 6: 50–89. *Terra Australis*. Canberra: Department of Prehistory, Research School of Pacific Studies, Australian National University.
Rosenfeld, A. 1986. The Aboriginal rock art of Australia. Paper prepared for the First World Symposium on Rock Art, Havana.
Sharpe, M. 1971. *Alawa phonology and grammar*. Canberra: Australian Institute of Aboriginal Studies.
Spencer, B. & F. J. Gillen 1899. *The native tribes of central Australia*. London: Macmillan.
Stanner, W. E. H. 1965. Aboriginal territorial organization. *Oceania* **36**, 1–26.
Ucko, P. J. 1983. The politics of the indigenous minority. *Journal of Biosocial Science*, **8** (suppl.), 25–41.
Ucko, P. J. in press. Subjectivity and the recording of Palaeolithic art. *Acts of the International Colloquium on Western Palaeolithic Rock Art, Perigueux, 1984*.
Wright, B. 1968. *Rock art of the Pilbara region, north west Australia*. Canberra: Australian Institute of Aboriginal Studies.

25 *Terracotta worship in fringe Bengal*

D. K. BHATTACHARYA

Archaeologically retrieved data and their contexts have normally been used to reconstruct the 'culture' which produced them. Yet the archaeologist's 'culture' has little or no information for a social anthropologist (Leach 1973). I do not propose any means of bridging this gap, but wish to record a simple ethnographic feature of a cult in a community in West Bengal, with the hope that similar studies from cross-cultural contexts might enable us to develop generalizations. This, in turn, may provide a deeper understanding of the varieties of terracottas known from prehistoric contexts in India and elsewhere.

Terracottas depicting various zoomorphic and anthropomorphic features are known to be worshipped all over India. I chose to study the present group because here the terracotta worship is connected with a pre-Hindu cult, there being no such association elsewhere in India, where this cult has been Hinduized and is still practised today. The cult involves the worshipping of *Manasha* (the snake goddess) without involving any specific iconic form for the deity. Further, we know that snakes and dragons occur almost invariably in ancient myths all over the world. In India a late Neolithic site (1375 ± 100 BC) from Bihar, called Chirand, has yielded a terracotta serpent – which is so far the only evidence we have of the prehistoric mind being preoccupied with snakes. The area of the present study is at the West Bengal–Bihar border, and the community studied, the Bauris, are generally believed to have migrated originally from Bihar (Risley 1915).

Bauris are a very low caste group in West Bengal, who may have until very recently been only tribal. They do not indulge in scavenging, but scavengers will not accept food or water from them. Risley considered them as a 'tribal caste'. The 1961 Census of India counted 501 269 of them in total. Of this, nearly 200 000 inhabit the district of Bankura, the area of the present study. Bankura is a rocky extension of Bihar which is highly laterized and is even today thickly forested. There are a few rivers which pass through the eastern extension of this rocky zone (usually referred to as Chotanagpur region), enter Orissa in the south and eventually meet the sea in the south-east of Cuttack. Agriculture is possible mainly along the alluvial stretches where the post-monsoon silt deposition is considerable. This, aided by seasonal rainfall, has led to the growth of scattered villages and small towns along these rivers.

One of the interesting features of this region is that the caste Hindu occupational areas are often interspersed by tribal huts, the latter being mainly adapted to the adjoining forest tracks. The Bauris no longer live outside the Hindu villages. Most are employed as labourers in agriculture or in road building, pond-cutting or even plying cycle-rickshaws for hire. Most Bauris have their settlements in areas which were given to them on the periphery of villages by the landlords, with the understanding that they would provide cheap agricultural labour to the owner. All family members work except the old, the infirm and children. Their settlements are mostly on fallow and infertile regions which are situated at one corner of the village. Heaps of refuse accumulate near their hut clusters, and pigs, dogs and occasionally hens are seen rummaging through the refuse and slush. The Bauris seem to have been pushed into the most inhospitable fringes of the village. Ignorance and starvation plague them. Quite a number of them are also lepers. In almost all villages one can see clusters of dirty, broken huts surrounded by slush resulting from lack of drainage, and pigs rummaging through heaps of broken pottery and generalized domestic refuse.

Bauris are highly sought after as medicine men (for conducting magical ceremonies) and also act as midwives. Their interaction with caste group Hindus does not extend beyond this level. For the role of barber or conducting rituals of life cycle, no Hindu – no matter how low in hierarchy – enters the Bauri society.

Essentially, Bauris are governed by a faith which believes in spirits, both benevolent and malevolent. Besides these chains of spirits which are usually referred to as *Kundra*, they have a profound veneration for water – both flowing and stagnant. Animals for which they have special respect are snakes and dogs. The former has been deified and almost totally dominates their ritual and festival cycle. The dog and a special variety of red-beaked heron (*kashyap bak*) are the other two animals which every Bauri respects, but these do not preoccupy much of their festivities. Of these, the dog seems to play a more important role in their life, as in many of their sayings the dog is referred to repeatedly. Further, a Bauri observes a period of mourning (ritual impurity) of 12 days when his pet dog dies. Incidentally, this is the same number of days of mourning that a Bauri observes when one of his parents dies. In the Hindu system the number of days for mourning is decided by the genealogical distance of the deceased from the ego. For most of their life-cycle rituals a Bauri picks up the practices of the neighbourhood. Those among them who have lived in the proximity of the Hindus have, in the course of time, picked up festivities and simple ceremonies of their neighbours, and similarly those living in the proximity of the Muslims have picked up Muslim customs.

Bauris have always enjoyed eating carcases of animals. Rats, frogs, pigs, snails and crabs provide their usual meat supply. During festivities these are further supplemented with a home-brewed wine called *haria*. They live in a joint family unless economic reasons force them to do otherwise. They allow multiple marriage, but in recent years its practice appears rarely because of economic constraints. Marrying one's elder brother's widow or wife's younger sister may be allowed, but a strict avoidance is practised with one's younger brother's widow. One's mother's brother plays a very important role in the society, and is given a high position of respect by the Bauri. The wife of one's mother's brother is so highly respected that one is not supposed to touch her even if one sees her drowning. Village endogamy is not forbidden, but it is generally avoided. Brideprice of a very nominal amount is expected in a normal negotiated marriage. Concubinage and loose bonds of cohabitation are also not unknown, although they do not form the rule.

Bauris are never known to have revolted against the king, the landlord or the law of the land as a group, unlike the Santhals and Mundas of the same region. Before the emergence of road traffic they were always used as palanquin carriers. During the various rules in the history of Bankura, be it under a king or a democratic government, the Bauris were never required to pay any tax or levy. This is primarily because they have never had cultivable land. It is a popular belief that, although the eldest son of a king used to rule over the Bauris, the second son, called the *Hakim*, had the right to use the Bauri unmarried women for his sexual pleasure. Apparently, the Bauris did not resent this and may even have accepted this exploitation as a privilege. However, it should not be forgotten that such oral histories originate mainly from the privileged community and, therefore the actual feeling of the Bauris for this form of actual and perpetual exploitation will never be known. To sum up, one can only repeat that the community has never shown any strong resentment towards the provider, and has always attempted to live in harmony with the dominant caste groups in spite of the usual oppression commonly known.

Bauris do not show any lack of organization for internal ordering. Even today they select an elderly and experienced person from among them as leader (*Mukhya*) who sits under a tree with other members of the community to settle disputes, to pronounce sentence and sometimes even to execute it. The offender has a right to seek judgement from the leader of a larger aggregate of villages if the village leader does not satisfy him. If the offender ignores all of these punishments he is promptly excommunicated.

Worshipping *Manasha* is by no means a peculiarity of the Bauris of West Bengal. It is found all over eastern India, although the manner of worship varies widely (Maity 1966). Among the Bauris as well, this difference is quite conspicuous. The Bauris of an adjoining district, Hoogly (Shasmal 1972) do not show any such preoccupation with the terracotta horses and elephants which form an inseparable part of the *Manasha* cult of the Bankura Bauris (Fig. 25.1). However, for Bauris all over West Bengal the chief cultural festival is always centred around this specific cult. Every Bauri village must have a specific place (*than*) for this worship. The object worshipped is a medium-sized earthen vase which shows three or four snake hoods in a row (called *Manasha Ghat*) (Fig. 25.2). It is cleaned every day and filled with fresh water from the river before the worship. During the end of August and the beginning of September the worship acquires a special festivity. Often this festivity extends over three days, during which goats are sacrificed and feasts are held. None of these worships is officiated by any Hindu priest. It is often the *Mukhya* who officiates at these rituals. In my fieldwork I came across one case of an old lady of the community

Figure 25.1 The terracotta horse worshipped along with the *Manasha Ghat*.

acting as priest, although there was a *Mukhya* elected for organizational leadership. The selection of a priest to officiate these festivities is often done by choosing the one who enters into *Jhupal* (trance). Terracotta horses and elephants are put on either side of the main object of worship – the vessel. Vermilion mixed with oil is smeared on the trunk and forehead of the animal figures.

These animal depictions are fairly stylized in form and are uniformly of the same style all over the district. For votive offerings, which are made both at the lesser *Manasha than* (which may be at any chosen area where the specific cactus *Euphorbia nerifolia* grows) to the large number of malevolent deities (*Kundras*), an entirely different kind of horse and elephant terracotta is made. These are much more stylized and oversimplistic in form (Figs 25.3 & 4). Intensive enquiries carried out during the present fieldwork could not reveal any kind of explanation for the presence of horse or elephant and their association with

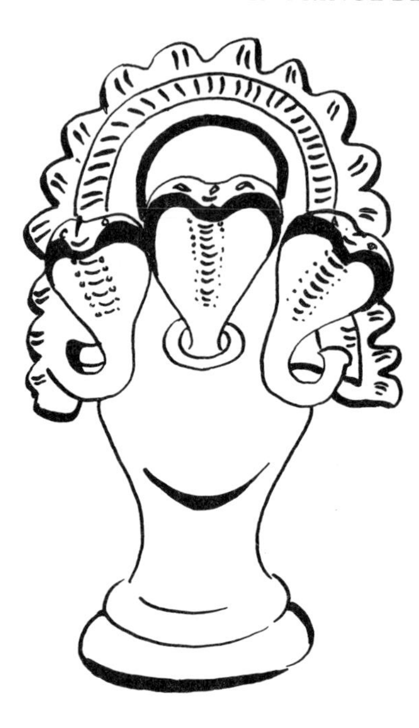

Figure 25.2 The *Manasha Ghat*, the main object of worship among the Bauris.

Manasha in the Bauri mind. An attempt has therefore been made in this chapter to uncover the mind that seeks the symbol. This symbol could have a root in the unconscious and may not be identifiable in the world of reality in the present context (Lévi-Strauss 1968).

The Bauris of Bankura are people who live on a rocky plain where good clay is not as readily available as elsewhere in West Bengal. A potter as a skilled professional, or for that matter a terracotta tradition in such a region, is therefore more of a novelty than a rule, whereas among the Bauris of Hoogly district, where alluvial soil abounds, the terracotta tradition does not play that dominant a role. In other words, symbolism can clearly be seen as seeking an expression through a medium which is not naturally abundant. Further, the Bauris themselves are incapable of preparing these objects and they depend totally on the Hindu caste of potters for this. That is, it can safely be assumed that the origin of the terracotta tradition in this region cannot be older than the historic period, even if the *Manasha* cult has an earlier origin.

There can be little doubt that the relationship of the cult and the terracotta tradition is similar to experience being related to fundamental categories of thought and action. Recently a study on the Hindu Puja has deliberated at length on this experience – mental category relationship. To quote Oster (1982):

> Symbols act to express concepts. Sets of concepts articulate around fundamental categories of thought and action. Categories are the final

Figure 25.3 The votive terracotta elephant.

> sources for the meaning of symbols. Categories relate to experience, they form and define experience. Conversely, symbols, concepts and ideologies deliberate in terms of particular cultural systems and so they may act as categories of analysis.

Perhaps the mental categories of the present community are implicit in their myths through which they seek a self-definition.

There are two interesting myths regarding the origin of the Bauris, which may be considered for understanding the thought categories. One of these shows their aspiration to belong to the clean Hindu caste rank, whereas the other reveals their conception of themselves being endowed with physical strength directly by the goddess of strength.

(a) Mahadev (Lord Shiva) lived with his wife Parvati at Kailash, a mountain in the Himalayan range. As Mahadev had no-one to do his work, he wanted to have a domestic servant, but he could not find a suitable person. So one day he made a small male effigy out of dirty excretions of his body and gave life to it. Gradually this effigy began to breathe like a living man and grew up. In the same way Parvati made a small female figure, as she had no companion or maid, and gave life to it.

The boy gradually became very strong, had a well-built body and could do any kind of hard work. Mahadev then wanted to get him married and asked Parvati to find a suitable bride for him, who could not be any ordinary girl because the boy had power and strength derived from Mahadev himself. Parvati was also thinking about the marriage of the girl she had created, and was in search of a suitable groom as a match. She then told Mahadev about this girl and eventually they were married. The other gods present in the marriage saw that the boy was not only strong and well-built,

Figure 25.4 The votive terracotta horse.

but also carried the mysterious power from Mahadev. This was a potential threat to their power. So they conspired and by deceit made him open a knot made of cow intestine. The boy could not open such a knot with the strength of his fingers, and went on to use his teeth without knowing what was touching his mouth. On hearing this Mahadev was very angry and cursed him into the lowest caste group. Bauris, the progeny of this mythical figure, thus came to be regarded as a low caste (Shasmal 1972). To the Bauris their divine origin brings their self-definition, their relation to the larger society being defined by the curse of their creator.

(b) The second myth says that the goddess Durga used to go to a river to bathe, carried by her favourite carrier, the lion. Once she took so much time that the lion showed his resentment, at which Durga became angry and kicked him. Since then lions have had a concave stomach. The lion was very hurt and his injured feelings affected Durga. When she started washing her body in the river she found there was an incessant stream of dirt ensuing. She realized that this was because she had hurt the feelings of her long associate, the lion. At once she asked for pardon from the lion and the dirt ceased, but the dirt already spread in the water was a potent part of Durga's body and hence could not be just dirt. Soon this turned into the Bauris and this explains why even today Bauris are found along the rivers.

Again they are traced from a prime source of mythical power from the Hindu belief structure. The myth goes on to say how they came to be used in carrying the palanquin of Mahadev during his marriage, and how Mahadev had to curse them to a life of poverty because of their laziness.

Both of these myths have many points of similarity and explain why the Bauri feels proud of his muscular body and physical strength. By bringing the divine sanction on this power, he wishes to make himself indispensable to agricultural caste groups in the neighbourhood. Furthermore, the depiction of his being called to carry Mahadev's palanquin attempts to legitimize his role and also, at the same time, to keep himself at a position higher than the lowest ranks within the agriculturists (like the Doms, Hari and Charmakars).

The ideological categories implicit in the above myths about the origin of the Bauris relate them to their material culture and behaviour in general. That is, they correlate with 'the informal logic of everyday life' (Turner 1975). They feel free to eat all those animals, dead or alive, which are generally considered unclean by any Hindu. Conversely, it can be said that these myths legitimize their continuing with hunting–gathering customs from a pre-Hindu period even when they have entered into a symbiotic relationship with the immigrant Hindu agriculturists.

In this chapter I wish to discuss the possible explanations for the Bauri cult of terracotta worship through neither structural nor functional perspectives. I wish to argue that no phenomenon can be discussed within a purely ahistorical point of view. Historical contact followed by natural growth can explain the arrival or disappearance of a material cultural object in a community. The object or symbol *per se* has seldom received adequate attention in structural analysis in ethnography. Hodder (1982) has succinctly summarized the continuous ignoring of the material object in structural approaches: 'In processual analyses of symbol systems, the artefact itself is rarely given much importance. An object may be described as symbolising status, male or female, or social solidarity, but the use of the particular artefact class and the choice of the symbol itself are not adequately discussed'. In the present study the emphasis has therefore been more on looking into the possible causes of the choice of horse and elephant terracottas among the Bauris, and finally on looking into the symbolic role ascribed to them.

Long before the arrival of the Hindu peasant in this region this forest track in Bankura had acted as a major route of contact, invasion and trade between the two centres of Early Historic capitals, viz., Magadh and Utkal. All of these human groups had to seek a course along the River Damodar or Kangsavati, primarily because they needed drinking water both for themselves and for the large number of animals they carried. These animals were mainly elephants and horses, besides some milking cows. Camels or ponies are not known to have been used. Of the animals carried, elephants and horses are given a great deal of decoration, either by painting or by mounting specially designed ornaments on them. Coming in a group, these decorated horses and elephants with their equally decorated riders could always produce a sense of awe and glory in the mind of the simple tribal forest-dwellers. It is difficult to believe that these contacts were limited merely to this distance-viewing. Any group of warriors passing through dense forests also looks to local people for direction, local knowledge, labour for cutting wood or feeding and bathing animals, and a horde of other similar activities. It is my contention that the Bauris had been regularly employed by these caravans from perhaps as early as 400 BC, if not earlier, and such contacts became increasingly regular by about AD 600. In all probability the *Manasha* cult before this contact was restricted to worshipping the *Euphorbia nerifolia* plant.

Around the seventh century AD the powerful Malla kings came to power over the combined regions of the present Bankura, Purulia and Midnapur districts. Their capital was built in Vishnupur, situated in Bankura. Malla kings ruled the region till the 18th century. However, after the 10th century various external invasions took place in the region, and these successfully fragmented and also weakened the Malla dynasty. The Bauris were therefore suddenly cut off from the usual contractual relationship with various kings' retinues in transit.

The Malla kings did not disown them altogether, but their work role was now structurally incorporated within the peasant economy – a newly evolved situation for the Bauris. The king would especially invite them on specific days to display their ability in snake charming, and would amply reward them. Automatically the entire community of the Hindus became their clients in snake-bite cure. Since snake-bite cure basically forms a psychosomatic therapy (effective only in preventing cardiac arrest because of shock in the case of non-poisonous snake bites), the Bauris had to recall their private religious cult of *Manasha* worship to the fore with demonstrative features of dance and trance. A great deal of psychologically effective features needed to be added to consolidate the confidence of the clients. Additional symbols of power and prestige probably evolved at this juncture.

Child delivery is another aspect which is shrouded, even today, by innumerable myths in villages. Twelve centuries ago the immigrant Hindus in Bankura were bound to be influenced by at least these myths, if not many more. Today one of the most commonly held causes of child mortality or death of the mother during delivery is attributed to the 'evil eye' of mortal men or evil spirits. Bauris were quite handy in acting as the mediator with these evil spirits, because of their strong belief in *Kundra*. Slowly their role as midwives started getting established. The myth of their origin being explained as being from the divine source of Mahadev and Parvati themselves, their entry into the inner quarters of a Brahmin at times of need was easily tolerated.

Finally, it will be clear why the Bauris, despite their physical proximity to such tribal groups as the Munda, Santhal, Kharia and Lodhas (who can by no means be termed pacifists), have never revolted against any kind of law-enforcement authority. Bauris have always been king's men. They have known and seen kings during their contact in the forest camps. They have always felt themselves to be a part of the king's inner circle of helpers for a period, lapsing into inactivity when the king and his gloriously decorated horses and elephants had gone away. It is during these periods of inactivity that the horse and the elephant started evolving as symbols of power (similar to royal powers) and also of economic well-being for the Bauris. Oral tradition may have maintained these symbols for a while before the caste Hindus started developing agricultural lands and villages on the fringe of the forests during the consolidation of the Malla kings. The oral tradition is now totally lost, but on being patronized by the Malla kings again the Bauris gave a tangible shape to their symbol. It is their *Manasha* worship that the new king patronized, and hence the terracotta symbol derived from their association with earlier kings appeared in the *Manasha than*. At the sites of *Kundra* worship these terracottas again serve as the best votive offerings, as these are their only link with royal connection, power and economic help.

In this respect the stylization of the horse in its terracotta form is quite revealing. It is given unusually long ears and a rather long and vertical neck, but the mouth is shown bridled with parts of the leash also represented (Fig. 25.1). The nostrils of the horses are shown flaring, as if it has had a long and tiring run. Even today horses used in royal entourages are decorated with a flowery stick standing vertically on the forehead along with the two ears. Seen from profile these decorations give an illusion of vertically standing long ears. The flaring nostrils show the long distance over which the horses may have travelled in their journey from Magadh. In this respect the elephants shown are much less stylized.

Once we can place the historical reasons for the choice of the symbols, many of the problems in understanding the Bauri cult start to become easier to comprehend. In prehistoric analysis, therefore, it would appear that dynamic processes of culture and the strategies of adaptation chosen by the community alone can help in the interpretation of symbolic objects. A mere stylistic or morphological description will serve no purpose in our understanding of the prehistoric mind, and hence the society. The terracotta horse and elephant worship among the Bauris of Bankura is a purely historic development. This should not be confused with the power symbol ascribed to the horse even today, because these uses of horse or Horse Power do not involve any cult or festivity as pivotal to life as the *Manasha* cult of the Bauris is.

In the light of the Bauri experience it would appear that the symbolic ascriptions sought for explaining terracottas from prehistoric contexts can be quite misleading or may be entirely wrong. It is more important to reconstruct the total economy before such ascriptions are attempted. In other words, the strategies of adaptation and the total available ecology within which such an adaptation is sought becomes equally important. Miller (1985) has quite successfully shown this process of the formation of categories in his study of pottery in a contemporary Indian village.

References

Hodder, I. (ed.) 1982. *Symbolic and structural archaeology*. Cambridge: Cambridge University Press.

Leach, E. 1973. Concluding address. In *The explanation of culture change*, C. Renfrew (ed.), 761–3. London: Duckworth.

Lévi-Strauss, C. 1968. *Structural anthropology*. London: Allen Lane.

Maity, P.K. 1966. *Historical studies in the cult of the goddess Manasa*. Calcutta: Punthi Pustak.

Miller, D. 1985. *Artefacts as categories: a study of ceramic variability in Central India.* Cambridge: Cambridge University Press.
Oster, A. 1982. *Puja in society*. Lucknow: Ethnographic and Folk Culture Society.
Risley, H. 1915. *People of India*. Calcutta.
Shasmal, K. C. 1972. *The Bauris of West Bengal*. Calcutta: Indian Publications.
Turner, V. 1975. Symbolic studies. *Annual Review of Anthropology* **4**, 145–62.

13 *Iron and beads: male and female symbols of creation. A study of ornament among Booran Oromo*

ANEESA KASSAM and GEMETCHU MEGERSA

Introduction

The cultural artefacts that people make and use and the things people do are the general basis for understanding what people think and how they view their world. People and cultures may disappear, but their material cultures often survive in the archaeological record, and can be used to reconstruct the past. Ornaments are one of the many artefacts which Oromo make and use in their daily life.[1] However, the term 'ornament' is an inadequate description for these objects, which Oromo call *nagata*, 'putting on; adorning'; *waan fayya*, 'beautiful things' or more rarely, *mard'aad* 'that which goes round'.[2] In Oromo, as in most other cultures of the world, ornaments are more than mere objects of self-adornment. In the early history of mankind they probably expressed deep-seated social, cultural and spiritual values, which the forces of 'progress' have either suppressed or retrieved by transforming them from symbols of 'pagan' belief and 'backward' behaviour into expressions of more 'civilized' thought. The following Boorana myth fully demonstrates the sacred nature of ornament.[3]

Myth of origin

A *hayyuu* of the Mataarri clan, Abbaa Yaya, returning home unsuccessfully from one of his campaigns for booty, came upon some members of the Booran community who were herding cattle. He inadvertently expressed aloud the wishful thought that, had they been the enemy, he would have attacked them and seized their animals.[4] Hearing this the *raaba* warriors immediately executed his wish, bringing death upon their fellow tribesmen.

For this sacrilege, for which they held the *hayyuu* responsible, the Booran 'punished' Abbaa Yaya by holding him upside down and swinging him back and forth by the hands and feet and chanting, *furaan furuntoo, furri yaya.*[5]

The *hayyuu* was a fat man, and this action of rocking him back and forth caused his huge belly to rupture, and as a result of this injury he died. However, his death had dire consequences for the Booran, for from his stomach emerged two scourges unknown to Booran until that time: ticks (*dirandissa*) and thorns (*goraati*), which began to cause widespread death in Booran. When they examined the stomach of the dead man, the Booran found there three other objects: a bead, called *buuran*; a thread, called *mataarri*; and another bead, called *c'iruwaan*.[6] The Booran did not know what to do, so they summoned the Mataarri clan and explained what had happened. First the Mataarri requested the two beads and thread found in the stomach of their clansman. They then decreed that the ticks would stop biting men and would bite cattle instead, and that thorns would remain on the trees where they had suddenly appeared, but would no longer be a cause of death. They would say no more, declaring that they would await the return of the *Qaalluu*, Mandada, who had disappeared, before pronouncing themselves.

After some time a man calling himself by various names appeared in several different parts of Booran country, then disappeared. Finally, he reappeared at a place called *Tulluu Nama Durii*, the 'Hill of Ancient Men', and instructed the Booran to bring their cattle before him, among which there should be a black-and-white spotted bull calf, so that he might bless them. The Booran suspected the man of trying to put a spell (*tolc-*, literally, 'make, do') on them. They again asked the Mataarri to intervene, asking them to kill the man. When the Mataarri came before the man, they knew he was the *Qaalluu* Mandada and, instead of killing him, asked him for his blessing. The *Qaalluu* asked the Mataarri for the *umu gurraatii* bead and the *mataarri* thread, and tied it around their necks and blessed them. However, the Mataarri were now faced with a dilemma. They could not kill the *Qaalluu* themselves, nor could they return without having accomplished their mission. So they seized a Konso and promised him a bull if he killed the *Qaalluu*.[7] The Konso plunged his spear into the *Qaalluu*, but he did not die.[8]

Until this day the Mataarri, whose *wayyu* (holiness) is great, are known as the *warr umu gurraatii* (people or owners of the black bead) and they never touch the *ditac'a* tree, with whose leaves the *Qaalluu* wiped his blood.[9]

Brief comment on the myth This myth, which forms part of a larger cycle centred on the person of the *Qaalluu*, depicts a conflict between spiritual and temporal power of historical significance. It involves a series of transgressions, the shedding of blood, and its consequences. At one level it takes a human victim and in what amounts to 'reading the entrails' appear objects symbolically representing life (the sacred beads) and death (ticks and thorns).

Levels of meaning

In Oromo Booran society ornament can be viewed as functioning at three different levels of society, namely:

(a) hierarchical;
(b) initiatory; and
(c) procreative.

To be able to understand the role played by ornament in identification at these three levels, it will be necessary for us to examine briefly the *gada* grades, and cultural practices of 'killing for honour', marriage and birth – interrelated concepts which regulate the life of ordinary men and women in society.[10]

Booran Oromo institutions and cultural practices

Traditional Booran Oromo society is composed of two opposed but complementary institutions known as the *Gada* system. These two institutions are the *Qaalluu* institution, representing spiritual authority, and the *Gada* (or *Aadaa* 'tradition') institution, representing temporal power. The head of the *Qaalluu* institution is the *Abbaa Muda* (Father of Anointment), and the head of the *Gada* institution is the *Abbaa Gada*. Both are ultimately responsible to the *Gumi Gaayo* (law-making assembly) and thence to *Waaga* (God). Under each of these dignitaries are officials, who are hierarchically ordered (Fig. 13.1). Both display distinctive insignia of office, which may be ornaments or other symbols of power and authority. The *Gada* officials have a mandatory term of eight years, but the office of the *Qaalluu* is hereditary. These two institutions regulate, from birth to death, the life of every male individual born into the society who passes successively through a number of grades, which correspond approximately to the natural ages of man. These are composed of ten eight-year periods, divided into two 40-year cycles, and fathers and sons who belong to the same patriline (*gogess*), of which there are five, follow one another at intervals of 40 years. Only one *gogess* is in power at any one time. This is the ideal system, but in reality a number of discrepancies, arising out of the theoretical framework and its practical application, tend to dislocate it. The transition from one grade to another entails changes in ritual status which are marked by rites of passage, and to which ornaments and styles of hair-dress correspond. Procreation should ideally take place in the senior warrior (*raaba*) grade, but to be worthy of doing so a man must have proved his virility by killing a trophy animal. For women, giving birth to a son is a feat equivalent to that of acquiring a trophy (cf. Bartels 1983, pp. 257–83). So, as these ritual changes equally affect the life of the female members of society, mothers and wives also don the appropriate ornaments.

With these sociopolitical and religious hierarchies in mind, let us now return to the role played by ornament in distinguishing officials and individuals at the three levels stated above.

Hierarchical level

The most important *Qaalluu*, or *Abbaa Muda*, is distinguished by the *laddu*, three iron bracelets worn on the wrist of the left arm. According to myth, iron was of

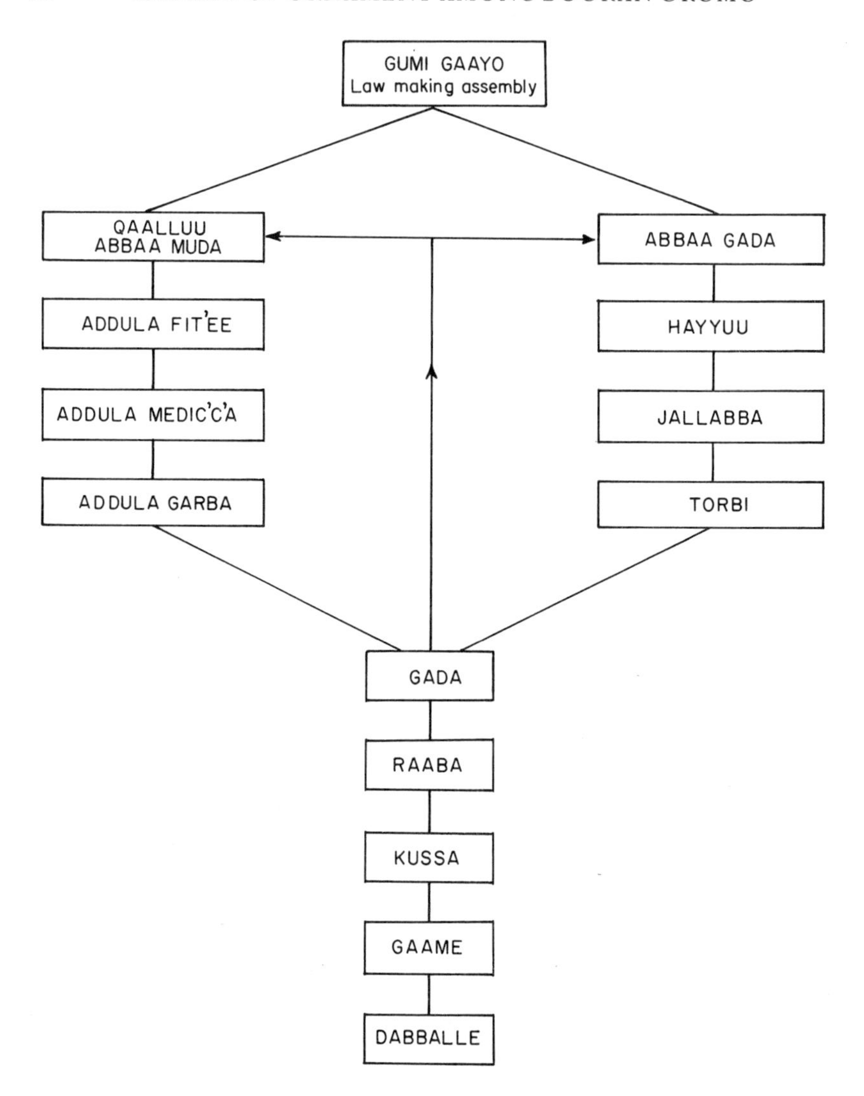

Figure 13.1 The *Gada* system.

meteorite origin and 'fell from heaven'. It is significant that the first *Qaalluu* is also said to have 'come down from heaven' (cf. Note 8). In Oromo there are a great number of ornaments made out of iron and its substitutes – copper, brass and more recently, aluminium – collectively known as *sibbilla*. Iron has various connotations, including that of protecting the wearer from evil forces, but in the present context it represents strength, divine power and resistance. The *Qaalluu* also wears an iron phallic-shaped horn (*kallac'c'a*) inserted into an ivory disc and tied around the head so that the horn rests erect on the forehead (cf. Fig. 13.2). The *kallac'c'a* is a symbol of fertility 'associated with religious wor-

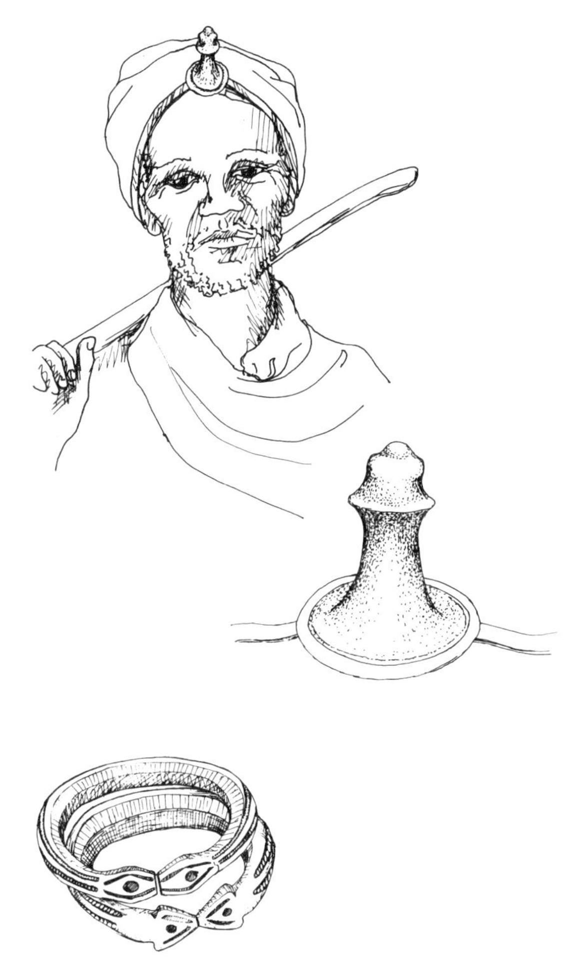

Figure 13.2 Booran elder wearing the *kallac'c'a* horn, close-up of horn, and snake-ended bracelets (*mirg mata bofaa*).

ship or kingship or both' (Baxter 1954, p. 372), and similar objects are found among other Cushitic-speaking peoples. Around his neck the *Qaalluu* wears a string of *buuran* beads. *Buuran*, as we have already seen, are considered particularly 'good' beads (cf. also Baxter 1954, p. 241). All of the parts of the body associated with these ornaments give an additional dimension of significance to them, symbolisms which will not, however, be fully developed here.

The *Abbaa Gada* wears virtually the same ornaments as the *Qaalluu*, the two men having almost identical status in their different realms of power, the only difference being one of number. The *Abbaa Gada* wears only one *laddu*, and his *kallac'c'a* is a double-horned one. However, the most distinctive symbol of power of the *Abbaa Gada* are the ostrich feathers by which he hands over and acquires power. Two parallel rituals of 'chase' are performed: that of a live ostrich and that of the outgoing *Abbaa Gada* by the incoming one. As Legesse (1973, p. 82) points out, ostrich feathers are generally a sign of political authority all over East Africa, related by their shape to the spearhead. For the Ancient Egyptians (Chevalier & Gheerbrant 1969, p. 88) the ostrich feather was a symbol of justice and truth, which may be equally evident here, as the *Abbaa Gada* is the highest judicial authority in the *Gada* institution.

The *hayyuu* 'councillors' (*addula*, *addula fit'ee*, *garba*, *hayyuu* and *hayyuu medic'c'a*) and their deputies (the *jallabba*) all wear, during their term of office, the ceremonial turban (*ruffa*), and carry the ceremonial staff (*hororo*) and whip (*liic'o*). However, their distinguishing mark of office is the skin wristlet (*medic'c'a*), through which they are appointed. The skin of stock specially slaughtered for the occasion is cut into strips, is first worn on the wrist of the *Qaalluu* or the *Abbaa Gada* and is then sent to the appointee. The wristlets are connected with sacrifice, and are also worn by ordinary Booran when they slaughter stock for peace and rain.

The *torbi* officers do not wear any distinguishing ornaments and are considered, despite their title, to be like any Booran, and wear like them *mic'iira* bracelets on the left arm. These are made out of three interwoven strands of metal, usually copper, brass and iron. They also wear the *surri*, the cloth turban of all married men, and a single *buuran* bead, interspersed with other types. The *ruffa* is worn on all ceremonial occasions, and all heads of households possess the *hororo* staff and the whip, *liic'o*.

Initiatory level

The *gada* grades cross-cut these offices, and it is from one of the patrilines that the officers are selected. Grade I is that of the *dabballe*, boys born ideally at the 'right' time in the cycle, who are therefore very special children who are highly protected. The term *dabballe* refers to their hairstyle, worn long like that of a girl and decorated with cowrie shells and *buuran* beads. In Oromo cowrie shells (*ellelaan*) are a symbol of the mother-and-child relationship, by their colour (that of milk), and are thought to have mnemonic properties, linked, like elsewhere, to the ear (cf. MacKenzie, 1926, pp. 139ff.). The *dabballe* are first reared by Waata hunter–gatherer surrogate parents, and are treated and dressed as girls, and are given derogatory names to protect them from evil (cf. Frazer 1918, pp. 168–98). The *dabballe* are 'among the principal mediators between man and god' and are 'invested with powers and attributes similar to the *Qaalluu* and other liminal persons' (Legesse 1973, p. 53). The mothers of *dabballe* have an equally privileged position in society, and wear the *gulma* – copper hairpieces fastened to the back of the head, sometimes with a *buuran* bead.

The following three grades are marked by changes in hairstyle. The fifth grade is that of the junior and senior warriors (*raaba*), and it is the latter who are ideally the fathers of *dabballe*. Such men wear the male equivalent of the *gulma*, an iron bracelet called *maldaa*. At the end of this period, in the first part of the *gada* grade, the official end of the procreative cycle is marked by circumcision and ear-piercing rites, these being symbolically equivalent acts, after which an earring is worn in the left ear, indicating proven ability as a man, a father, a warrior and a leader. In the second half of this grade *gada* elders are invested with ritual authority by making a pilgrimage (*muda*) to the *Qaalluu*.

In the next 40 years of his life a man gradually retires from active participation in the political affairs of the nation and dedicates himself to spiritual affairs. He goes first into partial (*yuuba* grade) and then full (*gadamoojii* grade) retirement. It is in this last grade that the *gadamoojii* elders put on a replica of the *kallac'c'a* and 'complete their heads'. Henceforth they belong to the sacred realm of women, are referred to by the female pronoun, and attain religious sanctity through their *kallac'c'a*. The wives wear an equivalent of the horn, called *benaac'u*, tied tightly to the centre of their backs, a symbolic representation of the son, through whom they have acquired indirect power. After the *gadamoojii* transition ceremony the *kallac'c'a* is kept upturned in a container of milk, and it will be worn by the heir of the elder, when he, in turn, succeeds to this grade.

Procreative level

Three important events mark the life of the male individual: killing, marriage and the birth of a son, each linked with the wearing of certain ornaments. For a woman each of these events has its equivalent and determines the type of ornament she will wear.

To be able to marry, a man must first prove himself worthy of becoming a husband and father by killing and emasculating an enemy or felling a wild animal, like an elephant, lion or buffalo, and returning with a trophy. Such a man wears a metal neckband called *gogessa*, an ivory bracelet called (*h*)*arbora* if the animal was an elephant, or a giraffe-skin necklet called *mart'a*. When he marries, his wife can display some of these ornaments on her own body, and she is also entitled to wear *kommee* (metal anklets). When a man marries, his wife receives other metal ornaments, bracelets (*meeti*), worn on the left arm, and necklaces (*galim*) decorated with medallions (*lira*). In Oromo iron is symbolically a 'dead' material, and is an appropriate gift, as marriage itself is seen as a kind of death, in which a husband 'kills' his wife by spilling her virginal blood. However, through this 'death' springs 'life', in the form of a child, ideally a son, who is like a woman's trophy, and through whom she establishes her right in her new clan. She can now wear bracelets on her upper right arm, the side of life, often in the shape of a double-headed snake, representing her double affiliations to the two moieties, *Sabo* and *Gona*, and the union of these opposites through marriage. Beaded necklaces are also worn upon the birth of the child, which traditionally are red and yellow (amber) in colour, standing for blood and regeneration and the child's healthy waste matter, respectively, the latter being a symbol of fertility in Oromo. These necklaces, like the *galim*, sometimes contain leather amulets (*kud'aam*) enclosing, before the advent of Islam, potent herbs to protect the wearer from the evil eye (*buda*) and other evil forces. These amulets are also worn by men and children, around the neck or on the upper left arm. At the birth ceremony of a son the mother wears a leather belt (*gollo*) decorated with small bells (*bilbila*) and wooden gourd tops (*buge*).[11] The *saga*, a dance ornament, similarly percussive, is worn around the wrist. The aluminium necklaces and bracelets (*gilgile*) worn for decoration also produce a pleasant sound when dancing. A married woman can also wear earrings (*gubee gurra*) and a ring (*gubee harka*), also worn by men, with the same meaning, as marks of social accomplishment. Children are decorated with beads and cowrie shells, wear necklaces of fragrant wood or seeds, to make them smell nice and, sometimes, a bell around the upper arm to protect them from harmful influences.

Thus, the ornaments of men, women and children are all connected with forms of fertility, and those of men and women boast of the social achievements of manhood and womanhood, of the pride of children successfully fathered and borne.

Conclusion

In this study of ornament we have examined how it functions at three different levels of society – not only as symbols of spiritual and temporal power and authority, but also as symbols of fertility, expressed through the male concept of iron and the female concept of beads. We have also tried to show, through the myth of origin of certain ritual beads and objects, and through the myth of the *Qaalluu*, the mystical nature of ornament and its deep religious value in the Oromo world-view, making it an integral part of *waan aadaa*, or 'things of tradition'.

Notes

1 The Oromo are an Eastern-Cushitic speaking people who live in Ethiopia, Kenya and Somalia and number between 18 and 22 million according to unofficial sources. All of the Oromo groups speak a mutually intelligible language and 'share core common cultural values and modes of thought' (Baxter 1985, p. 1). In conceptual terms they are composed of the Booran and Gabra (or Gabaro), representing the progeny of the first-born and that of the second-born sons of the mythical founder of the Oromo nation, Horo. The name Oromo is derived from the eponym Horo, which etymologically stems from the word *hora* (mineral water). It is preferred to the designation 'Galla', used in the ethnographic literature but repudiated by the people themselves. However, historical differentiation, economic, religious and other factors have tended to obscure the cognitive differences, which is especially evident among the Booran and Gabra of Northern Kenya. Here we take the Booran as representing the ideal image or model, from which necessary ritual differences have arisen, but many of our interpretations are valid for all Oromo.

2 None of these terms is really equivalent to 'ornament'. In Western Oromo silver jewellery is offered to a young woman during marriage negotiations, and *nagata*, from the verb 'to put on', indicates that she is engaged. *Fayya* is also used in greetings, in the sense of 'being well, healthy'. Our informants maintain that the word

mard'aad' is Oromo and not connected to *maridadi* ('fine, smart, beautiful', etc. in Swahili).

3 This myth was recorded by G. Megersa, and forms part of his unpublished Booran Oromo source materials. It was, unfortunately, not possible to present the myth *in toto* and we give here a paraphrased version.

4 Abbaa Yaya is also known as Baricha Gayo, and the Mataarri clan are still not allowed to nominate *hayyuu* due to this historical error.

5 Probably ideophones representing a swollen stomach.

6 There is a deliberate ambiguity in the original version of the myth about the *buuran*, *c'iruwaan* and *umu gurraatii* beads, three words for two objects due to their mysterious nature. The *buuran* is a dark blue, flat bead and is used to decorate several objects. The *umu gurraatii* (literally 'black bead') is a round bead of the same dark blue colour. In some Oromo groups beads (*umu*) are associated with the female divinity Ateta, called *ayo umtu* ('mother of creation'; cf. Knutsson 1967, p. 88), and it is tempting to see in the word for bead the verb *um-* ('to create'; cf. also the Arabic word, *um*, 'mother'). Black (*gurraac'a*, fem. *gurraatii*) has positive connotations for Oromo, and is connected with *Waaga*, their celestial God. *C'iruwaan* can apply to both types of beads. *Mataarri* is a thread consisting of three interwoven strands, as well as the name of the Booran clan from which the *Qaalliti* or ritual wife of the *Qaalluu* is still chosen today.

7 The Konso are Eastern-Cushitic agriculturalists who live in southern Ethiopia. Most blacksmiths in Booran are Konso.

8 The *Qaalluu* is the ritual leader of the Booran and is said to have 'descended from heaven'. According to different versions of the myth, he was 'found' in the wilderness by a Waata hunter–gatherer, had by his side a black cow and a spitting cobra. He was wearing the *laddu* iron bracelets and was wrapped in a black, white and red checked cloth, colours symbolizing the three life-giving liquids: water, milk and blood. Other ritual objects are also associated with his finding. There are five *gaalluu*, a supreme *Qaalluu*, who is the *Abbaa Muda*, and comes from the Karrayyu clan; the lesser *gaalluu* are all from the opposite, *Gona*, moiety. The *Qaalluu* myth can be found in Baxter (1954), Knutsson (1967) and Legesse (1973).

9 *D'itac'a* = *Psydrax schimperiana* (A. Rich.), Bridson, Rubiaceae.

10 For a fuller description of the Booran *Gada* system, see Legesse (1973) and Baxter (1978).

11 *Buge* = *Cucurbita lagenaria; lagenaria sphaerica* (Sond.) Naud., Cucurbitaceae.

References

Bartels, L. 1983. *Oromo religion. Myths and rites of the W. Oromo of Ethiopia. An attempt to understand.* Berlin: Dietrich Reimer Verlag.

Baxter, P. T. W. 1954. Social organization of the Galla of Northern Kenya. Unpublished PhD dissertation, Lincoln College.

Baxter, P. T. W. 1978. Boran age-sets and generation sets. Gada, a puzzle or a maze? In *Age, generation and time. Some features of East African age organizations*, P. T. W. Baxter & U. Almagor (eds), 151–82. London: C. Hurst & Co.

Baxter, P. T. W. 1985. The present state of Oromo studies: a résumé. Paper presented at the Institut national des Langues et Cultures orientales (INALCO), Paris, May 1985.

Chevalier, J. & A. Gheerbrant 1969. *Dictionnaire des symboles*. Paris: Laffont.
Frazer, J. G. 1918. *Folklore in the Old Testament*, Vol. 3. London: Macmillan.
Knutsson, K. E. 1967. *Authority and change. A study of the Kallu institution among the Macha Galla of Ethiopia*. Göteborg: Etnografiska Museet.
Legesse, A. 1973. *Gada. Three approaches to the study of African society*. New York: Free Press.
MacKenzie, O. A. 1926. *The migration of symbols*. London: Kegal Paul.

6 *The messages of material behaviour: a preliminary discussion of non-verbal meaning*

ROLAND FLETCHER

Introduction

People communicate using verbal and non-verbal meaning. Non-verbal communication (Mehrabian 1972, Argyle 1975, Morris 1977, Druckman *et al.* 1982) is generated both by the active behaviour of proxemics (Hall 1966, 1968, 1974) and kinesics (Hall 1959, Birdwhistell 1970) and by material behaviour such as the spatial arrangement of inert entities in a settlement (Fletcher 1981a, 1984). Verbal communication has until recently been entirely carried by the active behaviour of speaking or singing. Only in the past 5000 years has the storage and transmission of verbal meaning by material behaviour become fully established, first by writing and, in the present century, by various electronic devices.

Verbal communication is so characteristic of contemporary humans and so philosophically consequential (Wittgenstein 1953) that the substantial role of non-verbal communication in daily life is not readily recognized. As with the study of group behaviour and adaptation in other animal species (Barnard 1983), an understanding of non-verbal communication is fundamental for an ethology of our subspecies.

Because verbal meaning is crucial to our conscious intentions and is the most apparent immediate communication which we can individually exercise, it has been the subject of vigorous analysis. The 'deep structure', logic and expressiveness of verbal meaning have been the subject of profound enquiry, for instance by Chomsky (1957), Whorf (1956) and Leavis (1975), in the English-speaking tradition. We incline to view verbal meaning as the window into the human mind. With a humanistic preference for viewing our actions in terms of intentionality, verbal meaning has seemed to be the appropriate, sufficient and apparently even necessary foundation for understanding our cultural behaviour.

However, if non-verbal meaning also plays a fundamental role in the functioning of human communities (Hall 1977), then the predominance of verbal meaning interpretations is untenable. The presence of non-verbal messages and the non-verbal meanings which they carry specifies that verbal meaning must have a particular, not a universal, role in human life. Although verbal meaning is essential for the short-term, small-scale functioning of human society, it cannot be regarded as necessary or sufficient for an understanding of human interaction and communication on all timescales. Only by a reductionist argument, that knowledge of the smallest facet of human life is a prerequisite for all else, can the predominance of verbal meaning be sustained. An archaeological approach to the study of human behaviour cannot logically argue that only one scale of process, e.g. the ethnographic scale, is either proper or exclusively relevant. The potential of an archaeological approach to the past is that it can allow insights into the nature of human existence using a wide spectrum of timescales to identify the various processes which have been involved in creating our humanness (Bailey 1983, Fletcher 1981b, 1986). If these Time Perspectivist insights are applicable to our comprehension of the short timescale patterning of our daily lives, then we can ill afford to retain the predominance of verbal meanings in archaeological interpretation.

The case for non-verbal meaning

We usually understand meaning in verbal terms. Significance or difference and expressiveness are specified by words with values attached. For instance, the meanings attached to interpersonal relationships may be expressed verbally using terms like intimate, formal and distant. However, the behaviour is also assigned a relative meaning designated non-verbally by the spacing distances which the people use, whether they are aware that they do so or not. The non-verbal meaning of active behaviour, expressed as sensations varying from pleasure to distress, is produced without any need for verbal clarification. Indeed, such clarification can effectively demolish the meaning content of non-verbal signalling.

In different communities the proxemic spacing distances used may differ, often substantially. The actual distances used cannot be predefined by the verbal meanings ascribed to the interactions. A mother-in-law avoidance rule does not in itself tell you what spacing distance or positioning will be used. You cannot predict from a verbally declared specification of formal interaction what the actual distance used will be, though you can predict that it will be greater for public association than for an intimate conversation. Neither can you predict that the 'rule' will always be applied or that humans will consistently carry out the practice even when strict declarations are made about it. There is no simple correspondence between verbal declaration and actual behaviour. What people say and what they do are not the same.

Four basic points follow:

(a) that the non-verbal system is not sufficiently explicable in terms of the verbal system not reducible to it;
(b) that there may be a formal relationship between the non-verbal signals which are used, e.g. between the spacing distances in proxemic behaviour – to some degree the relative difference between the spacing distances can be predicted;

(c) there can be a mismatch between verbal meanings and non-verbal signals, e.g. inappropriate associations of interpersonal distances and verbal expression occur – they are part of the characteristic signal ambiguity of human social life; and

(d) verbal meaning cannot be a sufficient designate for the cultural functions of the human brain – if mind is considered, by definition, to be sufficiently comprehended through verbal meaning, then a very limited view of human-ness is being sustained.

We must therefore ask how meaning is to be comprehended in non-verbal terms, since it is clear that non-verbal signalling may possess its own internal formal coherence and is not reducible to the 'structures' of verbal meaning. A case can be made that non-verbal meaning must necessarily have an internal coherence of its own, otherwise consistent and repetitious modes of non-verbal expression could not be maintained. Since human communities are not generally aware of the nature of their own particular non-verbal message systems, human intentionality cannot act as the regulator of message consistency, nor can verbal meaning suffice, because of the lack of tight correspondence between declaration and action.

The specification of non-verbal meaning

Non-verbal meaning can be defined very simply by applying the same basic criteria which specify meaning verbally. The key is the designation of relative significance. For example, verbal meanings allocate position, rank, status, value, etc., to given social states by differentiation between them, specifying discrete categories for managing otherwise continuous variables and defining the content of the relationship between those categories (Goffman 1959). The verbal messages are carried by a grammar which precludes some ways of communicating (Whorf 1956). The grammar and sound periodicity of a language are levels of a hierarchy of 'deep structure' below the verbal meaning, but which nevertheless constitute meaning themselves. They constitute a meaning system because they designate relative value and specify discrete differentiations in an otherwise continuous spectrum of sounds and utterance frequency. Some sounds and deviations of speech are valued, others are excluded, some combinations are favoured, whereas others are delimited in use or excluded.

With non-verbal communication the same applies. This is most easily illustrated by proxemic patterns in active non-verbal behaviour. The behavioural meanings which affect us regardless of any conscious recognition of their occurrence are apparently carried by a 'deep structure' of interrelated distances which in some communities (e.g. white North America) consists of increasing size differentiation between the successively larger spacing distances (Hall 1966). We might view this as a corollary of the mechanics of the eye and brain, but it has not been shown by proxemic studies whether this is the only possible formal 'deep structure' for active non-verbal meaning. Although metrical interrelatedness can be viewed as a meaning system in the same way as a verbal grammar and sound periodic structure, it may have a much simpler formal content and is not time sequential like verbal communication.

Once non-verbal meaning is recognized for interpersonal spacing behaviour, it follows that the same applies to the spacing distances and arrangements used in material behaviour (Fletcher 1977). Verbal meaning may be ascribed to the size of entities such as residence units or their relative placement. However, by example from the above arguments it follows that the actual lengths of walls, widths of doorways, etc., are spatial signals constituting a message about the communities' cultural organization of space. The distances used should themselves be part of a formal pattern and specify meaning. That meaning is the metrical designation of which spacing distances will tend to be used, and the size and variation relationship between them. Different degrees and kinds of significance may be ascribed to the same distances in the material spatial messages of different communities (see Fletcher 1977, 1981a, 1984, for preliminary attempts to describe serial patterns in the settlements of agrarian sedentary communities).

Once recognized for material spacing behaviour, it then follows that similar material formal patterns of meaning should occur for colour coding, time differentiation by material means and the role of material barriers as segregators of sight and sound interaction. The material baffles which block sound transmission and prevent intervisibility generate a system of perceptual exclusions. We can specify on a methodological uniformitarian basis from mechanics and physics that materials have had these exclusion characteristics across the entire span of time that is relevant to the study of human beings. Provided that evidence of the material structures survives, we will also be able to describe the various arrangements of exclusion in different settlements. These arrangements can be analysed for their formal content, i.e. for the relationship between the exclusions that they generate. We can therefore make propositions that can be checked about those systems of exclusion as assemblages of meaning in the non-verbal sense described above, and can relate them to the behavioural trajectory of a community and the conditions of life in its settlement. Obviously route-access interaction frequency patterns are very different in a linear settlement (e.g. some North-West Coast and Eskimo settlements of North America) and in settlements with a grid-route system.

We have tended to correlate architectural patterns with social meaning expressed verbally (Preziosi 1979), but this is not an adequate approach. While striving to complement the complexity of human life, it does an injustice to the relationship between the different operational timescales of our various meaning systems. The approach seems to be elaborate only because we tend to take verbal meaning for granted. We do not readily perceive the other vast message patterns of community life with their own meaning systems, nor do we readily comprehend their autonomy. There is clearly a difference of scale and process in the relationship between what people actually do, the spatial milieu that they create, and the verbal declarations and expressions which are used to describe social life. For instance, human communities produce structures with very marked, identifiable material boundaries in conjunction with many different verbally designated social systems. Among the Ashanti (Fortes 1959) the residence arrangement is described in terms of brothers and sisters residing in the same building while the sisters send food to their husbands (someone else's brother) in another residence unit which can be some way across the settlement. The residence units are distinctly defined structures, often large rectangular compounds with interior courtyards and blank outer walls. Clearly, spatial definition is as important in the Ashanti residence pattern as it is in another very different social system used by the Tallensi (Fortes 1959), where a man, his mother, his wife and his children are the core domestic group in a residence unit with well-defined structural limits. The demands and normal patterning of the spatial component of community life are not reducible to the active social structure as expressed in verbal terms.

There should therefore be an entire structuralist approach capable of expressing non-verbal meaning without reference to the meaning categories, taxonomies or explanations applicable to verbal expression and human action understood in terms of those verbal meanings. The semiotics of the non-verbal meanings of material behaviour messages would be expressed in terms of frequencies, intensities and physical states such as distances, not a linear grammar as in verbal communication. Boolean algebra, set theory and topology, as well as quantified statements of serial order and degrees of variation, will be the appropriate modes of expression. The archaeological record is ideal for this enquiry, since we can even look at the evolution of these material meaning systems in ethological terms as aspects of biological behaviour.

The relationship between verbal and non-verbal meaning

Dynamics

A Time Perspectivist view specifies that material messages operate over longer timespans than do verbal and active signals. The former have a longer sustained signal presence and a generally slower replication frequency. Their meaning content and their 'deep structure' is therefore likely to change more slowly. Consequently dissonance can, and will, occur between material and active messages, because their rates of transformation and the specifics of their coding are different.

The implications of this are considerable. In any biological system the larger-scale, slower processes generate the selective pressure on smaller-scale, shorter timespan systems. The general class of material non-verbal messages will therefore exercise selective pressure on the more rapidly changing active and verbal message systems. The material messages are the milieu in which the active messages function, and are not adequately understood merely as derivative epiphenomena of active behaviour. Changes in non-verbal material messages will be necessary for the long-term functioning of a community. Within those bounds many different active signal systems might suffice, since they are only requisite for the short-term maintenance and stability of social functions. Furthermore, the dissonance between active and material messages will itself be a crucial generator of change. However, the central characteristic of a selection model is that no immediate delimited relationship exists between the two classes of message system. The verbal message systems are not bound to conform to the material non-verbal message format. The former should produce variants according to their own internal logic, not according to the dictates of a non-verbal context. All that the latter does is to select for or against the variants that any given verbal system can produce. An inherently unstable dialectical relationship is present in which new meanings can be generated when the two great meaning systems clash. The Time Perspectivist viewpoint does not allow social models either primacy or free rein. In many cases they are overspecified reifications of contemporary verbal constructions of reality. The selection processes in Time Perspectivism rule out a deterministic link between material and social phenomena. Verbal expression is a fundamental of human creativity, and is not predetermined by other aspects of community life or external environmental context. If it were so determined, then our attitudes to social and external environmental reality could not be consciously transformed.

Role of verbal messages

Since non-verbal messages patterns are in general not consciously apprehended by their users, some mediation is needed between them and the conscious mind. A profound social role of verbal meaning is to try and make the nature and consequences of active and material non-verbal behaviour comprehensible to the minds of the members of the community, and thereby apparently manageable.

Conclusions: some implications of non-verbal meaning

How do verbal and non-verbal systems interrelate? This can only be studied in contemporary contexts or where a sufficient material verbal record survives for analysis to be appropriate. The early literate civilizations and regions where oral tradition provides some linkage, as in Hawaii, will be invaluable archaeological contexts for such research. The interrelationship is a major issue of social process, and should not be diminished by the use of fallacious substantive uniformitarianism to impose associations from the present or the recent past on to the more distant past.

Meaning can be considered in archaeological contexts without reference to the putative verbal meanings with which we have tried to apprehend meaning in the material assemblages of human behaviour. If there is not a direct correspondence, then the imposition of verbal meaning on material behaviour is logically improper. If material non-verbal messages operate on longer timescales, then their functioning and nature can be analysed without necessary reference to the short timescale functioning of verbal meaning.

The 'structure' of meaning in material non-verbal messages would be the equivalent for cultural systems of the genetic code in biological systems. Since that meaning code is carried on the material component of human behaviour, it is directly accessible in the archaeological record. In contrast, the gene code is currently only indirectly observable in the palaeontological record. If archaeologists can break out of the tradition of understanding humans through verbal meaning, then there is great potential for fundamental research on the codes of non-verbal material meaning and their role in hominid behaviour.

Acknowledgements

My thanks to Tim Murray for discussions on the metaphysical foundations of archaeological theory and interpretation, and to Ben Cullen for discussion of the equivalence between genetic and material behaviour message codes, and their crucial differences.

References

Argyle, M. 1975. *Bodily communication*. London: Methuen.
Bailey, G. N. 1983. Concepts of time in Quaternary prehistory. *Annual Review of Anthropology* **12**, 165–92.
Barnard, C. J. 1983. *Animal behaviour: ecology and evolution*. London: Croom Helm.
Birdwhistell, R. L. 1970. *Kinesics and context*. Philadelphia: Philadelphia University Press.
Chomsky, N. 1957. *Syntactic structures*. The Hague: Mouton.
Druckman, D., R. Rozelle & J. C. Baxter 1982. *Non-verbal communication: survey, theory and research*. Beverly Hills: Sage.
Fletcher, R. J. 1977. Settlement studies. In *Spatial archaeology*, D. L. Clarke (ed.), 47–162. London: Academic Press.
Fletcher, R. J. 1981a. Space and community behaviour: spatial order in settlements. In *Universals of human thought*, B. Lloyd & J. Gay (eds), 97–128. Cambridge: Cambridge University Press.
Fletcher, R. J. 1981b. People and space: a material behaviour approach. In *Pattern of the past. Studies in honour of David Clarke*, I. Hodder, G. Isaac & N. Hammond (eds), 157–84. Cambridge: Cambridge University Press.
Fletcher, R. J. 1984. Identifying spatial disorder: a case study of a Mongol fort. In *Intrasite spatial analysis in archaeology*, H. Hietala (ed.), 196–223. Cambridge: Cambridge University Press.
Fletcher, R. J. 1986. Settlement archaeology: world-wide comparisons. *World Archaeology* **18**, 59–83.
Fortes, M. 1959. Primitive kinship. *Scientific American* **200** (6), 146–58.
Goffman, E. 1959. *The presentation of self in everyday life*. New York: Doubleday.
Hall, E. T. 1959. *The silent language*. New York: Doubleday.
Hall, E. T. 1966. *The hidden dimension*. New York: Doubleday.
Hall, E. T. 1968. Proxemics. *Current Anthropology* **9**, 83–108.
Hall, E. T. 1974. Studies in the anthropology of visual communication. *Handbook of proxemic research. Special publication*. Washington: Society for the Anthropology of Visual Communication.

Hall, E. T. 1977. *Beyond culture*. New York: Doubleday.

Leavis, F. R. 1975. *The living principle: 'English' as a discipline of thought*. London: Chatto & Windus.

Mehrabian, A. 1972. *Non-verbal communication*. Chicago: Aldine–Atherton.

Morris, D. 1977. *Manwatching: a field guide to human behaviour*. London: Cape.

Preziosi, D. 1979. *The semiotics of the built environment: an introduction to architectonic analysis*. Bloomington: Indiana University Press.

Whorf, B. L. 1956. *Language, thought and reality*. New York: The Technology Press of MIT/Wiley.

Wittgenstein, L. 1953. *Philosophical investigations* (transl. G. E. M. Anscombe). Oxford: Blackwell.

24 *Religious cults and ritual practice among the Mendi people of the Southern Highlands Province of Papua New Guinea*

THEODORE MAWE

The Mendi were first contacted by the Australian Administration in 1950 and had only limited Western-government rule by 1954 (see Lederman 1987). They inhabit a narrow valley area in the Southern Highlands of Papua New Guinea. Most Mendi are dark skinned, short and strongly built. They live in dispersed homesteads with clan or tribal group boundaries. The groups are patrilineal and are organized in kinship and descent formation. Nearly all members are primarily subsistence farmers or horticulturalists and secondarily pig herders, *kaukau* (sweet potato) being their staple diet supplemented by pork. Their socio-economic welfare has been and still is their major concern. Broadly speaking, this is the fertility of the people, their food crops and animals, as well as success in the manufacture, distribution and use of wealth. The ability to guide and control the socio-economic welfare of a group is the essential qualification for gaining power, authority or leadership.

Religion in Mendi is important, as it is in all Papua New Guinea societies. Nevertheless it is difficult to define. The people themselves have no general term for it, and it cannot be regarded as it is in the Western world as a separate culture entity, something pertaining to a special supernatural or transcendental realm within the Cosmos. Its explanatory myths or set of information is not different from or set apart from other forms of knowledge, nor is its ritual reserved for and performed on specific individual occasions. It is not something removed from the ordinary world of human affairs: it is best examined as one aspect of the total cosmic order that the people believe to exist.

The Mendi people see this order as being of two parts. The first is what we call the empirical, that which consists of the natural environment, economic resources (including animals, artefacts, etc.) and the human inhabitants themselves. The second part is the non-empirical, which includes spirit-beings and impersonal occult forces (including magic, sorcery, etc.). Thus, religion in the Mendi view is their putative relationship with spirit-beings and supernatural forces in the non-empirical part of the Cosmos. We can look at this in two ways: first, as a set of human beliefs about the nature of spirit-beings, occult forces as contained in myths and legends; and secondly, as a system of ritual techniques which the Mendi use in the attempt to communicate to their own advantage with these beings and forces.

This definition of religion does not fit into many others endorsed by a number of scholars. Malinowski (1961) sees a religious rite as an end in itself, which has no immediate or obvious objective. He regards magic as being pragmatically oriented. However, the Mendi religion is directed towards such things as the production of crops, raising pigs, hunting and fishing. Every myth and ritual act in Mendi has some specific practical purpose in view. Durkheim (1947) sees religion in a different way. For him religion was social and collective – its beliefs were symbolic and the rituals reinforced the social order. Magic was purely individualistic and isolated, and unlike religion had no congregation or church. This view also does not fit the Mendi life and religion, the reason being simply that the number of people engaged in any ritual is determined by how many are necessary to carry it out efficiently. Also, all Mendi beliefs rely on a common set of mental or intellectual assumptions and, furthermore, even if there is some degree of individual or group monopoly of myth and ritual, many members of Mendi society subscribe to all of its beliefs.

For Tylor (1903) and Frazer (1913) religion was essentially man's belief in spirit-beings who were superior to himself, whom he endeavoured to appease by means of ritual, thereby achieving freedom of action. Pure magic was man's belief that he himself, without the aid of spirit-beings, could control impersonal occult forces by using specialized ritual techniques.

This distinction only fits the Mendi situation to a certain extent. Whereas the rituals concerned with the dead are intended to appease them, the other spirit-beings and the associated rituals have no such intention, but rather ensure that what they desire will automatically be done. The same is true for magic. The category of magic which I am obliged to name as 'harm' magic (including sorcery witchcraft and other impersonal occult forces intended to harm or hurt people) has no need of aid from spirit-beings. The other category, which I term 'good' magic (including wealth-drawing magic, fertility magic and other types which are intended to obtain good things), was originally given to the ancestors by spirit-beings. So the definition of Tylor and Frazer only fits the Mendi situation in a limited sense.

Generally, all of these definitions bear little resemblance to real Mendi religious life. Westerners see religion and magic as isolated from culture, but this does not mean that such a concept should be regarded as universal. The Mendi – like many other Papua New Guineans – have special words for such things as myths, duties, spirits, magic, dead ancestors, various forms of rituals and sorcery. Yet they have no collective term for religion, nor do they have any term separating religion from magic.

The above attempt to define religion is to avoid using preconceived ideas from an alien culture and to study the facts through the eyes of the Mendi people themselves, taking into account only their experiences and the forces that have shaped their sociocultural order. This inevitably does not mean that the views of the scholars mentioned above will not be incorporated and endorsed, but rather the examination has got to be approached in the light of the views of the

Mendi people. Malinowski's view of religion can be correlated with a stress on the economic aspects of society, while Durkheim's correlates with a stress on social stability. Both emphasize the need for religion in situations of anxiety and stress due to certain socio-economic and political conditions. Tylor and Frazer see religion as part of a people's mental life, emphasizing their understanding of the world around them. Anyway, what is important and obviously of great concern for the Mendi people is where an activity or institution is strongly validated by myth and buttressed by ritual. Most Mendi take for granted those activities and institutions which have no associated myths or rituals.

I have written of spirit-beings and occult forces, and what these are to the Mendi. A fuller discussion of these and their main categories is necessary.

Spirit-beings can be explained in three categories. First, there are autonomous spirit-beings such as culture heroes and heroines, sky-beings (goddesses and gods) and demigods. All of these were believed to exist in the past from the time of creation, or from an early period, and to be the primary operative forces in the Cosmos. They are creative and regulative, and are thought to have introduced significant parts of the cosmic order (including culture). The *yeki* (sky-beings), which are known as gods and goddesses or angels, are thought to inhabit the sky and control meteorological phenomena such as rain, thunder and lightning. People still believe that they are in contact with human society and still influence its concerns. Culture heroes and heroines or demigods are important in the rituals attributed to them with the items of culture that they are thought to have invented.

The second category of spirit-beings are autonomous or self-governing spirit-beings: *su temo* (soil spirit), *ip temo* (water spirit) and *trip temo* (mountain forest spirit). These sorts of spirit-beings are regarded more or less as demons or some sort of natural spirits which exist, just as nature is. Although these beings have no doctrinal system of worship and ritual, they still influence human affairs. For instance, the *su temo* is concerned with ethics and moral codes of discipline. The *trip temo* is well known for 'eating' humans or stealing children, harming people, and so on. This category of spirit-beings the Mendi regard as of the natural order – they have no myth attached to them, and this explains why they have no rituals.

The third category of spirit-beings are the dead, and these are in two parts: the ancestral spirits and the recently dead. Whereas luck, good fortune and blessing are attributed to the ancestors, sickness and death are caused by the recently dead. Most sickness and death and other misfortunes are restricted to spouses, siblings and direct descendants.

Occult forces are impersonal, and most take the classic forms described by Frazer (1913), namely homoeopathic magic and contagious magic. Homoeopathic magic relates to the idea that something that is like another is created by that something, and any action taken on one of them will affect the other in the same way. Contagious magic assumes that the detached part of an object always remains in sympathetic contact with the whole object or, in a more clear sense, where two objects have been in close contact they will remain in sympathetic contact even when separated. Hence, any action taken on one of the two separated objects will produce identical effects on the whole or the other object. Both forms of sympathetic magic are thought to derive their power purely from ritual itself.

Unlike the above, which I have earlier referred to as 'harm' magic, there is good-purpose magic. This includes love magic, fertility (of humans, crops and animals) magic and wealth-drawing magical formulae. These forms, with the exception of love magic, are thought to have derived their powers from spirit-beings. The techniques and knowledge of the magical rites were invented and given to mankind by gods and goddesses, or sky-beings.

Ritual practice is the means whereby the Mendi people communicate with or manipulate spirit-beings and occult forces. Many of the rituals are often supported by observing taboos: for example, the restrictions attached to eating certain food, abstaining from sexual intercourse, restrictions on drinking water at certain times, and so forth. Without the observance of these taboos the ritual is usually deemed useless. Certain supernatural forces, such as the force of *saikil*, *kip* and the natural spirits *su temo*, *ip temo* and *trip temo* do not have any rituals, nor are there any taboos attached to them. They have no doctrinal system, nor are there any myths attached to them. The reason is simply that people cannot predict or control these forces to their own advantage. The force *saikil* is a force that saves or blesses, or it is the blessing itself. *Saikil* exists outside the processes of nature, and it is present in the atmosphere of life. It may attach itself to people and things and can only be seen by its works. The power *saikil* exists in its own right, therefore man cannot control or predict its events. When it appears man can say it is, so *saikil* is seen only by its works. An example will make this clear. If a tree falls towards you and misses you, by a centimetre or so, the *saikil* power is not the force that is in the tree that allows it to miss you, but rather is the force that allows for the tree to miss you. The following examples may clear any confusion:

> You would have got killed in the car crash but something that didn't want you to die saved you.

Suppose a plane crashed, killing all of the people on board except for one. The Mendi would refer to this incident as the presence of *saikil* on the part of the survivor. In fact there was a similar incident in Papua New Guinea, where a 2-year-old girl survived, all the rest including her parents died.

The force *kip* is concerned with the idea of luck and good fortune. *Kip* is the term for luck or the blessing itself, and to say one has got *kip* is to say one has got luck. When a person unexpectedly finds a material item which may have been totally lost he or she may say 'I got *kip*'. Regardless of where the material is found, the finder does not know who the owner is or any person who could lay claim to it, thus he or she says, 'I've been hit by luck'.

The power *kip* does not act on its own right because people believe their ancestors or God (as exclaimed today) would provide them with material wealth. As was the case for the force *saikil*, the people have no ritual, nor can they predict the events; that is to say, no-one performs any rite to achieve *kip*.

The power *kip* is a blessing, and such an event is unpredictable by mankind. So man does not question the idea behind *kip* to any great extent, because the power *kip* can only be seen by its works.

Returning to occult forces, many forms of sorcery exist. *Sokel* is one, and this is a rather mild form. When an envious person sees another with food or any desired material item but is not offered any of it, he or she may voluntarily or involuntarily swallow saliva and cause sickness and even death to the one with food. Hence, this sorcery acts as a weapon to fight greed and other sorts of selfish attitudes. The *sokel* can be assumed to restrain the rich from getting too rich, or in a clearer sense it fights inequality. Bigmen avoid being pinpointed by sorcerers simply by giving away their goods generously and thereby controlling a number of followers. They give their pigs out to relatives elsewhere, particularly to their sisters who have married out. Some even leave their highly valuable goods in the care of less-bigmen.

Other forms of sorcery which play a similar role are, first, *neomb*, which is a good example of contagious magic. The *neomb* sorcery involves the use of pieces of clothing, hair, excrement or fingernails from an intended victim, which are thrown into a sacred pond. In another version the material remains of the intended victim are put in a phial which hangs over the fire. As the fire heats the phial, so the victim becomes ill with a fever. The phial is then taken off the fire and buried. It is covered with a special leaf to fasten the soul inside.

The *memb* is when the sorcerer, in a concealed spot, hangs a bag with a stone bird on a double-branched stick and waves it from side to side in the direction of the victim while biting a worm and incanting spells. Later, the stick is broken into pieces (the stick symbolizes the bones of the victim). The victim may die a few days later, and few believe that the victims of this sorcery can be cured by any counteracting formula.

Another sorcery is the use of broken bottles, glasses and nails which are projected into the victim either to paralyse him or to kill him, but it is a recent introduction. The same is true for 'smoke' sorcery. Magicians puff smoke at the victim while saying harmful chants. The magically intoned or incanted smoke is inhaled by the victim, who gets affected.

What of good-purpose magic? This category of magic, unlike sorcery, has its origin in the spirit-beings, as mentioned earlier. The knowledge as well as the techniques are given to mankind by them. Fertility of the people, their food crops and their domesticated animals are of great concern to the Mendi people. As regards pig fertility, a piece of bespelled crystalline stone is used. Once every week or so a piece of this stone is flaked off and fed to the pigs, together with raw sweet potato, while saying expressive, magical chants called *mok nemongk*. The rubbing of ashes on pigs while saying magic chants is another example, and both are designed to make the pigs grow fat. Garden fertility involves the burning of the leaves of sweet potato intended for planting into ash which turns into soil. I suspect there is a magic formula attached to this too.

Other good-purpose magic includes that for hair and beard growth, for handsomeness and to attract the opposite sex. It was normal for Mendi men to have much hair as well as a long beard to draw the attention and admiration of women. Some men used bespelled sticks and paint (earth pigment) to daub their faces when they participated in *singsings* or certain public dances, so as to attract women. Another peculiar magic to attract women is for a man to roll a tobacco in which he mixes his pubic hair and certain bespelled leaves, which he gives to the girl concerned to smoke. This is intended to seduce the girl or to some extent marry the girl without having to pay brideprice.

More importantly, bigmen in Mendi use generosity magic as a means of drawing wealth. They use the *find* (literally: paint) which includes bat bones and special leaf fragments which are all mixed together. This potion is bespelled and used to daub their faces during special exchange ceremonies. When exchange partners see the markings, they become impelled to treat the bigmen generously.

Having said all of the above, it is worth mentioning that the practice of ritual is predominantly a male role. They have a complete monopoly, performing the rituals themselves to the absolute exclusion of women. Among males ritual is generally in the hands of experts or specialists, and to some extent bigmen. Although leadership is democratic and aspiring men force their way up competitively to the surface of affairs, it is not enough just to master all the secular activities. Leaders must also know and use the ritual secrets that guarantee success.

As has been illustrated, religion in Mendi is best seen as a functioning process. When recounted in myths and legends, spirit-beings validate the origin of the economic system and the sociopolitical system. Although myths and legends may appear fictions and to some extent historically worthless, the same intellectual approach given to the scriptures by the medieval population of Europe can be assumed.

Religion gives man the assurance that he can control, regulate and manipulate the cosmic order by means of ritual. Both myths and the associated rituals contain an absolutely unquestioned power and truth, and therefore all important economic, social and political undertakings are guaranteed by it. Hence, religion is applied as a form of explanation as well as a form of control over issues that produce the greatest anxiety and stress.

A deeper discussion of the spirit-beings and occult forces is necessary. I mentioned earlier that religion must be seen as one aspect of the cosmic order. The non-empirical is always closely associated with the ordinary physical world. The idea of it being supernatural is only in a limited sense. Many of the categories of spirit-beings described reside on the Earth, the exceptions being the sky-beings who live in the sky. The spirit-beings live in a separate sanctuary near human settlements; for instance the spirits of the dead, who reside among the family. Natural spirits who are associated with the soil, water and forest are regarded as the guardians of these provinces. They have existed since the beginning of nature, and thus they have no ending as long as nature exists. Whereas they are resistant to change just as the natural air is, they are thought to have the same human corporeal form as well as the same mental and emotional characteristics as those of humans. They are inhuman in that they can do things that are not possible to man. It is a fact that they exist anywhere and everywhere, and thus have no ending.

The dead spirits (or the spirits of the dead) are of human origin. They are part of mankind: man has a spirit which he leaves behind upon dying. Each spirit is restricted to its own group or family territory and its influence upon it. Their presence in the atmosphere is ascertained by their activities – certain whistles, laughs, footprints and excrements are interpreted by the Mendi as indicating the presence of these spirits. All illnesses and non-violent deaths are attributed to them. Their influence is restricted to their spouse, siblings and direct descendants. In addition, it is important to mention that leprosy is caused by their bites.

The rituals associated with these ghosts are merely to please or appease the angered ghosts so as to lessen their malevolent attacks. They are not a means of relieving specific illnesses. This activity is performed by an individual family or particular group, and only when illness or some sort of misfortune is realized. The ritual involves the killing of a pig whose blood is used to smear ancestral stones (including stone pestles, mortars and club heads) which symbolize the spirits. The heart of the pig is cooked in an earth oven under the skull. These activities are done with special prayers designed appropriately to please the ghost. Hence, the smell of the cooking pork or the smearing of spirit stones is regarded as the feeding of the ghost.

The sky-beings are distinguishable from the earth-spirits in that they are more light-skinned in colour (similar to Europeans) than the black earth-spirits. In fact, the Mendi regarded the first Europeans to enter Mendi as of the sky. The sky is believed to be a lake or pool on whose shores reside the *yeki* sky-beings. When the *yeki* beings strike the water, rain, thunder and lightning occur. More importantly, the fertility of the people and the prosperity of the clans is attributed to them.

Much of the ritual knowledge, particularly the ritual chants, has been given to mankind by them. Every fertility rite is accompanied by these special chants, which are essential for communication with the spirits. The practical rite itself is worthless without these archaic ritual formulae being chanted in the right manner, style and vocabulary as passed on to mankind by the *yeki*.

Although there are no myths attached to these spirit-beings, there are rituals enacted as means of placating and bargaining with them. The *yeki sen* ritual is one of these. In this case a newlywed couple may be asked to sleep together and, in the course of the activity, the husband is told to collect some of his semen in a gourd bottle. This is mixed with paint (earth pigment) and the resulting mixture is consumed. This is done while saying a ritual chant, namely the *yeki sen*. The popular belief is only when this ritual is enacted will the sky-being bless the couple to have children. Hence, couples without children perform this ritual to get assistance from the sky-spirits.

Another ritual is the *yeki to*, and this involves the whole clan or tribal group. Here a tower is built up to the sky, where a specialist may climb up and feed the essence of a pig to the sky-spirits. The specialist represents the group, and with special ritual chants he pleads with the *yeki* spirit to come down and assist them in situations of stress on human welfare, fertility, and the prosperity and the goodwill of the group.

Closely associated with the sky-beings are the culture heroes and heroines who are thought to have introduced certain aspects of the culture and disappeared to a place unknown. The famous *Sundo Owil* is a culture hero who is known to have been the first man on Earth. He is depicted in legend as introducing the arts of fire-making and cooking, showing women not to treat pigs as 'husbands' or, in another version, 'brothers'. He is also said to have shaped the sexual organs of women. *Owil*, after realizing that women acted strangely, in that they rubbed their bodies against the truck of banana stems as a means of relieving themselves of urine and waste, inserted sharp, flint-flaked blades against the truck. When, as usual, the women rubbed their bodies, they got cuts which formed their vulva and anus. More importantly he is thought to have introduced the sweet potato and various other crops. It is important to mention here that the sweet potato entered Papua New Guinea in the 16th century.

The sweet potato is of vital importance. This crop has a high yield compared with other crops at high altitudes, such as in the Mendi area. Its arrival allowed for more food to be produced than ever before, and consequently for an increase in the pig population and human numbers. This led to the major religious pig festivals that involve the mass slaughter of pigs. Men knew that, if they ever denied and ignored this important contribution by the culture hero, he would withdraw all of the items, leaving them to suffer. They therefore remembered this event in legend form, and attributed a religious rite to it. However, what people say is that they perform the ritual concerned as a means of avoiding hunger (due to dry weather or frost), when the gardens do not produce much food or when there are not enough pigs. These problems are believed to result from the culture-hero's annoyance or displeasure with the people. Therefore the ritual concerned is designed to appease and to some extent bargain with him.

I mentioned that *Sundo Owil* shaped women's sexual organs for the first time. This image explains the idea of sexual reproduction, which further suggests the growth of the human population. The image of the pigs as being treated as 'husbands' or 'brothers' and being well-cared for as such suggests that there were fewer pigs before the introduction of the sweet potato than after. *Owil* first showed them how to kill the pigs and eat them rather than keeping them as 'husbands' or 'brothers'. The sweet potato could have allowed for more than just enough pigs, and it could also support the growing population. Its presence thus allowed for the major pig-killing festivals and the elaborate exchange systems.

The ritual associated with these spirit-beings suggests the unity (oneness), stability and welfare of society. Many groups come together to perform the ritual, each represented by two people, having in mind that the cult is for all pervasive essences. No person attempts to enter this rite with an individual or personal motive. Everyone performs for the welfare and goodwill of society as a whole.

Whereas the welfare and economic aspects of society are explained by the sky-beings and the legendary culture heroes and heroines, morality is the concern of the spirits of the dead and the natural free-governing autonomous spirit. The 'natural' spirits do not have any myths, nor do they have any rites, although they do influence the moral rules and ethical code of discipline of individual people and families in society. People make the following statement as regards these spirits:

> Do not kill, do not steal, or do not ever think of doing anything bad against your territory men; the men you share land, river and forest with; hence the *su temo, ip temo* and *ar temo* will 'eat' you.

So morality and or ethical codes of behaviour are maintained by this category of belief. When the death of any person is suspect, oath-taking and divination techniques are applied to ascertain the nature of the incident. Divination techniques are also used to discover a thief or to locate a missing object. Whether the spirit-beings concerned are 'natural' spirits or the ancestors of the dead is in question. Presumably one of them is involved, but the people are not certain, therefore I have been forced to say there are no rituals attached to natural spirits who exist in nature. Hence, most natural spirits are demons, tricksters and pucks, who are well known for stealing children and harming people while they are alone in the forest, riversides or somewhere away from settlements. Many of the victims are poisoners, murderers, and the like.

Thus, it is possible to follow Malinowski's (1961) 'external' view and to show that from the 'inside' Mendi religion appears to function to give Mendi people assurance in the control of all socio-economic welfare. Religion allows them to have a feeling of control over the problems which stand out beyond their powers, and which thus produce the greatest anxiety and stress. For the Mendi religion is the guarantee of success in all important economic, social and political activities, and its successful practice ensures strong group unity.

References

Durkheim, E. 1947. *The elementary forms of religious life*. New York: Free Press.

Frazer, J. G. 1913. *The golden bough*. London: Macmillan.

Lederman, R. 1987. *What gifts engender: social relations and politics in Mendi, highland PNG*. Cambridge: Cambridge University Press.

Malinowski, B. 1961. *The dynamics of culture change*. New Haven: Yale University Press.

Tylor, E. B. 1903. *Primitive culture*. London: Murray.

9 *Sites as texts: an exploration of Mousterian traces*

LUCY JAYNE BOTSCHAROW

An archaeological site is like a text in an unknown language. Like a written text, archaeology is fixed discourse (Ricoeur 1976, 1981). Just as writing fixes the 'said' of speaking, so a given site fixes the 'said' of doing. The ostensive reference – the situation surrounding the act of discourse – is lost. The actions of certain people have left their traces in the dirt, and these have become documents of human action. The task of the archaeologist is to recover these documents or texts, and then to try to decipher and interpret them. Decipherment is difficult and interpretation may be impossible, but if one is to 'read' the history of man's past, then an attempt must be made: to fail to do so is to leave archaeology with only the sterile remains of unread texts.

Sites are made up of traces left by people in the course of daily life. The presence of the archaeologist is an accident. If the materials in sites are documents, then they are documents that were meant to be read by contemporary, not future, readers. Moreover, they are fragmentary documents. Because the discourse in a site is always inadvertent and partial, there will always be aspects of culture and social organization which will not be retrieved. Nevertheless, if an archaeological site is a text, then it should be possible to read at least portions of that text.

Culture, as it is used here, refers to a shared system of codes or meanings, communicated through symbols and signs and enacted in behaviour. To modern humans almost everything is a sign of something else, and these signs are related through syntagmatic and paradigmatic associations (Jakobson & Halle 1956, de Saussure 1966) into systems. These systems in turn form basic codes which give meaning to any particular unit within the system.

It is possible that there were simple sign-systems in earlier cultures, and that these were generated by contrast and association in much the same way that modern codes are created. If this is so, then there should be evidence of paradigmatic and syntagmatic relationships in early sites. Here the material remains of Mousterian sites will be treated as tangible remnants of pre-existing signs-systems which, in any given site, form a fixed text. The Mousterian sites described below were chosen because they are capable of yielding decipherable messages. A comprehensive survey of all Mousterian sites is not intended.

Spatial hierarchies in Mousterian sites

Space and spatial boundaries are clearly of significance at Molodova I (USSR). Molodova I consists of an oval arrangement of mammoth bones, which measure approximately 10 m × 7 m (Klein 1966). One segment, to the south-east, looks as though it may have been an opening or entryway. The area outside the circle was much less dense in artefacts than the interior was. Within the interior there is evidence of the differential use of space. Most cores, flint detritus and kitchen debris were found in the northwestern half of the oval, whereas the southeastern half contains relatively more artefacts and less debris. Hearths within the oval are scattered. One is centrally located, whereas the remainder are primarily in the southeastern portion, coinciding with the denser distribution of flint artefacts. It appears as though this was the area in which food was prepared and consumed, and in which other domestic activities probably took place. The northwestern portion seems to have been mainly a refuse deposit.

Space in this site was divided into three levels of differentiation. At the first level is the distinction between the site and its surrounding area. This is a level of distinction that Molodova I shares with other Mousterian sites, and with some pre-Mousterian sites as well (Botscharow 1982). The occupants of Molodova I made a basic distinction between what was their camp and what was not their camp. Such a distinction is more than a simple utilitarian occupation of space, because the same space was repeatedly occupied year after year. Returning to the same general locality may be a necessity; returning to the same spot is not, at least when the site is an open-air one. It is a tradition.

Within the site of Molodova I yet another distinction has been made between the feature's interior and its exterior. Differences in distribution and density attest to this. The interior of the oval was used for cooking, for what appears to be a good deal of tool manufacture, and probably also for sleeping. However, large-scale food preparation seems to have been done outside in what appears to be the rear of the structure. Finally, there is a spatial division within the structure. Interior space appears to have been divided into a dwelling area and an area for debris.

This division of space appears to be utilitarian. However, it should be noted that even utilitarian classification implies a cultural code (Sahlins 1977, Boon 1983). There is a collection of tasks to be done, and there is an area of space in which to do the tasks. When space is divided along functional lines it means that space has been classified and given meaning in accordance with the tasks performed in it. If this was not so, then the use of space would be haphazard, and that is not evident here. Tasks and space have been treated isomorphically – one has been classified by reference to the other. Physical space has been given meaning as social space, and social space is given localized expression by physical space.

Level 17 of the cave site at Cueva Morin (Spain) also shows internal differentiation (Freeman 1978). It is divided by a dry stone wall. The section of the cave between the wall and the entrance is rich in artefacts. Tool-type distributions here are distinctly bounded. This seems to have been the inhabited part of the site. By contrast, the rear section is sparse, and such artefacts as there are are generally distributed throughout the area. It seems to have been used for refuse.

Like Molodova I, there is a three-part categorization of space at Cueva Morin, although it is organized in a slightly different way. The first division, as at all Mousterian sites, is the distinction between camp and not-camp. The second is internal to the cave and is between the front and rear, a distinction which is strongly marked by the presence of the wall. This wall marks the distinction between the living area and the refuse area. Finally, the habitable area is divided into activity areas. The artefact clusters at Cueva Morin seem to indicate a more complex classification of activities than at Molodova I, which lacks artefact clusters.

The distinction between living space and refuse areas seems to have been an innovation of the Mousterian. It is apparently absent in earlier sites. If this is so, then this distinction represents an increase in the complexity of use of space from earlier times. Modern *Homo sapiens* mark some kind of distinction, no matter how weak, between living space and refuse space (for example, see Ascher 1977, Binford 1978, Yellen 1977). Garbage, although a by-product of human activity, is seen by modern humans as being not fit to live with. It must be given its own space. There are many Mousterian sites which do not seem to distinguish between living space and refuse space, but a few do, including Cueva Morin and Molodova I. In such instances space in general takes on a tripartite division into uninhabitable nature and habitable space. Human space, in turn, is divided in some sites by the separation of the area in which people actually lived from areas into which they threw their refuse. In some sites the rotten has been distinguished, if not from the cooked, at least from the cooking. It is possible that a simple and basic code has been developed here, reminiscent of Lévi-Strauss' (1966) 'culinary triangle'.

Social categories in Mousterian sites

Burials are the best-known evidence of symbolic behaviour in Mousterian sites. Although relatively few Mousterian sites contain deliberate interments, a few, such as Teshik Tash (USSR) (Movius 1953), La Ferrassie (France) (Heim 1976, Vandermeersch 1969) and Shanidar (Iraq) (Solecki 1971, 1975) show elaborate treatment of the dead. Burials, in contrast with technological activities, are more easily identified as symbolic behaviour because they are so obviously non-utilitarian. However, it must be noted that, whereas burials may seem non-utilitarian to outside observers, they can be extremely utilitarian to those who practise them, and can be felt to be as necessary as the manufacture of stone tools. This is not to deny the symbolic nature of burials, but to point out the less obvious symbolic component in utilitarian behaviour.

The issue regarding the relation of burials and social organization is a contested one (see Shanks & Tilley 1982, for a summary), but it seems clear that Neanderthal burials do not seem to be obvious reflections of social organization, power or social rank. However, whatever other status distinctions may have been present in Mousterian societies, there is always one kind of distinction which is crucial in burials – the distinction between the living and the dead. No matter what other distinctions may have been present in Mousterian burials, the important thing about them is that they concerned the dead. Burials create a demarcation between the dead and the living. The unburied dead create a conceptual quandary for categorizing beings: they are both here and gone, both human beings and refuse. They are ambiguous because they cross boundaries. They must be put in their place. There are many places where the dead can be put in order to separate them from the living. One place is to bury them. As indicated above, Neanderthals were probably capable of drawing boundaries between things. Classification and categorization entail the drawing of distinctions and the creation of contrasts. The residents of some Mousterian sites drew a distinction between living space and garbage, and between activity areas within living space. It is also possible that some drew a distinction between living people and dead people.

Of particular interest are the burials at Shanidar cave, since these burials afford the possibility of identifying contrasting sets of social categories among the deceased. Most informative is what appears to be a multiple burial of two adult males, two adult females and an infant (Solecki, 1971, 1975). The greatest amount of *post mortem* attention was lavished on a male, Shanidar IV. In contrast with the other burials, which contained no such grave goods, Shanidar IV was found in association with various pollens and branches, none of which could have been there naturally (Leroi-Gourhan 1975, Solecki 1971). The pollen came from a variety of flowering plant. It was found over, under and around Shanidar IV. He must have been lying on a bier of branches and flowers and must have been covered by flowers.

The burial of Shanidar IV resembles Western burial customs, but this apparent similarity by no means indicates that the residents of Shanidar cave had the same ideas regarding death that modern Western people have. It is highly unlikely, although not impossible, that flowers had the same meaning in a Mousterian culture as they do in a modern Western one. It cannot be too strongly stressed that there is no way of knowing the ostensive reference of any Mousterian symbolic act or object. Since symbols are arbitrary, the possible number of meanings of a given symbol are infinite, and there is nothing intrinsic about flowers and branches to associate them with death or burials.

The important thing is that these flowers symbolize something. They can be nothing other than symbolic. We cannot assume that the people of Shanidar had a concept of a soul or an afterlife, or of something we could call religion. However, we can assume that this man was in some way significant. We may even speak of differential status at Shanidar because this burial contrasts with those of others in the group. If the other male, Shanidar V, was contemporary with Shanidar IV, as he seems to be, then there must have been status distinctions of sufficient importance among grown men that Shanidar IV received an elaborate burial whereas Shanidar V did not. If Shanidar V is not a contemporary, then we can only posit that adult males were in some way differentiated from women and children. In any case it appears that people at Shanidar categorized themselves at least by age and sex, and this distinction is in accordance with what we know of modern foragers. It is a minimal but important distinction between types of people. If there were also some kind of distinction between adult men, then Shanidar went beyond the minimum to more-elaborate social categories.

Burials are rites of passage. They both mark and bring about the transition from life to death. Among modern men burials do not exist in a ritual vacuum. They exist within a system of related rituals in a contrastive set. If Neanderthal burials were, as they seem to be, rites of passage, then it is possible that they, too, existed within a set. Among modern men these other rites vary from culture to culture, but they frequently involve some ritual, no matter how simple or how delayed, of birth. The coupling of rituals of birth and death makes a logical pair, since both are biological facts and one is the inverse of the other. If the dead are ambiguous, then so are the newborn, who pass from non-existence to existence. Each event is a major, final event, and the events of life in between are minor compared with one's entrance and exit. Modern men mark many boundary transitions with rites of passage, creating clarity where there had been ambiguity. We know that Neanderthals had at least one rite of passage. Did they have at least one other? If they did, it may have been a ritual of birth.

Conclusion

This summary should be sufficient to indicate that it is possible to read Mousterian texts to some extent. It is also possible that cultural codes did exist in the Mousterian, and that they included contrasts between the raw, the cooked and the rotten, as well as between the dead and the living. They may also have included contrasts between types of human activity, types of rituals and types of humans. It appears that classification and analogy were used in the Mousterian, and it is at least possible that sets of oppositions were organized into underlying cultural codes based on association and contrast.

It appears that sites can be read from texts, and it is possible that our knowledge of prehistory can be added to by this type of reading. Readings of any sort may vary, and it is the richness of the text that makes alternate readings possible. At this stage the results of the reading are less important than the act itself. A misread text still has life, whereas an unread text is truly dead.

References

Ascher R. 1977. Time's arrow and the archaeology of a contemporary community. In *Experimental archaeology*, D. Ingersoll, J. E. Yellen & W. MacDonald (eds), 228–40. New York: Columbia University Press.

Binford, L. R. 1978. Mortuary practices: their study and potential. In *An archaeological perspective*, L. R. Binford (ed.), 208–43. New York: Seminary Press.
Boon J. 1983. *Other tribes, other scribes*. Cambridge: Cambridge University Press.
Botscharow, L. J. 1982 Paleolithic semiotics: behavioral correlates to speech in Achuelan sites. Paper presented to the Premier Congrès International de Paléontologie et Paléoanthropologie, Nice, France.
Freeman, L. G. 1978. The analysis of some occupation floor distributions from earlier and middle paleolithic sites in Spain. In *Views of the past: essays in Old World history and paleoanthropology*, L. G. Freeman (ed.), 578–616. The Hague: Mouton.
Heim, J. L. 1976. Les hommes fossiles de la Ferrassie (Dordogne). *Archives de l'Institut de Paléontologie Humaine*, Tome 1, mémoire 35. Paris: Masson & Cie.
Jakobson, R. & M. Halle 1956. Fundamentals of language. *Janua linguarum*, Vol. 1. The Hague: Mouton.
Klein, R. 1966. The Mousterian of Russia. Unpublished PhD dissertation, Department of Anthropology, University of Chicago.
Leroi-Gourhan, A. 1975. The flowers found with Shanidar IV, a Neanderthal burial in Iraq. *Science* **190**, 562–4.
Lévi-Strauss, C. 1966. The culinary triangle. *Partisan Review* **33**, 586–95.
Movius, H. L. 1953. The Mousterian cave of Teshik-Tash. *American School of Prehistoric Research* **17**, 11–71.
Ricoeur, P. 1976 *Interpretation theory*. Fort Worth, Texas: Christian University Press.
Ricoeur, P. 1981. *Hermeneutics and the human sciences* (transl. J. B. Thompson). Cambridge: Cambridge University Press.
Sahlins, M. 1977. *Culture and practical reason*. Chicago: University of Chicago Press.
Saussure, F. de 1966 (1911). *Course in general linguistics* (transl. W. Baskin). New York: McGraw-Hill.
Shanks, M. & C. Tilley 1982. Ideology, symbolic power and ritual communication: a reinterpretation of Neolithic mortuary practice. In *Symbolic and structural archaeology*, I. Hodder (ed.), 129–54. Cambridge: Cambridge University Press.
Solecki, R. 1971. *Shanidar: the first flower people*. New York: Alfred A. Knopf.
Solecki, R. 1975. Shanidar IV, a Neanderthal burial in northern Iraq. *Science* **190**, 880–1.
Vandermeersch, B. 1969. Les sepultures Néandethaliens. In *La Préhistoire Français*. Tome I: *Les Civilizations Paléolithiques et Mésolithiques de la France*, H. de Lumley (ed.), 725–7. Paris: Centre National de la Recherche Scientifique.
Yellen, J. E. 1977. Cultural patterning in faunal remains: evidence from the !Kung Bushmen. In *Experimental archaeology*, D. Ingersoll, J. E. Yellen & W. MacDonald (eds), 271–331. New York: Columbia University Press.

2 *Style and changing relations between the individual and society*

POLLY WIESSNER

Archaeological interpretation can be either more or less objective. There are several ways in which greater objectivity can be achieved. Perhaps the first and most important way is through careful observation which goes beyond the variables chosen to support or reject an hypothesis, and in which variation and exceptions are treated seriously as indicators that additional factors may need to be considered. A second means of increasing objectivity that is worth exploring is the use of universally found human cognitive processes and strategies of human behaviour to set guidelines and limits for archaeological interpretation.

In the past two decades researchers have sought cultural universals that could directly link human behaviour to material culture, and have reached the conclusion that few such simple correlations exist because of the role played by history and cultural context in the patterning of material culture (Hodder 1982). However, such findings do not imply that 'universals' in human behaviour have little application for archaeological interpretation, but rather that they should be used at a more general level of analysis, to set guidelines and limits. For instance, even though studies that have tried to link the floor area of habitation sites to the number of occupants have come to the conclusion that there is great variation in spacing from society to society, this does not mean that a general rule for respect of the space of others is invalid. Thus, departures from standard uses of space, such as encroachment, may suggest important changes in social relations. Numerous 'cultural universals' have been identified in human societies, including territoriality (whether socially or physically defended), the existence of a norm of possession and respect of rules governing possession, the tendency of people to rank others in terms of their social and physical abilities, as well as universally found human cognitive processes that result in common patterns of perception and communication (for a good summary of these see Eibl-Eibesfeldt 1984). All of the above-mentioned cultural 'universals' are very general principles that can be manifested in a wide variety of ways from society to society. Here I take one basic cognitive process that has been identified in social psychology, that of social identification via comparison, propose that it constitutes the underlying behavioural basis for style in material culture, and then go on to develop from it guidelines and limitations for the interpretation of data on stylistic variation in artefacts.

Style and personal and social identification

Before turning to style, let us take a brief look at the process of identification via comparison. There is a vast literature in social psychology on this subject, and so much evidence has accumulated on the need of humans to establish a self-image through social comparison that it is considered by many authors to be a basic cognitive process in man (Lemaine 1974, Tajfel 1978, 1982, Turner 1975). Through comparing themselves with similar others, people evaluate their characteristics and abilities against those of others surrounding them, not in any absolute terms, and develop a self-image which they try to present positively to others. The value of this process is obvious – in order to be socially competent, people must know where they stand relative to others, and to a certain extent must have this position accepted by others. Although identification via comparison appears to be a basic human cognitive process, the content of identity and dimensions chosen for comparison are recognized to be culturally and historically determined (Wetherell 1982).

Both personal and social aspects of identity play important roles in the formation of self-images. On the one hand, people are unable to form self-images in the absence of social identity derived from membership in one or more social group (Tajfel 1982). On the other hand, an element of personal identity appears to be equally important and when put in situations of extreme conformity, individuals strive to differentiate themselves from similar others (Fromkin 1972, Lemaine *et al.* 1978). Social and personal identity can be switched on by certain situations, social identity being the mechanism that makes group behaviour possible. People have also been found to have a strong desire to present positive self-images to others in order to obtain self-esteem and self-recognition. This motivation may be linked to the evolution of reciprocity in that those who can present positive images to others will be more likely to be successful in relationships of delayed reciprocity that are critical for economic security.

Following previous work, I suggest that style is one of several means of communication through which people negotiate their personal and social identity *vis-à-vis* others, whether it be to project a certain image, to mask an aspect of identity, or to raise questions about a person's identity. The mechanism underlying stylistic development and stylistic change would then be social and corresponding stylistic comparison. For instance, in choosing dress for certain occasions, people make stylistic decisions by comparing styles with others, and correspondingly comparing themselves with the people with whom they associate those styles. Then, knowing the context of the occasion and the image that they would like to project, they choose a style that would communicate relative identity, whether consciously or unconsciously. To say that style largely deals with projecting aspects of relative identity may seem to be a very limited view of style. However, it should be noted that other forms of non-verbal behaviour, such as facial expressions and spatial behaviour, also serve almost exclusively to communicate relationships of relative identity.

Implications for archaeology

If style is seen as a means of communication used in the fundamental human cognitive process of identification via comparison, then what are the practical implications of this for archaeology? What can be gained from seeing style in this perspective? First, it provides a behavioural basis for looking at all aspects of style in all cultures (Wiessner in press). In recent years some attempts have been made to define different aspects or kinds of style (Sackett 1982, 1985, 1986, Wiessner 1983, 1985) with the underlying assumption that style may encompass several different kinds of behaviour. However, if style is regarded as having one underlying behavioural basis, then efforts to deal with the different aspects of style should concentrate on questions concerning conditions around social and stylistic comparison that lead to qualitatively and quantitatively different uses of style for communication, rather than classifying style according to its qualities. For instance, the dividing line between Sackett's isochrestic and iconological variation may become blurred once it is recognized that isochrestic patterns of variation may be due to the fact that the artefact plays a very minor social and symbolic role in a society. As a result it incites only a very low rate of social and stylistic comparison, and has only very vague social referents attached to it. However, change that increases an artefact's social and symbolic import may in turn lead to frequent and intense social and stylistic comparison, stronger social meanings becoming attached to a given style and, as a result, iconological patterns of variation. Thus, it is conditions that come into play during social and stylistic comparison and affect the frequency and intensity of comparison, the concreteness of stylistic referents and the nature of stylistic statements made as an outcome of comparison that generate the different aspects or kinds of style. If we can use our understanding of social and stylistic comparison to be more explicit about how context and conditions affect style, then we should also be able to derive information about these from stylistic studies.

Secondly, when style is seen as having its behavioural basis in identification via comparison, the roles of history and cultural context cannot be ignored, since cultural and symbolic structures define people and styles as comparable, and identity is negotiated in terms of these, not in any absolute terms (Wiessner 1984). Interpretation of stylistic data should take place only after as much of a past cultural context has been understood from other classes of data. Due to the role of history, stylistic studies will yield better results when directed at looking at change in patterns in styles over space and through time, than at any one single point in time.

Thirdly, if style is seen as a means of negotiating personal and social identity, then this supports the use of style to provide information on groups, boundaries and interaction. However, it also cautions that style can only do so within the realm of those who are defined as comparable, under certain conditions such as frequent comparison (Wiessner 1984) and in the context of certain relationships. Perhaps the single most important factor here is the social and symbolic role of an artefact – changes in patterns of stylistic variation through time and over space can be generated both by a changing social landscape and by changing roles of an artefact that make it more or less subject to stylistic and social comparison.

Finally, if style is a means by which persons negotiate and communicate personal and social identity *vis-à-vis* others, then this points to a new potential use of style in archaeology – as an indicator of the balance between the interests of the individual and society. The balance between individuals and society has long been an important issue in the social sciences. This is because, for any society to be stable, some balance between individual and social interest must be achieved. Where this balance point lies depends on social, economic or political conditions. Situations that switch on a strong sense of social group identity include fear, intergroup competition, and the need for co-operation to attain social, political or economic goals, or imposed political control. Those that switch on a strong sense of personal identity would include inter-individual competition, options for individual enterprise and breakdown in the social order that would force individuals to find solutions to their own problems. If style is a means of negotiating identity relative to that of those surrounding one, then change in the amount of personal and social expression in a given artefact in a region through time should give some measure of changes in the conditions mentioned above, personal and social expression being measured by heterogeneity or homogeneity, respectively, in artefacts. A few examples from different cultures will illustrate this point.

The first example, one of dress among the Eipo swidden horticulturalists of eastern Irian Jaya, illustrates how certain situations switch on personal or social aspects of identity. As in many highland New Guinea societies, the Eipo have a strong, conscious sense of identity towards the group that co-operates in a number of economic activities as well as in defence. They also have a strong sense of individuality, particularly among men, who constantly compete for status (Heeschen *et al.* 1980). Details of everyday and ceremonial dress were recorded from films taken by the Max-Planck Institut in 1975, before missions were established in the area. In everyday dress there was a fairly high degree of personal expression, depending on the activities of individuals. Some men wore virtually no decoration and others paraded about well-adorned. In intravillage dances during pig exchanges there was some increase in homogeneity of dress, in that most participants made an effort to wear some form of standard ceremonial headgear, although individual expression was still high. Depending on current concerns, some men, mainly middle-aged men who would be competing for status, wore full ceremonial dress, others dressed more spontaneously, adorning themselves with ordinary feathers, leaves and berries worn in ways to amuse. Others, mostly old men, participated but did not bother to dress. Finally, in the large, long-planned intervalley exchange and feast dances, dress showed a much greater degree of social group expression and homogeneity (Table 2.1). The dancers had all made an effort to obtain highly valued items such as bird-of-paradise feathers, cassowary feathers and nassa shell headbands. All dancers had similar face-painting and were grouped according to similarity in dress. As can be seen in Table 2.1, for most categories of items, particularly those of cer-

Table 2.1 Dress of male dancers at the intervalley dance of the Large people in Eipomek compared with that of the intravillage dance at Dincrkon, Eipomek.

Item of dress*	Percentage of dancers wearing item		Number of different types of item worn in dance †	
	Intervalley (n = 22)	Intravillage (n = 12)	Intervalley (n = 22)	Intravillage (n = 12)
feathers	100	57	2	5
headbands	91	64	2	4
necklaces	77	79	2	4
nose decorations	77	43	2	1
ear decorations	23	7	1	1
armbands	68	71	2	2

*Feathers and headbands are considered to be largely for ceremonial occasions. A variety of necklaces, arm, ear and nose decorations are worn in everyday life as well as on ceremonial occasions.
† Different kinds of feathers would include highly valued bird-of-paradise feathers and cassowary feathers, the only two types found in the intervalley dance, as well as less-valued feathers from other birds. Each kind of feather would be considered a different type. Types of necklaces would include cowrie shell necklaces, marsupial tooth necklaces, orchid fibre necklaces, quill necklaces, etc.

emonial dress, many more types are used per category in the intravillage than in the intervalley dance. In the latter case the fact that all of the dancers could co-ordinate their dress, and that each individual was well-connected enough to obtain the valued shell and feather decorations for the dance, conveyed an impression of group strength, unity and wealth. Each individual stood to benefit from showing identity with a wealthy and unified group, in terms of promoting exchange and discouraging warfare, as groups from other valleys were potential enemies. Similar observations on personal and social expression in ceremonial dress have been described by Strathern & Strathern (1971).

A second example of change in personal and social expression in artefacts can be taken from developments in housing decoration in northern Vietnam in the late 1970s and early 1980s. This period was one of considerable change as the country emerged from the Vietnam War and in 1980 began major organizational changes in the economy. In Quang Ninh Province, east of Hanoi, farming co-operatives were altered and land was divided between families on the stipulation that a quota of the produce be given to the government, and what was produced above this quota could be sold either on the free market or to the state. The result was an increase in initiative and income at the family level, and a boom in the number of houses built. These houses were built of home-made cement blocks, and they were decorated by family, friends or relatives according to the desires of family members. Table 2.2 summarizes changes in house

Table 2.2 Decoration of Vietnamese house fronts for houses built in 1976–9 and 1980–3. (All houses recorded had building date above their doors.)

	1976–9	1980–3
no decoration	4	3
one motif	6	5
two motifs	3	7
three motifs	1	6
four or more motifs	0	2
painting*	0	4
Total	14	27

*Motifs and painting differed, in that motifs consisted of geometric designs of raised plaster, whereas painting consisted of painted non-geometric features such as flowers, birds, etc.

decoration from 1976 to 1983 from data collected on the decoration of houses while driving from the port of Ha Long, through Quang Ninh Province, to Hwon Tach. As can be seen in Table 2.2, decoration became more elaborate and heterogeneous in the 1980s, with brightly painted designs incorporating new motifs beginning to appear in 1982–3. This increase in decoration and individual expression was noted even by casual observers, and coincided with a number of conditions: (a) a less pressing need for co-operation during peace-time and relief from fear; and (b) more economic opportunities at the family level and a rise in prosperity.

A third example that also involves a marked increase in individual stylistic expression with changing conditions can be taken from !Kung San beadwork (see Wiessner 1984, for a more thorough discussion). With the introduction of glass beads to the San during the 19th century or before, new designs were adopted as glass-beaded headbands gradually replaced ostrich-eggshell beaded headbands. The broad design repertory that was established by the 1950s remained essentially unchanged in northwestern Botswana and northeastern Namibia until the late 1960s, when a San settlement scheme was set up at Tsumkwe in Namibia and glass beads became more widely available. Although some stylistic innovation was occurring in other San areas then, the most radical increase in individual expression took place at Tsumkwe among !Kung who were settled on the government scheme. Stylistic differentiation at the level of the individual occurred to the point where traditional design structure was broken and many new headbands exhibited stylistic disorientation. This surge in personal expression can be attributed to a number of factors including: (a) an attempt by San to maintain individuality in a large community where many people have the same skills; (b) social disorientation caused by a breakdown in traditional norms and values; (c) new opportunities open to individuals, particularly wage labour for men; (d) the changing economic role of women; and (e) increased availability of beads, more-widespread beadworking and thus enhanced stylistic comparison. It might be noted that although some conditions in all three examples leading to increased personal stylistic expression were similar, that each situation was unique. Nevertheless, in the three cases the factors that 'switched on' personal aspects of identity fell within the range of those mentioned earlier.

Concluding remarks

In conclusion, I hope that the above discussion encourages the exploration of 'universally' found cognitive processes and strategies of human behaviour for their potential use in increasing objectivity in archaeological interpretation. Such cultural 'universals' have been found to be of little use to archaeologists in the past decade because of the level of analysis at which they have been applied – to establish one-to-one correspondences between behaviour and patterning of material culture. However, they may prove to be very helpful at a more general level – to establish guidelines and limits for archaeological interpretation. For instance, viewing style as communication in the process of identification via comparison has made it possible to outline several such guidelines. Perhaps the most important of these is the suggestion that in stylistic studies it is time to go beyond looking at information that style can give on groups, boundaries and interaction alone, and to expand the limits of stylistic interpretation to look at individual and group expression in style as a source of information on changing relations between the individual and society through time. As with all archaeological interpretation, causes of increases or decreases in stylistic variation will not be straightforward, because patterns of variation can potentially stem from several sources, i.e. different social conditions, the effect of exchange, the symbolic role of an artefact and so on. Conclusions drawn can only be checked against evidence from other categories of data. Nevetheless, looking at changes in personal and social expression in artefacts through time may allow archaeologists to make use of a much wider range of material that is not suitable for answering questions about groups, boundaries and interaction because of problems such as low sample sizes, inadequate dating or material being available from a few sites only in a region.

Acknowledgements

I would like to thank Dr. I. Eibl-Eibesfeldt, Dr Volker Heeschen and Dr Wulf Schiefenhovel of the Max-Planck Institut for making their films of the Eipo of Irian Jaya and their ethnographic notes and observations available to me.

References

Eibl-Eibesfeldt, I. 1984. *Die Biologie des Menschlichen Verhaltens*. Munchen: Piper.

Fromkin, H. L. 1972. Feeling of interpersonal undistinctiveness: an unpleasant affective state. *Journal of Experimental Research in Personality* **6**, 178–85.

Heeschen, V., W. Schiefenhovel & I. Eibl-Eibesfeldt 1980. Requesting, giving and taking: the relationship between verbal and non-verbal behavior in the speech community of the Eipo, Irian Jaya. In *Verbal and non-verbal communication*, R. M. Key (ed.), 139–66. The Hague: Mouton.

Hodder, I. 1982. *Symbols in action*. Cambridge: Cambridge University Press.

Lemaine, G. 1974. Social differentiation and social originality. *European Journal of Social Psychology* **4**, 17–52.

Lemaine, G., J. Kasterztein & B. Personnaz 1978. Social differentiation. In *Differentiation between social groups*, H. Tajfel (ed.), 269–99. London: Academic Press.

Sackett, J. R. 1982. Approaches to style in lithic archaeology. *Journal of Anthropological Archaeology* **1**, 59–112.

Sackett, J. R. 1985. Style and ethnicity in the Kalahari: a reply to Wiessner. *American Antiquity* **50**, 151–9.

Sackett, J. R. 1986. Isochrestism and style: a clarification. *Journal of Anthropological Archaeology* **5**, 266–77.

Strathern, A. & M. Strathern 1971. *Self-decoration in Mount Hagen*. London: Duckworth.

Tajfel, H. (ed.) 1978. *Differentiation between social groups*. New York: Academic Press.

Tajfel, H. 1982. Introduction. In *Social identity and intergroup relations*, H. Tajfel (ed.), 1–11. New York: Academic Press.

Turner, J. 1975. Social comparison and social identity: some prospects for intergroup behavior. *European Journal of Social Psychology* **5**, 5–34.

Wetherell, N. 1982. Cross-cultural studies of minimal groups: implications for the social identity theory of intergroup relations. In *Social identity and intergroup relations*, H. Tajfel (ed.), 207–40. Cambridge: Cambridge University Press.

Wiessner, P. 1983. Style and social information in Kalahari San projectile points. *American Antiquity* **48**, 253–76.

Wiessner, P. 1984. Reconsidering the behavioral basis for style: a case study among the Kalahari San. *Journal of Anthropological Archaeology* **3**, 190–234.

Wiessner, P. 1985. Style or isochrestic variation? A reply to Sackett. *American Antiquity* **50**, 1–224.

Wiessner, P. in press. Is there a unity is style? In *The uses of style in archaeology*, M. Conkey & C. Hastorf (eds). Cambridge: Cambridge University Press.

1 *Post-modernism, post-structuralism and post-processual archaeology*

IAN HODDER

Post-modernism

We are already post-modern . . . when we finally become free of the frame of the modern movement, when the morphology does not have to follow the function. . . An architecture which . . . has created a new reality as if we would do the shopping for the week in the 'hypermarket' of the memory – pieces of classic architecture, comics, and sets . . . mixed.

Manuel Blanco 1985. *La Luna de Madrid*. Madrid.

It was only in the 1970s that the historical limits of modernism, modernity and modernisation came into sharp focus. The growing sense that we are not bound to *complete* the project of modernity . . . and still do not necessarily have to lapse into irrationality or into apocalyptic frenzy.

Andreas Huyssen 1986. *After the great divide: modernism, mass culture, post-modernism*. Indiana University Press.

The freedom to consume a plurality of images and goods is equated with freedom itself. . . As we make images and consume them, we need still more images; and still more.

Susan Sontag 1978. *On photography*. Allen Lane.

There is a new depthlessness, appearance is everything. . . All culture becomes a parody of past forms.

Sandy Nairne 1987. *State of the Art*. Chatto & Windus.

There's a superabundance of explanations and purposes to suit any inquisition, any situation. That isn't the problem. The problem is to select from an almost infinite spectrum of reasons why. . . The answers are all around you. The head is drenched with thoughts and images that supersede one another with such rapidity that writing and even speaking become intolerable. . . You don't what any image, you want to be transparent, a projection almost seen on a cloud of cigarette smoke. And you know as you say it that all you're doing is to make another kind of image. . .

Mark Boyle 1986. *Beyond image: Boyle family*. Arts Council of Great Britain.

The false search for the 'real' her is exactly what the work is about. . . The attempt to find the 'real' Cindy Sherman is so unfulfillable, just as it is for anyone, but what is so interesting is the obsessive drive to find that identity.

Judith Williamson 1983. *Screen*. London.

Women are never acceptable as they *are* . . . at a deeper level, they (we) are somehow inherently disgusting, and have to be deodorised, depilated, polished and painted into the delicacy appropriate to our sex.

Lisa Tickner 1978. *Art History* 1.2.

Society is a battlefield of representations, on which the limits and coherence of any set are constantly being fought for and regularly spoilt.

T. J. Clark 1985. *The painting of modern life*. Thames & Hudson.

A society without power relations can only be an abstraction. Which . . . makes all the more politically necessary the analysis of power relations in a given society, their historical formation, the source of their strength or fragility, the conditions which are necessary to transform some and abolish others.

Michel Foucault 1982. In *Art after modernism: rethinking representation*, B. Wallis (ed.) New York: New Museum of Contemporary Art.

It is thoroughly engrossing for an archaeologist, a student of cultural change, to be living through the apparent 'birth' of a new cultural style. Yet it is surprising how difficult it is to define and understand what is happening. The more I try to tie down post-modernism, the less coherent it seems. I see 'it' happening all around me – in architecture, art, literature, philosophy, fashion and music. However, I feel uncomfortable with many of the analyses of it that I read. There is, of course, a growing literature by cultural analysts seeking to capture the new essence and create a theory out of the disparate events (for example, Nairne 1987, Jameson 1984, Lyotard 1984, Appignanesi 1986). Yet somehow the growth of the style seems bigger than any individual analyst's attempts to characterize it. Ultimately it engulfs any attempt to fix it. It runs on freely, following laws that we all know but that none of us can understand. However, still I try to grasp it, understand it and control it within my structured text.

The various strands of post-modernism are alluded to in the above quotes. First, there is a sense of disillusion with the projects of science and progress. Since at least the Enlightenment, but also to some degree since the classical Greek world, there has been a notion of progress towards some better state, latterly through scientific and technological as well as through social advance. However, modernism – the high point of this development – did not deliver any eradication of inequality, poverty, inhumanity and exploitation.

Secondly, modernism is seen as having produced alienation, cynicism and detachment. Particularly in modern architecture, the individual became lost in an identical, sterile and dehumanizing world. The search for symbols of the past within post-modern architecture has, among other things, the aim of reintroducing 'meaning', including irony and parody, into everyday life.

Thirdly, a number of changes in society since World War II can be seen to have produced a new relation between people, meanings and images. The terms abound: post-industrialism, world capitalism, consumerism, media society and planned obsolescence. The rate of fashion and style change has increased massively. Advertising and the media penetrate ever further into our lives. People become separated from their images of themselves. The images proliferate, and anyone can be a 'star for a day'. The images seem to be divorced from any meaning. Signifier is separated, floating free from signified. There is little remaining difference between 'high' and 'low' culture, or between fine art and *kitsch*. In contrast with modernism in which the meaning was in the functional form, now the facade is everything.

Fourthly, there is an awareness of the ways in which interest groups, whether these be multinationals or individuals, manipulate images in order to gain and maintain political, economic or social advantage. There is an increasing understanding that the creation of any discourse, whether in speech, clothing or fine art, is involved in power relations.

Yet when looked at in detail, these four points break down into a conflicting set of problems and questions rather than into a coherent set of answers. This new style concerns what we worry about in contemporary society. No overall solution is offered. For example, on the one hand there is an attempt in post-modern architecture to find an older 'meaning' for cultural products by plundering the past for classical columns and Egyptian motifs. At the same time the proliferation of de-contextualized images, the free play of signifiers, appears to constitute a radical critique of any attempt to find meaning – since everything is superficial image. Equally, some artists are convinced that the only truth left is to reach beyond image to find reality, while at the same time accepting that reality is itself only an image. Power, too, presents a contradictory situation. On the one hand power is present in all imaging and in all discourse, but to create a critique of power in a new discourse is itself to create a new power. Should we play the game of power, or somehow seek to step outside it altogether? Can we fight for a cause, while at the same time seeing that cause as no more than another image?

A brief account of one particular group of artists – the Boyle family – will accentuate these ambiguities and contradictions in a context which is of particular interest to archaeologists, and of particular relevance to this book. In an introduction to a recent exhibit of the Boyle family's work at the Hayward Gallery in London, Mark Boyle (1987) begins with an expression of radical doubt, part of which is quoted above, concerning the relationship between art and interpretation. The polysemy of the art object, and the way explanations of the artist's work seem to 'take off' into a multiplicity of debates has clearly led to a revulsion towards the creation of meaning and a cynicism towards interpretations, images and signs. Interpretations are seen as related to prejudices and preferences, manipulating the image. One reaction taken by many post-modern artists is to become overly critical, and to politicize the image. However, the reaction of the Boyle family is to go 'beyond image' to some 'reality'. They want only to say of their art 'there is this, there is this, there is this'. 'As far as I can be sure there is nothing of me in there. [The paintings] present as accurately and objectively as I can manage certain sites randomly selected, isolated at one moment' (Boyle 1987, p. 8).

The Boyle family thus worked under the name 'The Institute of Contemporary Archaeology'. In the late 1960s they blindfolded friends and members of the public and invited them to fire darts at a map of the world. Each randomly selected site was then visited, and so as further to remove subjectivity of choice, a metal right angle was thrown in the air, and where it landed became the corner of their square 'canvas'. An exact copy was made of the Earth's surface – the sand, mud or concrete painstakingly transformed into paint and resin, strengthened with a fibreglass backing. These little random pieces of reality, frozen in time, were then displayed in galleries as art.

In this almost scientific concern with making an accurate replica of the Earth's surface, the Boyle family talk of 'digging' our environment, just as an archaeologist does. It is of course one of the central paradoxes of archaeology that the objects dug up are concrete and real things, yet it is so difficult to ascribe any meaning to them. The Boyle family exploit this distance between an event and our interpretations of it. Their pieces of the Earth's surface that are hung in an art gallery seem a mockery of traditional art and its interpretation. Their 'archaeological' approach 'problematizes' the whole process of representation. Even the 'reality' in their fibreglass canvases is ultimately only an image of something beyond itself, charged with meaning.

The work of the Boyle family is particularly relevant to this book and to the event from which it derives – a 1½ day session at the World Archaeological Congress in Southampton 1986. It was as if darts had been thrown at a map of the world, identifying a random set of archaeologists from more than 70 countries. Of course human action is never random, and in many ways my analogy with the Boyle family event is false. The World Archaeological Congress had been carefully planned, and many people were involved in making choices about who could attend, including governments, national archaeological services, visa departments, the organizers of the Congress and myself. Nevertheless, I did not hand-pick all of the participants in my session according to theme or approach. I solicited few of the papers, and I knew the work of very few of the participants. Even though, in rejecting some of the contributions to the Congress to produce this book (see Preface), I placed some coherence on the chapters, the end-result reflects much of the variability of the original Congress session itself. I had made limited attempts to define subthemes and to control what perspectives would dominate the discussion at the Congress. The participants arrived, more than 50 of them, as if at random, with different backgrounds, aims and expectations, to participate in a session on 'Material Culture and Symbolic Expression'. The event was quite unpredictable, and indeed there were a number of unexpected and difficult moments during the course of the 1½ days. Certainly there was much misunderstanding, and little overall coherence. The end-result was a pastiche of contributions, interjections and movements – rather like the random pieces of the Earth shown in the Boyle family exhibition.

The event, then, was as 'open' and as 'real' as it could possibly be. The attempts made by the chairpeople of the discussions to keep the participants to any one theme were often frustrated. Because of the large size of the session and the multiplicity of special interests present, there was no time for the discourse to be set, defined and dominated. Each participant experienced the event in different ways and went away with different experiences. The overall result was decidedly 'post-modern' in its mixing of decontextualized, almost meaningless statements, and in the plurality of images which the participant was free to consume. The session was also self-reflexive. Anyone who attended the Congress had been forced to think hard about political issues concerning South Africa and academic freedom. The meeting was clearly political. The mix in each session of Western and Third World, West and East, and male and female was a directed attempt to erode established power relations.

Post-structuralism

Many of the corners of post-structuralism are reminiscent of the tensions at the centre of post-modernism. However, post-structuralism brings us closer both to the study of material culture and to the critical analysis of archaeological events such as conferences and books.

Post-structuralism is again an uncertain term. As used here, the term is mainly associated with a group of French writers including Foucault, Barthes, Derrida and Ricoeur. Of the many and complex strands of argument followed by these authors, I wish to emphasize only certain themes. In particular I want to characterize a central concern within post-structuralism as a movement from language to text. As Tilley (Ch. 14, p. 185) demonstrates, post-structuralism developed out of a critique of structuralism, which was itself based on Saussure's analysis of language. Many of the aspects of this critique concern the distance between an abstract language and a particular concrete text written in that language.

There are two aspects of texts that will be discussed here. The first is that a text has to be written, and the second is that it has to be read.

(a) Within structuralism a sign has meaning by being placed in an abstract and internally structured code of presences and absences, similarities and differences. Thus 'white' is the opposite of 'black' and different from 'while'. The structured sets of differences in the language are separated from the activity of speech – *parole*. It is this separation of *langue* and *parole* which makes the analysis of symbolic structures so difficult, and which accounts for the inability of structuralism to deal with social and structural change and with human activity as a creative process.

In writing a text one does, of course, use rules, structures and grammars. The text may be an article or a book, but we can also talk of spatial texts or material culture texts. Here again, rules and structuring principles (up–down, left–right, inside–outside) are employed in the organization of activities in space and in the production of pots, bone residues, burial ceremonies, and so on. However, the creator of any of these texts does not want to be understood in relation to an abstract code. He or she also wants to be believed, respected, distinguished, listened to, or whatever. In other words the text is produced to *do* something and to have some tangible social effect. Thus, the writing of a text is rather like a performance. It is 'staged', using the rules, but manipulating them in relation to social ends.

Consider, for example, a member of the royal family planting a tree or a politician cutting a ribbon in order to open a new motorway. We can all go around cutting ribbons and planting trees. These acts, when carried out in a formal public setting, do not simply have meaning in relation to an abstract set of opposed signifiers. They also have meaning in relation to their stage setting. For example, it is important in the formal occasion that the ribbon cutter or tree planter is of high status, that reporters and the public are watching, that the institutions that have paid for the motorway or nature reserve have asked the member of the royal family or the politician to be present and so on. In other words the 'writing' of 'texts' (such as cutting a ribbon or planting a tree) depends on institutional contexts.

Not everyone can write a text. For example, look at the reviewing process for prestigious archaeological journals. The ability to write or to act in a certain way is intimately linked to power. Again, it is not simply a matter of following the rules. Symbolic structures and power structures certainly exist, but in any one situation the structures can be put into practice to a greater or lesser effect. The contexts in which action takes place, particularly less-formal contexts than the events of ribbon cutting and tree planting described above, never repeat themselves exactly. The rules have always to be used strategically, competently and situationally. There is always a concrete context for text production. Indeed, the writing of the text strategically links structure and context.

Thus, the emphasis on writing texts takes us from abstract language to the relations of power and the contexts of action which are structured by and reproduce language.

(b) A text also has to be read, but it is clear that there is no 'right' way to read a text. Indeed, we often read things 'into' a text. The text itself has no meaning at all outside of its reading. Culture as text requires reading. A text is thus ambiguous and polysemous.

Indeed, it can be argued that as members of a cultural world we are caught in a network of signifiers relating to other signifiers in an endless sequence. Thus, in giving meaning to a text we simply refer to other signifiers. For example, in explaining the meaning of the colour 'red' we might say it means 'blood', but what does 'blood' mean? It suggests 'danger'. What does that mean? The opposite to 'safety'. And so on. Each signifier is only understood in relation to other signifiers.

When language is considered in the abstract it certainly does seem to have the ability to 'run on' like this so that any individual reader can make new links and make new interpretations. In fact, a dictionary often does have a 'surplus' of meaning in the long lists of definitions given for any one word. It is context which allows us to fix meanings. It is the context in which a signifier is used (written) which screens out the polysemy and limits the interpretation.

The context of the reader or the participant in an event will affect that person's reading of the event. In many cultural events the contexts of the reader and that of the writer are closely tied. For example, in speech acts the 'reader' is present, listening to the words as they are spoken. Speech is spoken *to* someone. The speaker can emphasize, point, recapitulate, and so on. However, writing and material culture are often read in quite a different, 'distant', context from that in which they were written.

The reading of an event is therefore never finished. Particularly in the case of long-lived monuments in the past, we must assume that they were continually open to new interpretations and to new meanings, as they are today.The context in which an event is read is continually changing. There is therefore always something specific and particular to any full interpretation of an event. It is not enough simply to read the varied structuring principles implicated in the writing of an event, it is also necessary to see how context was used to give a particular meaning in a particular case. There are few rules for doing this. It is an imaginative and interpretive enterprise, understanding the event in relation to that which is immediately around it, including power structures and special interests.

The ability to fix readings returns the argument to writing texts. To be able to fix meanings is to have power, since all symbolic meanings can also be written or read to have social meanings. The example of this book is appropriate. Faced with a disparate set of contributions from all parts of the globe I reject some and ask for others to be rewritten. I construct coherent themes within which to wrap them. This introduction relates the more ambiguous contributions to the central themes. The authority invested in me as editor of a worldwide set of papers, given further prestige through publication by a significant firm of publishers, has to be 'brought off' using established skills. Even if many of the editorial rules have been codified by the publishers in their attempt to control the authors and editors, I can still succeed or fail, to a greater or lesser degree, in my application of the formal and informal rules in the context of this particular book. My own power and prestige derive precisely from my ability to control the free flow of signifiers, and to link structures together in this particular strategic context. It is the management of the relationship between structure and context which both depends on and creates power.

Post-processual archaeology

The move from language to text in post-structuralism sidesteps the old dichotomy between, on the one hand, normative, culture-historical, idealist archaeology and, on the other hand, processual, culture-ecological and materialist archaeology, and leads to a post-processual phase in which these dichotomies are broken down. Indeed, it is precisely the relationships between the two sides of these dichotomies that become the aim of study.

The opposition between adaptational accounts and structuralist accounts which has led to a recent rearguard reaction on the part of die-hard processual archaeologists (for example, Binford 1982), and which has been followed by the placing of this opposition at the centre of study within post-processual archaeology, can be seen as a trend within this book. So here I will begin to place the contributions to this book in a coherent developmental theme. I will return to read this writing in a critical way at the end of this chapter.

The context determines

One way to characterize the processual approach towards symbolism and meaning is to say that the economic and social context produces particular symbolic expressions. At least it is argued that the social and economic context should be studied in order to understand the symbolic, projective or information processing subsystem. The use of material symbols to express social roles is discussed in several chapters in this book – as, for example, in the work of Kleppe (Ch. 4, pp. 195–201) and Pilali-Papasteriou (Ch. 5, pp. 97–102). In this latter case Minoan figurines are studied to show that female headgear expresses societal-wide solidarity, whereas male dress indicates hierarchy. Such work is closely related to Sackett's (1985) 'iconological' approach, best exemplified by Wobst (1977). As an example of the generalizations that can result from this approach, in this book Hulin (Ch. 3, pp. 90–6) argues that religion and social systems are mutually reinforcing, and that religion adapts to innovation in the social realm.

Certainly symbol systems do in some sense have to be 'adapted' to their social and economic context. There is always a danger of a tendency towards behaviourism, however, as in Wiessner's (Ch. 2, pp. 56–63) discussion of the way in which a context 'switches on' a particular response. What is 'switched on' will normally depend on a whole series of historical and structural factors, and on human intention and strategy: the types of factors to be discussed below. However, Wiessner is right to argue that there are universals in the way in which humans create meanings within social contexts. Thus, she suggests that humans have a need to establish a self-image through social comparison.

The main problem with the view that social context determines meaning is that it takes 'the social' as already given. For example, consider the explanation for pot type 'A', that it symbolizes a chief – but what is a chief? In a particular case one might reply: the chief is a person with pot type 'A'. There is no social reality in being a chief that can be separated from the cultural symbols which create chieftainship. The notion of chief is not a separate social reality against which symbols can be compared, but it takes shape through the interplay of meaning structures and power structures, as will be discussed below.

The structure determines

Several chapters in this book describe an abstract code of meaning which appears to exist before action and divorced from context. For example, Kassam & Megersa (Ch. 13, pp. 23–32) argue that in their study male is to iron as female is to beads. Hall (Ch. 12, pp. 178–84) discusses the interesting example of the Winnebago moieties where ball-headed warclub is to flat-headed warclub as sky is to earth as male is to female, etc. Male–female oppositions are also described by Biaggi (Ch. 11, pp. 103–21). The structures appear as abstract codes even though they involve social relations between men and women.

The prior existence of an abstract system of thought is discussed by Criado (Ch. 22, pp. 79–89), and by Llamazares (Ch. 10, pp. 243–9) in her argument that rock art is structured as a language into a grammatical code. Botscharow (Ch. 9, pp. 50–5) also suggests that sites, including Palaeolithic sites, are constructed using an abstract code that is previous to and in some sense determines action. As a result the symbol can be seen as arbitrary. The specific choice of symbol that is made has only to fit into the structured set of oppositions. As Kobylinski (Ch. 8, pp. 122–9) argues, in Polish philosophy too, the symbolic is seen as separate from the technological and the practical.

'The fallacy of the antecedent self', discussed by Richardson (Ch. 15, pp. 172–7), easily leads to the view that the structure entirely determines the self. Lemonnier (Ch. 7, pp. 156–71) argues persuasively that much technological action is directed by an implicit image of what should be. In this sense, then, the first artefact fixes the form (*ibid.*) or, as discussed by Richardson (Ch. 15, pp. 172–7), 'the stone defines the hand'.

It is not necessary to follow a linguistic analogy in identifying overarching structures of meaning. Fletcher (Ch. 6, pp. 33–40) argues that material culture should be studied as organized by a non-verbal semiotics organized in terms of frequencies and distances. There is an abstract code, which in this case includes proxemic codes, which informs the way we construct the material world. It is by considering the ways in which material culture is similar to, yet different from, language that we can begin to break down the notion of abstract and determining codes. Many of the chapters in this book discuss the relationship between material culture and language. Even in linguistic studies it is now realized that texts are not simply produced by an abstract code, as was discussed earlier in this chapter. However, the consideration of material culture takes us closer to an integration of structure, context and action.

Material culture versus language

First, it can be argued that material culture meanings are less logical and more immediate, use-bound and contextual than meanings in language (see, for example, Botscharow, Ch. 9, pp. 50–5). Thus material culture meanings are often non-arbitrary. Certainly, as noted by Layton (Ch. 18, pp. 1–11) and demonstrated by Kubik's dot-and-line motifs (Ch. 23, pp. 210–32), much material culture is not obviously representational and has little figurative or iconic content. However, even in Kubik's example there is a possibility of an historical link to the use of sand signs by hunters. Most material culture does have meanings through being associated with practical uses in specific contexts. Language, too, has contextual meanings, but we seem to depend more on context in relation to material culture than on abstract 'grammars'. This point is made by Kobylinski (Ch. 8, pp. 122–9).

Secondly, perhaps because material culture is often more practical and less immediately concerned with abstract meaning, the meanings it does have are often non-discursive and subconscious. This point is discussed by Melas (Ch. 17, pp. 137–55), and it raises the issue of the overall relationships between discursive and non-discursive knowledge, and between the formal and practical control of meanings.

Thirdly, if material culture meanings are often practical and subconscious, then it is hardly surprising that it becomes difficult to be unambiguous in assigning meaning to material symbols. The polyvalence, polysemy and ambiguity of symbols are stressed in this book by Kobylinski (Ch. 8, pp. 122–9), Layton (Ch. 18, pp. 1–11) and Tilley (Ch. 14, pp. 185–94). The ambiguity derives partly from the non-discursive nature of much material meanings and partly from the greater contextuality noted above. Another difference between material culture and language also contributes to ambiguity. Speech and writing are linear. The reader knows where to begin, and follows the words through one by one in an ordered sequence. Faced with a room of objects, on the other hand, there is no set order or pattern to the way in which reading takes place. Actions, movement or convention may in some way 'lead the eye through' any complex setting, but the complexity of the message has a much greater potential for ambiguity than in language.

Fourthly, once produced, a material symbol often has considerable durability, unlike the spoken word. The same spoken sound is often repeated for centuries, even though the meaning may change, in the same way that Kubik's fleeting drawings in the sand are part of a very long tradition of similar depictions (Ch. 23, pp. 210–32). However, most material objects of the types studied by archaeologists have a long duration, which means that the control of material symbols is an effective social strategy in the control of meaning and hence society. Yet there is a concomitant danger, already discussed above in relation to texts: the material object soon becomes divorced from its context of production and it can be taken into new contexts of use. The meanings of objects may change as they move into new contexts. The ambiguity has a greater potential for increase in regard to material culture, simply because the object is more durable than the spoken word.

There are therefore reasons to argue that material culture meanings are more contextual and practical than language. The study of material culture thus raises, even more acutely than in the study of language, the relationship between structure and context.

Structure, context and agency

It is difficult to argue that there is any predetermined relationship between general structures of power, structures of meaning, and particular contexts of action. Indeed, the relationship between structure and context has to be set in motion by human action, creating contexts and drawing on structures. The need to include the agent in archaeological theory is discussed by Melas (Ch. 17, pp. 137–55), while Richardson (Ch. 15, pp. 172–7) describes how material culture and the organization of space are actively used to, for example, create a sense of 'culture'. Wiessner (Ch. 2, pp. 56–63) emphasizes contextual decision-making and the agent's monitoring of the effects of action.

If the agent is to be allowed a role in linking meaning structures to contexts, it immediately becomes necessary to consider the structures and relations of power which inhibit or permit such activity. A number of chapters in this book explore the way in which dominant groups manipulate meanings in particular contexts in order to increase or maintain power. Their power is not based on any 'reality', but on some construction of reality. For example, Bhattacharya (Ch. 25, pp. 12–22) shows why, in a particular historical context of meanings and power relations, particular shapes are chosen for terracottas in worship. The elephant and horse shapes are used for the terracotta votive offerings because they are the only link to royal connection, power and economic help. Mawe (Ch. 24, pp. 41–9) shows how every myth or ritual action in Mendi has some specific practical purpose. Religion in Mendi is seen as a functioning process, partly involving male dominance and the dominance of big men. Kubik (Ch. 23, pp. 210–32) and Layton (Ch. 18, pp. 1–11) both show how the elaboration of meanings associated with material culture can be used to maintain control by seniors through the control of esoteric knowledge.

Meaning structures are thus created and re-created in the context of specific power relations through the strategies of agents. Equally, structures of power are created and re-created in the context of specific historical meanings. Any particular event creates a new context of action in which these two types of structure (symbolic meaning and power) are brought together, separated or otherwise manipulated in relation to each other. Understanding of the particular event thus depends on an understanding of the history of that event – that is, the structures of meaning and power which the event brings into play. Davis (Ch. 16, pp. 202–9) emphasizes that history is important if we are to avoid explaining mind by mind. Teague (Ch. 21, pp. 130–6), Sanders (Ch. 19, pp. 233–42) and Yates (Ch. 20, pp. 249–61) provide elegant analyses of how a specific historical context provides the setting in which agents can manipulate and create particular cultural products.

Method

A final strand of post-processual archaeology to which I wish briefly to refer concerns philosophy and method. There has been much discussion in the literature over whether past historical meanings can ever be reconstructed with any rigour. There are two, necessarily linked, paths which lead in the direction of a positive resolution to this problem. A third path argues that the very attempt to 'reconstruct' the past is false.

The first response to the demand for methodological rigour in interpreting past meanings is to put one's trust in Melas' 'external' analyses (Ch. 17, pp. 137–55), involving the search for and use of universal statements. Davis' thought experiment in Chapter 16 (pp. 202–9) is a useful one: could an Aurignacian be taught to use a word-processor? For many of us there is a feeling that he or she could. We feel drawn to universal statements of the type expressed by Wiessner in Chapter 2 (pp. 56–63). It also seems reasonable to argue that meaning is always constructed by humans using methods such as association, difference and context. This 'external', 'objective' knowledge must be part of our methodology.

The second response is to argue that Melas' 'internal' analyses must also be strived for. I have argued above that human action involves the strategic linking of structure and context. Since structure and context can never remain identical from one moment to another, the linking has always to have some component of creativity. To understand that creativity will always involve an imaginative and creative effort on the part of the analyst. Biaggi (Ch. 11, pp. 103–21) rather than making external comparisons in order to recover symbolic meaning, examines internal associations. Kobylinski (Ch. 8, pp. 122–9) places an emphasis on the internal analysis of the text. An internal, emic analysis does not only involve the identification of associations and contrasts, and the comparison of these with external knowledge. It also necessitates a creative moment – a sensitivity to the particularity of the context.

Thirdly, however much we think that we understand a past culture, that understanding always has its own context in the present. Archaeology is not only a reconstruction of the past, but also its construction, and this point is discussed by Tilley in Chapter 14 (pp. 185–94). We are thus brought back to the writing of the past, and to the writing of this book.

This book

In the above account of post-processual archaeology I have oversimplified a complex debate. It would be possible to summarize even further the main points I have made in a simple diagram.

This simple scheme has been identified at three levels of discussion: the wider world of post-modernism, the philosophy and social theory of post-structuralism, and the specific world of post-processual archaeology. My strategy here has been to naturalize the points that I have been making by giving them a universality. Further, if I analyse my analysis, I can argue that the growth of post-processual archaeology in the context of the growth of post-modernism is an example of the manipulation (by me in this case) of particular contexts within wider frameworks of meaning in an attempt to create power. I have therefore tried to provide a coherence, in which all of the pieces fit nicely into a larger, legitimating whole.

I have tried to make this book coherent by mentioning each of the chapters in relation to a set of themes. This is the common editorial round. The contents page that I would have produced by this method is as follows.

Introduction

1. *Post-modernism, post-structuralism and post-processual archaeology* I. Hodder

Section A *Symbolic expression in the social context*

2. *Style and changing relations between the individual and society* P. Wiessner
3. *The diffusion of religious symbols within complex societies* L. C. Hulin
4. *Divine kingdoms in northern Africa: material manifestations of social institutions* E. J. Kleppe
5. *Social evidence from the interpretation of Middle Minoan figurines* A. Pilali-Papasteriou

Section B *Structures of meaning*

6. *The messages of material behaviour: a preliminary discussion of non-verbal meaning* R. Fletcher
7. *Bark capes, arrowheads and Concorde: on social representations of technology* P. Lemonnier
8. *Ethno-archaeological cognition and cognitive ethno-archaeology* Z. Kobyliński
9. *Sites as texts: an exploration of Mousterian traces* L. J. Botscharow
10. *A semiotic approach in rock-art analysis* A. M. Llamazares
11. *The Priestess Figure of Malta* C. Biaggi
12. *The material symbols of the Winnebago sky and Earth moieties* R. Hall
13. *Iron and beads: male and female symbols of creation. A study of ornament among Booran Oromo* A. Kassam and G. Megersa

Section C *Meaning, power and agency*

14. *Interpreting material culture* C. Tilley
15. *The artefact as abbreviated act: a social interpretation of material culture* M. Richardson
16. *Towards an archaeology of thought* W. Davis
17. *Etics, emics and empathy in archaeological theory* E. Melas
18. *The political use of Australian Aboriginal body painting and its archaeological implications* R. Layton
19. *Organizational constraints on tattoo images: a sociological analysis of artistic style* C. R. Sanders
20. *Habitus and social space: some suggestions about meaning in the Saami (Lapp) tent ca. 1700–1900* T. Yates
21. *Heresy and its traces: the material results of culture* K. Teague
22. 'We, the post-megalithic people. . .' F. Criado
23. *Tusona ideographs – a lesson in interpretive objectivity* G. Kubik

24. *Religious cults and ritual practice among the Mendi people of the Southern Highlands Province of Papua New Guinea* T. Mawe
25. *Terracotta worship in fringe Bengal* D. K. Bhattacharya

I have retained the numbering above in the listing of chapters in the actual contents page printed at the front of this book. However, that numbering, relating as it does to the scheme I have created in this chapter, bears no relation to the initial event for which most of these contributions were written. In fact, hardly any of the points discussed in this 'editorial' chapter were discussed in the Southampton meeting. More importantly, most of the points are not the main concern of any individual author. Rather, faced with a rather varied set of contributions, I have followed the frequent editorial practice of creating a coherence and placing myself at the head of the contents list – the starting point (I would have hoped) for discussion of these contributions.

In addition, the chapters are organized above in a clear developmental sequence. Each section of the book moves towards the ultimate pinnacle – the final section in which the most up-to-date and 'approved' theories and approaches are displayed. Of course I have also deleted many contributions from the book, and there are many other procedures I have used in order to control the text. The end-result is a writing which uses and creates power through the control of meaning.

This point is especially clear in the organization of chapters within each section of the above contents list. It is possible to argue that synthesis and generality of application are important attributes of academic prestige in Western writing. In other words, academic archaeologists of high 'visibility' normally are the ones who write successful syntheses or theoretical or methodological statements which set the tone for more-detailed work. The referring or citation networks demonstrate this most clearly. Within each section in the above contents list the chapters have been organized from the general to the particular, and this is a strategy frequently used by editors. The general or abstract chapters are placed *first*, so reconstructing the importance of the theoretical. It is also not difficult to see that the ordering places authors who are white and Western 'first', 'above' and 'higher than' those from the Third World. In the 'writing' of this text, relations of power and dominance are re-created and social categories are valued.

It therefore becomes necessary to 'write' this book in a way that criticizes and limits at least certain dimensions of power. I have taken my cue from the Boyle family. I wish to create this book as just another image, containing many images within it, which can be 'read' in many ways. The aim is to return the meaning to the reader who must 'work at' creating his or her own meanings out of these diverse contributions. For those who wish to follow my scheme I have provided it here. However, the structure I have provided inadequately captures the context in which the contributions were produced. That context, the World Archaeological Congress at Southampton in 1986, had as its prime, hard-fought purpose the breakdown of Western domination of archaeological discourse.

In order to limit that Western domination within this text, the printed ordering of the chapters has been chosen at random. The Southampton Congress, and this book, are not of course random events, but the notion of randomness was the nearest I could get to the ideals that I wanted to follow. These ideals include self-critical awareness of this as a constructed book involved in strategies of power, the critique of Western domination of the control of meanings in archaeological writings, and more generally the use of material culture (including this book) as a means of linking the control of meaning to the control of people. The random ordering in the contents pages at the beginning of the book seems to place 'terracotta worship in fringe Bengal' on the same level and in the same category as 'etics, emics and empathy in archaeological theory'. Perhaps that is as it should be.

References

Appignanesi, L. 1986. *Postmodernism*. London: Institute of Contemporary Arts, Documents 4 & 5.

Binford, L. 1982. Meaning, inference and the material record. In *Ranking, resource and exchange*, A. C. Renfrew & S. Shennan (eds). Cambridge: Cambridge University Press.

Boyle, M. 1987. *Beyond image: Boyle family*. London: Arts Council.

Jameson, F. 1984. Postmodernism, or the cultural logic of late capitalism. *New Left Rev.* **146**, 53–92.

Lyotard, J.-F. 1984. *The postmodern condition: a report on knowledge*. Manchester: Manchester University Press.

Nairne, S. 1987. *State of the art*. London: Chatto & Windus.

Sackett, J. 1985. Style and ethnicity in the Kalahari: a reply to Wiessner. *American Antiquity* **50**, 151–9.

Wobst, M. 1977. Stylistic behaviour and information exchange. University of Michigan Museum of Anthropology. *Anthropological Paper* **61**, 317–42.

22 *'We, the post-megalithic people . . .'*

FELIPE CRIADO

To a blues guitarist,
in a symphonic orchestra.

Let me occupy the territory of megaliths once again. By doing that I will not claim to produce any definitive and conclusive 'explanation' of this topic, the reasons being not only the limitations of the present work and writer, but also, and more generally, the awareness that this text is written by a context (a 'post-megalithic' one) which is part of a longer history which lacks names or protagonists. There are some privileged topics visited periodically by the qualified specialists of our culture. Perhaps Megalithism is one such. New contexts will arise which will produce new explanations. Finally, the value of this profusion of discourses will probably be to mirror the knowledge within which we are situated, the discourse which owns us, the power which crosses and splits our praxis.

I will not offer a critical review of previous approaches to Megalithism here; such a critique has been made by various writers (Hodder 1982b, 1984, Midgley 1985). However, by assembling the major implications of such works I will establish the space through which this chapter claims to move itself, the general objectives it aims at, and the basic orientation which will be chosen.

In the past 15 years most explanations of megaliths have been either functionalist or structural–symbolic. In relation to both positions I would argue that whereas the functionalist approach made useful contributions to the problem of megaliths by focusing on their spatial-territorial dimension (Renfrew 1973, 1976, 1983, Fleming 1971, 1973, Chapman 1981), this perspective was unrelated to an adequate theory dealing with the symbolic and ideological phenomena involved with megaliths; the epistemological framework did not provide a conceptual mechanism suitable for such explanations. (For a critique, see Hodder 1982a, c, Miller & Tilley 1984b, or, for a specific criticism of functionalist explanations about megaliths, Hodder 1984.)

On the other hand, structural–symbolic archaeology uses the correct theoretical categories with which to discuss this theme (Hodder 1984, Tilley 1984, Shanks & Tilley 1982). However, in losing the reference to megaliths as territorial events it has also failed to take account of one of the most important elements of the context of these monuments.

My proposal, lying between both positions, attempts to view megaliths as 'territorial symbols which are also socially active', and to understand them as phenomena involving a 'spatial dimension'. They were the material signs by which the particular configuration of space and time of the megalithic groups (their specific construction of a social landscape) was expressed.

Any society constructs time and space in distinct and specific ways. We must account for the specific configuration produced through megalithic activity, by looking both at the internal order of the thought within which megaliths are embedded and at its differences from other ways of shaping time and space. From a theoretical–methodological standpoint this implies looking at megaliths as not being 'territorial' or 'social' markers, or 'power-ideology expressions' (Larsson 1985, pp. 107–10), but as 'events' (Sahlins 1985) or 'happenings' of thought.

Why is it necessary to use the concept of thought to analyse megaliths? I will give two reasons for doing so. First, from a general perspective, because any specific time and space shaping is articulated within a particular framework of thought. Secondly, clearly, megaliths reflect not only a time and space configuration, but more generally the way megalithic groups thought this configuration.

Further, I will propose that the shape of time and space, signified through megaliths, signals the very discontinuity between a system of thought which I identify with the '*sauvage pensée*' as defined by Lévi-Strauss, and a different form of thought, no longer '*sauvage*'.

To give concrete meaning to both proposals ('megaliths as events of thought' and ' "megalithic" thought versus savage thought') it is necessary to define the concepts involved in them. Moreover, their definition implies two different levels of analysis: a theoretical–epistemological and a theoretical–practical one.

Epistemological–theoretical basis: thinking thought

About thought

To begin to think thought, we must use this concept as defined by Lévi-Strauss, i.e. a notion which involves the total system of meanings of a culture, including their relations, structure and transformations, a system through which society 'is thought' (Lévi-Strauss 1966, 1978, 1981). There are several writers whose works, retaining Lévi-Strauss' basic approach, are suitable for thinking thought in prehistory. So next I will define the notion as it is going to be used in this chapter, summarizing ideas from different authors (mainly Foucault 1971, 1974, Clastres 1979, Sahlins 1985, and structural archaeological works, Hodder 1982a, b, Miller & Tilley 1984a).

First of all, thought must not be confused with ideology as defined by structural archaeology. Clearly in this latter approach ideology appears in the very specific field where the interaction between power, the symbolic and society is played. However, the real force of ideology lies not only in its ability to 'hide', 'misrepresent', 'mystify' and 'naturalize', but in the fact that, to maintain order, ideology appears as an 'active force', a positive factor, a principle of building which constructs the social reality, working above general principles of symbolic meaning (Hodder 1982a), and creates categories which punctuate social settings (Miller 1985) or acts back on the social plan and causes a new dynamic (Shennan 1982).

I propose that it is insufficient to view megaliths as 'ideological' phenomena. In so far as the structural archaeological interpretation of them as a 'way of inversion, disguise or distortion of social reality' (Hodder 1982a, p. 200) is simply a way of developing our understanding of Megalithism, it can be accepted as a valid heuristic device (see also Shanks & Tilley 1982, Shennan 1982, Tilley 1984, Braithwaite 1984). However, if we accept this as a definitive explanation, the approach arrived at would be as decontextualized as the diehard functionalist statement that megaliths functioned as 'territorial markers'. Burial may be 'an idealized expression of relations of power' in a society, the dead may be manipulated by the living for propaganda, hiding or misrepresenting social inequality, the past in general may be used to legitimize the present (Parker Pearson 1982, pp. 110–12), but by emphasizing these points we are in danger of arriving at a simplistic approach resulting in such naïve statements as 'myth is the opium of the savage' (Clastres 1981, p. 57) or 'megaliths are the opium of prehistoric people'. I would suggest that ideology is not just a prodigious and sophisticated mechanism to 'say no' (so sophisticated that it can forbid while affirming, order while offering alternatives: Foucault 1977). Ideology lies within the space of thought, which has an order, a language, a vocabulary, a logic and an infinite richness, which are weakened if all attention is centred on its manipulative character, and functional dimensions.

About event

To move beyond the last point towards an adequate concept of thought, we can use Sahlins' (1985) notion of event. This, being a relation between a happening of everyday life and an underlying structure (i.e. the symbolic relations of cultural order), allows the practical realization of the cultural categories in a specific historical context, and vice versa. This categorization (similar to Foucault's concept of happening: Foucault 1971, 1974, Bermejo Barrera 1986) means that any new situation must be incorporated into the culture through a pertinent adjustment of its structure, as this structure must read the new situation with an extant vocabulary. Otherwise this culture could not conceptualize the new situation. Simultaneously, the new context influences the incorporation of new senses in the old vocabulary, before it returns to the underlying structure with a mixture of new features. This implies the possibility of structural change within culture. However, reciprocally, the structure becomes a condition of possibility for change and transformation.

The phenomenon just mentioned occurs frequently in every culture. As it is not possible to analyse these examples here, suffice it to say that the conclusion arising from them is always the same: new things are thought with old categories of the culture. Is this the result of the manipulation of ideology to avoid changes, or the result of the obsessive conservatism of cultures? I would rather view this stability as a structural condition of survival. The structure–

context dialectic establishes the setting for performances. The familiar vocabulary domesticates the unfamiliar situation. Etymologically 'to domesticate' means to bring home. So structure becomes the infrastructure which makes change possible, both in thought and in life. Its vocabulary and grammar become a condition of possibility of the social reality. This vocabulary can be used ideologically to prevent or induce changes which support emergent power structures. However, the vocabulary, structure and system of thought are beyond the strictly ideological field.

It is now possible to draw some conclusions from this brief theoretical discussion. First, clearly there is a thought beyond ideology and to restrict the symbolism of the cultural order (i.e. thought) to the very specific field of the interaction between power, society and thought (i.e. to ideology), is to deny the actual existence of this universe of thoughts. In short, thought is an 'argument to think life'.

Secondly, a knowledge of the configuration of such thought before analysing its practical outcomes seems necessary. However, this does not imply a causality or determining priority of thought over the other fields of culture. From a theoretical precautionary perspective, we should simply say that thought is often considered the best (if not the only) way to think cultures.

Thirdly, putting both considerations together and applying them to our topic, I propose that it should be recognized that megalithic monuments may or may not be an expression of the strategies of power within a particular society, but there is no particular necessity that they should be so. Before considering such an hypothesis, it is necessary to look at them as 'happenings of thought'.

Finally, an important point which emerges here is the possibility that power and ideology, since they are experiences of particular historical contexts, are not 'universals'. Unfortunately, this cannot be discussed here.

Theoretical–practical basis: the savage thought

Whether or not I propose that megalithic monuments signal the discontinuity between savage and post-savage thought, it is necessary to define what constitutes savage thought, and what data allow for its use in prehistory. This is imperative if megaliths are to be considered as 'monuments against the savage'.

Lévi-Strauss has shown the inner logic, and internal functioning of what he calls the '*sauvage pensée*' (Lévi-Strauss 1958, 1966, 1978, 1981). However, his framework fails to clarify the diachronical dimension of thought and the social context beyond conceptual categories.

Clastres (1979, 1981) has defined the societies with savage thought as 'primitive societies', i.e. human cultures which are 'total social facts', where it is not possible to identify specific levels of social activity, so that no determinism exists between different arenas of social unity. The most characteristic and universal feature is the absence of an organ of political power divided from society. A primitive society is a totality and oneness.

As Clastres says, the traditional view of 'primitive' groups is that they are limited by intrinsic centrifugal tendencies. Contextual analysis reveals that these are, in fact, safety valves of the society. The key to their survival is the clear differentiation made between 'us' and the 'other', the understanding of which becomes important, as it defines one's own society as a totality and unity. The plurality of 'happenings' in these societies is the way the society exorcises change and keeps itself undivided and egalitarian: 'The key to the functioning of the system is to emphasize repetition and inertia. But to achieve it, the system is in complete movement and dynamic' (Clastres 1981, p. 213).

Most primitive societies have a strong territorial sense, which must be understood as a space of exclusivity through which fragmentation, self-identification and difference are all emphasized. The definition of territory is not an economic act but a strategy against the 'other'.

Religion and myth are the media through which primitive societies deploy power to remain undivided (Clastres 1981, p. 159). The discourse of the society establishes an order which compels society to remain the same. This order does not come from individual human beings; if it did, it would not be respected. It is a 'given discourse', given by gods or ancestors (see below), not made by a dominant group or something similar. The discourse is not a manipulative ideology, but is the safety of society: 'instead of providing a "superstructure", it is inherent in the primitive social being' (Clastres 1981, p. 159). Therefore, an ideology for one dominant power does not exist here; 'the nature of primitive societies excludes the possibility of such discourse' (Clastres 1981, p. 173).

Clastres remarks on the identification of the individual with the whole project of society, but a topic he has not dealt with is the position of women in such an existential framework, since it is possible that their views of society differ from those of the men (Damm 1987). This would be a subject for further analysis.

I will attend now to the shape of time and space involved in the thought of the primitive societies. The best way to see the shape of time in primitive societies is through an analysis of death. Primitive societies stress a distinction between two kinds of dead: the old (ancestors) and the new (dead relatives). The living society recognizes a close proximity to the ancestors who occupy the time of myth. This mythical time provides the rules of the society and its mythical discourse (as seen above). To keep these rules is a condition of survival for society. To implement the mythical past, the ancestors' time is made present, denying the flux of time and emphasizing cultural continuity. It re-actualizes once and always the old order as given by the ancestors. The continuity held by the mythical discourse, and wanted by society, finds a practical expression through the negation of everyday time that the primitive society signals in its discourse (Clastres 1981). Myth is a mechanism to kill time, its flux being a danger to any society, but what is relevant is the shape of the mechanism used for killing time (Lévi-Strauss 1981).

The best expression of the danger involved in time is found in the attitudes towards the 'new dead'. These are the opposite of the ancestors because, instead of consolidating continuity through the reference to a mythical past which denies the present, they brutally reveal the everyday destructive effect of time's discourse. So, the relationship between living society and the new dead becomes a linkage of distancing, even occultation. All of the rites around death claim one objective: to forget. A number of burial customs perform the role of hiding death: the most exaggerated being endocannibalism (Clastres 1981, p. 75), but including customs like the disposal of the dead on posts or trees, in canoes, or just on the floor (see Jenness 1955). Bearing this in mind, the lack of evidence for elaborate burials in many archaeological contexts should be conceptualized as a 'true' lack which tells us a great deal about the society and the thought wherein these burials do not appear. On the other hand, the presence of megaliths would become more meaningful, revealing a discontinuity.

Myths clearly establish the position of man in the environment. For primitive societies we have the configuration of the culture within nature as emphasized by Lévi-Strauss (1981). Such a 'thought position' is not contradicted by the many economic practices wherein the effect on the environment is negligible.

Thinking the savage thought in (pre-)history

I will briefly apply this theoretical–practical apparatus to archaeology. It is imperative to rethink the Neolithic, moving beyond its traditional conceptualization as a time of changes and revolutions. The idea that the Neolithic was the beginning of a different relationship between man and environment should be avoided. In proposing this, I am not saying that such a feature does not exist, but rather that the traditional idea which situates such an achievement at the very beginning of Neolithic is incorrect.

In place of such an approach, any rethinking of the Neolithic should view it as a time of discontinuities, with at least two 'breaks': in traditional terms, one of these discontinuities would be the primitive agriculture of the early Neolithic, and the other the 'secondary neolithic revolution' (Sherratt 1981).

Why do I propose this re-reading? What are the data which support it? From the above discussion about thought, it does not seem possible to think the differences between both discontinuities in infrastructural terms. Instead, if the analysis is approached from the perspective of thought, it becomes possible to see the different conceptualizations about the man–environment relationship which appear in both discontinuities; further this reveals the close relationship which situates the 'Mesolithic' and the 'Neolithic' in the same discontinuity.

Recent archaeological data suggest that the distance between Neolithic and Mesolithic should be drastically reduced (Burenhult 1984). According to them there was a complex of activities involving sophisticated plant management and environmental manipulation which can all be classified under the common denomination of gardening (Larsson 1985, Sherratt 1981). Referring to the 'Mesolithic' context in North America, it is clear that if some cultures did not use agricultural resources in sophisticated ways, it was simply because they chose not to rather than because they were under the pressure of environmental constraints (Ford 1979).

Apparently, then, the Neolithic precedes agriculture. However, I would say that the Neolithic way of thought precedes the Neolithic way of life. I propose that savage thought, concerned with situating man as an extension of nature, emphasizes that the first condition for the survival of society is to keep nature in its right, 'natural', order. The first economic practices of environment management do not contradict such criteria, but respect them. Sometimes it has been stressed that the first changes made to the natural environment were 'conservationist-oriented', initiated to help nature to maximize its possibilities without introducing elements of distortion. An example of this is the symbolic conceptualization of fire among some North-American Indians. Fire is not viewed as the destruction of nature, but as a way of restoring natural order (i.e. removing the profusion of weeds and shrubs: Day 1953).

It is now possible to draw some conclusions.

(a) There is a clear 'discontinuity' between savage thought and the system of thought of post-savage societies.
(b) The savage thought establishes a correspondence between Mesolithic and some Neolithic groups. The shape of time and space appearing in it points out a general identity in the economic practices of both kinds of groups. This shape did not allow the occurrence of monumental constructions for displaying death or breaking the man–nature extension.
(c) The new thought, appearing after this 'savage' one, has a new shape of time and space, conceptualizing man–environment relationships differently, allowing for a new kind of economic praxis. This discontinuity is signified through various cultural elements and symbols, including the megalithic monuments whose presence signals a particular historical context wherein they should be understood.
(d) Before leaving the 'savage' space, I would suggest that there are some data to propose that the savage thought was probably a fairly late development in the history of mankind. However, this thought is beyond the scope of this chapter.

Thinking the 'post-savage' thought behind megaliths

It now becomes easier to account for megaliths as the actual and factual expression of a system of thought which replaces the savage one and allows the 'construction of a new landscape'. However, one thing is clear: my approach explains almost nothing about megaliths. This, far from being a mistake, is a necessary consequence of conceptualizing megaliths as a 'happening of thought'. The dimension of thought is given primary consideration and, later, the dimension of 'happening'. Megaliths belong to a system of thought which occurs in various contexts, so that it is only by looking at them as a single element of a 'group of transformations' (Lévi-Strauss 1958, 1981) that it is possible to define the actual thought that they signify. It should be emphasized that such thought allows for widely differing solutions and historical contexts within it. However, until we can understand both terms of our concept completely, it will be impossible to translate the particular context of megaliths. We must ignore much of the specifity of megaliths at this stage.

We saw that the symbolic order of primitive societies reads man as a 'gardener'. Therefore, the social landscape becomes one shaped by nature and occupied by men, in harmony. Nature is the condition of culture, but equally culture is the condition of nature in that there is no firm division between them. In contrast, who is the man behind the social landscape of 'domesticated thought' (Goody 1977)? Clearly the answer is the farmer, the peasant. He is the one who needs to control the territory, who becomes a slave of it and of natural accidents, so that, whenever possible, he uses his culture to domesticate land. It is important now to dominate not help nature. Rather than legitimizing itself through nature, thought composes order in it. (The next stage is to appropriate it: with fences, not merely extending symbolic metaphors around the territory, but with the impressive and unambiguous measure of field systems. The appearance of field systems linked to megaliths is now meaningful (Caulfield 1978, 1983).)

In this context it seems more productive to think of megaliths as territorial symbols, and to incorporate the clear evidence that often they were or are limits. With this approach, correcting the simplistic interpretations of functionalist theories appears easy: the function of the megalith is not to be a limit, but the limit is a 'function' (in the algebraic sense) of the megalith. Using data from my fieldwork, it is possible to suggest that megaliths often use natural signifiers to shape the specific configuration of space that is involved. Repetitive links between megaliths and natural limits or borders could then be understood as a way to incorporate the natural organization of the environment within the social organization of the landscape.

A comparison between primitive and state–peasant societies in South America reveals the same contraposition that is found between savage and megalithic groups. Amongst the Andes Indians the overall relationship with the Earth, with the landscape understood as 'productive' (the Mother Earth, the fields of the community . . .) is coherent with economic practices which are different from those of the Forest Indians. Such considerations are far removed from the conceptualization involved in the primitive societies' notion of territory (i.e. the field of identification with nature and the contrast with other groups: Clastres 1981, pp. 67–97). This disjunction is also maintained in other features, like the appearance of monumental constructions to organize the social landscape (i.e. the concept of *wak'a* is important here (Clastres 1981, pp. 89–91, Manani Condori 1986), the displaying of death and the concept of time found in these cultures.

The change in the concept of time from the savage to the domesticated thought can be studied through the rites of death in post-savage societies. In opposition to the forest societies, the cult of the new dead in the Andes is very important. The relationship with the new dead reinforces the continuity between the worlds of the living and the dead. This is a totally different pattern of relationship with the dead from that in a primitive society wherein death, a danger to the living, was hidden and forgotten. The continuity of the living society is stressed in the Andes by reference to the 'new dead' and to the ancestors. This stress on the continuity is expressed through a physically visible territorialization of relations (cemetery, *wak'a*). What emerges here is a concept of time quite different from that found in primitive societies where time and the past were mythical, situated beyond society, from which society originated. The survival of these societies depends on emphasizing the relationships with this 'founding time' and negating the 'living time'. However, in the Andes time develops from the ancestors' time and progresses towards 'now'. Any breakdown of such time must or can be incorporated within the present to secure unity and continuity of society.

As a general summary it could be said that megaliths, the first monuments to dominate nature, made for all time and to unify ancestors, the new dead and society, construct a 'post-savage' landscape by implementing new concepts of time and man–environment relationships. This overview of the 'thought setting' wherein megaliths appear suggests that it is a prerequisite for the understanding of the contexts of megaliths. A step beyond this and a subject of further analysis is an enquiry into the way in which the variability within Megalithism is linked to ideological–power–social relationships that are played out in this setting (Criado Boado n.d.).

It is ironic to finish this chapter with a reference to its writer, who chose at the start to keep himself out.

Acknowledgements

Behind the mysterious happening of a chapter in a book there are several different happenings and individuals who, through the tyranny of the writer, are condemned to silence. I would wish that they could appear throughout the chapter rather than be 'enclosed' in these aseptic references. Comments and discussions with Grant Chambers, Charlotte Damm, Ian Hodder, John Muke, Nandini Rao and Chris Tilley proved very useful for this piece of work. Grant Chambers and Nandini Rao corrected my English too. This chapter was written while I was visiting the Department of Archaeology, University of Cambridge, in 1986, enjoying a 'Xunta de Galicia' (Spain) scholarship. I would like to thank both institutions for providing me with their research facilities.

References

Bermejo Barrera, J. C. 1986. *A morte da historia. Ensaio de historia teórica*. Vigo: Galaxia.

Braithwaite, M. 1984. Ritual and prestige in the prehistory of Wessex, *c*. 2200–1400 BC. In *Ideology, power and prehistory*, D. Miller & C. Tilley (eds), 93–110. Cambridge: Cambridge University Press.

Burenhult, G. 1984. The archaeology of Carrowmore. Environmental archaeology and the megalithic tradition at Carrowmore, Co. Sligo, Ireland. Theses and Papers in North-European Archaeology, Institute of Archaeology, Stockholm.

Caulfield, S. 1978. Neolithic fields: the Irish evidence. In *Early land allotment in the British*

Isles. A survey of recent work, H. C. Bowen & P. J. Fowler (eds), 137–43. Oxford: BAR British Series 48.
Caulfield, S. 1983. The Neolithic settlement of north Connaught. In *Landscape archaeology in Ireland*, T. Reeves-Smith & F. Hamond (eds), 195–215. Oxford: BAR British Series 116.
Chapman, R. 1981. The emergence of formal disposal areas and the 'problem' of megalithic tombs in prehistoric Europe. In *The archaeology of death*, R. Chapman, I. Kinnes & K. Randsborg (eds), 71–82. Cambridge: Cambridge University Press.
Clastres, P. 1979. *A Sociedade contra o Estado. Investigacoes en antropologia polîtica*. Porto: Ediçoes Afrontamento (Paris, 1979).
Clastres, P. 1981. *Investigaciones en antropologia politics*. Barcelona: Gedisa (Paris, 1980).
Criado Boado, F. n.d. Las culturas megaliticas de la fachada Atlántica peninsular y sus relaciones con el marco natural. PhD in preparation. To be submitted to Departamento de Historia 1, Universidad de Santiago.
Damm, C. 1987. An appeal for women in archaeology. *Archaeological Review from Cambridge* **5**(2) (in press).
Day, G. M. 1953. The Indian as an ecological factor in the northeastern forest. *Ecology* **34**, 329–46.
Fleming, A. 1971. Territorial patterns in Bronze Age Wessex. *Proceedings of Prehistoric Society* **37**, 138–66.
Fleming, A. 1973. Tombs for the living. *Man* **8**, 177–93.
Ford, R. I. 1979. Gathering and gardening: trends and consequences of Hopewell subsistence strategies. In *Hopewell archaeology: the Chillicothe Conference*, D. S. Brose & N. Greber (eds), 234–8. Kent: Kent State University.
Foucault, M. 1971. Orders of discourse. *Social Science Information* **10**(2), 7–30.
Foucault, M. 1974. *The archaeology of knowledge*. London: Tavistock (Paris, 1969).
Foucault, M. 1977. *Discipline and punishment*. London: Allen Lane (Paris, 1975).
Goody, J. 1977. *The domestication of the savage mind*. Cambridge: Cambridge University Press.
Hodder, I. 1982a. *Symbols in action. Ethnoarchaeological studies of material culture*. Cambridge: Cambridge University Press.
Hodder, I. (ed.) 1982b. *Symbolic and structural archaeology*. Cambridge: Cambridge University Press.
Hodder, I. 1982c. Theoretical archaeology: a reactionary view. In *Symbolic and structural archaeology*, I. Hodder (ed.), 1–16. Cambridge: Cambridge University Press.
Hodder, I. 1984. Burial, houses, women and men in the European Neolithic. In *Ideology, power and prehistory*, D. Miller & C. Tilley (eds), 51–68. Cambridge: Cambridge University Press.
Jenness, D. 1955. *The Indians of Canada*. Ottawa: National Museum of Canada.
Larsson, M. 1985. *The Early Neolithic funnel-beaker culture in south-west Scania, Sweden. Social and economic change, 3000–2500 BC*. Oxford: BAR International Series 142.
Lévi-Strauss, C. 1958. *Anthropologie structurale*. Paris: Plon.
Lévi-Strauss, C. 1966. *The savage mind*. London: Weidenfeld & Nicolson (Paris, 1962).
Lévi-Strauss, C. 1978. *The origin of table manners*. London: J. Cape (Paris, 1968).
Lévi-Strauss, C. 1981. *The naked man*. London: J. Cape (Paris, 1971).
Mamani Condori, C. 1986. Historia y Prehistoria: ¿dónde nos encontramos los Indios? Unpublished paper submitted to The World Archaeological Congress, Southampton.
Midgley, M. S. 1985. *The origin and function of the earthen long barrows of Northern Europe*. Oxford: BAR International Series 259.

Miller, D. 1985. *Artefacts as categories*. Cambridge: Cambridge University Press.
Miller, D. & C. Tilley (eds) 1984a. *Ideology, power and prehistory*. Cambridge: Cambridge University Press.
Miller, D. & C. Tilley 1984b. Ideology, power and prehistory: an introduction. In *Ideology, power and prehistory*, D. Miller & C. Tilley (eds), 1–15. Cambridge: Cambridge University Press.
Parker Pearson, M. 1982. Mortuary practices, society and ideology: an ethnoarchaeological study. In *Symbolic and structural archaeology*, I. Hodder (ed.), 99–113. Cambridge: Cambridge University Press.
Renfrew, C. 1973. Monuments, mobilization and social organization in Neolithic Wessex. In *The explanation of culture change: models in prehistory*, C. Renfrew (ed.), 539–58. London: Duckworth.
Renfrew, C. 1976. Megaliths, territories and populations. In *Acculturation and continuity in Atlantic Europe*, S. J. de Laet (ed.). *Dissertationes Archaeologicae Gandenses*, XVI, 198–220.
Renfrew, C. 1983. The megalithic monuments of western Europe. In *The megalithic monuments of western Europe*, C. Renfrew (ed.), 8–17. London: Thames & Hudson.
Sahlins, M. 1985. *Islands of history*. Chicago: University of Chicago Press.
Shanks, M. & C. Tilley 1982. Ideology, symbolic power and ritual communication: a reinterpretation of neolithic mortuary practices. In *Symbolic and structural archaeology*, I. Hodder (ed.), 129–54. Cambridge: Cambridge University Press.
Shennan, S. 1982. Ideology, change and the European early Bronze Age. In *Symbolic and structural archaeology*, I. Hodder (ed.), 155–61. Cambridge: Cambridge University Press.
Sherratt, A. 1981. Plough and pastoralism: aspects of the secondary products revolution. In *Patterns of the past*, I. Hodder, G. Isaac & N. Hammond (eds), 261–305. Cambridge: Cambridge University Press.
Tilley, C. 1984. Ideology and the legitimation of power in the Middle Neolithic of southern Sweden. In *Ideology, power and prehistory*, D. Miller & C. Tilley (eds), 111–46. Cambridge: Cambridge University Press.

3 *The diffusion of religious symbols within complex societies*

L. CARLESS HULIN

Introduction

This chapter represents an initial meditation on the processes through which intrusive religious concepts, paraphernalia or practices are absorbed into indigenous religious systems. It has grown out of my research into the non-industrial peasant cultures of the pre-Christian Near East. These cultures are characterized by numerous small agricultural communities standing in a dependent relationship to cities, where power is concentrated in the form of divinely ordained kingships, economically powerful priesthoods and the merchant classes (Sjoberg 1960).

During the first half of the 20th century, diffusionism (i.e. the view that most cultural traits emanate from a limited number of sources, and are transmitted by means of contact between peoples) was taken to account for most culture change. When it became clear that this was a somewhat simplistic theory, the entire concept fell into disuse among archaeologists, although geographers and anthropologists continued to refine the concept. Recently, revived interest among archaeologists has concentrated on the more tangible aspects of the process, i.e. the distribution of stylistic traits and technological items (see Davis 1983, for a full bibliography). However, the diffusion of *ideas* remains an undeveloped concept. The cross-cultural comparison of religious artefacts still tends to be justified on the (diffusionist) basis of degrees of visual similarity, rather than by known patterns of social interaction. Syncretism is used as a model of, rather than a model for, the diffusion of religious symbols.

Diffusion and social structure

Clearly, in general terms, the degree of interaction between communities must determine the amount of diffusion possible (Foster 1962). However, since *individuals* are the agents of diffusion, and individuals move in socially proscribed circles, the potential for diffusion of any innovation is affected by the relative advantage and mobility of the social circle to which those individuals belong. Although the identification of complex social stratigraphy in the material record in absolute rather than relative terms is notoriously difficult (for example,

Cowgill *et al.* 1984, Chapman & Randsborg 1982, McGuire 1983), activities performed at the individual, household, sodality and community levels are recognizable (for example, Flannery 1976). For the purposes of this chapter, individuals, households and village-based sodalities are classified together as the small group (SG). The monarch, his court, army commanders and religious leaders constitute the large group (LG). Crude though these divisions may be in social terms, they serve as useful minimum concepts which may be applied to the archaeological record.

In the type of social system under consideration, all fundamental policy decisions which affect the economic social and religious life of village communities are made externally, by city-based LG powers (Foster 1962). Therefore the parameters of SG decision-making are restricted to those areas not accessed by the LG, i.e. local issues. It follows that any innovation, the acceptance of which fundamentally alters village life, represents a threat to LG authority processes (see below). Consequently, the potential for diffusion from the SG to the LG is limited by the compatability of SG and LG interests. For example, a process which increases production, and therefore the wealth of all parties, is likely to be generally acceptable, whereas a process which increases the autonomy of the SG is likely to be resisted by the LG. At a first glance it would appear that innovation accepted by the LG has the potential for widespread diffusion, by virtue of its power in the community. However, acceptance at an LG level leads to universal diffusion only if the innovation increases the benefits to the LG while at the same time posing no threat to its authority by increasing SG autonomy.

Diffusion and religious structure

One of the functions of religion is to explain the real and unreal world, ordering and validating community experience in terms of its own explanation (Durkheim 1957, Geertz 1965, Radcliffe-Brown 1939). Religious and social systems are therefore mutually reinforcing, and one might expect diffusion patterns within religious systems to mirror those of the state. In the ancient Near East, theological and sociopolitical realities were contiguous (Frankfort 1948, Ahlström 1982). Political territories were regarded as the property of the gods. Kings ruled either on behalf of the gods or as divine beings themselves; often they held important posts in the religious hierarchy. In sanctifying such kingships, the religious system ratified existing social realities, including the stratification upon which LG power depended.

Social stratification is maintained partly through the control of information, knowledge and actions based on these (Berger & Luckmann 1967). In pre-industrial cities the priestly groups usually controlled the flow of information by providing teaching personnel (Sjoberg 1960). In the religious system, information becomes canonical and consequently incontrovertible. Any innovation presents a potential threat to the symbolic universe as put forward by the ruling élites. Extreme threats are likely to generate extreme responses: threatened systems will resist innovation as a matter of policy, as did the Jews under Antiochus

(*I & II Maccabees*, esp. *I Maccabees* 2, vv.19–22). In such cases diffusion is unlikely to occur.

Clearly, acceptance of an innovation necessitates validation from the host system. Adoption of an innovation requires either an alteration of the meaning of the innovation or of part of the religious system. Competing deities may be integrated by means of a reinterpretation which denies their uniqueness; thus the Greeks in Egypt equated Amun with Jupiter and Osiris with Dionysus (Herodotus II, p. 2).

As in the secular sphere, the potential for diffusion within the religious system depends on the relationship between the SG and LG spheres. Social stratification is expressed in the religious system by the presence of practices either peculiar to or more commonly found in one social level than another. In the ancient Near East most of the rituals involving royalty, the senior priesthood and other members of the LG were predominantly concerned with LG issues, e.g. the fertility of the land and livestock, and national security. Small-group rites localize these issues, reducing concerns to such matters as the fertility of the immediate district, or personal health (Pritchard 1950). This stratification of roles and concerns reduces the likelihood of diffusion from the LG levels, since there is less unity of interest and concern. Indeed, the SG may be considerably ignorant of all but the practical application of its own religious duties (Sperber 1975, Ladurie 1978); the more highly educated members of the élite group enter the clergy at high levels, whereas the lower positions tend to be filled by poorly educated individuals from the same low-status group as the congregations which they serve (Sjoberg 1960). As a result there is often a considerable difference between the folk-rites of the SG and the more formal observances of the LG, which adheres more closely to the ideal norms of society.

Large-group interest may dictate the limited acceptance of an innovation. Ahaz introduced a 'foreign' altar into the temple in Jerusalem as an expression of his symbolic subjugation to the Assyrians (*II Kings* 16, vv. 10–16), an act demanded by the victorious Assyrians as a matter of course (Pritchard 1950). As such it had no discernible effect on the Yahwist cult as a whole, despite the outrage of the prophets, since access to the temple was an LG privilege. However, innovation at an LG level may spread to those sections of the community that share or aspire to LG aims. For example, in New Kingdom Egypt, as a consequence of royal patronage (which was itself a political expression of Egyptian military superiority), certain Asiatic gods were adopted by the court and thereafter by royal-tomb builders. The army embraced the worship of the warlike goddess Anat. However, by contrast the mass of Egyptian society seems not to have come into contact with the Asiatic gods at all (Carless Hulin 1982). The significance of a recognizably diffused element present in all levels of society is that, if it can be shown to have originated in the LG, then its dispersal throughout the community as a whole must represent an act of will on the part of an LG, acting towards its own advantage. For example, the Tyrian queen Jezebel promoted the cult of Melqart in Israel at the expense of Yahwism in an effort to secure a power base favourable to Sidon (*I Kings* 18, vv. 4–19).

Since innovation promoted by the SG represents a threat to the realities imposed by the ruling élites, the potential for diffusion from this level depends on the relationships between different social strata (see above). Douglas (1970) has argued that the relationship between sacred and secular systems and the relationship between public obligation and individual negotiation (group and grid) determine the receptivity of society to symbolic meaning. Wiessner (in Ch. 2) maintains that the degree of social and symbolic significance invested in an artefact determines the amount of stylistic variation expressed. Significance is seen to be determined by social, economic or political conditions – factors equivalent, I would suggest, to the value placed on various acts by the LG stratum. This relationship also governs the willingness of society to accept 'alien' symbols, in that the more forcibly the socioreligious norms are imposed, the less room there is for SG expression. Powerful religious institutions develop 'theories of deviance' designed to prevent challenge to the existing system. Aberrant individuals may be accused of demon-possession, or madness; they are killed or 'cured'. Alternatively, 'rising' deities may be defeated in theological battles, or denied theological reality (Berger & Luckmann 1967). Should diffusion at an SG level become significant, it may be (explicitly or implicitly) designated proper only for those of low status to worship, thus confining the spread of an innovation to those strata. Niebuhr (1969) noted that denominations and sects represent the accommodation of religion to the caste system. Alternatively, deities may amalgamate, thereby checking the ascendancy of a potential rival; the legends of the Near East record numerous modifications of this type.

Where some measure of SG autonomy is favoured, innovation is encouraged in its spread through the system. For example, in Samoa the Congregational Mission conversion programme proved successful, because the strongly individual church structure was compatible with patterns of village authority. The more hierarchical Catholic mission had less impact (Brown 1957). Alternatively, where LG authority is strong but remote, deviant or alien theories may take root. It was noted above that a large porportion of SG communities are relatively ignorant about fundamental religious tenets. It is clear that in the 14th century AD the inhabitants of Montaillou, France, confused the tenets of Catholicism and Albigensianism, and saw no difficulties in this; indeed, the local Catholic priest was a leading heretic (Ladurie 1978).

Talmon (1969), in a study of millinarianism, noted that such cults, while finding their support in all levels of society, particularly attract those who suffer from a radically different relation between social aspirations and the realities of life. Obviously this is more likely to occur within the SG, especially in times of social or economic uncertainty or deprivation. At such times the SG will tend to be receptive to alien phenomena simply *because* such elements do not belong to the system which has proved unsatisfactory to SG members.

Since theological and sociopolitical reality are contiguous, a significant innovation accepted in the social system inevitably also has ramifications within the religious system. As religion serves to legitimate existing social categories, it is necessarily resistant to change; for a religious system to alter perceptions of socioreligious realities is to undermine its own power base. Therefore, in countenancing change, religion is *adaptive* rather than innovative. For example,

Knapp (1986) demonstrated that the transformation from an isolated village-based culture to an international city-oriented metal-producing society in Cyprus (1700–1400 BC) involved an absorption into the belief system of a number of symbols derived from the metallurgical industry. Clearly the structure of society was changing so fundamentally that religious ideology had to modify itself in order to maintain its authority, and it did so by identifying its interests with those of the newly emergent group. Sjoberg (1960) suggests that religion re-interprets itself only when society changes slowly; rapid social development is more likely to lead to social collapse (cf. Drennan 1976).

Objects and diffusion

When trying to determine the significance of the presence of a diffused element, it is important to recognize the distinction between the diffusion of theology and the diffusion of ritual. An object of the cult (i.e. a *focus* of worship), plays a more active role in religious life than a cult object (i.e. an artefact used in the *act* of worship). The former, by its nature, is more scarce in the material record than the latter. One might suppose that the adoption of a deity does more violence to existing systems than does the diffusion of practice, since a 'new' deity requires greater efforts of accommodation at a theological or mythological level, whereas the practice need do no more than 'find favour' with the gods.

Is it possible to predict the circumstances under which an element will diffuse, given the conditions of contact, and 'fit' with the host system described above? Ultimately, the successful diffusion of a symbol rests on its relevance to, and fit with, the host value system. However, Ortner (1973) has defined two broad classes of symbol: elaborating and summarizing. Elaborating symbols are conceptual parables which serve to explain theological reality by analogy to known phenomena; their utility makes them recurrent; their frequency rarely makes them sacred. Summarizing symbols represent conceptual distillations, explicable only in the context of cultural information shared by the whole community; given their rarity, they are generally revered. Ortner argues that summarizing symbols, being culture-specific, are culture-bound. However, Goodenough (1954) suggested that they are more likely to be diffused by virtue of their distillation, becoming associated with general ethical concepts unfettered by cultural boundaries. Certainly images do cross religious boundaries. For example, a mosaic from Paphos, Cyprus, celebrates the dawn of the age of Dionysus; the infant god is shown with his mother in a posture which echoes that of the Virgin and Christ-child (Daszewski 1985). Although little work has been done in this area, it would seem that those elements which most readily diffuse (i.e. those that are not imposed) are those which most easily accommodate a change of meaning, and thus have arguably only weak links with their original significance.

Conclusion: diffusion and the archaeological record

The common assumption that the presence of a recognizably alien religious symbol within an indigenous system represents an intact and comprehensive acceptance (diffusion) of that innovation is clearly simplistic. Religious systems do not conform to realities presented in ancient texts which mostly record LG beliefs. Practice and beliefs are socially stratified. Members of the various social strata operate different strategies in order to deal with intrusive elements, and some of those (e.g. 'syncretism' in its Classical sense) or 'particularization' (the confining of innovations to specific strata) necessitate the manipulation of meaning away from its original sense. Even the translation of the innovation into terms equivalent to host values becomes, in effect, a denial of innovation. Therefore, it is preferable to interpret symbols within the context of the host culture, and not on the basis of visual similarity with other cultures across space and time, unless an unbroken link can be proven.

References

Ahlström, G. W. 1982. *Royal administration and national religion in ancient Palestine*, 3–4 and n. 54. Leiden: Brill.
Berger, P. & T. Luckmann 1967. *The social construction of reality. A treatise in the sociology of knowledge*. Harmondsworth: Pelican.
Brown, G. G. 1957. Some problems of culture contact with illustrations from East Africa & Samoa. *Human Organization* **16**, 14–21.
Carless Hulin, L. 1982. The worshippers of Asiatic gods in Egypt. *Papers for Discussion* **1**, 269–78.
Chapman, R. & K. Randsborg 1982. Approaches to the archaeology of death. In *The archaeology of death, new directions in archaeology*. N. R. Chapman, I. Kinnes & K. Randsborg (eds), 1–24. Cambridge: Cambridge University Press.
Cowgill, G. L., J. H. Altschul & R. S. Sload 1984. Spatial analysis of Teotihuacan: a Mesoamerican metropolis. In *Intrasite spatial analysis in Archaeology*, H. Hietala (ed.), 154–95. Cambridge: Cambridge University Press.
Daszewski, W. A. 1985. *Dionysos der Erlöser. Griechisch Mythen im spätantiken Cypern*. Mainz/Rhein: Philipp von Zabern.
Davis, D. D. 1983. Investigating the diffusion of stylistic innovations. *Advances in archaeological method and theory*, Vol. 6, M. B. Schiffer (ed.), 53–89. New York: Academic Press.
Douglas, M. 1970. *Natural symbols*. London: Barrie & Rockliff.
Drennan, R. D. 1976. Religion and social evolution in formative Mesoamerica. *The early Mesoamerican village*, K. V. Flannery (ed.), 345–64. New York: Academic Press.
Durkheim, E. 1957. *The elementary forms of the religious life* (Engl. transl.). New York: Free Press.
Flannery, K. V. 1976. Religion and social evolution in formative Mesoamerica. In *The early Mesoamerican village*, K. V. Flannery (ed.), 333–45. New York: Academic Press.
Foster, G. M. 1962. *Traditional cultures and the impact of technological change*, Vol. 25, 46–7. New York: Harper & Brothers.

Frankfort, H. 1948. *Kingship and the gods*. Chicago: Chicago University Press.

Geertz, C. 1965. Religion as a cultural system. In *Anthropological approaches to the study of religion*, M. Banton (ed.)., 1–46 Association of Social Anthropologists Monographs No. 3. London: Tavistock.

Goodenough, E. R. 1954. *Jewish symbols of the Greco-Roman world*, Vol. 4, Ch. 2. Bollingen Series XXXVII. New York: Bollingen.

Herodotus *The Histories*, Book II, 29 (1948 edn), Ph.- E. Legrand (ed.). Paris.

Knapp, A. B. 1986. *Copper production and divine protection: archaeology, ideology and social complexity on Bronze Age Cyprus*. Studies in Mediterranean Archaeology Pocket-book Series, Vol. 42. Göteborg: Aström.

Ladurie, E. L. R. R. 1978. *Montaillou*. Harmondsworth: Peregrine Books.

McGuire, R. M. 1983. Breaking down cultural complexity, inequality and heterogeneity. *Advances in archaeological method and theory*, Vol. 6, M. B. Schiffer (ed.), 91–142. New York: Academic Press.

Niebuhr, H. R. 1969. The social sources of denominationalism. In *Sociology and religion. A book of readings*, N. Birnbaum & G. Lenzer (eds), 314–8. Englewood Cliffs, New Jersey: Prentice-Hall.

Ortner, S. B. 1973. On key symbols. *American Anthropologist* **75**, 1338–46.

Pritchard, J. B. (ed.) 1950. *Ancient Near Eastern texts relating to the Old Testament*. Princeton: Princeton University Press.

Radcliffe-Brown, A. R. 1939. *Taboo* (The Frazer Lecture.) Cambridge: Cambridge University Press.

Sjoberg, G. 1960. *The preindustrial city. Past and present*. New York: Free Press.

Sperber, D. 1975. *Rethinking symbolism* (Engl. transl. A. L. Morton). Cambridge: Cambridge University Press.

Talmon, Y. 1969. Pursuit of the millennium: the relation between religious and social change. In *Sociology and religion. A book of readings*, N. Birnbaum & G. Lenzer (eds), 238–54. Englewood Cliffs, New Jersey: Prentice-Hall.

5 *Social evidence from the interpretation of Middle Minoan figurines*

ANGELIKI PILALI-PAPASTERIOU

The first publicly organized cult in Crete emerged around 2000 BC in the Peak Sanctuaries. The 52 recently identified sanctuaries, dispersed mainly through east and central Crete, were situated near settlements or palatial centres. Most were frequented during the period of the Old Palaces, as well as during the first phase of the New Palaces (1900–1600 BC). Only in a few of them (e.g. in Jouktas) was the cult continued through the whole Minoan period (Peatfield 1983, Rutkowski 1986, pp. 79f.). The main offerings in Peak Sanctuaries were male and female figurines. These figurines, conceived as symbols of an ideology, may reveal multiple evidence about the religious and social concepts of the Middle Minoan period.

Numerous figurines in all the Peak Sanctuaries were found mostly broken, in a layer of ashes between the rock crevices, along with other votives of similar character. Their size, their gesture, their dress and the absence of other specific attributes strengthen the suggestion that they represent votaries and not cult idols (Platon 1951, pp. 156–7, Renfrew 1985, p. 23).

The main iconographical features of these figurines are their dresses and especially their headdresses. Items of dress belong to a category of material culture which would play a part in information flow and information exchange in many different contexts (Wobst 1977, pp. 329, 331). The emitted messages should be linked to the rules and processes of the socio-economic and ideological structure of the whole society (Hodder 1982a, p. 193, 1982b, pp. 204f.). These messages, as many cross-cultural examples reveal, could participate in processes of social differentiation. This differentiation concerns the uniqueness of rank or status of an individual or the social and economic group affiliation (Wobst 1977, p. 328).

The social context, from which these Minoan artefacts come, is that of a strictly organized hierarchical system, centralized mainly in four palatial centres (Knossos, Phaistos, Mallia and Zakros), and probably in several smaller regional centres (Cherry 1984, pp. 32f.). The dedication of votaries at the Peak Sanctuaries is a part of defined cult ritual among the rural population of Crete – a population which is incorporated in the hierarchical system. The existence of social differentiation among the votaries becomes more evident if we accept the direct or indirect relationship between the establishment of that religious practice and the palatial system (Peatfield 1983, p. 277, Cherry 1984, pp. 34–5). Therefore the question to be tackled is how and to what extent this social differentiation is expressed through the depicted dresses in the Minoan figurines.

As far as the male dress goes, none of the types depicted in the Minoan representation seem to be specific to a certain social rank or status, except perhaps for the ritual dress (Sapouna-Sakellaraki 1971, pp. 92, 97, 100, 110, 115, 121, 123). It is generally assumed that the specific items of a high status are richly decorated dresses, daggers, shoes, long and elaborate hair and particularly jewellery (Sapouna-Sakellaraki 1971, pp. 97, 119, 123, Verlinden 1984, p. 138). Wobst (1977, pp. 332, 335) suggests that the messages emitted through some of the above items, with the shortest visibility, express an individual's position along a ranked scale such as wealth, status or age. This suggestion could be admitted for the Minoan figurines as well, since they come from a hierarchical social context. Among the 34 male clay figurines from Petsofas, only six carry specific items of high status. Museum of Herakleion, Crete (Her. Mus.) 3408, 4873 wear necklaces, Her. Mus. 4880 a necklace and a dagger, Her. Mus. 3409, 3407 a dagger and shoes and Her. Mus. 3425 a necklace, a bracelet and shoes (Sapouna-Sakellaraki 1971, nos 10, 13, 9, 14, 18, 12, Verlinden 1984, p. 68). The dissimilar distribution of items can probably be explained as an indication of an even more refined differentiation.

Another item of high status is the dagger. Among the male figurines from the Peak Sanctuaries only a few carry daggers: namely ten figurines, among the 34 from Petsofas, one from Piskokephalo, some from Karphi and none from Maza (Fig. 5.1a, Sapouna-Sakellaraki 1971, nos 4–6, 8, 9, 11, 14, 16, 18, 23, 54c, 27, 29, 30). This sample indicates that the dagger was not an indispensable element of the male dress. The same conclusion is deduced from the distribution of daggers in the Early Minoan and Middle Minoan tombs of Mesara. It is suggested that the daggers are represented in roughly one out of every five burials (Branigan 1970, appendix 2, Whitelaw 1983, pp. 334–5, e.g. Platanos A, 300 burials, 75 daggers, Hagia Triada A 200–300 burials, 50 daggers). Therefore it is evident that the daggers had a restricted use and were perhaps the exclusive possession of a specific segment of the population, mature men or family heads (Whitelaw 1983, p. 343, ref. 16). The evidence of a rising 'militarism' in the Aegean during the third millenium BC in relation to the emergence of the palatial system in Crete, later, may indicate the function of the dagger more as a mark of an emerging warrior's rank rather than as a simple symbol of political authority or as a weapon of display for any rich and important man (Renfrew 1972, p. 394).

The main feature of the female figurines is the impressive headdresses. The elaborate rendering of these headdresses in contrast with the schematic representation of the facial traits, even if some of them were painted, may conceal a special symbolic meaning (Platon 1951, p. 129, ref. 84, Buchholz & Karageorghis 1971, nos 1215, 1217, 1218, Hood 1978, p. 105). During the Old Palace period most of the female figurines carry hats of Petsofas type, while in the New Palace period the long hair or the elaborate hairdressings predominate (for example, Hood 1978, fig. 86, Verlinden 1984, p. 137, pl. 16). According to

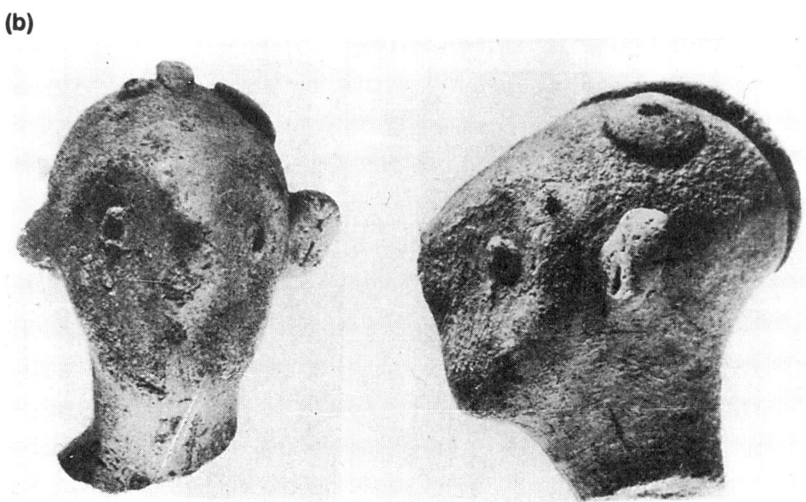

Figure 5.1 Male figurines from (a) Petsofas and (b) Jouktas.

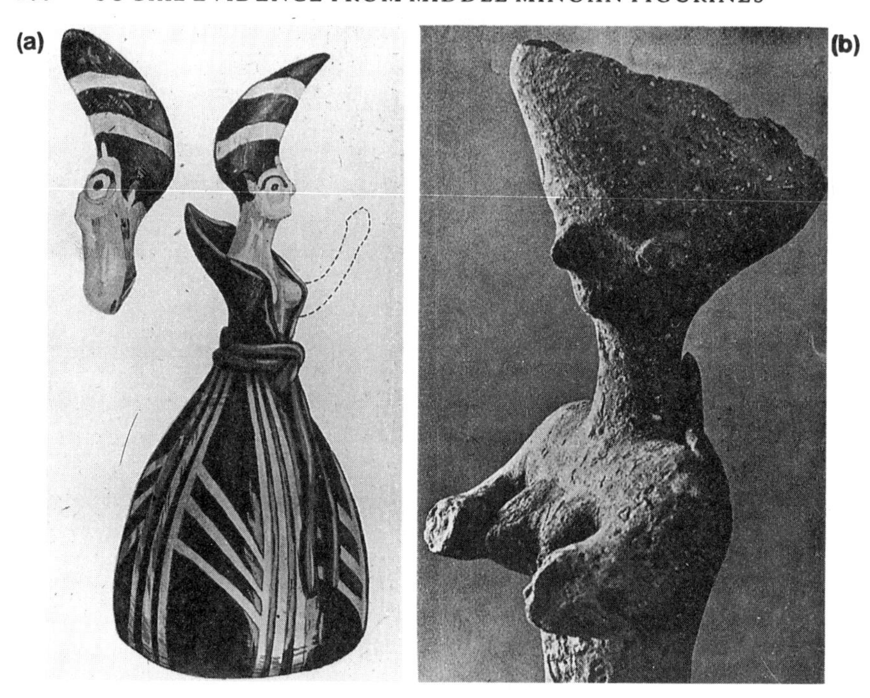

Figure 5.2 a, b Female figurines from Petsofas.

ethnographic examples, hats are supposed to be appropriate to take on messages of social group affiliation, because of their great visibility (Wobst, 1977, pp. 332–3). This suggestion could be tested, archaeologically, through the study of the typology and the distribution of the Minoan hats. The following types of hats can be observed.

(a) Hats with the front brim raised above the forehead, in shoe-horn shape. The upper edge is often curved forwards. The hat is attached far back on the head by its back margin, whereas the posterior surface is concave without indication of hair (Myres 1902–3, p.370). this type with several variations, particularly in size, appears at the Peak Sanctuaries of Petsofas (Fig. 5.2a), Jouktas (for example, Her. Mus. 21269, 21971), Tylisos (Her. Mus. 16945), Prinias (Museum of Hagios Nikolaas, Crete (Hag. Nik.) 6013), and at Mallia Petras, Phaistos and Kommos (Détournay *et al.* 1980, p. 103).
(b) In the second type of hat the brim is turned up all round so as to form a deep bowl. This type is found at the Peak Sanctuaries of Petsofas (Fig. 5.2b), Jouktas (Her. Mus. 21925, 21918, etc.), Tylisos (Her. Mus. 16920, 16946), Prinias (Hag. Nik. no No.), Maza and Karphi (Platon 1951, p. 107, 143). These two types of hats are dispersed through east and central Crete and, furthermore, may coexist in the same sanctuary. It is therefore evident that a common style exists in the four palatial centres, as well as in the regional centres. This homogeneity in the form and the distribution of hats

may be interpreted more as a message of a common cultural identity than as a message of social affiliation. The predominance of specific items of dress from 2000 BC onwards is related to processes leading to the formation of a common cultural behaviour, which was an indispensable factor for the establishment of a concrete social system, namely the hierarchical palatial system. However, a social differentiation of women expressed through items of dress may be expected, since these female votaries participate in an hierarchical system. Some hats of the first type in relation to other elements, as the decorated dress or the girdle, may indicate a female of high status (Fig. 5.2a). Besides, the fact that figurines having this specific type of hat are found in the palatial region (e.g. Mallia and Phaistos) points in the same direction.

In contrast with the female figurines, the male ones do not usually wear hats. A great number of them are represented hairless (Verlinden 1984, p. 67, ref. 31), whereas some figurines of this category carry other items, like daggers or jewellery, probably showing a high status (e.g. Petsofas, Sapouna-Sakellaraki 1971, nos 11, 12). On other figurines the hair is indicated with a long lock along the median line. This single lock is depicted in the figurines of Jouktas (e.g. Her. Mus. 21919, 21255) and Petsofas (e.g. Myres 1902–3, pl. X, 2). Sometimes this lock is combined with bun-like discs (e.g. Jouktas, Fig. 5.1b). Other figurines have only one, two or three bun-like discs set along the median line or in different order. These discs probably indicate tufts of hair or single locks in schematic rendering. A similar indication of hair is very common in the Minoan representations (for example, Evans 1964, II^2 fig. 496, III fig. 211, 308b, IV^2 figs 391, 536, Sapouna-Sakellaraki 1971, no. 56, pl. 17b). Some figurines of this group carry also specific items like daggers (Fig. 5.1a).

Men's hairstyle does not seem to have the same meaning as women's hats. The suggestion that the different male hairdressing may indicate differentiated status needs to be supported with more evidence. It has been assumed that the figurines with single locks represent young people of high status (Sapouna-Sakellaraki 1981, pp. 503, 505, Marinatos 1984, pp. 37, 109). However, it is difficult to accept this view, since this kind of hairstyle appears on a great number of votive figurines, some of which may not necessarily be related to young males. Nevertheless, this is a matter that needs further investigation.

If our hypothesis is correct, then it is evident that only the women carry items which give messages about cultural identity. Could this distinction be related to a matrilineal system, or is it the result of incorporating women within a system in which social differentiation was based mainly on male status (Nixon 1983, pp. 237–8)? This problem could be elucidated only through further analysis of the whole structure of the Minoan society.

Acknowledgements

I wish to express my special thanks to Professor G. Chourmouziadis, Dr I. Hodder and Dr S. Andreou for their advice.

References

Branigan, K. 1970. *The tombs of Mesara*. London: Duckworth.
Buchholz, H. G. & V. Karageorghis 1971. *Prehistoric Greece and Cyprus*. London: Phaidon Press.
Cherry, J. F. 1984. The emergence of the state in the prehistoric Aegean. *Proceedings of the Cambridge Philological Society* **210**, (N.S. no. 30), 18–48.
Détournay, B., J.-C. Poursat & F. Vandenabeele 1980. *Fouilles executées à Mallia. Le quartier Mu II* (Etudes Grétoises XXVI). Paris: Librairie Orientaliste Paul Geuthner.
Evans, A. 1964. *The palace of Minos at Knossos*, Vols I–IV (reprinted). New York: Biblo & Tannen.
Hodder, I. 1982a. *The present past*. London: B. T. Batsford.
Hodder, I. 1982b. *Symbols in action*. Cambridge: Cambridge University Press.
Hood, S. 1978. *The Arts in prehistoric Greece*. Harmondsworth: Penguin.
Marinatos, N. 1984. *Art and religion in Thera*. Athens: Mathioulakis.
Myres, J. L. 1902–3. The sanctuary-site of Petsofa. *Annual of the British School at Athens* **IX**, 356–88.
Nixon, L. 1983. Changing views of Minoan society. In *Minoan Society, Proceedings of the Cambridge Colloquium 1981*, O. Krzyszkowska & L. Nixon (eds), 237–42. Bristol: Bristol Classical Press.
Peatfield, A. A. D. 1983. The topography of Minoan peak sanctuaries, *Annual of British School at Athens* **78**, 273–8.
Platon, N. 1951. To Hieron Maza kai ta Minoika Hiera Korifis. *Kretika Chronika* **E**, 96–160.
Renfrew, C. 1972. *The emergence of civilisation*. London: Methuen.
Renfrew C. 1985. *The archaeology of cult. The sanctuary of Phylakopi*. The British School of Archaeology at Athens. Supplementary volume No. 18. London: Thames & Hudson.
Rutkowski, B. 1986. *The cult places of the Aegean* (2nd edn). New Haven: Yale University Press.
Sapouna-Sakellaraki, E. 1971. *Minoikon Zoma*. Athens: Bibliothiki tis en Athines Archaeologikis Eterias, Nr 71.
Sapouna-Sakellaraki, E. 1981. Hoi toichographies tis Theras se schesi me ti Minoiki Kriti. *Pepragmena Δ ' Kretologikou Synedriou 1976*, Vol. I, 2, 479–509.
Verlinden, C. 1984. *Les statuettes anthropomorhes crétoises en bronze et en plomb du IIIe Millénaire au VIIe siêcle av. J.-C.* Archaeologia Transatlantica IV. Louvain-la Neuve, Belgium: Art and Archaeology Publications, Collège Erasme.
Whitelaw, T. W. 1983. The settlement at Fournou Korifi Myrtos and aspects of Early Minoan social organization. In *Minoan society, Proceedings of the Cambridge Colloquium 1981*, O. Krzyszkowska & L. Nixon (eds), 322–45. Bristol: Bristol Classical Press.
Wobst, H. M. 1977. Stylistic behavior and information exchange, Papers for the Director: research essays in honor of James B. Griffin, C. Cleland (ed.). *Anthropological Papers of the University of Michigan* **61**, 317–42.

11 *The Priestess Figure of Malta*

CRISTINA BIAGGI

This chapter challenges the current reconstruction of the Maltese 'Priest Figure', contending that it is in fact a Priestess Figure. I have taken into account the basic fragments of the 'Priest' and shown how they can be reconstructed into a 'Priestess Figure', and I examine the resulting implications to Maltese religious thought and ritual, and to the Maltese Late Temple scenario.

The so-called 'Priest Figure' of Malta (see Fig. 11.3) was found by Themistocles Zammit in 1917 on the floor of apse 15, near a double-shelved niche of the Tarxien Centre temple. This niche is in front of the double-spiral screen which cuts off the secluded Holy of Holies parts from the rest of the temple. According to Evans (1959), this figure (Fig. 11.1) was probably 60 cm high, the head being 11.5 cm and the skirt 22 cm. The figure is made of clay, evidently moulded on a core of straw, which burned away, leaving the interior hollow. It is the best-preserved of three such clay figures, all found in the Tarxien Centre (Fig. 11.2). Zammit says the following about the 'Priest Figure':

> At Tarxien a part of the sanctuary is shut off from the remainder and is reached by a flight of stone steps which ascend to a platform leading to the inner rooms. There are indications that the section thus separated from the main building was put to a use different from that of the remainder. It was, perhaps, a specially holy place to which only a priest or official was in the habit of penetrating. Here were found remains of figures of a character different from that of the objects revealed in other sanctuaries. These figures are roughly wrought of unbaked clay, but are nevertheless realistically rendered. They are clothed in robes reaching from neck to feet with pleated skirts. The heads have survived complete, but are detached from the statues. There is nothing to indicate the sex of the statues themselves, but one, at least, of the heads is surely a portrait and represents a male.
>
> (Zammit 1924, p. 76)

Evans, who worked on the Maltese material in the mid-1950s, had this to say about the 'Priest Figures':

> To call these, as I have, priests . . . may perhaps be regarded as unwarrantable, since having no written records, we cannot prove that this

Figure 11.1 'Priest Figure' from Tarxien Centre. Clay, 60 cm high. (Evans 1959, pl. 60.)

(a)

(b)

Figure 11.2 Clay fragments of two other 'Priest Figures' found at Tarxien. (a) Head 9.3 cm (b) skirt, left 16.5 cm, right 10 cm. (Evans 1971, pls 40 & 50.)

Figure 11.3 Unrestored 'Priest Figure' found at Tarxien. Clay, 60 cm. (Zammit 1924, pl. XIII.)

Figure 11.4 Globigerina limestone heads found in the Hypogeum. Left, 10.9 cm high; right, 9.1 cm high. (Evans 1959, pls 55 & 56.)

> is what they were. Yet this is the impression these figures have made on all students, and it seems inherently quite likely. The figures interpreted as priests are only three, and these are incomplete. . . . Their sex is inferential, since the chest region is missing in all cases, and the lower part of the body is covered with a bell-shaped skirt, somewhat like that of the cult figures [the Stone Goddess images], but reaching to the feet. The dress above, therefore, might lead one to imagine that they were a further variety of cult figures, were it not for the heads, which are preserved in two instances. The better preserved of these, when contrasted, for example, with the two stone heads from the Hypogeum [see Fig. 11.4], impress one as being that of a male, and very possibly a portrait. It may be mentioned also, in passing, that they were found in the inner part of the middle temple at Tarxien, the part supposedly cut off from the general public, which may be an argument in favour of their being priests.
> (Evans 1959, p. 145)

The reconstruction of the 'Priest Figure' was executed in 1975, two years before the completion of the archaeological museum, by Busutil, the restorer of the museum, and under the auspices of Evans. Evans, who believed that the fragmented figure represented a male, was doubtless influenced by Zammit.

Based on the assumptions of these two archaeologists and the subsequent reconstruction of the 'Priest Figure', a whole belief system concerning Maltese

Figure 11.5 Sumerian Priest Figure, 2700 BC, gypsum, 72 cm. (Amiet 1980, p. 360, fig. 258.)

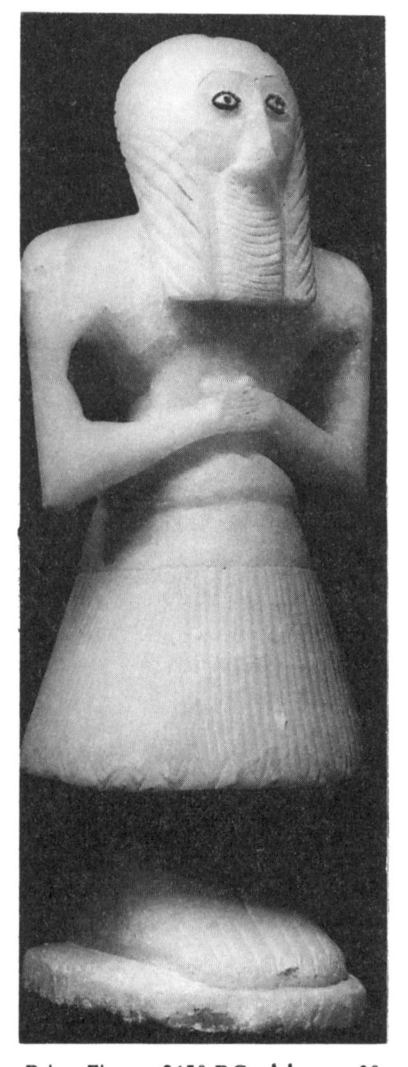

Figure 11.6 Sumerian **Priest Figure, 2650 BC, alabaster, 30 cm.** (**Am**iet 1980, p. 364, fig. 263.)

religion and ritual practices has developed and is to be found both in the scholarly and popular literature. Some examples follow.

When Trump discusses, in his book on Malta, the causes of the sudden demise of the Maltese temple civilization, he mentions that 'The increasing evidence for priesthood . . . could be quoted as a possible cause of internal revolt' (Trump 1972, p. 21). However, in another part of the book he does state that, even though ' . . . the clay figure . . . is often described as "the priest," . . .

Figure 11.7 Sumerian Priest Figure, 2400 BC, calcareous brescia, 53.8 cm. (Amiet 1980, p. 364, fig. 290.)

there is no clear basis for this identification' (Trump 1972, pp. 47, 97). In the popular literature we find the following: 'It is probable that the controlling group was an elite class of priests . . . ' and 'The priestly class may have become too conservative. . . ' (Blouet 1984, pp. 26–8). 'This person [the traveller] will then hear the mystical oracular utterings of the priest echoing through the once covered temples. . . ' (von Makensen 1981, p. 2). The temples were ' . . . apparently run and directed by priests' (Lewis 1977, pp. 25–31).

Why did Zammit and Evans call these fragmentary pieces which are devoid of sex, priest figures instead of priestess figures? Why did they attribute masculinity to images which have no indication of sex whatsoever?

From their stances and their clothing, the three fragmentary Maltese figures must have reminded their discoverers of the Sumerian priest figures, also known as orants, who appeared in the middle of the 4th millennium BC. As can be seen from the illustrations (see Figs 11.5–11.7), the flounced skirts and clasped hands of the Maltese are reminiscent of the Sumerian figures. Both are in frontal poses. However, while the legs and feet of the Maltese figures are hidden by full-length skirts, the Sumerians' skirts are three-quarter length, revealing legs and feet slightly apart, planted squarely under the skirt.

There are glaring differences between the Maltese and Sumerian figures. The Maltese figures are not as refined, which may be due to the material and technique used. The Maltese had probably not refined the technique of making large clay figures on a core of straw, and the figures may not have been considered as important – maybe they were meant to represent assistants in the ritual practices. The most important difference between the two is the fact that the Sumerian priest figures are most often bearded or bald. The skirt is waist high, leaving the chest nude. There is not enough of the Maltese 'Priest Figure' to surmise whether the chest was covered or left bare. The Sumerian priestesses (see Figs 11.8–11.10) are depicted in exactly the same frontal poses as the males, with hands clasped in front. However, their dress, which covers their breasts, is slung over one shoulder, leaving the other bare as in a Roman toga. The hair is often piled or bunched up on top of the head, in contrast with the males, who are either bald or who display locks that float on their shoulders. Priestesses' breasts are not delineated under their togas. In fact, there is no indication of their femaleness other than their differences in dress and their lack of a beard.

There is a similarity in the skirt pattern between the Sumerian and Maltese figures, even though the Maltese seem simpler. In both there is an indication of patterned folds in the material. The Sumerian Figures 11.7, 11.9 and 11.10 show a more complicated pattern, perhaps indicating animal fur or bird feathers, which would be appropriate for a special skirt used for ritual events.

To add some further insights into the sex and meaning of the fragmented Maltese 'Priest Figure'. let us compare it with the small intact Priestess Figure found in the Hypogeum. Two Priestess figures were found in the Oracle Room of the Hypogeum. Each is shown sleeping on a couch, with a pillow beneath her head, and is naked to the waist. The best-preserved one, known as 'The Sleeping Lady of Malta', is made of brown clay with a polished surface that shows traces of red ochre (Fig. 11.11). Her skirt is decorated with incised lines ending in a sort of fringe. She is turned on her side, in a naturalistic sleeping position, her voluminous right forearm under her head, her left one draped over her heavy breasts and touching her right arm. Though she is treated naturalistically, the Priestess shows a disproportion between the small head and upper part of the body, and the enormous swelling hips and thighs, ending in relatively small calves and feet. Her disproportion is similar to that of the

Figure 11.8 Sumerian Priestess Figure, 2700 BC, gypsum, 59 cm. (Amiet 1980, p. 360, fig. 257.)

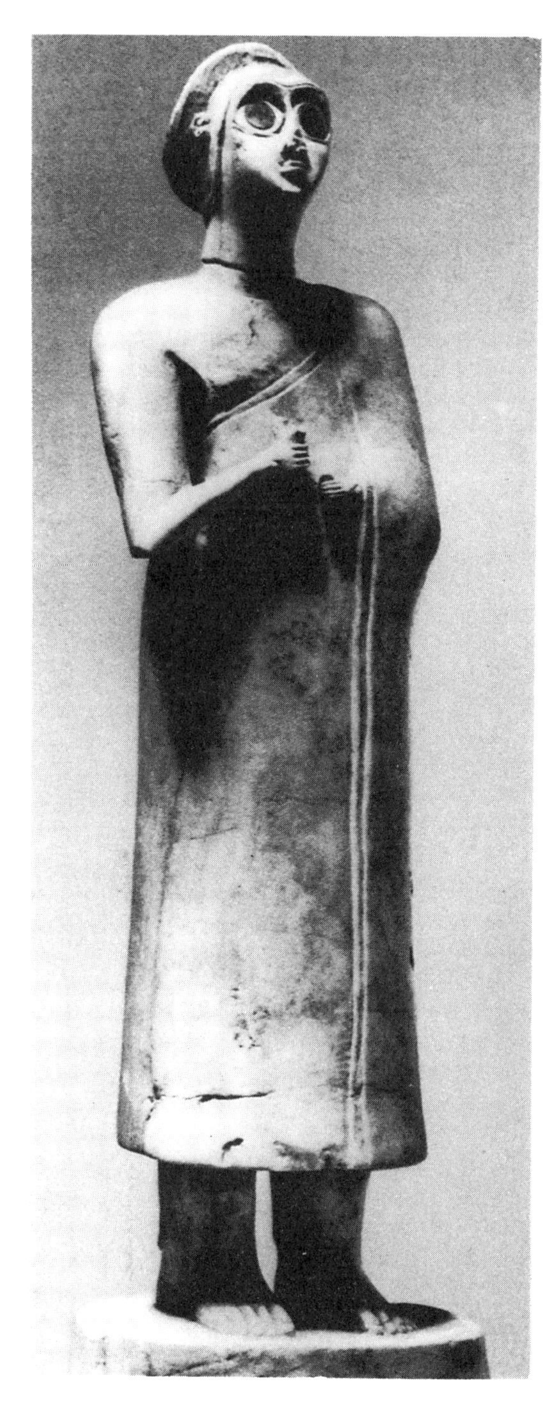

Figure 11.9 Sumerian Priestess Figure, 2500 BC, limestone, 14.9 cm. (Amiet 1980, p. 361, fig. 263.)

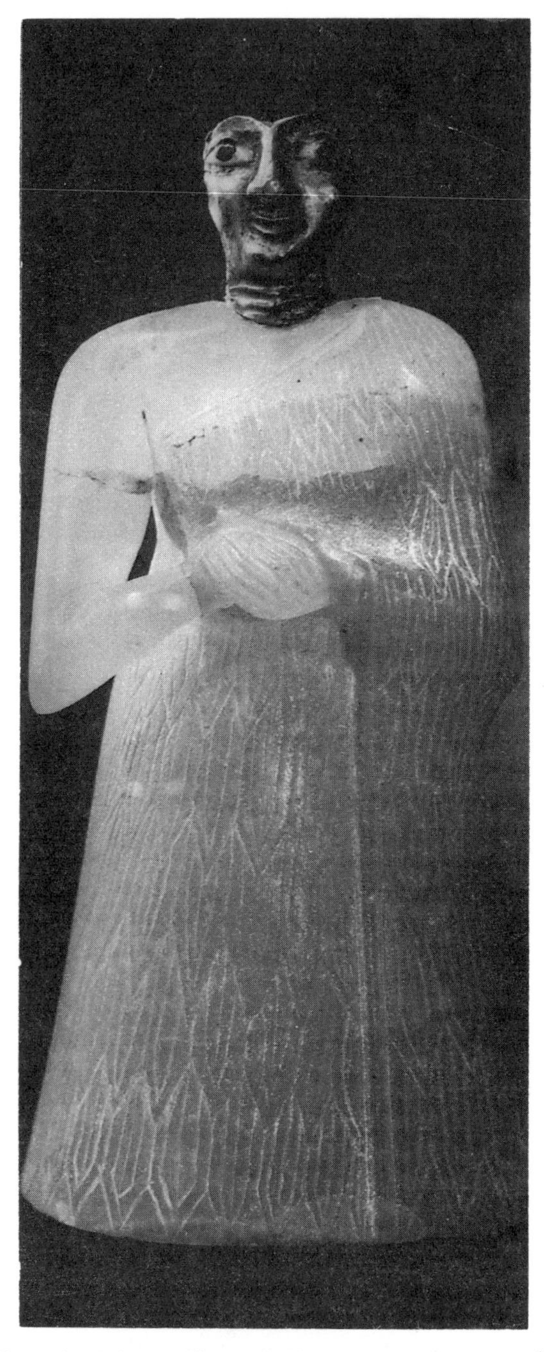

Figure 11.10 Sumerian Priestess Figure, 2550 BC, green argonite and gold, 15.2 cm. (Amiet 1980, p. 361, fig. 264.)

Maltese Goddess images made of stone. She is six times smaller than the 'Priest Figure'. The skirts of the 'Priest' and Priestess figures are slightly different, possibly suggesting a different function. The 'Priest's' skirt is pleated, whereas the Priestess does not seem to be wearing a real skirt. Rather, she seems to be covered by a short cover with a pleated border. Since she is nude on top, it seems that she is sleeping nude except for a coverlet (see Fig. 11.12). This coverlet has a similar border to that found on the skirt of the large seated Goddess from Tarxien, which is made of limestone and was supposedly about 2 m high (Fig. 11.13).

There are basically two varieties of Maltese stone figures; nude and clothed. These probably represented two aspects of the Goddess, perhaps invoked at different times and for different reasons. Although both of these types lack primary sexual characteristics (perhaps because female characteristics were signified by other factors such as opulence: Biaggi 1985, p. 16), the sleeping Priestess and the Venus of Malta (Fig. 11.14) both display definite breasts. Since the 'Priest Figure' seems to be the same sort of figure as the Sleeping Priestess – they are both clay and are similarly clothed – it is possible that the figure also had well-defined breasts.

What do the similarities and differences among the various types of figures discussed indicate about their function and meaning? How does viewing the 'Priest Figure' of Malta as a 'Priestess Figure' (see Fig. 11.15) change one's perception of Maltese religious thought? What does this suggest about the religion of the Great Goddess in Malta?

Figure 11.11 Sleeping Priestess found in the Hypogeum. Clay with traces of red ochre, 7 cm high, 6.8 cm wide, 12.2 cm long (Evans 1959, pl. 57.)

Figure 11.12 Sleeping Priestess found in the Hypogeum, viewed from above. (Ugolini 1932, p. 578.)

Figure 11.13 Seated Goddess from Tarxien. Globigerina limestone, 2 m high. (Photograph by Charoula.)

The fact that the Sleeping Priestess shares her exaggerated body proportions and her type of skirt with the Seated Goddess from Tarxien suggests a close relationship to the Goddess images. Her small, compact size, the fine delineation of her shape and her red ochre colour indicate an important func-

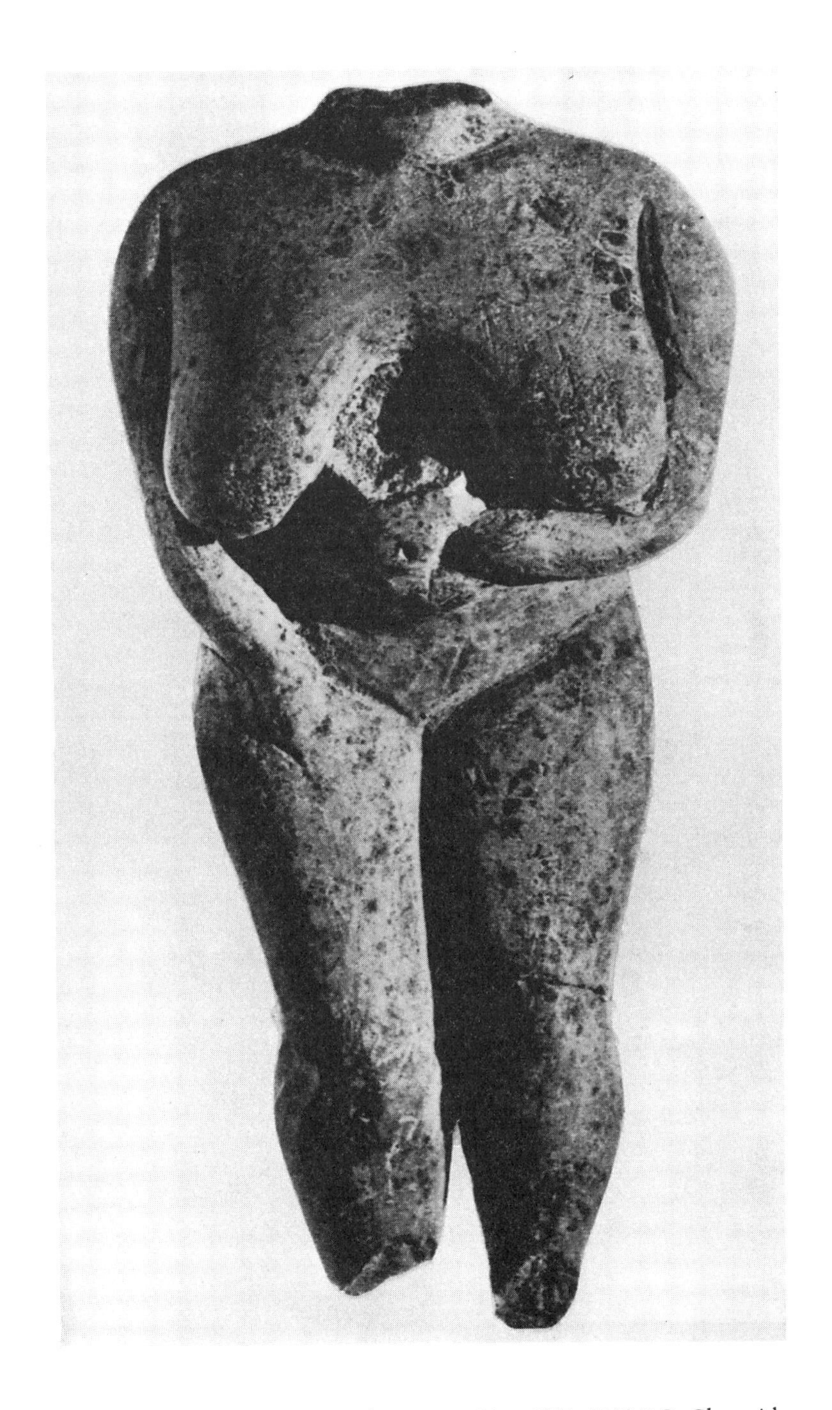

Figure 11.14 Venus of Malta, found at Hagar Qim, 3000–2500 BC. Clay with traces of red ochre, 12.9 cm high, 6.5 cm wide. (Evans 1959, pl. 65.)

Figure 11.15 Priestess Figure from Malta, reconstructed by the author. Clay, 60 cm high. (Photograph by Cristina Biaggi.)

tion as intermediary to the Goddess. Perhaps she was a sort of Delphic Pithia – depicted in a state of dream incubation – adept at interpreting dreams and giving oracles (Ugolini 1932, p. 584).

The much larger 'Priestess Figure', her frontal stance with hands clasped in front, implies a certain important function in the ritual of the Great Goddess, perhaps as orant or spiritual stand-in for the worshippers, as is the case of the Sumerian figures. That they were found in special areas of the temples near the double-spiral screen which separated the public from the Holy of Holies suggests the importance of the strong and specialized role that the priestesses must have acquired towards the end of the Tarxien period. If viewed as a Priestess, the 'Priest Figure' emphasizes the priestly specialization, the hierarchical structure that Maltese religion perhaps developed towards the end of the Temple Building period.

However, perhaps the *de facto* or symbolic role of the male was also ascending in Maltese religion towards the end of the Temple Building Period. The Phallic Niches that appeared at this time may suggest the appreciation and acknowledgement of the role of the male for his contribution towards the continuation of life and the cycles of nature (see Fig. 11.16). Yet the representation of the disembodied phallus in the pit marked niches suggests that this talented member still belonged to the magic retinue of the Maltese Goddess, who was considered both male and female (Gimbutas 1981, p. 9).

One feature that appeared in the Hypogeum and seems to be important in determining the influence of the male role in later Maltese religion needs to be mentioned – the Oracle Hole. Tour guides to the Hypogeum always stress the fact that only a deep male voice is effective in the Oracle Hole. This seems to imply that the male must have assumed a certain exclusive importance in Maltese religious ceremonies, perhaps as the intermediary voice of the Goddess.

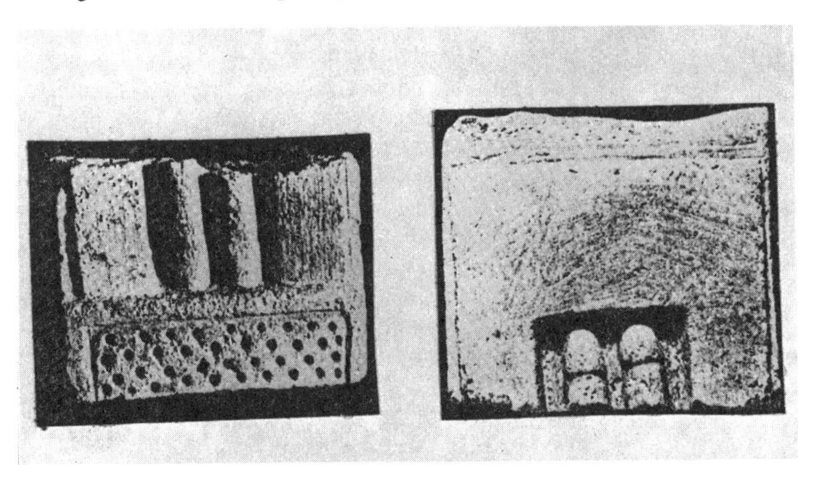

Figure 11.16 Phallic Niches found at Tarxien. Both show traces of red ochre and are made of globigerina limestone. Right, 14 cm high; left, 11 cm high. (Evans 1971, pl. 50.)

Does this mean that the Goddess suddenly made use of a male voice to transmit her utterings? We can assume that in a female-identified society such as Malta the male became included in this way – that the Goddess could choose to speak also in a male voice as well as in the female voice of her priestesses, just as she also contained male elements such as the phallus in her gynandrous repertoire of attributes.

The significance of the Oracle Hole needs further exploration. It is raised here because it seems to be a pivotal point in the discussion of Maltese religion, and is directly concerned with the presence and influence of priests and priestesses in the religion of Malta. That it has only been used effectively by a deep male voice may have a number of explanations, including the fact that no trained female voices have sufficiently tested the acoustic properties of the Oracle Hole. It would be interesting to test the voice of a Bormliza, a specialized Maltese female singer of ancient tradition with a wide range and a very loud voice (McLeod & Herndon 1975, pp. 87–8). Until such a test is carried out, any conclusions made concerning the acoustic properties of the Oracle Hole remain in the realm of conjecture.

How does viewing the 'Priest Figure' as a Priestess change the Maltese scenario? The Maltese had a female-centred culture and worshipped a Great Goddess. Priestesses perhaps guided temporal as well as religious matters. In time, and with the increase in population and perhaps a move towards greater specialization, the influence of the priestesses increased; they became more specialized and perhaps less available to the general public. This may account for the depiction of larger yet less-refined priestess figures found in the secluded parts of the Tarxien Centre. If one interprets the evidence from the Oracle Hole in a certain way, then men became more active in religious practices. If, on the other hand, a school of trained female oracle singers or Bormlizas made their appearance, then one can surmise that a high degree of specialization grew among the priestesses.

I think that, despite evidence that the male became included in Maltese religious practices, his presence and influence were harmonious and not at odds within the egalitarian Goddess-worshipping cultures of the Late Tarxien Temple Period. The change from a female to a male identification appeared later in Malta, and started with the bronze-wielding Tarxien Cemetery groups who appeared about 2000 BC. I maintain that the 'Priest Figure' was, in fact, a Priestess Figure, an acolyte or even a Bormliza to the Maltese Great Goddess.

References

Amiet, P. 1980. *Art of the ancient Near East*. New York: Harry N. Abrahams.

Biaggi, C. 1985. The significance of the nudity, obesity and sexuality of the Maltese goddess figures. Paper given at Archaeology and Fertility Cult in the Ancient Mediterranean Conference at the University of Malta.

Blouet, B. 1984. *The story of Malta*. Malta: Progress Press.

Evans, J. D. 1959. *Malta*. London: Thames & Hudson.

Evans, J. D. 1971. *The prehistoric antiquities of the Maltese islands*. London: Athlone Press.
Gimbutas, M. 1981. 'The monstrous Venus' of prehistory or goddess creatrix. *The Comparative Civilization Review* **10** (3), 1–26.
Lewis, H. 1977. *Ancient Malta*. Gerrards Cross: Colin Smythe.
McLeod, N. & M. Herndon 1975. The Bormliza, Maltese folksong style and women. *Journal of American Folklore* **88** (347), 81–100.
Trump, D. H. 1972. *Malta: an archaeological guide*. London: Faber & Faber.
Ugolini, L. M. 1932. La dormiente di Malta. *Daedalo* **12** (7), 575–85.
von Makensen, H. 1981. *Golden Malta*. Malta: Printex.
Zammit, T. 1924. Neolithic representations of the human form from the islands of Malta and Gozo. *Journal of the Royal Anthropological Institute of Great Britain and Ireland* **54**, 67–100.

8 *Ethno-archaeological cognition and cognitive ethno-archaeology*

ZBIGNIEW KOBYLINSKI

Application of the Hempelian deductive–nomological model of explanation to archaeology (as was proposed by the American *New Archaeology*) requires knowledge of a number of well-confirmed laws or law-like statements describing sociocultural systems and their material, archaeologically visible remains. Before it reaches an archaeologist, information on the past sociocultural reality has gone through a succession of stages, during which it has been subject to various transformations and reductions. These are: (a) the sociocultural; (b) the depositional; (c) the post-depositional; and (d) the archaeological. It is only the last of these stages that is subject to the will of an archaeologist, who can select optimal methods of excavating and recording. The description of these transformations should be expressed in terms of relatively universal rules, related neither to time nor space, but only to the sociocultural (socio-economic in particular) and environmental conditions. Consequently, the further development of archaeology requires the construction of an archaeological theory. This theory should consist of a system of interrelated statements describing the trajectories of processes at work from the past sociocultural reality to the present archaeological evidence. These trajectories would probably vary according to the actions of some prerequisite independent factors. A hierarchy of such factors conditioning a given phenomenon can be called its 'essential structure' (Nowak 1977).

It is evident that the formulation of laws, which according to Popper should be carried out by posing *a priori* hypotheses and verifying or refuting them empirically, can be performed only when it is continuously possible to measure (on a certain, at least nominal, scale) the values assumed by variables in the course of a process. To formulate the theory of a phenomenon, it is also necessary to be able to manipulate the variables influencing the course of a process. This experimental procedure consists of assigning different values to variables, and in eliminating the effect of the remaining independent variables, considered to be of secondary importance (the so-called *ceteris paribus* clause).

Archaeology, when it sets out to build the framework of its theory by following the line of the highly developed empirical sciences, cannot limit itself to observing only the final stage of the transformational chain and reconstructing on this basis the conjectural reasons. In other words, archaeology cannot limit itself to the traditional *ex post facto* procedure only – it has to look for 'research laboratories' where these transformations can be studied in action experimentally. However, the past is by definition unobservable, because time is anisotropic. Due to ethno-archaeology the modern society (both 'primitive' and 'civilized') appears to be the only possibility for such a laboratory.

Although ethno-archaeology cannot ensure the possibility of really experimental observation, it enables one to replace the manipulation of independent variables by the accurate control and measuring of these variables. Repetition of such observations in different sociocultural and environmental contexts establishes a quasi-experimental research procedure, which is much more reliable than the *ex post facto* approach. Such a quasi-experimental testing of hypotheses describing the essential relationships between sociocultural, environmental and 'archaeological' factors seems to be the most promising possibility for ethno-archaeology.

The theoretical assumption underlying the applicability of knowledge gained in the course of observations carried out in modern communities to the archaeological past is the conviction that processes (both the natural and the sociocultural) of the same type follow the same rules, irrespective of time and space. There is no doubt that natural processes (e.g. sedimentation, erosion or decay of organic waste) occurring under the same conditions are always uniform. It is much more difficult to justify the same course for cultural processes. For this purpose the following arguments are applied. The common neurophysiological basis of individual perception and behaviour, the existence of universal structures of thinking conditioning human behaviour, or the principle of rationality in human activities, guarantee the same behaviour under the same conditions. All of these arguments can be reasonably criticized. It is also impossible to accept the extreme approach of 'unilinear evolutionism' (contained implicitly in works by White, Parsons, Bellah or Levy), claiming that the contemporary 'archaic' or 'primitive' societies are characterized by properties which once used to be typical of the prehistoric ancestors of contemporary European societies.

Hence, in my opinion, ethno-archaeology is not just a new form of reasoning by analogy, because such a reasoning requires previous proof of a structural identity between compared phenomena or processes. In the case of ethno-archaeology the making of such an assumption is not based on the results of any empirical investigation, but on 'metaphysical belief' (Watson 1979). Thus, the drawing of analogies for the explanation of prehistoric phenomena from the modern pre-class and non-urbanized communities, would have no justifying grounds. Rather, ethno-archaeology is the quest for universals in sociocultural systems related to each other in, for example, the conditions of the natural environment or in the level of development of productive forces. It is an experimental field where the existence of such universals can be tested. Thus, my answer to Gould's question: 'is uniformitarianism necessary' (Gould & Watson 1982) is 'yes', but I believe that this affirmative answer does not mean that the principle of uniformitarianism should be recognized as a law of science with universal validity. Rather, by way of ethno-archaeological observations one should seek the range within which the phenomenon in question is subject to the same rules. Moreover, ethno-archaeology provides a unique opportunity for determining the factors which essentially condition the specific form of the phenomenon, constant over some range, and for building the framework of the theory of this phenomenon.

The question can be asked whether, in such a model of the cognitive situation of ethno-archaeology, inductive or hypothetico-deductive strategies are appropriate for the construction of theory. Since Popper's time at least, it has been known that the image of an empirical fact introduced by a researcher into the scientific circulation is burdened by theoretical assumptions expressed explicitly or, more often, implicitly. Thus, methodologically, the research procedure described for example by Hempel (1968) is doubtless more valid: the identification of an empirical fact requiring explanation, the posing of an explanatory tentative hypothesis, the deduction of empirical implications from this hypothesis, the collection of facts to confirm or refute the hypothesis, possibly the posing of a new hypothesis, etc. The difference between this explanatory scheme and the model introduced into the social sciences by Marx (and interpreted by Nowak, 1977) lies in the fact that the latter recognizes that the main factor (the essential cause) of the phenomenon under study cannot be grasped empirically, since the effect of this factor is disturbed by a number of side factors influencing the 'surface' of this phenomenon. Hence, it is necessary to formulate ideal hypotheses with a number of contradictory ideal assumptions stating the lack of influence of the side factors, and their gradual suppression, until the level accessible to direct observation has been reached.

Ethno-archaeological data can serve both as an empirical basis for the formulation of an ideal hypothesis and as empirical material against which a hypothesis, proposed on the basis of other reasons, is tested. Thus, ethno-archaeological data can function both in the 'context of discovery' and in the 'context of justification', to use the distinction once made by Reichenbach (1938).

Moreover, ethno-archaeological observations should clarify the controversy between cultural determinism and indeterminism. A number of students, in their critical evaluation of the excessively optimistic first generation of 'new archaeologists', state that the nomothetization of archaeology, and also of all the social sciences, is hampered by the unlimited possibility of choice in the realm of social life, arts, beliefs, etc., and that no evidence has been found to indicate that any specific choice is governed by rules which can be conceived of in the form of laws. Hence, a number of philosophers, from Dilthey to Ricoeur, have proposed various psychological methods of interpretation of cultural phenomena. In turn historical materialism is a theory consisting of statistical laws (in the broader sense of the notion, i.e. those which do not contain any accurate definition of probability), and of selective–adaptative laws which, while leaving a considerable role to accident, determine which 'random' choices can become common and established in social systems with given essential structures (Klawiter 1978). Social micro-indeterminism does not imply the indeterminism of macroprocesses, although here also the determinism is perceived as probabilistic rather than as exceptionless (Amsterdamski 1983).

In addition one can assume, by following the Polish philosopher Kmita (1985), the distinction between two spheres of culture: technico-utilitarian and symbolic. Both spheres include three layers of different ontological status: the ideal, the behavioural and the material (Chmielecki n.d.). The distinction between the two spheres of culture is based on the identification of the existence of two kinds of human activities: simple technico-utilitarian activities and those which are meant to be interpreted. The latter require the inter-subjectively established rules of cultural interpretation which, when fixed in social memory, form the sphere of symbolic culture. The material products of such activities acquire, as a consequence of the existence of these rules, a semiotic value.

A student from outside a given sociocultural system, who wants to know and understand the sphere of its symbolic culture, can: (a) ask members of the sociocultural system to verbalize the meaning of activities and to explain the semiotic value of the products of those activities: (b) directly observe series of activities meant to be interpreted and reactions to them, and on the basis of these observations identify their meaning, and thus also the semiotic value of material products; (c) analyse the products of activities meant to be interpreted and attempt to identify their semiotic value and, also, indirectly, the meaning of the activities as a result of which these products have emerged. The latter possibility is the only one that an archaeologist has at his disposal. Ethno-archaeology enables him to use both of the former approaches.

It is necessary to ask whether it is possible to understand the symbolic culture of a specific system in an 'archaeological' way. The question is complex and has to be broken into a few parts. Above all it is necessary to ask whether the product accessible to archaeological analysis is the same product which functioned in a living sociocultural system, and if it is not, whether the features of the product which carry its semiotic information are still recognizable. A bronze figure of a god found during archaeological excavation is the same figure that once functioned in cultural circulation and it has not been deprived of its identity in the course of site formation processes, although it could have become isolated from its meaningful cultural context. However, stones scattered irregularly in a cultural layer are no longer the stone ring marking the boundary of a sacred zone; a batch of sherds is not identical to a ritual vessel in which, once a year, a ritual dish was cooked; and rectangular arrangements of post-holes are not the same as a ritual meeting house. Thus, in a large number of cases it is extremely difficult, or even impossible, to identify a product as having a semiotic value. Many objects of primary technico-utilitarian function could also have important meaning in social communication, difficult or even impossible to define. Such an identification is possible when, for example, an object normally functioning in technico-utilitarian contexts, such as a boat, is found in situations which are evidently non-utilitarian, such as in a grave furnishing. That is why statistical analyses of the coexistence of features and artefacts in common contexts are so important.

Subsequently, it is necessary to ask whether in a studied culture there were transformational rules attributing a constant semiotic value to specific products (or quantitative–qualitative–spatial arrangements of these products) so that knowledge of these rules would always permit a correct understanding of the cultural meaning of a given product. Contrary to the arbitrary systems of conventional signs, in which the relationship between a sign and its meaning is univalent, the rules of cultural interpretation according to which the material products of non-industrial societies acquire a semiotic value, are often polyvalent in nature. In culture the same meaning can be expressed in various ways; at the same time the same behaviour or product can have different meanings, depending on the whole situational context. The reason for this is that the rules of syntax in cultural communication are mostly 'dramatic' – the meaning of one object can be modified by another. Studies of the historical development of the meaning of a given product, however important for understanding the dynamics of culture, provide no assistance in identifying the specific meaning, since variability during this development can lead to a total change in the original meaning: 'The whole development process of the use of a star symbol can suggest its increasingly strict connection with religious and magical ideas until suddenly, when placed on a red banner, it flutters with a perversely different meaning' (Stomma 1981).

Moreover, some activities, gestures or symbolic products can carry whole knots of semantic associations that are recalled simultaneously through representational or symbolic thinking (cf. the meaning of boat in symbolic culture in Medieval Scandinavia: Kobyliński n.d.). This results from the specificity of symbolic thought, which probably dominated in societies studied archaeologically, but is present to some extent also in the mind of modern 'civilized' man. The symbolic way of thinking has often been described by adjectives such as 'analogic', 'preverbal', 'sensory' or 'emotive' (cf. Beck 1978). This type of thinking is based on uniform sensory experience, preceding the differentiation into types of sensory qualities (touch, hearing, sight, etc.). The existence of this type of original experience is confirmed, for example, by the phenomenon of synesthaesia, and by the results of the surdopedagogic practice. The historical difference between symbolic and 'categorical' or 'abstract' thinking should not be seen as a simple sequence of developmental stages, because both are probably generic in man. Rather, the difference should be situated in the different hemispheres of the brain (cf. Piaget *et al.* 1967, Maruszewski 1970, Paredes & Hepburn 1976). One should speak rather of a continuous and fluid transition from the preponderance of the analogical to the preponderance of the abstract mode of thinking, as a result of the evolution of the functional asymmetry between brain hemispheres and of social training through positive–negative reinforcement (cf. Kobyliński & Połubińska 1980).

Symbolic thinking results not in signs, invoking a conventional connection between them and the signified reality, but in symbols. A symbol is a representational, multivocal sign which is semantically opaque, i.e. in the words of R. Jakobson, it has a poetic function or, as Soviet semioticians would have it, it is self-reflective and has a high modelling capacity (Zalizniak *et al.* 1977). A symbol directly denotes sensory perceptions and evokes emotional–motivational states, and therefore is perceived as identical with its referent. The central symbols of a semiotic system, which denote directly the most important values of a given culture, are the material records of the 'memory' of the sociocultural system. A paradox of symbolic thinking is that at the same time symbols do not cease to be material objects, sometimes of technico-utilitarian function, and can be used as houses, boats, swords, etc.

The mental processes involved in creating and using symbols are predominantly visual. This kind of social communication is non-verbal, and in fact verbalization often cannot help in understanding the meaning of symbol. A symbol which is verbalized ceases to be a symbol (Czerwiński 1973, p. 129). To articulate symbolic meaning in language means to translate it into the logic of verbal categories. In this process much of the original meaning is lost. 'No contemporary Christian can explain all the meanings (affective, behavioural, cognitive, cultural, historical etc.) adhering to the image of the cross' (Marshack 1979, p. 304). This means that even asking the participants of symbolic communication can be of no assistance in studying the meaning of material symbols. The private meaning can be often only a part of the public, cultural meanings.

Some interesting ideas for symbolic (ethno-)archaeology can be drawn from the works of the contemporary Soviet structural–semiotic 'school of Tartu'. Marxian structuralism does not accept the thesis of the invariability of cultural structures. Rather, what unites this structural semiotics and the 'classical' structuralism of Lévi-Strauss (irrespective of the difference of opinion on the phylogenesis of semiotic phenomena) is the conviction that there exist 'deep' structures of thought, which form the space of factors significant for cultural semiotic codes. These structures should be identified by way of statistical analysis of cultural 'texts', where one should find the nature of the coexistence or exclusiveness of some significant units (ornamentation, shape, spatial arrangement, etc.). Such an internal analysis of a 'text' permits its syntactical rules to be described, and thus the semiotic relationships to be determined. It should also allow a student to unburden himself of his own system of cultural values and of his own image of the world (cf. Kobliński & Połubińska 1982). However, the determination of the meaning of a particular sign or group of signs, is a matter of 'considerable courage' (Wasilewski 1981). It is exactly here that one should see the role of ethno-archaeology as providing knowledge of sets of values in cultures of various types. These values are always symbolized, and knowledge of the most frequent forms of material symbolization of these values, together with knowledge of external and internal sociocultural factors determining a specific form of symbolization can be obtained.

The cognitive situation becomes even more complicated when we go from the study of monosemantic cultures, i.e. those which operate with only one modelling symbol system, to the study of polysemantic cultures (the notions proposed by Lem 1965). Here the central values are not identified by way of uniform reactions to a common set of symbols, but by identification with values symbolized in ways characteristic of small social groups. The overlapping of these small groups (social microstructures) forms the consistency of the system (cf. Shils 1975). Thus, a correct understanding of such a culture requires an appropriate determination of its internal homo- or heterogeneity, and the resulting mono- or polysemanticity. The identification of archaeologically visible indicators of these two different states of cultural systems is another task of ethno-archaeology.

An ethno-archaeological theory of symbolic culture should be a system of interrelated statistical statements describing universals in the creation, use and discarding of symbols. However, if we accept the interpretation of dialectics proposed here, universals should not be understood as really universal, but rather as 'historically universal'. This means that they are phenomena of the same essential structures, which are relatively stable but historically changeable. A general theory of this kind can be exemplified by Plechanow's model of the social creation of symbols, applied in some archaeological works (cf. Kobyliński n.d.). However, general theory must be accompanied with a specific explanatory model describing all of the factors influencing the particular situation.

The role of ethno-archaeological observations in this research procedure of formulating general ideal laws and then making them more specific by applying them to given phenomena cannot be overestimated. Particularly, thanks to the ethno-archaeological observations of human reactions to symbols, it is possible to understand the pragmatic aspect of symbolic communication, or 'symbols in action' (Hodder 1982). This seems to be the most important aspect of studies on symbolic systems, because the dynamics can be revealed in this domain, as opposed to the relative stability of syntactic and semantic structures.

References

Amsterdamski, S. 1983. *Nauka a porzádek świata*. Warszawa: Państwowe Wydawnictwo Nankowe.

Beck, B. 1978. The metaphor as a mediator between semantic and analogic modes of thought. *Current Anthropology* **19**, 83–97.

Chmielecki, A. (n.d) Kultura duchowa – refleksje ontologiczne, In *Myśl przez pryzmat rzeczy*, Z. Zobyliński, B. Lichy and P. Urbańczyk (eds). Warszawa: PTAiN (in press).

Czerwiński, M. 1973. *Magia, mit i fikcja*. Warszawa: Panstwowy Instytut Wydawniczy.

Gould, R. A. and P. J. Watson 1982. A dialogue on the meaning and use of analogy in ethnoarchaeological reasoning. *Journal of Anthropological Archaeology* **1**, 355–81.

Hempel, C. G. 1968. *Podstawy nauk przyrodniczych*. Warszawa: Państwowe Wydawnictwo Nankowe.

Hodder, I. 1982. *Symbols in action*. Cambridge: Cambridge University Press.

Klawiter, A. 1978. *Problem metodologicznego statusu materializmu historycznego*. Warszawa: Państwowe Wydawnictwo Nankowe.

Kmita, J. 1985. *Kultura i poznanie*. Warszawa: Państwowe Wydawnichwo Nankowe.

Kobyliński, Z. n.d. Things as symbols: boat in the Early Medieval culture of Northern Europe. *Archaeologia Polona* (in press).

Kobyliński, Z. and K. Połubińska 1980. Świadomość: myśl–jezyk–wyobraźnia. In *Świadomość i rozwój*, J. Lipiec (ed.), 174–86. Kraków: Krajowa Agencja Wydawnicza.

Kobyliński, Z. and K. Połubińska 1982. Konflikt systemów wartości jako problem metodologiczny nauk antropologicznych. In *Człowiek i świat wartości*, J. Lipiec (ed.), 177–93. Kraków: Krajowa Agencja Wydawnicza.

Lem, S. 1965. *Filozofia przypadku*. Kraków: Wydawnictwo Literackie.

Marshack, A. 1979. Upper Palaeolithic symbol systems of the Russian Plain: cognitive and comparative analysis. *Current Anthropology* **20**, 271–311.

Maruszewski, M. 1970. *Mowa a mózg*. Warszawa: Państwowe Wydawnictwo Nankowe.

Nowak, L. 1977. *U podstaw dialektyki Marksowskiej*. Warszawa: Państwowe Wydawnictwo Nankowe.

Paredes, A. J. and M. J. Hepburn 1976. The split brain and the culture-and-cognition paradox. *Current Anthropology* **17**, 121–7.

Piaget, J., P. Gréco, B. Inhelder and P. Ol´éron 1967. *Inteligencja*. Warszawa: Państwowe Wydawnictwo Nankowe.

Reichenbach, H. 1938. *Experience and prediction*. Chicago: Chicago University Press.

Shils, E. A. 1975. *Center and periphery*. Chicago: Chicago University Press.

Stomma, L. 1981. Metoda strukturalna w etnologii. In *Metody etnologii*, 119–35. Warszawa: UW.

Wasilewski, J. S. 1981. Semiotyczne badania symboliki. In *Metody etnologii*, 137–57. Warszawa: UW.

Watson, P. J. 1979. The idea of ethnoarchaeology: notes and comments. In *Ethnoarchaeology*, C. Kramer (ed.), 277–87. New York: Columbia University Press.

Zalizniak, A., W. Iwanow and W. Toporow 1977. O możliwościach strukturalno-typologicznych badań semiotycznych. In *Semiotyka kultury*, E. Janus and M. R. Mayenowa (eds.), 67–83. Warszawa: Państwawy Instytut Wydawniczy.

21 *Heresy and its traces: the material results of culture*

K. TEAGUE

The importance of human remains and associated material for the interpretation of social and cultural systems is self-evident. However, one of the major problems in medieval archaeology is the suppression of the practice of burying grave goods, which resulted from the establishment of Christianity. This lack of evidence is offset by the gains provided by the historical record and surviving illustrative material. Provided that this material is used ethnographically as well as in historical and art historical terms, the gain in terms of information is enormous (de Bouard 1969, Audouze & Leroi-Gourhan 1981).

However, the validity of the historical record must always be in question. The record is a 'survivors' version, in this case that of the Western Church. The establishment of Christianity in Western Europe led further than the mere suppression of practices to the active seeking out and destruction of offensive material and people, even posthumously. The process was institutionalized in the medieval Inquisition.

The suppression of un-Christian practices and ideas was part of the Church's attempt to gain dominance and impose social control on Western European society. This attempt, which was formulated in the 11th century during the Gregorian Reforms and the investiture conflict, reached a peak during the reign of Pope Innocent III (1198–1216) when religious dissent – heresy – was declared treason.

Among the numerous heresies of the 11th–14th centuries, that which attracted most attention was the dualist heresy of the Cathars, also known as the Albigensian heresy, after its localization in southwestern France, near the town of Albi. The Cathar heresy involved a belief in two gods or principles, good and evil. The material world and the physical body were despised as the work of the evil god. The Cathar congregation was divided into perfect members, male and female initiates who practised asceticism, and believers who followed an ordinary life-style. Supporters of the heresy decried the rituals and organization of the orthodox Church and secular institutions such as marriage and oath-taking. The heresy was eventually suppressed by a combination of crusades and inquisitorial action.

The Cathar heresy had profound effects on contemporary social and cultural life, including the foundation of preaching orders such as the Dominicans and the political unification of France, effects which persist in various forms in Western Europe today. It has been studied extensively (Russell 1965, Walther

1965), and should therefore provide easy access for further study except for the vexing problem of the lack of physical evidence noted above. As far as we know, bodily remains, art and artefacts relating to the heresy are non-existent, apart from the ruined fortress of Montsegur, although other fortresses were held by supporters of the heresy. The authorities were at pains to burn unrepentant heretics and to exhume and to burn the remains of people who were posthumously suspect of heresy. One is thus reliant on textual evidence to construct a model of heretical views of human nature and its circumstances (Wakefield & Evans 1969).

Historiographical discussion of the Cathar heresy divides broadly into two approaches. On the one hand, heresy is seen as a cultural problem; on the other hand, heresy is seen as the result of socio-economic conditions, e.g. deprivation. Both approaches use an implicit racial or ethnic model, the 'Cathars' or 'Albigensians' are discussed as a unit or entity, often in emotionally loaded terms. The heresy was a 'cancer' (Griffe 1971), an 'alien' belief system (Leff 1967), which took root in the 'cracks' of medieval society (Moore 1977) and led towards 'race suicide' (Runciman 1955, 1984). Such views, expressed by modern historians, are often identical with those of medieval clerics and must surely arouse the suspicion of the anthropologist.

A straightforward sociological approach (Berger & Luckmann 1966) is no solution, since this may take certain factors as given, e.g. that medieval Europe was a 'Christian society'. Although this is true it requires considerable qualification. If heresy was so widespread in Western Europe, it is difficult to see this society as entirely 'Christian'.

My problem is to adopt an analytical position which will allow a reinterpretation of the Cathar heresy without too many assumptions or preconceptions about its nature. The difficulties in defining religion and ritual cross-culturally are notorious, largely due to cultural specificity and bias. Nevertheless, the management of the body in life and its disposal after death are physical and social problems facing all societies. It has been demonstrated that items of material culture are strategic points from which to analyse and examine various aspects of sociocultural activity (Ucko 1969). The choice of an 'artefact' such as the body is therefore of considerable strategic value, its centrality both as social metaphor and symbol well argued (Douglas 1973, Hertz 1960, Mauss 1936).

Douglas (1973, p. 93) distinguishes 'two bodies' of a person: the physical individual and the social, and argues that 'the social body constrains the way the physical body is perceived . . . ', with the physical body being a battleground where the problems of social control and the relationship between the individual and society are fought out.

In the medieval context the fit between concepts of the individual and society was very close. Medieval society in Western Europe was strongly man-centred. The dominance of this theme ran through all aspects of culture, from the emphasis on figurative motifs in art to the division of society into the three estates of 'those who work, those who fight and those who pray', i.e. peasants, knights and clerics.

Knights and peasants were incorporated into society by birth. Entry into the clerical estate was a secondary incorporation from the other two estates. Since the religious life was taken as the ideal for all Christians, this led to an inherent structural dilemma. Peasants, who served as a labour force for the other two estates, were often seen as 'monstrous' or brutal in nature by the others, e.g. in the *chansons de geste* and pilgrims' guidebooks (Sumption 1975).

The 'physicality' bias in medieval culture was emphasized in the knightly estate. The function of a knight was to fight with arms and armour from horseback. In northern France, where feudalism was more strongly developed, initiation involved vows of allegiance and placing one's hands between those of the overlord. In southern France such vows were rarer, although here, as elsewhere, a knight proved his estate by means of his skill and strength. In the 'Usages of Barcelona', operative in southern France from the 11th century, a knight's oath was devalued to that of a burgher's when he ceased to fulfil his military functions (Mundy 1954). Knights often ended their life by withdrawing into a monastery.

The third estate, 'those who pray', catered both for its own salvation and for the continuing socialization of the other two estates. Clerics performed the cycle of Church rituals, including those of baptism, marriage and death, for the laity. One should note that all of the sacraments connected with these key stages in the life cycle were under debate and development during the Middle Ages. The Church also provided other means of social control for the other estates, including penance, the Peace of God, pilgrimage and crusade, as well as ruling on marriage.

However, the ideal of the religious life was that which was supposed to be practised by the monastic clergy who had separated themselves from this world and practised methods of bodily control: celibacy, abstinence in diet and other asceticisms, as means towards salvation. Christianity, from its relevation, has focused on the body as a dominant theme. The Last Supper is relived in the central sacrament of the Church when the bread and wine become the body and blood of Christ. The death of Christ on the cross is seen as the supreme symbol of sacrifice and mediation between God and mankind.

A corollary of this physical theme has been anxiety about the body, its functioning and behaviour, especially in sexual matters. It was quickly assumed in Christian thought that the Tree of Knowledge represented carnal knowledge, and that Adam and Eve fell from innocence because of their presumption in this regard, hence their expulsion from Eden and mankind's predicament.

Mistrust of sexuality was advocated by St Paul, whose views have persisted as a major influence in Western thought and attitudes. The Cathar heresy, like Buddhism, reduced this anxiety by positing a process of reincarnation which enabled people to approach salvation on a long-term basis. This was in contrast with orthodox Christian thought, which increased anxiety about salvation by allowing only one chance – this life – in which to reach heaven or hell.

In the Middle Ages the Church faced this uncertainty about salvation in an acute form. On one hand, there was the model of a sanctified body which would be physically resurrected in perfection at the (imminent) Judgement Day, on the other was a view of the body as lustful, sinful and violent. To compound the issue, not even the holiest of men could be certain that they would be saved. The conflict between the physical and social bodies along this crucial dimension was thus extreme. The Cathars avoided this dilemma by positing a spiritual rather than a physical resurrection. For the Cathars the body was the work of the devil, and would return to the decay it deserved.

The taming of the physical body by asceticism in Christianity was fostered by the development of the eremetic life in Egypt from the 3rd century and of monastic communities in Cappadocia by St Basil in the 4th century. Eastern Turkey, Syria and Iraq was also the region in which dualism developed in various forms from about the start of the Christian era until the Middle Ages.

The Western Church termed the Albigensians 'Arians' and 'Manichaeans'. I am not concerned here with the historical problems of the putative connections and derivations of these dualist cults, although one should note that contemporaries, e.g. St Anselm in the 13th century, saw the Cathar heresy as derivative from the Manichaean. Nevertheless, I should sketch the features of dualist cults contemporary with the Albigensians for comparative purposes.

Manichaeans proper were present among the pastoralist and agricultural communities of central Asia from soon after the cult's foundation in the 3rd century until the 14th century, when the cult was finally ended by the adoption of Islam in eastern Turkestan. In central Asia the dualists were also organized into communities of 'perfect' or initiated members and supporters, like those of the Cathars in Europe. The Manichaean communities existed peacefully alongside Buddhists, Zoroastrians, Nestorian Christians, Saivites and eventually Muslims, in the oasis towns of the Silk Road (Le Coq 1985, Snellgrove 1978).

The Manichaeans stressed the importance of literacy and written work to propagate their beliefs, and, like orthodox monks in the West, practised manuscript painting and illumination, being influential on later Iranian, Indian and possibly Tibetan art. Such artistic production contrasts strongly with its absence among the Cathars, who appear to have been more iconoclastic than the Cistercians. It is debated whether this paucity was due to the destruction of all such traces by the authorities in the West (Vicaire 1971).

In the Balkans, between the 10th and 15th centuries, dualists were termed 'Paulicians', 'Bogomils' and 'Patarenes', and a similar organization of communities of initiates and supporters existed (Obolensky 1948). In Bosnia a number of rock carvings on funerary monuments, stechaks or bilig, are debatably attributed to the Bogomils. The style of these figurative carvings shows similarities with carvings from Hatra near Mosul, and Bard-e-Nechandeh in the Zagros mountains, dating from the time of the Parthian empire (Bacon 1971, Frye 1962).

The punishment for holding dualist beliefs in all of its contexts towards the West, i.e. in Iran, Iraq, the Byzantine empire, the Balkans and Western Europe, tended to be violent. In Western Europe heresy, especially the Cathar heresy, was seen as a cancer, a physically infectious disease which had to be removed from the body of society. The taint persisted in deceased individuals, who were exhumed and burnt, and in the descendants of heretics, who were not allowed to hold public office for four generations, in theory. Torture to extract information from heretics was eventually adopted in western Europe in the 13th century. The Church, facing the difficult problem of defining or proving heresy, was led to pay particular attention to physically incriminating behaviour: expressions and gestures, as well as attendance at heretical rituals, as indices of heretical beliefs. Heretics who abjured their beliefs received a variety of penances including pilgrimages, wearing distinctively marked clothing, or imprisonment, varying in severity according to social status and degree of involvement in the cult.

The violent eradication of heresy runs parallel to similarly crude treatments of disease in contemporary society (McCall 1979), and requires interpretation from the viewpoint of wider cultural factors, which I merely indicate here. One index of such factors is the changes which were occurring in medieval art, where the physicality bias was marked. From the 11th century onwards, the monastic orders gave an 'enormous impulse' (Hubert 1963, Huyghe 1963, Olschki 1966) to the cult of saints, i.e. the housing of their physical relics in tombs, which in turn led to the development of monasteries as centres of pilgrimage. The development of iconographic mural painting further expressed and embellished this impulse. Transformations in the iconography of Christ were also marked, from the Romanesque representations of Christ in majesty, which were a striking feature of the churches of southwestern France, such as Moissac and Conques, towards the Dominican depiction of a humanized, tortured Christ on the Cross of the 13th century, e.g. in St Sernin, Toulouse.

While stressing the human attributes and physical qualities of God and the saints, the Church was also stressing the dominance of the sacred. For this purpose new representations were developed. In the 12th century in French art, angels and 'a prevalence of gruesome, individual demons' appeared for the first time. The triumph of divinity over the demonic became the greatest symbol available in daily life (Tillich 1978). Concurrent with this 'demonization' of art, at the height of the 12th century Renaissance, came the social and ideological 'closing of the gates' of Western Europe against foreign influences, and widespread moral panic about the spread and number of heretical cults which were anathematized at the III Lateran Council in 1179 (Heer 1974). In these circumstances the Church was issuing contradictory messages. The increased emphasis on the humanity and physicality of God was presented against long-held views which disparaged the physical body and this world. This disparagement, stemming from the Pauline tradition, reinforced by the Augustinian tradition, had been reiterated by other notable churchmen. Pope Gregory the Great (590–604) had taught that while man was in this, physical, body he was in exile from God and must expiate the rebellion of the angels and the Fall from Grace. Peter Damian, Cardinal Bishop and advisor to several popes stated, in 1050, that 'matter is foul, the world is corrupted by sin . . . only the world of the spirit is' (Brooke 1971), a view which was identical with Cathar views two centuries later (Wakefield 1974). In the 12th century St Bernard reinforced again the disdain for this world which was held by some sections of the Church.

Given such orthodox devaluation of this world and the physical body, it is difficult to accept modern interpretations of the dualist heresy as a 'cancer', despite their echoing medieval views. Fraud, the fair appearance hiding foulness, was a problem to orthodox Christian and heretic alike, and each accused the other of this sin.

The Cathar heresy, by disparaging the physical nature of man, extended contemporary contempt for the body but offered a more manageable and certain view about salvation than orthodoxy. By offering initiation as a deathbed rite, in the absence of orthodox clerical, pastoral visits and the administration of last rites by the orthodox Church in southwestern France, one could argue that the Cathar heresy was functionally positive for local society by giving guidance on the disposition of the body in life and death. Such practices, along with the logical consistency of dualist views of the world, must account in part for the cult's local popularity and support.

Sociological interpretations aside, and returning to the physical evidence, I should conclude by referring again to the fortress of Montsegur. During the Albigensian Crusade the numerous châteaux held by the knightly supporters of the Cathar heresy were beseiged and subsequently destroyed. Only one of these fortresses, Montsegur, is strictly specific to the cult. In 1204 leaders of the heresy were given permission by the lord holding this place to refurbish or rebuild Montsegur. This fortress then served as the cult's headquarters until its siege and fall in 1244.

Montsegur has been studied since then in a variety of ways, and from various premises, in attempts to derive or deduce the esoteric teachings of the Cathars, e.g. that the heresy was a cult of the sun or light (Niel 1962). Today, although only a ruined shell of a building, Montsegur serves as a multifunctional symbolic site: the focus of Occitanian or local identity and nationalism, a centre for pilgrimage by neo-Cathars and tourists, and for the congregation of practitioners of alternative cults and ideologies in the village nearby, e.g. yoga, T'ai Chi and acupuncture, which focus on physical approaches to life's problems.

If one takes away the 'layer' of tourism, one may still observe the polarities of ideological and political alignment expressed through physical action. Local nationalists march to Montsegur to hold rallies expressing their dissent. Orthodoxy produces counter-behaviour, e.g. in Aix-les-Thermes, a valley town in the same region, a recently instituted festival is that of the Feast of St Louis, which includes boundary walks and patriotic songs expressing loyalty to the wider society of France, led by the town priest.

Discourse over the centuries has shifted or expanded from one code of behaviour and categories: heresy, to include other codes: alternative lifestyles and political dissent, yet discourse still employs physical or bodily modes of expression centred on a symbolic site. The centrality of material culture in interpretation is self-evident.

References

Audouze, F. & A. Leroi-Gourhan 1981. France: a continental insularity. *World Archaeology* **13**, 170–89.

Bacon, E. 1971. *Archaeology: discoveries in the 1960s*. London: Cassell.
Berger P. & T. Luckmann 1966. *The social construction of reality*. London: Penguin.
de Bouard, M. 1969. The Centre for Medieval Archaeological Research. University of Caen. *World Archaeology* **1**, 61–7.
Brooke, C. 1971. *Medieval Church and society*, 146–7, 152–3. London: Sidgwick & Jackson.
Le Coq, A. von 1985. *Buried treasures of Chinese Turkestan*. Hong Kong: Oxford University Press.
Douglas, M. 1973. *Natural symbols*. London: Penguin.
Frye, R. N. 1962. *The heritage of Persia*. London: Wiedenfeld & Nicolson.
Griffe, E. 1971. *Le Languedoc Cathare de 1190 à 1210*, 11. Paris: Letouzey & Ane.
Heer, F. 1974. *The medieval world*. London: Sphere.
Hertz, R. 1960. *Death and the right hand*. New York: Free Press.
Hubert, J. 1963. Romanesque art. *Larousse encyclopaedia of Byzantine & medieval art*, R. Huyghe (ed.), 263, 270, 280. London: Hamlyn.
Huyghe, R. (ed.) 1963. *Larousse encyclopaedia of Byzantine & medieval art*, 314. London: Hamlyn.
Leff, G. 1967. *Heresy in the later Middle Ages*. Manchester: Manchester University Press.
Mauss, M. 1936. Les techniques du corps. *Journal de la Psychologie* **32**, 271–93.
McCall, A. 1979. *The medieval underworld*. London: Hamish Hamilton.
Moore, R. I. 1977. *The origins of European dissent*. Allen Lane.
Mundy, J. H. 1954. *Liberty and political power in Toulouse 1050–1230*. New York: Columbia University Press.
Niel, F. 1962. *Montsegur, temple et fortresse des Cathares d'Occitanie*. Grenoble.
Obolensky, B. 1948. *The Bogomils*. Cambridge: Cambridge University Press.
Olschki, L. 1966. *The Grail Castle & its mysteries*, 65. Manchester: Manchester University Press.
Runciman, S. (1955) 1984. *The medieval Manichee*. Cambridge: Cambridge University Press.
Russell, J. B. 1965. *Dissent & reform in the early Middle Ages*. Berkeley: Publications of the Center for Medieval and Renaissance Studies I.
Snellgrove, D. 1978. *The image of the Buddha*. Serindia: Unesco.
Sumption, J. 1975. *Pilgrimage: an image of medieval religion*. London: Faber & Faber.
Tillich, P. 1978. *A history of Christian thought*, 148–9. London: SCM Press.
Ucko, P. J. 1969. Penis sheaths: a comparative study. *Proceedings of the Royal Anthropological Institute* **2**, 27–67.
Vicaire, M.-H. O.P. 1964. *Saint Dominc and his times*. London: Darton, Longman & Todd.
Vicaire, M.-H. O.P. 1971. Notes et discussions. *Le credo la morale et l'Inquisition*, E. Privat (ed.), 391–2. Toulouse. Privat.
Wakefield, W. L. 1974. *Heresy, crusade and Inquisition in southern France 1100–1250*, Appendix 5. London: Allen & Unwin.
Wakefield, W. L. & A. P. Evans 1969. *Heresies of the High Middle Ages*. London: Columbia University Press.
Walther, D. 1965. A survey of recent research on the Albigensian Cathari. *Church History* **34**, 146–77.

17 *Etics, emics and empathy in archaeological theory*

E. M. MELAS

Introduction

How do we know what is – or was – in another person's mind? Such a question is critical in cognitive psychology and the philosophy of mind. Accordingly, the most fundamental question in cognitive archaeology and anthropology is how to gain access to an alien belief system, and especially the world-view of primitive or prehistoric peoples.

When first dealing with a strange tribe, whose language is inaccessible or unknown to us, their theories concerning the world around them would remain unknown. Similarly – even if we share their language – we cannot imagine what, for instance, a specific African tribe means when members speak of washing their souls. The degree of understanding of such a statement will inevitably depend on our familiarity with their cognitive or mental map (as defined by Renfrew 1982, 1986). Suppose that here the interpretation and systematization is carried out by outsiders, through scientific observation of the behaviour associated with specific beliefs. The question arises of whether an explanation thus achieved is adequate and satisfactory; also, to what extent and in what ways must such an explanatory account be constrained by actors' accounts or perhaps by those available to actors in general in the community.

These are the main ideas or issues, and the basic relevant questions, on which this chapter focuses. It is obvious that we are dealing with two separate and seemingly inconsistent methods of enquiry, an 'external' and an 'internal' one. What we argue here is for a compromise of the two approaches, necessitated by their complementarity. Both are useful aids in theory building, depending on how fruitful they might be in a given context for providing understanding and insight. As Bell (1986) argues, methods in general should be taken as useful epistemological tools and not as ideologies or as empirical claims debatable upon grounds of truth or falsity. After all, knowledge in the social sciences, and not only in the humanities, can never be said to be absolutely true or false, no matter which method is used. A certain degree of subjectivity, relativity and partiality is always involved, and no investigation ever results either in absolute success or in complete failure. No archaeologist or anthropologist has ever concluded an enquiry or come back from a field trip with the following report: their concepts are so explicit and straightforward that they are absolutely comprehensible; or they are so alien and their material record so inherently inaccessible that it is impossible to describe their social life – kinship system, etc. – language, land tenure or ritual. There is never a claim for absolute success or a total admission of failure. In normal practice there should only be admission of partial success or partial failure of comprehension.

We will begin by defining what, in the context of this chapter, is meant by etics, emics and empathy. After outlining the principal tenets of these concepts and contrasting them with each other, their benefits for, and their limits to cognitive archaeology will be discussed, depending on how and in what contexts they are worthwhile assumptions for the generation and testing of theory (first three sections). The next two sections serve as a conceptual background for the discussion of internal explanation and its integration with external explanation of the two subsequent sections. The idea of such an integration forms the principal tenet of this contribution.

Etic reality and emic reality

In an existential or anthropological sense, the terms emic and etic were first introduced into anthropology by Harris (1968, 1976, 1979). Within the context of his cultural materialist version of Marx's great model, Harris distinguished etics from emics; that is, the behavioural from the mental dimension of human conduct.

Etic reality is also often called 'the extrasomatic base', and normally refers to material evidence of behaviour. That is, it consists of domains or operations whose validity does not depend on the demonstration of conscious or unconscious significance or validity in the mind of the native. What constitutes etic reality for Harris is a two-dimensional thing. There is, on the one hand, the so-called infrastructure, i.e. etic behavioural modes of production and reproduction, such as technical skills. However, there are no valid criteria for what constitutes infrastructure, and therefore different materialist perspectives have the option of popping any part of the social system in and out of the infrastructure to suit their convenience (Harris 1979). The so-called structure, on the other hand, comprises the domestic and political economy.

Emic reality refers to non-material factors, and consists of domains and operations that are real and meaningful – but not necessarily conscious – to the natives themselves. This is a corollary to the notion of 'first-person knowledge', i.e. of the reflective standpoint of the agent who possesses knowledge and beliefs referring to objects that – like phenomenological variables – are modified by his or her beliefs about them (Hampshire 1982). There is also a distinction between behavioural and mental emics. The first refers to cultural actualities, such as art, music, literature, advertising, rituals, sport, games, hobbies, science and social organization. The second consists of cultural dispositions and psychological attitudes, such as conscious or unconscious cognitive goals, intentions, categories, rules, plans, values, symbols, philosophies and beliefs about behaviour. All of these can be elicited from the participants or inferred by the observer.

It is unnecessary to repeat that the question of the importance and causal primacy of either etics or emics pervades the philosophical and anthropological literature. Most philosophers of action propound a kind of behaviouristic reductionism, by introducing the concept of basic or primitive action. Any human action is reduced to the status of a mere event that could be recorded by a scientific observer. Actions are thus cashed into the currency of physical events, as seen by what we may call the event-watcher. In line with such an assumption is Davidson's (1980) dictum that 'we never do more than move our bodies, the rest is up to nature'. The implication is that etic reality and experience dominate the scene, whereas emics are rendered obsolete or non-existent. However, it is counter-argued that actions thus considered relate to basic events, such as bodily movements, rather than to basic actions. These basic events in human conduct might perhaps be called 'robot-actions', 'humanoid events' or 'actvents' (Baier 1985).

On the other hand, many psychologists and philosophers consider phenomenological variables to be significant in human existence. The inner world of the individual is thought to be much more closely related to – and to have more influence upon – his or her behaviour, than the observable environmental stimuli (Rogers 1964). The reductionist notion of action as physical event is opposed by seeing actions as intentionally staged events. Underlying these events, active mental postures are postulated, such as intentions exercising some recognizable ability or competence. As a result, 'we never do less than we can be recognized to have intentionally done . . . is due to the culture, as well as the nature, of which we are part' (Baier 1985). It is evident that the importance of emic reality is here underlined.

Etic approach versus emic approach

We now turn to defining the methodological aspect of etics and emics. The terms were borrowed from linguistic methodology, where they derived from the contrast between phonetics and phonemics: the etic approach dictates that the physical patterns of language be described with a minimum reference to their meaningful function within the language system, whereas the emic approach takes full account of functional relationships, setting up minimal contrastive units as the basis for a description. When dealing with human social life, the communication of meaning in any interpersonal relation is subject to the distortions arising in the subjective world of the person being observed and those arising in the subjective world of the observer. How can such a communication be dealt with scientifically? Such a question, asked by psychologists (Wann 1964), points to the broad, everyday dimension of the etics–emics controversy.

To put it briefly, the etic approach in anthropology is meant to be the process of acquiring knowledge through observation. It seeks understanding by using categories of analysis that do not necessarily coincide with the mental templates – cognitive standards, belief systems, ideologies and moral orders – of the subjects.

This epistemological position stems from Enlightenment rationalism, with its beliefs in universal laws of human nature, in all-embracing scientific methods for accumulating truths, in intellectual and moral progress; and with its mistrust of subjectivism and arbitrariness. Etic explanations are subject to transcultural standards of rational appraisal. It is assumed that there is a strong core of human cognitive rationality common to the cultures of all periods and times (Hollis & Lukes 1982).

In everyday experience an etic perspective depends on the standpoint of the observer, who acquires knowledge of objects or persons that exist independently of anyone's knowledge or beliefs about them. The discoveries of the natural sciences are used to explain actions under appropriate descriptions, appropriate that is to orthodox causal explanations (Hampshire 1982).

The basic assumption underlying the emic approach is that what is true can only be determined within a style of reasoning, and more specifically the style which judges other cultures only by their, not our, standards. It follows that emic analysis in anthropology is meant to offer a kind of insight similar to that which natives have of themselves. Such an understanding may be gained by considering what subjects think and say about their beliefs, intentions, etc., rather than by observing behavioural patterns. In other words, one takes into account the native's rather than the enquirer's – imported – conceptions. Emic perspectives arose from the previously ethnocentric assumptions of 19th century anthropology, and were further developed within Boasian individualism and relativism.

The above definition of emic method implies that emics lead to a form of intentional or internal explanation through translation of utterances and interpretation of associated actions. Interpreting what people do when they 'believe' something is taken to be parallel to what they mean when they utter sentences indicative of their actions. However, there are complex relations between what people think or say they believe or desire, and what they actually believe or desire (Hampshire 1982). It also often happens that what they do may be intelligible, but not what they say. As Gellner (1982) put it, 'how different one finds the savage seems to hinge largely on whether one goes by what he does (which is not strange – he acts in the same world as we do, and in a similar way), or by what he says (very odd by most translations)'.

It is thus asserted that translation – i.e. explaining culture A in the language of culture B – in this context is more important than, and precedes, interpretation. According to Hall (1977) we cannot interpret prehistory without making a conscious attempt to understand the nature of humans as symbol-using social animals. To identify what people believe, we need to translate the meaningful symbols of their beliefs into familiar categories of comprehension, thus linking meaning to truth conditions. At the level of self-conscious, codified and diversified civilization there are codified criteria of valid belief, which must be decoded. Interpreting such beliefs looks, then, like decoding them, especially in cases where the whole point of the symbolism appears to be mystery rather than clarity. Such cases – like, for example, those of magic and religion – may be subject to cognitive but not to rational assessment, representing ways of dealing with information that exceeds our perceptual capacities (Lukes 1982).

There are therefore always inherent difficulties in translation. In emic explanations the thought to be traced is usually entrenched in a particular language and vocabulary, and languages are diverse and not easily translatable into each other. This entails that we often cannot correctly specify in our language the contents of other people's beliefs and intentions.

The difficulty increases when we are dealing with cultural aspects where societies are free to indulge in their fantasies. Such aspects are mythology, cosmology, metaphysics, sociopolitical and ritual organization. Here intercultural differences are enormous and translations sometimes sound very odd, due not only to mistranslation, but probably also through the view translated, which may be completely different from ours, and thus incomprehensible (Lukes 1982). Nevertheless, a good measure of translatability exists at the same time, which facilitates the highlighting of this divergence (Gellner 1982). However, it must be emphasized that translatability does not mean agreement.

Let us now consider the priority controversy between etics and emics as methods. This problem, like its corollary concerning etic and emic reality, is ever present within anthropology and archaeology. The etic approach appears to be more favoured and dominates the relevant literature. Its main advantage is considered to be the fact that it offers a style-neutral, and thus objective, standard of reasoning. However, there are difficulties in the application of the model. Such a difficulty arises, for instance, from the etic notion that until the explanatory model of the scientist is constructed, the social system under study has no objective structure. Critics of Harris' etics emphasize that this method appears to be no less subjective than the emic method, because the external observer unintentionally imposes present-day or personal ideology on the ancient material or on alien cultures; and there is a wholesale ethnocentric imposition of conceptions of Western science, which obscures rather than reveals social reality (Leone 1981).

On the other hand, the benefits of methodological emics have often been stressed, notwithstanding its inadequacies and limitations. Advocates of the emic approach maintain that ethnographically or archaeologically revealed phenomena may not be adequately explicable without considering the mental templates and beliefs of their creators; and that anthropologists working from a native-centred point of view would bring fewer preconceptions to the explanation, and would thus be more likely to come to an understanding of the phenomenal world of their subjects as it exists. They maintain that the guiding spirit of an emic approach is to rid oneself of preconceptions about universal structures, so that the data may be analysed objectively to reveal the true universal structures (Rogers 1964, Kay 1970).

It follows that, in using emics, the objective loss is not such as to exclude objectivity from the service of science. Emic units of analysis can, indeed, have a place in the framework of scientific, descriptive anthropology, which demands a truly scientific approach to the sociological study of beliefs. Such a scientific approach to alien cultures, as well as to our own, requires the grasping of it from within. This implies that objectivity is an internal standard (Feleppa 1986, Lukes 1982, Barnes & Bloor 1982).

The critics of emic analysis counter-argue that, given its presupposition of accurate translation, such an analysis is not free from interpreter imposition, especially if he or she presumes that it is possible to mirror the semantic–cultural substratum. This weakness reveals the relativistic nature of the approach, considered to be its most serious disadvantage. According to Newton-Smith (1982), the truth of relativism entails the impossibility of translation. As a consequence relativism ends by depriving the natives of translatable beliefs, and fails as an explanation, generating more puzzles than it solves.

We reach the conclusion that both etic and emic analysis impose alien structures on the culture or language being studied. It is evident that both standpoints, the internal as well as the behaviouristic, have their limitations. Also, theorists who claim final authority for the internal source are no less in error than the behaviourists, who claim that only the evidence available to any observer yields genuine knowledge about actions and mental attitudes.

Furthermore, both analyses suffer from indeterminacy, be it translational or physical. Translators can produce 'right' answers, but they cannot warrantably say that they are true; and different translation manuals can always be employed. Such a translational underdetermination presupposes, and is additional to, physical underdetermination: there can be factual differences about meaning – or anything else – only if there are differences in physical macro- or microstructure (Feleppa 1986).

However, how are we to remedy such an indeterminacy and inadequacy in the explanation methodology of the social sciences? The only answer is rather to be sought in a newer philosophy of science which will not be fearful of finding room for the person, both the observer and the observed, in his or her subjective as well as his or her objective mode. First we will have to admit that any successful translation, and indeed interpretation, of beliefs presupposes at least some common rationality. Then we will proceed by interpreting alien people and their cultures as instances of very widespread correlations between inputs and outputs, correlations which are specified in a terminology shared by many or most interested observers. At a more elementary level we could perhaps gain some understanding by watching their behaviour and visible expressions of feelings (Hampshire 1982).

Empathetic model

Empathy could be defined as a peculiar mode of explanation, dependent neither on intuitive penetration nor on subsumptions under generalizations. As such it must be associated with the German verb *verstehen*, rather than with the noun *Einfülung* implying psychological involvement, i.e. projection of the self into the feelings of others, or even into the being of objects. In psychology empathy is used as a tool to check interpersonal understanding, or to check with a colleague 'our understanding' of something out there (Wann 1964).

When applied to the explanation of the human past, empathy should be distinguished from methodological individualism. The latter focuses on cognitive factors alone, whereas empathy rests on the assumption that humans may feel and think in the same or very similar ways. Therefore empathy aims at grasping cognitive, affective and spiritual elements of human experience (Bell 1986). In the philosophy of history, empathetic method is usually associated with Collingwood, who argued in support of the model as follows. Past acts, works and situations are dead, unless the historian or the archaeologist can understand the thoughts that lie behind them. Such understanding can only be achieved in so far as the explanation-seeker can relive, re-enact and reconstitute the thoughts of the past people in his or her own mind. One achieves some kind of contact – through empathy, not sympathy implying agreement – with these people. Thus he or she will arrive at an imaginative (as a creative process, not to be confused with imagery) understanding of the minds of the people dealt with, and of the thought behind their historical acts or cultural activities.

By way of a short definition, then, empathy could refer to the ability to put myself in someone else's shoes. Collingwood (1946) views empathy as 'an activity of thought, which can be known only insofar as the knowing mind re-enacts it and knows itself as so doing. To the historian, the activities whose history he is studying, are not spectacles to be watched, but experiences to be lived through in his own mind'. By drawing attention to the criterion of intelligibility or correctness, advocates of empathy argue that to explain an action or a situation it is enough to show that it follows rationally from an agent's thoughts. In that way the enquirer will be able to identify relevance with a certain degree of confidence (Dray 1964).

From the above analysis it becomes clear that the use of empathy offers great potential especially in the study of preliterate peoples. It appears to be one of the most interesting and worthwhile tasks in prehistoric research, although a difficult and complex one. However, the limitations of the model are obvious and there are always problems not only with its application, but even with its conceptual delineation. As a result it has become a highly controversial issue within archaeology. The main point most critics emphasize is its simplistic historicism and extreme relativism, and that it is not a methodological model of explanation at all, but merely an analytical fashion, a means of generating ungrounded explanatory hypotheses (for example, Hempel 1965). Therefore, according to Hempel and his followers, the empathetic approach to explanation does not embody an alternative to – and is not different from – the covering law explanatory form.

For Bell (1986) empathy's only criterion of truth is 'self-referential' theory; that is, intuition. That is why empathetic portraits, although they might yield insight, do not lead to much understanding beyond the portraits themselves. Such portraits are contrasted with conjectures on which assessments can be made, and new and further insights gained. Like actual portraits, they are a final product, not a sketch that can be tested, altered and used to gain further perspectives.

Science – explanation – understanding

Science is regarded by many today as a relative term, and scientific models or paradigms are taken to be subjective and changeable according to circumstances, such as scientific revolutions, etc. It is thus argued that science does not reproduce reality, but rather distorts it through imposition and abstraction (Kuhn 1964, Feyerabend 1978). With regard to the social sciences, and particularly to anthropology and prehistory, there is a widely held view that enquirers work on commonsense knowledge relating to preliterate cosmologies, and that only the hard sciences can possibly produce scientific knowledge (Hollis & Lukes 1982). Such a scepticism about science allows us to believe that conceptually archaeology is a science to the extent that it finds things out, makes important discoveries and expands our knowledge; the knowledge of the human past and not of nature's past. However, what is wholly impossible are radical developments or fundamental discoveries, such as the hard sciences make. We thus waste our efforts, if we retain any inappropriate picture of the capacity and expectations of our subject. In that sense archaeology is not a hard science, and the 'archaeological laws' that it employs are nothing more than general statements covering universal but trivial regularities. With respect to its methodology, archaeology may again be called a science only in a loose common sense: it uses principles of collecting evidence, deduction, experimentation, etc., which have become part of the methodical exploration of all knowledge. However, owing to the nature of its record, archaeology increasingly calls on more-rigorous scientific techniques of the natural sciences (such as geology, zoology and botany), for the models dealing with its record have to be largely technological, evolutionary and economic.

In the human sciences there appears to be an asymmetry between explanation and understanding. Explanation – which seems to be more compatible with the physical sciences – is one-dimensional; something an investigator does to account for a phenomenon by using a cause–effect formula. Such explanation has a predictive character, and can be deduced from mere correlation with covering laws. This kind of explanation may account for variation without an understanding of its behaviour. Besides, there is the problem of 'empty' explanations – i.e. commonsense tautological ones – conveying no understanding. Understanding, on the other hand, often requires more than giving true statements about causes. Given the distinction between causes and reasons, understanding involves reasoning of beliefs associated with a particular phenomenon. It also involves making intelligible the material connections between particular deeds and intentions of the agent, etc. Understanding in that sense can be employed trans-historically as well as cross-culturally, and assumes a two-dimensional character as referring to the know-how, to rules of intelligibility employed by both the enquirer and the participant.

It follows that, in the human sciences, explanation alone is insufficient. The ideal is to combine explanation and understanding, to produce explanatory understanding. This is better achieved by integrating internal explanation, which I believe is an integral part of understanding, and practical inference, in the sense of establishing an intelligible material connection between the elements of the agent's action, that is his or her deed and the relevant necessary and sufficient conditions, including situational motivation, intention and means-to-the-end-belief. The insight given by such an integrative understanding can probably be supplemented through etic analysis.

Forms of explanation

There are admittedly two irreducible kinds of activity in the world, corresponding to two distinct explanation models: action or mental activity and causality or behaviour (cf. Bock 1980, pp. 183–5, Baier 1985, pp. 40–9). The one model is clearly suitable to actions – and their apparatus of purposes and motives – and the other to physical causation. Accordingly, the enquirer needs to refer both to what is thought normal or appropriate, and to what normally occurs.

In accordance with this distinction – and given the non-coincidence between the material and non-material aspects of culture – when talking of explanation in archaeology and anthropology we mean three things: (a) explanation of actions or of material remains by reference to the thoughts of individual agents; (b) explanation of the institutional setting, i.e. the social and political background, in which those deeds, artefacts and beliefs have substance; (c) explanation of physical events – such as the desolation of a city or the gradual wasting away of a countryside – in which deeds and beliefs played some, but by no means the whole or even the most important causal role.

It is against this conceptual background that the issue of an emic and empathetic approach to archaeological interpretation must be seen. Within such a theoretical framework the philosophy underlying the rationale of internal explanation may be illuminated and partially modified, thus becoming more suitable to meet the requirements of a reliable and convincing explanatory process.

Emics and empathy clearly belong with the first type of explanation ((a) above) – without being totally irrelevant to the other two ((b) and (c) above) – and must be viewed in connection with an archaeology of mind, the mind of individual agents and participants. Emic analysis and empathy appear to be the right way of investigating mind, and constitute a valid source for the mental and spiritual life, especially of prehistoric man. By keeping in mind the distinction between the three types of explanation, we will be able to form a clear idea of the emic and empathetic approaches, avoiding misunderstanding and confusion. This confusion usually results from two basic misconceptions. Emics and empathy are either rejected out of hand as epistemically non-existent methodological tools, or their role is overestimated, by putting an overemphasis on intentionalistic explanations.

On the other hand, explanations of the second and third type can hardly be based on an intentionalistic model: there are various kinds of sociocultural phenomena, such as happenings in social institutions and ecosystems, of which individual persons are largely, perhaps wholly, unconscious and irresponsible. Such factors and happenings constitute the material aspects of a culture, in other words the etic reality or etic units of analysis, which mainly consist of the kinds of behaviour and activity related to subsistence, economy and technology. There is little doubt that the nature of these phenomena allows for the application of an etic approach for their reconstruction, that is by observation, and through ecosystemic and evolutionary models employing a covering law scientific methodology.

From the above analysis it becomes clear that in the study of man there is room for both forms of explanation. Presently, however, there is, especially in prehistory, an overwhelming predilection for the etic or external approach. This is mainly due to the fact that the evidence available to the prehistoric archaeologist – products of technology and the incidental outcome of subsistence patterns – almost exclusively reflects the material aspects of the people under study. This, along with the high value set by the present age on material culture and technology, tends to overemphasize the role of the etic approach, and to produce a materialist view of the prehistoric past.

Internal explanation

We have already referred to both emic and empathetic approaches as forms of intentional or internal explanations; explanations, that is, which trace connections of thought and try to interpret other cultures, languages and theoretical schemes from within (cf. Hollis & Lukes 1982, p. 1). The two methods share some common goals, as well as the assumption that human experience has been as vitally important in prehistory as it is today. The basic assumption behind both models is that the enquirer and the people – past or present – whose material culture or belief system is studied, share a common language of experience. The only difference is that in anthropology this kind of sharing is direct, whereas in archaeology it is achieved indirectly, by means of mental processes, i.e. through speculation and imaginative re-enactment. In other words, empathy involves the assumption of getting around as a participant in another period (which is probably not possible); on the other hand, the emic approach implies the notion of getting around as a native in another, contemporary culture (which probably is possible).

Thus, both empathy and emics are methodological models which try to reach explanatory judgements by appealing not to general laws, but to processes of internal understanding; that is, by referring to the participant's or native's thoughts, and by establishing internal rules of intelligibility or appropriateness connecting these thoughts with a particular behaviour, which results in the action to be explained.

Apart from the difference already mentioned, there is a contrast in the application of the two models. Emics, like methodological individualism, with which it appears to be identical, focuses on making – often tenuous and conjectural – statements based on cognitive factors alone. Such statements are open to empirical investigation and other types of criticism. On the other hand the empathizer develops not only cognitive, but also affective and spiritual orientations; and his or her claims are not subject to testing procedures similar to those of cognitive conjectures reached through emic analysis.

The notion of internal understanding is subject to a certain ambiguity, and has been subjected to dialectical pressure. To avoid confusion it would be useful to say at once what the empathetic and emic model excludes, rather than what it involves.

It is not meant to be an intuitive process; that is, seeing the connection of thought and action directly and immediately. Such an assumption implies that advocates of the method invariably stand for subjectivism and lack of checking, and for the use of intuitive rather than verified claims. Internal understanding is, rather, meant to be an explanatory deliberation and penetration involving two basic things. On the one hand, inductive reconstruction of the agent's thought and of alternative courses of action through interpretation of behavioural evidence. Such evidence can be elicited from the material and ethnographic record, against which conjectures and translation enterprises may be – at least partially – assessed. On the other hand, it involves empirically warranted demonstration that the deed is plausibly determined by that thought.

It does not imply a literal identity of agent's and enquirer's thoughts, of their rules of intelligibility, but merely the ability to follow these rules. Adoption of the subject's point of view does not mean agreement and actual sharing of particular concepts and rules by enquirer and subject (cf. Davidson 1980, pp. 238–9, Lukes 1982, p. 262). A certain kind of conceptual identity is, of course, inherent in internal explanations, but not in the sense of direct precondition, as an *a priori* attainment. It is established by appealing to understanding, and not vice versa: one argues to it, not from it.

It is not a psychoanalytic model, relying on alien psychoanalytic categories and rules emphasizing unconscious motivation. It does not mean sympathy, that is to share with the subject's feelings, beliefs, social horizons and view of the world. Therefore, it is not concerned with duplicating or reproducing the relevant rules of intelligibility, but merely with assimilating them.

World unity versus man's diversity

The points raised above must be seen in connection with the reflective historical consensus that, despite the uniqueness of the world, and the universality and regularity of nature, there are transcending differences in periods and cultures (for example, Gellner 1982, p. 186). Differences may be minor and explicable at the sensory and motor levels, but very great at the level of self-conscious, codified civilization. This has been accepted even by sociobiologists who allow that, while retaining a human nature formed long ago, we have become socially and culturally different from our hunter–gatherer forebears and contemporaries (see Bock 1980). The investigator has therefore, as an important aim, the revelation of feasible ways of organizing experience and the social world that are different from those with which he or she is familiar. However, anthropological understanding would be impossible under the complete rejection of a 'science of human nature' and of all notions of trans-historical and cross-cultural generalizations. This rejection would imply that the cognitive equipment of societies differs radically. Collingwood (1946) is often taken to hold such an extreme view by saying that the development and differentiation of mind in the historical process results in a marked heterogeneity over time in the thoughts and deeds of human beings.

We thus arrive at the necessity of an assimilationist model and at the underlying notion that differences in material culture and in certain aspects of human behaviour do not imply an overall lack of uniformity in non-material concepts; that is, in mental processes and spiritual categories. Cultural significance may not be universally shared, but it is potentially and necessarily sharable. Collingwood himself has allowed for some relative homogeneity in delimited periods of history, otherwise, even the facts and attendant attitudes of the 20th century would be incompatible with the historian's picture of life for that period. The logic which leads to an assimilationist argument could be framed as follows.

In the process of internal understanding we entertain thought-connections. However, how can we have any basis for believing that they are in fact those of the people we are studying? As already implied, three different solutions have been offered, based on similarity or dissimilarity assumptions. The first assumption propounds an absolute similarity model, based on the acceptance of a 'science of human nature' and of a 'fundamental constitution of the mind', as suggested mainly by Hume, Mill and Hempel (see Martin 1977, p. 20f.). Accordingly, Dilthey (1964) tries to bridge the gap by asserting that we can understand only those minds that are similar to ours: 'The fact that the investigator of history is the same as the one who makes it is the first condition which makes scientific history possible'.

On the contrary, the second solution proposes an absolute dissimilarity scheme, as exemplified by Collingwood's 'process view of mind'. The latter suggests that, given the trans-historical and cross-cultural diversity, the move to similarity does not work. As already mentioned, this theory suffers from the logical defect of being contradictory and incompatible with the notion of internal understanding and with scientific knowledge in general, since cultures would not be comparable (Martin 1977, Bock 1980). It must therefore be accepted and, in a modified version, integrated into a more comprehensive theory. The basis for such a theory is offered by the third solution, favouring a partial similarity model. As Berlin (1954) put it, 'the modes of thought of the ancients or of any culture remote from our own are comprehensible to us only in the degree to which we share some, at any rate, of their basic categories'. This implies an acceptance of some common features uniting all men of all societies, and the universality of the principle of a certain humanity bound up with some concept of rationality, which minimizes unintelligibility (Hollis 1982, Lukes 1982, p. 265).

Thus, we have arrived at the notion of a common humanity or psychic unity of some sort, which promotes the epistemological unity of mankind (Gellner 1982, pp. 182, 199, Hollis 1982), and allows for a certain kind of cross-cultural generalization and for an explanatory understanding of alien cultures. This notion underlies the assimilationist account of internal explanation, which could be argued for as follows.

Assimilationist account of internal explanation

We assume that beneath superficial qualitative differences, there must be a solid bedrock of shared traits and characteristics of mental and behavioural ways, which enable people of one culture to understand those of another. In other words, the ability to judge the appropriateness of alien deeds, by calculation of plausibility, implies a certain uniformity and familiarity between the subject's and enquirer's ways of responding, thinking and acting, under specific internal or external stimuli.

This assertion appears to be compatible, although not identical, with the idea of a 'science of human nature' and of an 'objective historical consciousness'. However, while there exist certain general principles which are the same whether we study the past or the present, and which enable us to explain the former through the latter, there are always attitudes and mental states which do not apply to people in all times and places. Even in relation to hungry and thirsty people, or in the area of sex, few truly universal generalizations can be made.

It could be conveniently said that the assumption of such a psychic unity of humanity finds expression at three levels of human reality: behavioural, spiritual and mental. All three levels belong to the sphere of psychology, whose fundamental laws are relevant here.

At a purely behavioural level there appear to be general propositions concerning human nature; that is, a fundamental set of judgements about the characteristic responses human beings make to the various challenges set to them in the course of their lives, whether by natural conditions, or by their fellow human beings. However, it seems that the only genuinely characteristic and uniform responses would concern reflex behaviour, rather than decided actions.

At the spiritual level there are certain rules of general validity, concerning emotions as well as feelings and passions, which (according to Hume) are naturally alike in every individual, and constitute the regular springs of human action and behaviour. Among these feelings we may mention fear, insecurity and existential anxiety, animosity and aggression, love and hatred, ambition, etc.

At the mental or cognitive level we postulate general statements, concerning rationality, that is inescapable modes of thought, original associative operations of mind. Such hypothetical statements may correspond to the principles of practical inference – as defined above – and to Collingwood's 'absolute presuppositions'. These principles can be regarded as synthetic (i.e. necessarily but not analytically true) epistemological *a priori* propositions, in Kantian terms, i.e. assumed, not discovered. They are, that is, operative in all thinking people in all times and places. Moreover, they are unchanging, always asserting some sort of necessary relationship: for example, the statement 'men must think the world under the category of causality' is *a priori*. Although it is not an ungrounded proposition, by being unspecific it is not a prescriptive conceptual representation. It is non-empirical, and hence not subject to confirmation or falsification.

Undoubtedly, it is this mental horizon of our common humanity that plays the most significant role in the process of internal understanding. Such an understanding can be genuinely cross-cultural to the degree in which explanatory categories or concepts of general applicability are constructed from personal experience of actions done today, as well as through social inheritance and generalizations built up over the generations. It is to these generalizations we now turn.

From the above presentation, it follows that instead of rejecting cross-cultural generalizations, we have to formulate and use them in such a way that they cover, as general formulae and classification headings, non-homogenous phenomena of human thought and behaviour. As we have seen, the logic of internal explanation does depend on some sort of existential regularity generalizations, especially in so far as the probabilistic establishment of relevance is concerned. Such generalizations may take the form of a law statement, but only in a broad and loose sense. They are not free-standing, and have no independent empirical existence on the order of Hempelian covering laws, allowing for a deduction of a particular deed. Thus, they are not general laws, unless we count inductive statistical laws of high probability as general covering laws.

We have already referred to generic human traits, which must lie behind human actions. These common traits may correspond to Descartes' universal rules (in Baier 1985, p. 37), and could be defined as action-universals (Gellner 1982, pp. 183–4, 195, 200). The latter may involve universal principles – i.e. general terms and categories – of action and intention. Such principles include purposes, beliefs and deeds under generic material descriptions. Martin (1977) and Hampshire (1982) define these general principles as generic assertions – thoughts or concepts – of appropriateness or correctness, or material rules of intelligible or plausible connection; that is, connection between purposes, beliefs, deeds, etc., which constitute the action elements. Such principles are meant to be strategic hypotheses whose application renders what subjects do and say intelligible, by means of a bridgehead argument for interpretation. Such assumptions are organized by rules of consent to which a rational person cannot fail to subscribe (Hollis & Lukes 1982).

Such generic assertions or rules of appropriateness can be internal or external, as they may be directives either referring to the native's know-how, or to the investigator's explanatory proficiency. In the latter case they may also be conceived as instruments for data-gathering.

With regard to internal rules, it is true that within the context of ethnographic enquiry, usually the participant cannot articulate the rules of intelligibility that he or she follows in conducting everyday affairs (cf. Smith & Jones 1986); he or she does not seem to use them explicitly. However, actually he or she appears to be following them implicitly, at least to the extent that he or she could say whether something was being done correctly, thus explaining and giving a coherent and continuous picture of his or her conduct, which makes sense because if a person has the know-how, he or she knows that in normal conditions the act succeeds. Also, in having a belief, he or she has reasons backed by fundamental assumptions about the ordering of the Cosmos. Such assumptions are embedded in the theoretical culture, in which understanding the universe and coming into tune with it are inseparable activities (Baier 1985, pp. 22, 37). This is the case, for example, with rules used by priests or by practitioners of magic, witchcraft or healing, by chiefs or by farmers. The native normally knows his or her kinship terminology, theory of disease and curing, and whole-world view so well that he or she applies them effortlessly and automatically. Having learned them from childhood, he or she may never have followed explicit rules in becoming skilled in their use.

To such a theoretical framework correspond the methodological models of empathy and emics. The latter refers to a translation process aiming at extracting the factual meaning of alien belief systems from symbolic, and particularly linguistic, expressions of emic cultural phenomena. A similar process is involved in evidence-based empathy, which draws symbolic meaning from extralinguistic entities, from non-verbal customs, and taboos and artefacts.

It appears, on the other hand, that the receptor-culture or the investigator – given the implicitness and vagueness of the rules of the participants, and especially those of past people – requires the help of explicit rules and narratives to start with. Rules serve the end of scientific knowledge, by offering an external understanding; that is a non-participatory explanation through mere reciting of rules, without any familiarity with the practices, the activities and skills involved. Such an explanation requires that it will be a necessary first step to look for those connections of thought and beliefs which look familiar and plausible to the enquirer in making up his or her own mind. This logic underlies the methodological premises of etics, according to which rules of appropriateness, concerning both etic and emic phenomena, are established by behavioural evidence alone, provided through observation of these phenomena.

Following this distinction between source-culture and receptor-culture standards of appropriateness, we may differentiate between a participatory and an investigatory understanding. However, the question arises of who is the final judge of appropriateness – the participant or the investigator? A certain solution could perhaps be reached through the following considerations. If the native to a particular period or culture can formulate the rule, and explicitly tell us the rationale or principles of intelligibility inherent in his or her actions, we would be able to take account of his or her behaviour by following those terms. If not, we can do nothing but construct hypothetical rule statements, which more or less accurately formulate certain objective features in the society under study. We may evaluate these statements by their ability to account for – or predict – behaviour that natives accept as real, appropriate and meaningful, or scholarly immersion in the society under study suggests as such. Thus, the epistemic requirement of explicit rules, for the social scientist to start the explanatory procedure, appears to be fulfilled. However, in the process, he or she may learn those things so well that he or she can dispense with rules, which he or she can easily forget as well. He or she may begin to select appropriate behaviour automatically, like learning a new language or game, without applying the rules. There is nothing, logically, that prohibits him or her from going native, from getting around in the native culture and attaining the participant's know-how. In this case we are dealing with a different sense of internal understanding, which nevertheless approaches the one of the native. It may also count as sufficiently scientific in so far as the knowledge it provides is based on explicit and intelligible rules. The ability to follow these rules affords an indirect, but valuable confirmation of the soundness of the explanatory praxis.

Internal and external explanation: integration

We have thus arrived at the notion of complementarity and integration, promoting a pluralism of models. From the above presentation, it is becoming clear that emic notions become etic simply because they are or may be cross-culturally instantiated. That is, emic notions, once incorporated in the ethnographic description apparatus for some culture, become part of an etic kit usable by other enquirers (Feleppa 1986). It follows that as etic and emic reality are integrated on a theoretical level, so must be the experience-distant and experience-near methodological schemes. In the final analysis a society or a culture is nothing but what is said or thought about it – by those who observe it, as well as by those who compose it. Observation alone fails to reveal meaning and culture, and so does mere reliance on participant's assertions or on empathetic reconstruction. That is, the meaning of what those interpreted believe is not simply whatever they say or whatever the empathizer believes; but nor is the interpreter free to assign any meaning his interests or theories may dictate (Lukes 1982). Both etic and emic analysis depend on fruitfulness, and whereas this may speak on occasion in favour of emic analysis, it may favour a purely etic analysis in other contexts. After all they are both methodological tools and not empirical statements. Also, as Bell (1986) has shown, any method is assumed because of its appropriateness. It is the investigator's task to find out what is of value in each by taking account of their positive elements.

What seems to emerge as inevitable is an idea of emics acknowledging the observer's interests. Emics must go beyond what subjects say or consciously think, as suggested by the 'phon-emic attitude' detectable in the unguarded speech judgements of native speakers who may have a complete control of their language in a practical sense, but have no sensible, consciously systematic knowledge of it. According to a Weberian attitude underlying emic analysis, emics should complement etics, the idea being that anthropology seeks to unify emic perspectives into a systematic, comparative theory of culture, based in large part on etic theoretical notions (Bock 1980, Feleppa 1986).

Under such an integrative assumption we may be able to overcome the historical dichotomy between the polar positions of naturalism or positivism and historicism or idealism. This dichotomy appears to be a difference in emphasis, rather than a categorical difference which reflects on the truth and falsity of the opposing positions. The assimilationist account we propose could be justified as follows. To the extent that the ultimate concern of archaeological and anthropological explanation is towards a reconstructive and explanatory understanding of human behaviour, and both explanation and behaviour involve human minds – both of the subjects and of the investigators – emics and empathy will always be present (often only implicitly) and indispensable in the explanatory process. It is taken for granted that minds and thoughts are normally involved in human behaviour (at least from the appearance of *Homo sapiens*), rendering that behaviour intentional, as opposed to animal behaviour.

This, I believe, must not be taken as contradictory to the scientific aspirations of archaeology, nor to the generalizing prerequisites (i.e. trans-historical and cross-cultural principles) of the objective standards of explanation. As already stated, the insights and understanding acquired through this perspective constitute a significant contribution to scientific knowledge, the term scientific here being relative to man and not to nature. Such a contribution is always welcome, and finds expression in two areas of enquiry. First, in fieldwork, where sites and their function, as well as local resources and their exploitation, can be identified (see, for example, Hanks & Winter 1986). Secondly, in establishing patterns of past behaviour through interpretation of excavation data.

Undoubtedly, the subjective element is inherent in explanations, which are never beyond doubt or conclusive in any final sense, since individual minds (of the agents) express – through language or material symbolism – their views on their historical and cultural matters, or are approached and construed by individual minds (of the enquirer). However, relatively objective standards can always be achieved, depending on the investigator's competence, skill and proficiency; in other words, on his or her ability to empathize and to translate properly, and to confirm his or her assertions by means of probabilistic reasoning. Yet on many occasions, for a truly comprehensive explanation, there will be a need for hypothetico-deductive testing and for additional etic information based on observation–behavioural evidence. This last requirement marks the point where the two approaches converge. Of course, the explanatory procedure may occasionally start the other way round, that is from the outside. Again, however, the same principle of complementarity will prevail. Both methods may coexist, and there is not just room, but a proper place, for each, depending on the particular kinds of questions asked.

Conclusion

The pragmatically oriented pluralism advocated here can be summarized in the following way. There should not be any radical distinction between different frames of reference, such as between seeing an alien culture or period in its own terms versus our terms or categories. In an adequate explanatory practice any imposition of the latter must be avoided, whereas alien utterances and behaviour must be incorporated into categories comprehensible to us. Also, rules already indigenous to our practice must be reformulated on the basis of native rules. By assimilating instances from other stocks, we will bring their intentions, beliefs and actions under the same family of rules, which in principle both investigator and participant can use. Thus, by drawing together and assimilating material rules of intelligibility from different cultural settings, we will reach a truly trans-historical and cross-cultural understanding.

Such an assimilationist model at the cognitive level implies the necessity for a compromise between the extreme positions of behaviourism or objectivism, on the one hand, and existential phenomenalism or contextualism, on the other hand. This leads to a comprehensive and opportunistic pluralism asserting that the best views are the eclectic ones; that is, the theories which will prove to be genuinely heuristic, leading to the discovery of significant functional relationships having to do with human life as it is.

Acknowledgements

This chapter owes much to Professor Jim Bell and to Dr Ian Hodder, both for encouragement and constructive criticism. Mr Peter Lee has also offered useful suggestions.

References

Baier, A. 1985. *Postures of the mind: essays on mind and morals*. London: Methuen.
Barnes, B. & D. Bloor 1982. Relativism, rationalism and the sociology of knowledge. In *Rationality and relativism*, M. Hollis & S. Lukes (eds), 21–47. Oxford: Blackwell.
Bell, J. 1986. Methodological individualism in cognitive archaeology. Theoretical Archaeology Group Conference, London, 15–17 December.
Berlin, I. 1954. *Historical inevitability. Auguste Comte Memorial Trust Lecture No. 4*. Oxford: Oxford University Press.
Bock, K. 1980. *Human nature and history: a response to sociobiology*. New York: Columbia University Press.
Collingwood, R. G. 1946. *The idea of history*. Oxford: Oxford University Press.
Davidson, D. 1980. *Essays on actions and events*. Oxford: Clarendon Press.
Dilthey, W. 1964. *Pattern and meaning in history*. New York: Harper & Row.
Dray, W. 1964. *Philosophy of history*. Englewood Cliffs, New Jersey: Prentice-Hall.
Feleppa, R. 1986. Emics, etics, and social objectivity. *Current Anthropology* **27**, 243–55.
Feyerabend, P. 1978. *Science in a free society*. London: New Left Books.
Gellner, E. 1982. Relativism and universals. In M. Hollis & S. Lukes (eds), *Rationality and relativism*, 181–200. Oxford: Blackwell.
Hall, R. L. 1977. An anthropological perspective for eastern United States prehistory. *American Antiquity* **42**, 499–518.
Hampshire, S. 1982. *Thought and action*. London: Chatto & Windus.
Hanks, C. & B. Winter 1986. Local knowledge and ethnoarchaeology: an approach to Dene settlement systems. *Current Anthropology* **27**, 272–5.
Harris, M. 1968. *The rise of anthropological theory*. New York: Crowell.

Harris, M. 1976. History and significance of the emic–etic distinction. *Annual Review of Anthropology* **5**, 329–50.
Harris, M. 1979. *Cultural materialism: the struggle for a science of culture*. New York: Random House.
Hempel, K. 1965. *Aspects of scientific explanation and other essays in philosophy of science*. New York: Free Press.
Hollis, M. 1982. The social destruction of reality. In *Rationality and relativism*, M. Hollis & S. Lukes (eds), 67–86. Oxford: Blackwell.
Hollis, M. & S. Lukes (eds) 1982. *Rationality and relativism*. Oxford: Blackwell.
Kay, P. 1970. Some theoretical implications of ethnographic semantics. *American Anthropological Association Bulletin* **3**, 19–34.
Kuhn, T. S. 1964. *The structure of scientific revolutions*. Chicago: University of Chicago Press.
Leone, M. P. 1981. The relationship between artifacts and the public in outdoor history museums. *Annals of the New York Academy of Sciences* **376**, 301–14.
Lukes, S. 1982. Relativism in its place. In *Rationality and relativism*, M. Hollis & S. Lukes (eds), 261–305. Oxford: Blackwell.
Martin, R. 1977. *Historical explanation: re-enactment and practical inference*. Cornell University Press.
Newton-Smith, W. 1982. Relativism and the possibility of interpretation. In *Rationality and Relativism*, M. Hollis & S. Lukes (eds), 106–22. Oxford: Blackwell.
Renfrew, C. 1982. *Towards an archaeology of mind: an inaugural lecture*. Cambridge: Cambridge University Press.
Renfrew, C. 1986. The mental map as a theoretical entity. Theoretical Archaeology Group Conference, London, 15–17 December.
Rogers, C. R. 1964. Toward a science of the person. In *Behaviorism and phenomenology*, T. Wann (ed.), 109–40. Chicago: University of Chicago Press.
Smith, P. & O. R. Jones 1986. *The philosophy of mind: an introduction*. Cambridge: Cambridge University Press.
Wann, T. W. (ed.) 1964. *Behaviorism and phenomenology: contrasting bases for modern psychology*. Chicago: University of Chicago Press.

7 *Bark capes, arrowheads and Concorde: on social representations of technology*

PIERRE LEMONNIER

The technological activity of societies always brings into play a combination of four elements: matter on which an action is directed; objects ('tools' or 'means of work', including the human body itself); gestures and movements organized in operational sequences; and a specific 'knowledge', conscious or unconscious, that may be expressed or not. These elements comprise a system, and are the basis of the diverse technologies in any given society (Gille 1978, Lemonnier 1983).

That archaeologists recover only a small part of a technological system in no way lessens the fact that all these elements are required for the formulation of an anthropological theory of material culture (or 'technological systems', or 'forces of production'). It would be absurd and disastrous for palaeozoological studies to forget that fossil fish were once in water. Indeed, without the gestures which move it, without the matter on which it acts, and without the knowledge involved in its use, an artefact – the everyday bread of archaeologists – is as strange as a fish without water.

The concept of a technological *system* should then be the starting point for any tentative social theory of material culture. In short, the anthropology of technology is the study of the relationships between technological systems and society, with two requirements. The first requirement is to beware of forgetting that these relationships are not one way: they should be studied through the *reciprocal* effects of a technological system and the social system of which it is a part. The second requirement is that the variations in material culture which hold our attention should not only be the so-called 'stylistic' ones, those dealing with technological traits aimed mainly to communicate information, but also those concerned with the most physical aspects of material culture, i.e. those first involved in the action on matter or energy.

It is obvious that technological systems have reciprocal relationships with the social systems to which they belong. As emphasized by Mauss (1983), technological phenomena are full social phenomena, a conclusion that leads to questions concerning the social dimensions of technologies themselves. Also, one should not just consider the various *constraints* that technologies have on a society. One approach focuses on those constraints which deal with the most material conditions of reproduction of a society, based on an inventory and study of the productivity (output approach). The notion of 'level of forces of production' has been the most sterile aspect of this approach. Other social constraints deal with the bringing into play of forces of production, especially those resulting from particular social relations of production. In fact, in the first approach one only asks what a society can produce, at which cost and with which means of action on matter. In the second approach the material context of human social life is only taken into consideration through the relationships that take place between individuals or social groups when they use these technologies: the types of cooperation, the sexual division of labour, the conditions of access to means of production, etc.

Both of these approaches in term of constraints are definitely necessary. Nevertheless, they both take into account only the *effects* of technological actions on society. Of course, when reading economic anthropology, one suspects that material culture, technologies, are certainly produced and used by human beings; but the social dimension of technologies – i.e. in what aspect they are social phenomena – is not considered. With a very few exceptions, technologies are always considered as a *given*, the nature and organization of which remain unknown.

Thus, moving from the old tradition of identifying discontinuities in material culture with particular social groups, archaeology now investigates the social conditions of the appearance, and use, of material culture. This is the focus of 'symbolic' archaeology. Unfortunately, most often it is the 'stylistic' features that are considered, not the more 'functional' aspects of action on matter (quotation marks remind us that style has also a function). The question of which dimensions of material culture are meaningful is correctly asked, but the answers to it seem to me to be overly simplistic. The necessity for a 'contextual' archaeology is obvious, but very often goes along with hasty generalizations of results that are as much contextual. Thus, it is indeed an important achievement to demonstrate, in particular cases, that relationships may exist, between particular aspects of material culture and particular features of social organization, especially when these results are through actual fieldwork, thereby adding to our knowledge of living technological systems. However, every social theory of material culture should *also*, necessarily, explain the specificity of these relationships, why they exist in the given case, *and* try to understand cases when they do *not* exist. Contextual archaeology will long have to fight with counterexamples.

The examination of the social dimensions of production and transformations of material culture suggests that societies sometimes choose between equivalent technological answers. Sackett's (1982) research has led him to somewhat similar conclusions. He also suggests, unfortunately without developing the idea, that style and function may be two aspects of the same question, considered from two different but complementary points of view. We shall see that a similar proposition constitutes one of the basic questions of an ethnology of technological systems. We are nevertheless obliged to state that Sackett only considers 'useless' traits, and that style has no function for him, except perhaps that of making the life of archaeologists easier. Still, there are other aspects of technological systems that are accessible to archaeology – the physical dimensions of action on matter and energy, reconstruction of movements and even technological knowledge – which unfortunately have not received adequate attention.

What about ethnologists? Except for piling up objects which merely collect dust, their interest in material culture rarely takes the form of a study of the relationships between technology and society. When it does, it is the effects of technologies on societies which are considered (e.g. that of irrigation, net hunting, etc.), not the social dimension of technologies in themselves. The one exception is that of studies of the immediate informational aspect of material culture. Types of buildings, canoes or pipes have long been mapped to delimit homogeneous 'cultures'. This is a well-known approach in archaeology as well, about which there is not much to comment, because of the paucity of what it can tell us about the social conditions of production of a technological system.

On the other hand, from Bogatyrev (1971) to Wobst (1977) ethnological studies of costume fit more closely to the goals of an anthropology of material culture. The fitting, colour, shape or material of a given piece of clothing have been interpretated as elements of codes communicating social information about the ethnic origin, sex or status of the bearer. Recently, Wiessner has suggested the hypothesis that material culture might play an active role in affirmation of ethnic identity, in terms that the ethno-archaeologist Hodder would not disapprove. Furthermore, she investigated – in my opinion, without finding an answer – the question of the link between the nature of the messages transmitted through traits of material culture and the nature of these traits. The technological features which she considered deal, by definition, solely with the informational dimension of material culture.

On social representations of technological systems: the Anga case

At first glance the 70 000 Anga seem to belong to the same 'culture'. They are divided into 30 or so local groups speaking related languages (although not mutually intelligible) and sharing the same kind of social organization: acephalous tribes with patrilineal clans, age classes and a strong male dominance. All are horticulturalists of sweet potato, taro and banana, and raise semi-domestic pigs. However, if one has a close look, things display less uniformity than appears at first glance, in social organization as well as in technological systems (Lemonnier 1982, 1984a, 1986).

Ranging from the shape of grass skirts to the fitting of headdresses, some traits of Anga material culture display 'stylistic' differences, immediately visible, that refer more or less directly to ethnic identity, age class, sex or status of the bearer. However, variations are also observed in domains of technological action in which one would assume, wrongly, that more uniformity would be found. Among the Anga – as, no doubt, in other places – it is not only traits of dress or decoration that vary from one group to another, but also for example the way in which people move red-hot stones or brands without burning their hands, protect themselves from cold or open a new garden in the forest. Another observation is that, as far as we know, many of these variants are independent of the ecological, and in a certain way the technological, context in which they appear. It is thus impossible to correlate climatic features with the degree of protection against cold or humidity offered by the various types of houses encountered (single- or double-walled), or with the use of beaten bark to protect one's body: some Kapau go with a naked torso in one of the most humid and cold places in the region, whereas other Anga are wrapped in one or more bark-capes, although they live in a far better climate. According to which bank of a river they inhabit, some people use a given type of pig-trap (dead-fall trap) while others do not, although they all share the same type of ecosystem and are familiar with the making and use of this particular type of trap. Tribes permanently at war with each other would either use or leave aside quadrangular barbed arrows.

Even horticulture, which one might assume takes similar forms throughout huge areas of New Guinea, varies astonishingly from place to place. In seven highland societies which are comparable from the point of view of the species grown as well as the ecosystems exploited, and which all use the same three key operations when opening a new garden – i.e. burning of cut trees and shrubs, building a fence to protect the garden from semi-domestic and wild pigs, and planting seeds and shoots – the sequence of opening a garden changes according to the society in which it takes place. Thus one will find burning–fencing–planting among the Baruya and Watchakes, burning–planting–fencing among the Langimar, Simbari and Yoyue, and fencing–burning–planting among the Menyeand Kapau. Certainly we are now quite far from nose decorations and bead necklaces! Here the subject is no longer status marking or ethnic identity, but burning, death by haemorrhage and torn bowels (barbed arrows), and pneumonia (no bark-cape on shoulders), not to speak of possible variation in the productivity of hunting or agriculture.

Their dealing with the most physical dimension of material culture and their independence from the ecological context in which they are used is not the only interesting feature of these variations. They also form *combinations* – i.e. sets of traits that show concomitant variability – the distribution of which is a *non*-random one, although these traits are *technologically* (physically) *independent*.

As far as we know, there is no compelling technological (material) link, direct or indirect, between the shape of an Anga arrow, the transverse section of the bow which shoots it, the ground-plan of the house where the hunter lives, the use or non-use of bark-capes or the order of the operations for opening a new garden. Nevertheless, among the Anga these various technological traits share approximately the same non-random distributions. In other words, everything happens *as if* the local forms of these physically independent technological traits were systematically associated with one another. Having eliminated any simple ecological or 'geographical' determinism, since in this respect any of the traits considered could appear anywhere, under any of a variety of forms, there are only three ways of explaining the observed distribution: (a) to assume that the distribution is random, even though the probability of such a pattern arising by chance is so low that this hypothesis has to be rejected; (b) to attribute the distribution to historical factors, which is a way of sending the technological or general social logic of the phenomena observed back to an inaccessible past; or (c) to suggest the hypothesis that societies select an 'ideal' (Godelier 1986), and sometimes arbitrary (from a physical point of view), ordering of the technological domain.

This last hypothesis means that social representations of technologies exist that go beyond 'mere' know-how. In other words, like other social phenomena, technologies are also, in part, systems of meaning. What could be the function and mode of functioning of such a system? I only have *partial* explanations at hand which elucidate the variations of single technological traits, but I do not yet see the logical links between different traits even though they often clearly co-vary with each other.

For instance, it would be possible to consider some of these technological features as ethnic markers, and say that the shape of their grass-skirts, or of their bow and arrows, is a way through which the Anga mark their differences. This hypothesis is certainly true in part. It nevertheless leaves us with a series of difficult questions: why should Anga ethnic identities be expressed by a given artefact (grass-skirt, headdress, rattan-belt, etc.), and not by another one, or through body postures, or other means external to material culture?

The intertribal division of labour, which is necessary to maintain trade relations between groups (Lemonnier 1981) is a possible explanation of other particular variations in Anga material culture. This is certainly the reason why, for example, one group specializes in the production of vegetal salt, while others specialize in bark-capes, or bows that the first group might otherwise itself produce. Is this a sufficient reason to link the *use* of beaten-bark to some necessity of intertribal trade? It certainly is not. Another fundamental social phenomenon, the opposition of male and female worlds (Lemonnier 1984b), plays a role here in the use of bark products for ropes, skirts and capes, expressed through the choice of vegetal species, the sex of the producers, and the age and sex of the users.

Ethnic identity, intertribal trade and male–female relationships: here are three partial explanations of the Anga technological system, but how can we go from one explanation to another? Which of these relationships actually accounts for the variations? Again, I do not know the answers to these questions, and it will take many more years of fieldwork to try to understand the logic of Anga social representations of technologies, especially by listening to what the Anga say of their material culture.

These data lead me to suggest, following Hodder (1982) and Lévi-Strauss (1973), the hypothesis that material culture also works as a system of meaning, but I would do it in quite different terms. The aspect of meaning is not confined just to traits which directly carry meaning; it also applies to those technological traits directly involved in action in the material world. Moreover, I consider that this dimension of meaning rarely takes simple forms. Contrary to Hodder (1982, pp. 68–74), for instance, I do not think that the decorations on a calabash express social relations in any simple, direct manner.

A new question arises, then: is it possible to predict which traits of material culture will be used in a system of meaning and which traits will be left out? In other respects nobody doubts that the 'ideal' ordering of the technological domain in terms of social representations must be compatible with other social relations, with other social phenomena, but what are the underlying causal factors, or the logic of this ordering? Nobody knows.

Because they deal with action on matter, a domain of constraints *par excellence*, technologies might seem to be outside the domain of the arbitrary. Although there is considerable range for arbitrary choices in particular domains of technology, there nevertheless is considerably less latitude for arbitariness than in the world of myths, for instance. The crucial question of an anthropology of technological systems then becomes: given the existence of social representations of technologies, up to what point do they arbitrarily constrain choices made by societies among possible modes of action on matter? These social representations have an obvious influence on 'style', that is to say on those technological traits that carry immediate information and are non-utilitarian in physical action on matter. Up to what point can they play a role in the choice of features directly involved in action on matter, and thus influence the transformations of technological systems and societies? In other words, are there domains of material culture more prone to arbitrary variability than others? This question pinpoints an issue of central concern to all scholars who are interested in developing a social theory of material culture, be they ethnologists or archaeologists.

A glance at aeroplanes: more social representations of technologies

The following case deals with a particular technology of our modern industrial societies. It shows that representations of technologies play a part even in our 'high-technology' world, and illustrates the question: up to what point can representations of technology play a part? This example is about the history of aviation, a domain in which we think the constraints of the natural world have a particularly heavy weight[1] and a domain which has been handled by highly specialized talented engineers since the beginning.[2] An aeroplane would not seem to be a technology with much latitude for technological choices except for those that had been previously planned, and only its 'decoration' would be likely to bear stylistic information (figures and letters for identification, airline logo and upholstery). As in the case of an adze or a bear-trap, the shape of a plane expresses several of its physical functions, particularly those adapted to flying and carrying a payload: wings for lift; fuselage for payload; engines for movement; ailerons, fin, rudder and elevators to stabilize and direct the flight; etc. Yet, if one looks at the history of aviation, and considers only successful aircraft which flew and met their designers' expectations, the diversity of technological answers is striking.

Consider, for example, the location of engines on propeller-driven civilian transports, already a limited sample: the propeller can be tractive or propulsive,

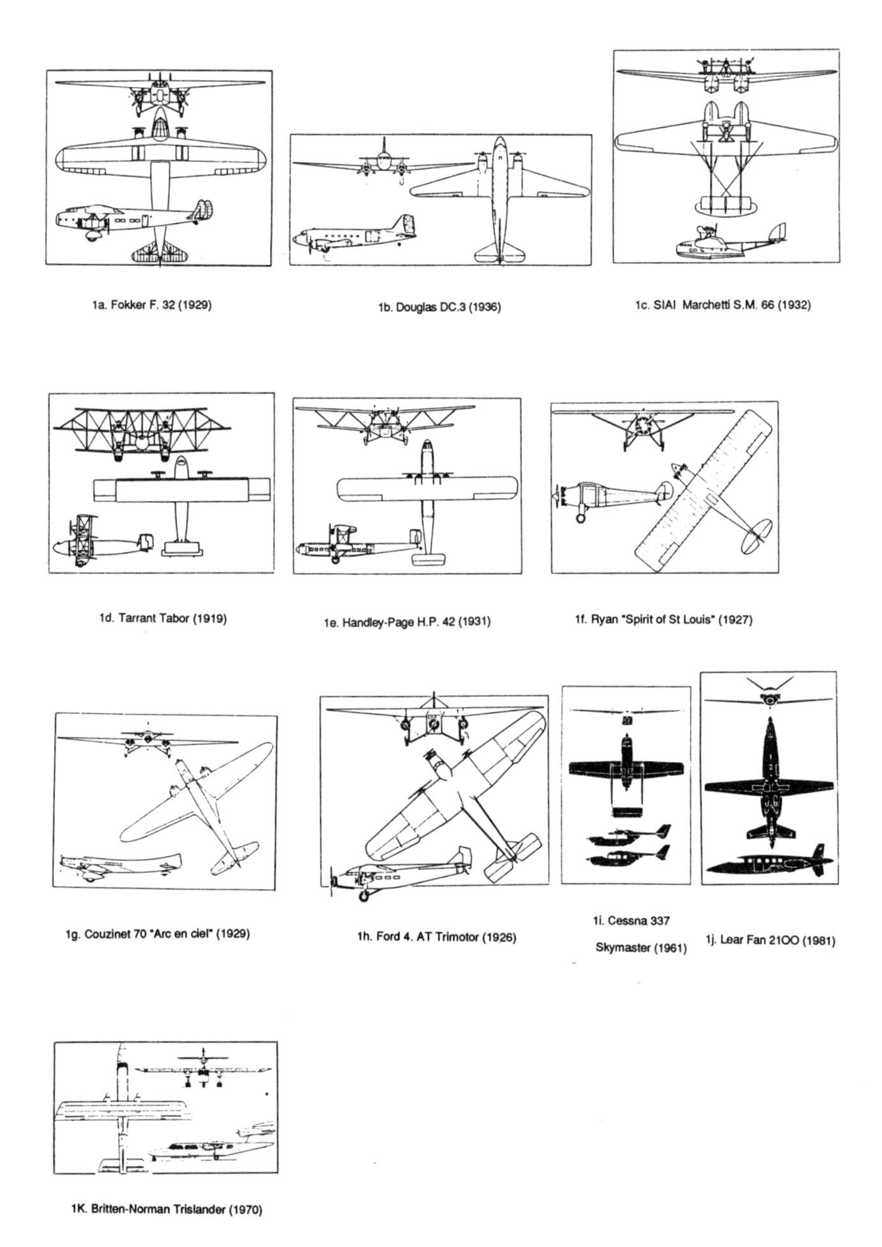

Figure 7.1 Location of engines on propeller aeroplanes.

the engine(s) can be located under the wing (Fig. 7.1a), inboard on the wing (Fig. 7.1b), above the wing (Fig. 7.1c), between the wings of a multiplane (Fig. 7.1d), in each of the wings of a multiplane (Fig. 7.1e), at the bow of the fuselage (Fig. 7.1f), in the fuselage and inboard on the wings (Fig. 7.1g), in the fuselage and under the wings (Fig. 7.1h), at the bow and at the back of the fuselage (Fig. 7.1i), at the back of the fuselage (Fig. 7.1j) or inboard on the wings and included in the fin (Fig. 7.1k). Engines number from one to eight, and even to 12 (Fig. 7.2)!

A comparable diversity of technological answers is found for other functions as well: for the wings (shape, location and number), the tail-plane (with or without, at the back or at the front of the body), the landing-gear, etc. Passengers also are sometimes found in quite surprising places: in the floats of a floatplane (Fig. 7.3a), in two fuselages (Fig. 7.3b) and even in the wings, partially (Fig. 7.3c) or totally, if we include the once-planned civilian version of a Northrop bomber (Fig. 7.3d).

In order to narrow the scope of possible variations, we shall now focus on a single type of plane: the high-winged twin-engine light transport (less than ten passengers) aeroplane. Figure 7.4 shows clear differences between aircraft designs. The general case is an aeroplane with flat or in-line engine, tractive propeller and body reaching the tail-plane. However, we also find three propulsive propellers (Piaggio P136 and P166, and Querandi), two radial engines (Antonov, Grumman) and two short fuselages (Miles and Antonov), not to mention the flying-boat versions (Grumman and Piaggio P136), the use of turboprops or the strange body-located engines of the Dornier.

Thus, when one narrows the scope of discussion, new fields of variability appear, which is a common feature of studies of technology. Nevertheless, all variations discussed so far deal with functional aspects of the aeroplane, and not with style or the communication of information between social groups. Every technological trait so far mentioned contributes fundamentally to the functioning of the aircraft – that is, its ability to move a payload in the air. *A priori* none of these traits marks any particular social or ethnic identity, nor does it carry any kind of information except, perhaps for a specialist, as an indirect clue of the designer's particular school of thinking. These variations do not even give clear information on a given age of aeronautics since, with few exceptions (multiplanes, great number of engines and passengers located in floats), all of the designs mentioned so far are still commonly used. All of these technological features nevertheless show great diversity, which does not (or did not) prevent these planes from regular flying. Indeed, some of them flew faster and further, and with more safety and less expense, than others, but all are (or have been) efficient technological artefacts coping with their users' requirements.

Each designer is certainly convinced that he or she has found a better solution to various design problems than his or her colleagues, and there have been obvious improvements as a result of the growth of technological know-how. Yet these improvements hardly concern the general choices of location reviewed here. Instead, they concern particular domains. In addition to relative cuts in costs, these include regular ameliorations in aerodynamic efficiency and

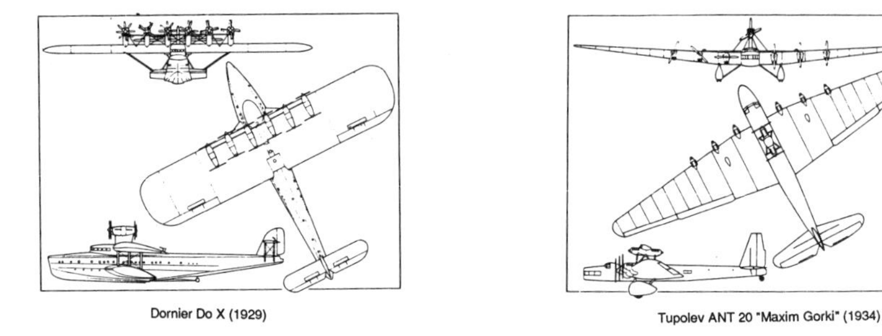

Figure 7.2 Giant multi-engined aeroplanes.

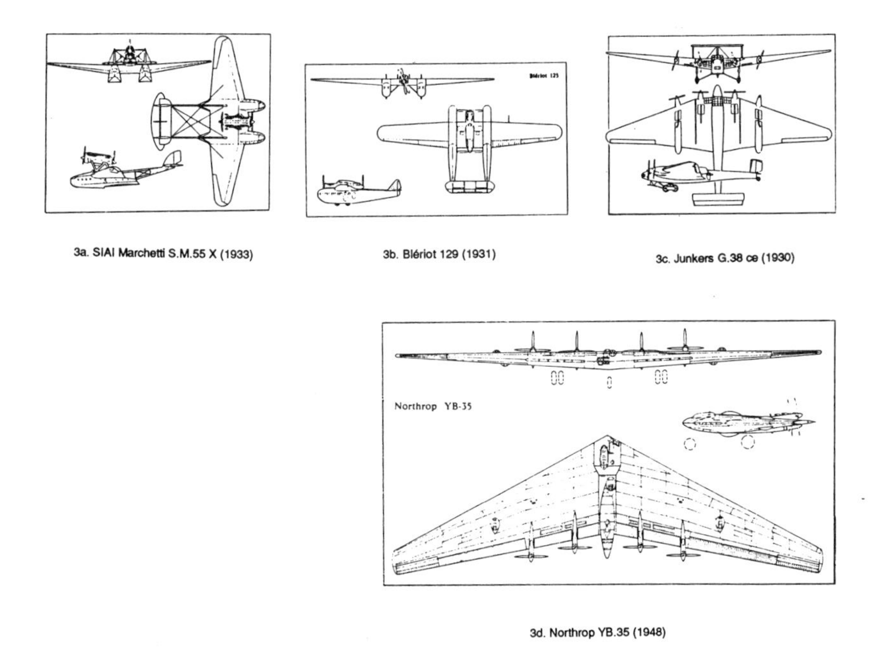

Figure 7.3 Location of passengers.

weight of aircraft, as well as the power output and fuel consumption of engines, and of course safety. They led to gains in speed, range and capacity, and to reductions in accidents and costs.

Thus, for example, although first designed in 1910 by Dunne (Fig. 7.5a), no 'flying-wing' has yet reached series production,[3] in spite of their obvious advantages in several respects: suppression of fuselage and tail-plane, possibly leading to aircraft that cannot be stalled or spun (Wooldridge 1985); and important savings in 'structural' weight. Cutting down the weight of an aircraft would allow iteither to carry the same payload further, by having more fuel inboard, or to increase the payload for a given distance. Locating the horizontal

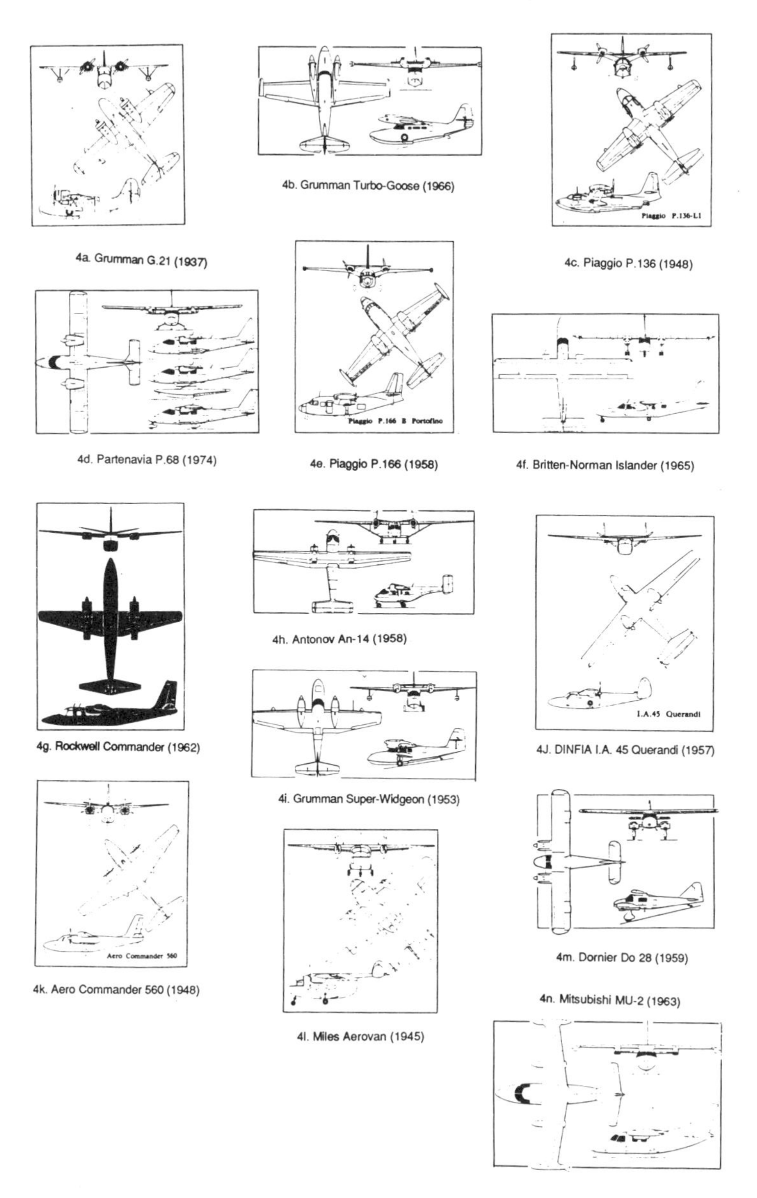

Figure 7.4 Light high-wing twin-engined aeroplanes.

stabilizer in front of the main supporting wing ('canard' plane) also diminishes the weight of an aircraft, for comparable lift ability. Although they date from 1909, and even from the Wright brothers' 'Flyers' gliders, canard foreplanes are still only being used on a few fighters, and on amateur do-it-yourself planes (Rutan VariEze and Quickie Aircraft Corporation Starship) or as projects

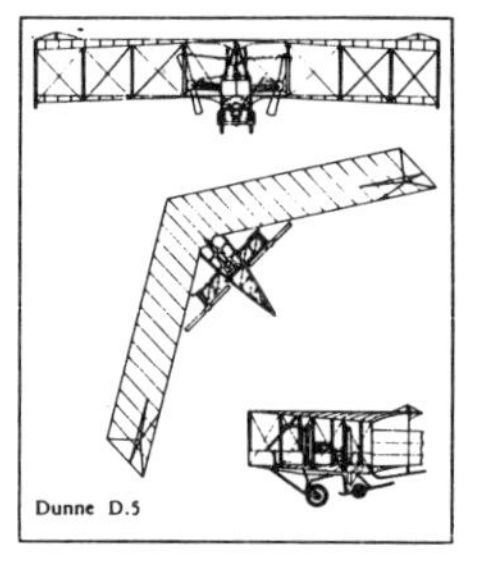

a. Dunne D5 Flying-wing (1910)

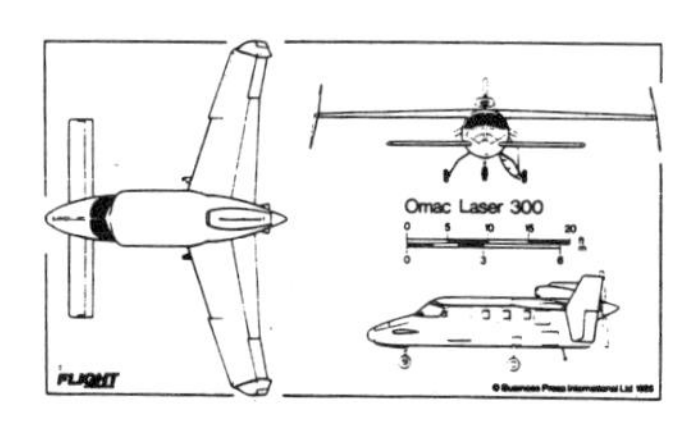

b. Laser 300 "canard" plane.

Figure 7.5 Dunne D5 Flying-wing (1910) and Omac Laser 300 'canard' aeroplane.

(Avtek 400, Gates–Piaggio Omac Laser 300 – Fig. 7.5b). Although a limited case, one should note that 'wingless' planes are even more rare (Lifting body, Martin Mariette X24).

We must wonder, then, why particular technological features are held back by aeronautic designers. Are these formulae or devices dismissed because of their inefficiency, or for other, non-physical reasons, in the realm of fashion or of the ideas people have of what an aeroplane is 'supposed' to look like? Are they representations of this particular technology that have nothing to do with the physical or mechanical principles that aviation brings into play, or with economic considerations?

Obviously one cannot make any design fly. Laws of aerodynamics and resistance of materials create constraints with which designers and builders have to deal, using the know-how of the time. Thus, Phillips' Multiplane (1904) was a complete failure (Fig. 7.6a), even though the same inventor was to make the first powered (and controlled?) flight ever to take place in England (1907, 157 m), with a more complex version of engine-driven venetian blinds (shutters) (Fig. 7.6b). Aircraft with persienne-wings in series had *a fortiori* no future, as Count Caproni was to learn to his cost in 1921, with the failure of his Triple Hydro Plane (Fig. 7.7) (Taylor 1981, pp. 8–13; *Air Classic Special Report* 1985, pp. 72–7). Similarly, showing apparently everything to be successful – except it was flying in the *opposite* direction to what its look might classically lead one to imagine – Nixon's Nipper (Fig. 7.8) was also a loud failure (Taylor 1981, pp. 9, 11), yet, Santos-Dumont had been the first man ever to fly more than 25 m with his 14 bis, a biplane aircraft sharing with the Nipper the use of a canard foreplane and propulsive rear engine. The Multiplane, the Triple Hydro Plane and the Nipper were just too close to the margin of aeronautics laws.

On the other hand, there are some aircraft that had no success for reasons other than their ability to fly. Here I do not mean planes that were outclassed by their opponents, or whose original purpose was no longer of interest when they were ready for series production (a common situation for military aircraft). Rather, I am now considering aircraft that are as efficient as, and sometimes more efficient than, their opponents. Two planes already mentioned

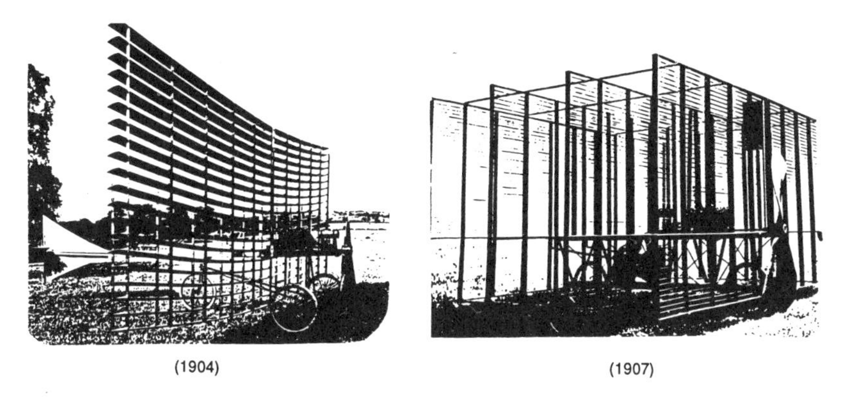

Figure 7.6 Phillips Multiplane.

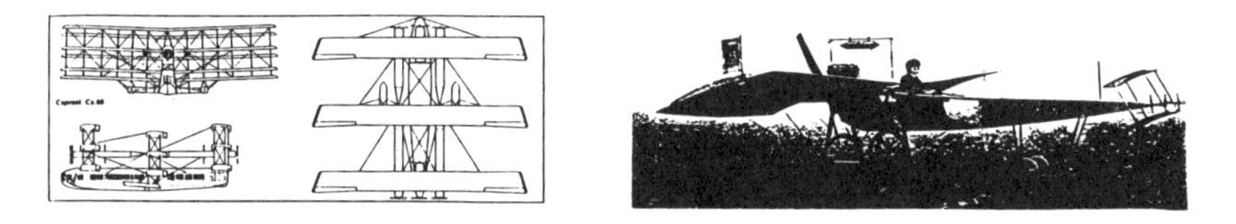

Figure 7.7 Caproni Ca 60 Transaero (1921). **Figure 7.8** Dixon Nipper No. 1.

illustrate this. Cessna's C137 Skymaster (or 'push–pull') and Mitsubishi's MU–2 were both failures in spite of their unquestionable qualities, and were possibly even superior to similar aircraft. In the case of trouble with one of its two engines, their longitudinal location maintains the Cessna's lateral stability, whereas ordinary twin-engine planes have a tendency to spin, with obvious fatal consequences if this happens during take-off. Notwithstanding this basic quality, mistakes in the use of the aircraft (e.g. attempts to take off on only one engine), as well as its unusual appearance and, mainly, the kind of safety given by this aircraft, which did not fit the male image that a pilot has of a twin-engine,[4] made the Cessna C137 a commercial failure.

Mitsubishi's MU–2 was also an 'odd-looking machine' (Fig. 7.4n). However, once again the aircraft was definitely a successful piece of technology, as shown by its ability to take off from short grass airstrips as well as its top speed, which outpassed by 100 knots (180 km/h^{-1}) its best competitors. On the other hand, its small wings (which allowed its high speed) and a particular use of high-lift devices (flaps) gave it an unusual silhouette and required new piloting procedures which, together, led to its commercial failure: 'Along the way the MU–2 became controversial because it is unique' (MacMcClellan 1985, pp. 40–2). These two contemporary examples show how the social representations of the aircraft itself, on the one hand, and the weight of routine in using it (i.e. the technological knowledge of the time), on the other hand, led to the dismissal of shapes which, although quite odd, were perfectly adapted to their purpose. In this case skilled technician–users (the pilots) were the ones who turned down these aircraft. Moreover, no aeroplane-maker today is likely to re-introduce these particular bright ideas.

Designers themselves, at least most of them, only produce machines that fit their own representation of what an aircraft should look like. In the introduction to his *Fantastic Flying Machines*, Taylor writes: 'While a few prove dead-ends technically, others were inspired, only their radically *unusual appearances* preventing series production' (Taylor 1981, p. 7, emphasis added).

In the same way, D. Kucheman, the head of the aerodynamics department in the Royal Aircraft Establishment between 1966 and 1971, when the yet unseen shape of the supersonic transport (SST) Concorde was designed, talks of 'the traditional reluctance to accept novel concepts on their technical merits' (in *The aerodynamic design of aircrafts*, quoted by Owen 1982, p. 39). The particular design that Kucheman suggested violated a basic principle of aircraft design, the law proposed by G. Cailey (1796–1865) according to which each main function of a plane has to be effected by separate components. Kucheman was proposing a partial integration of wings and fuselage, so that the latter would contribute to the total lift. Though not incorporated into the Concorde, this proposal was employed in today's Rockwell's B1 bomber, a plane designed for the greatest possible efficiency. The civilian SST illustrates this last observation: the higher the performance demands are, the narrower is the scope of variability. We have to keep in mind that in the beginning of the 1960s, when the SST project was taking shape, it was still a critical and dangerous exercise to reach supersonic speed, even with a military plane. Although non-pressurized, a way to eliminate the risk of explosive depressurization, American B58 Hustler bombers frequently disintegrated in the air when an engine failed at supersonic speed. One can easily imagine the unparalleled difficulties encountered by the engineers who wished to fly 100 passengers safely across the Atlantic at Mach 2 in a pressurized cabin! Facing new and extremely difficult problems – designing a shape that would reduce the heat resulting from kinetic energy, but, at the same time, handle well at low speed; withstanding tremendous differences in pressure between the interior and exterior of the cabin; cooling of the cabin interior and 'systems' – the scope of possible designs obviously narrows. For example, multiplanes or fixed landing gear are no longer viable options. The 'slender delta' plane is more compelling at Mach 2 and technological choices now switch to the thousand problems to be solved to make a slender delta SST fly. Figure 7.9 illustrates this convergence of shapes toward a single type when the laws of the physical world, as well as the technological knowledge of the time, leave nothing but a narrow margin within which to manoeuvre.

A comparison between the racing float-planes of the Schneider Coupe (1913–1931) and the best fighters of World War II shows a similar phenomenon of convergence. The search for an optimum between power and speed led, given the time and available technological knowledge, to similar shapes and configurations.

Thus, a look at modern 'high-tech' brings us back to a well-known principle in the ethnology of technology, the weight of *tendance* (tendency) in the words

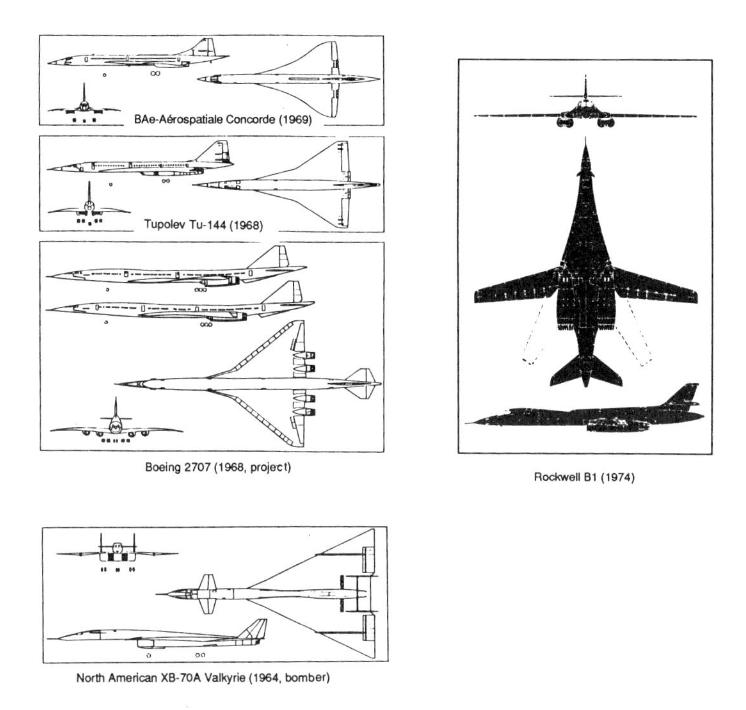

Figure 7.9 Heavy supersonic aeroplanes.

of Leroi-Gourhan (1943: 27). To him, the more a technological feature is concerned with the *premiers degrés du fait* (first degrees of fact) – those dealing with the action on matter and energy toward which a given technology is aimed – the less it is subject to variation. When this technological action takes place among technological principles which are themselves very compelling, the scope of possible variations is narrowed ever further. However, within these limits imposed by the physical world, choices are still possible, the logic of which has nothing to do with the 'objective' knowledge brought into play, or with any style or communication of information. Inboard computers and 'fly by wire' technology have allowed us to fly aircraft that are far more unstable than the flying-wing of the canard plane, for instance. At a time when a 2 or 3 per cent saving in fuel determines the success of an aircraft among airlines, one or the other of these formulae could perhaps lead to an important increase in profits. They are not in any agenda so far. Thus, in 1985, when Boeing presented the design for a 150-passenger canard plane among proposals for other propfan- (transonic propeller) equipped projects, the specialized newspapers immediately suspected a tall story rather than a workable project! Among the possible designs for a propfan plane, the canard has only a small chance of being developed, mainly because such an aircraft does not look like a 'classical' flying machine. Similarly, among the 'stealth' bomber projects of the 1980s, the Northrop flying-wing proposal is said to have been put forward just to trick the Soviets!

The social representations playing a role in these choices refer to domains other than the mere knowledge of the principles of action on the material world. Thus, in our so-called 'technical'(?) and efficient societies, the conception an engineer has of what a given artefact should be is heavily influenced by already existing designs. As Quilici (pers. comm. 1985) put it, 'the first operating artefact congeals the genus, which can only be the sole and good one'. It then takes time for the *tendance* to take over and for new and more-advanced technological shapes to be developed. What about other societies? How much do such social representations weigh on the transformation of the technological systems studied by archaeologists and ethnologists? These are the questions which I suggested earlier, and which have to be asked again and again. The example of modern aeronautics corroborates the existence of forms of technological thought other than those related directly to the physical aspects of action on matter or the stylistic meaning of decoration on artefacts.

Notes

1 Heavier than air, in fact.
2 The image of the designer as a joyous improvisor or 'flying mad man' that we often associate with the ones who made the first 'small step' is an historical untruth. The Wright brothers made minute studies of Octave Chanute's (the designer of many gliders) work, and they had made years of experiments with biplane kites (1899) and gliders (1900–1902) before they succeeded in their first flight 'with engine, of long continuance, and controlled, taking off from a flat terrain', in December 1903 (Hart 1980, pp. 34–9). It is among drawing-boards and patents that aviation was born (Culick 1979, Chadeau 1986).
3 The prototype of the flying-wing of the American aeroplane-maker Northrop goes back to 1928. Facing more-conventional opponents, none of his machines reached series production (Taylor 1981, pp. 34–45, Angelucci & Matricardi 1983, p. 396, Sweetman 1985).
4 'One of the biggest problems in marketing the skymaster was overcoming its image as an airplane for wimps. Centerline thrust was not macho, according to Ted Moody, Cessna's manager of product support and airworthiness' (Thurber 1983, p. 40). It may also be possible that the high level of noise in the cabin did not match the 'class' one expects from such a private plane for businessmen in a hurry.

References

Air Classics Special Report 1985.2. Fabulous Flying Flops.
Angelucci, E. & P. Matricardi (eds) 1983. *L'encyclopédie des avions civils du Monde des origines à nos jours*. Paris: Fernand Nathan.
Bogatyrev, P. 1971 (1937). *The function of folk costume in Moravian Slovakia*. Paris, La Haye: Mouton.
Chadeau, E. 1986. Poids des filières socio-culturelles et nâture de l'invention: l'aéroplàne en France jusqu'en 1908. *L'Année Sociologique* **36**, 93–112.

Culick, F. E. C. 1973. The origins of the first powered, man-carrying airplane. *Scientific American* **241**, 86–100.
Gille, B. 1978. *Histoire des techniques*. Paris: NRF.
Godelier, M. 1986. *The mental and the material*. London: Verso.
Hart, C. 1980. Cerfs-volants et planeurs. In *Encyclopédie de l'Aviation*, 22–39. Paris: CIL.
Hodder, I. 1982. *Symbols in action. Ethnoarchaeological studies of material culture*. Cambridge: Cambridge University Press.
Lemonnier, P. 1981. Le commerce inter-tribal des Anga de Nouvelle-Guinée. *Journal de la Sociétè des Océanistes* **36**(70–1), 39–75.
Lemonnier, P. 1982. Jardins Anga. *Journal d'Agriculture Traditionnelle et de Botanique Appliquée* **29**, 227–45.
Lemonnier, P. 1983. L'étude des systèmes techniques: une urgence en technologie culturelle. *Techniques et Culture* **1**, 1134.
Lemonnier, P. 1984a. L'écorce battue chez les Anga de Nouvelle-Guinée. *Techniques et Culture* **4**, 127–75.
Lemonnier, P. 1984b. La production de sel végétal chez les Anga (Papouasie Nouvelle-Guinée). *Journal d'Agriculture Traditionnelle et de Botanique Appliquée* **21**, 71–126.
Lemonnier, P. 1986. The study of material culture today: towards an anthroplogy of techniques. *Journal of Anthropological Archaeology* **5**, 147–86.
Leroi-Gourhan, A. 1943. *Evolution et techniques. L'homme et la matière*. Paris: Albin Michel.
Lévi-Strauss, Cl. 1973. *Anthropologie structurâle deux*, Ch. 1: *Le champ de l'anthropologie*. Paris: Plon.
MacMcClellan, J. 1985. The odd squad: Mitsubishi MU-2, an odd-looking machine. *Flying* **112**(4), 40–2.
Mauss, M. 1983. Les techniques du corps. In *Sociologie et anthropologie*, M. Mauss (ed.), 365–86. Paris: PUF.
Owen, K. 1982. *Concorde. New shape in the sky*. London: Jane's Publishing Company, in co-operation with the Science Museum.
Sackett, J. 1982. Approaches to style in lithic archaeology. *Journal of Anthropological Archaeology* **1**, 59–112.
Sweetman, B. 1985. Avions indétectables. *Interavia* **11**, 1207–12.
Taylor, M. J. H. 1981. *Fantastic flying machines*. London: Jane's Publishing Company.
Thurber, M. 1985. The odd squad: C337. *Flying* **112**(4), 37–40.
Wobst, M. 1977. Stylistic behavior and information exchange. *Papers for the Director: research essays in honor of James B. Griffin*, C. E. Cleland (ed.), 317–42. New York: Academic Press.
Wooldridge, E. T. 1985. *Winged Wonders. The Story of the Flying Wings*. Washington: Smithsonian Institution Press.

15 *The artefact as abbreviated act: a social interpretation of material culture*

MILES RICHARDSON

The objective of post-processual archaeology (Hodder 1985), if one may so suggest, is the same as interpretive anthropology in general, to confront the question of meaning, not meaning in a passive, structuralist sense, but meaning in an active, experiential sense: how we, flesh and blood, two-legged primates make sense, how together we construct a reality in which *we*, creatures of mindless nature, *are*.

The secret to the capacity to make meaning lies in the artefact. Beginning as an object that is out there, embedded and indistinguished from the rest of nature, fixed first by sight and then touched by the magic of the hand, the artefact, in its artifice, becomes a 'collapsed act', a structure whose response is given in advance (Mead 1972, pp. 121–2, 368–70). Thus, more than a geological specimen and more too than a technological device, the artefact is a document that describes our past, an image that reflects our present, and a sign that calls us into the future.

This consideration of how artefacts achieve social meaning, how they constitute the world in which we are, forms itself around the social behaviourism of George Herbert Mead. This chapter begins with a brief overview of the Meadian position, moves to a more detailed accounting of Mead's concept of the act, relates that interpretation to the experiential world of the Spanish-American plaza, and concludes with a note on the relevance of the argument to post-processual archaeology.

Social behaviouralism

An American pragmatist who taught philosophy at the University of Chicago during its rise to prominence in the early 20th century, George Herbert Mead (1863–1931) is an especially congenial figure for anthropologists. His derivation of the self and the mind from social interaction, and his insistence that both self and mind are essentially linguistic, symbolic phenomena, and consequently both have emerged only in the species who talks, are ontogenetic recapitulations of the human phylogenetic record.

Another way in which Mead is congenial to anthropologists is that in contrast with visual, cerebral thinkers, he is a tactual, muscular philosopher (Miller 1973a, pp. 103–4). The hand, according to Mead, approaches the brain in importance in accounting for emergence of self and mind. Like other animals, we humans live within the rich flow of sensory experience. Unlike other animals, however, such as the dog, which moves unconsciously from sensing his environment to consuming it, we stop the flow with our hands; we manipulate the object we have extracted from the flow, and from the resistance the object provides, we reflect upon the encounter.

Still another manner in which Mead is compatible with anthropology is his holism. He avoids the 'phenomenalistic fallacy' of positing a self before social behaviour; similarly, he shuns the 'behaviouristic fallacy' of reducing consciousness to physical stimuli (Miller 1973b). Consequently, for Mead, 'objective reality cannot be defined as wholly external to the organism (materialism) or wholly internal (subjective idealism), but rather it is the product of organism–environment interaction' (Lewis 1981, p. 132).[1]

The act

From the Meadian perspective 'the unit of existence is the act . . .' (Mead 1972, p. 65). In the reality of acting, the dependence of the organism on the environment is causal. At the same time the dependence of the environment on the organism is perceptual. Nature acts on us; however, through our acts we define nature. This reciprocity is existence.

Among organisms the reality of the act is the gesture. This is especially true among sexually reproducing species in which the continuing of life itself is dependent on the appropriate response. The gesture is even more characteristic of mammals, and our own gregarious, primate order. In the 'conversation of gestures' animals respond to each other's responses. The meaning that a gesture has is in the response that another animal makes. The response of the other animal separates the gesture of the first from being that animal's exclusive, private experience. The gesturing is becoming social.

Among animals other than humans, gesturing remains strictly an exchange. In a dog fight the dogs are *not* giving voice to their emotions; they are responding to one another's snarls. A snarl is a response to an earlier snarl and is itself a stimulus for a return snarl. The snarling is social-like, but it has not become a social object. It has not become an artefact (Strauss 1964, pp. 156–7).

Among humans the conversation of gestures becomes objectified so that the conversation, now cast into vocal gestures – that is, speech – assumes a position at a distance from the interior of the speakers. This distance permits the speakers to gesture to themselves as they gesture to one another, and in so doing become objects of their own gesturing.

Being objects of our own gesturing, we humans develop a self. The possession of a self permits us to interpret our own acts from the standpoint of one another. As we speak to each other we assume the role that the other is playing, and from that perspective we interpret our own responses. From that interpretation we, together, assume selves relevant to the course of acting engaged in, and distinct from other courses of action and our other selves.

In interpreting our actions from the position of one another, we distinguish between self and other. Together, as a group, we interpret our responses not simply as a series of individual selves, but from a more comprehensive, generalized other. We transform the flow of social experience into an object and, from the position of that object, we define the course of action we are in. We objectify the experience of social interaction to form a generalized other from which we then construct an interpretation of our actions. In the same manner we distinguish between self and other, we distinguish the generalized other we are presently constructing from previous and future generalized others. In this process the generalized other becomes a constellation of acts collapsed into symbols which then inform our behaviour and give it particular character.

In the formation of the generalized other we determine the character of our actions and, Mead argues, in this determination, physical objects play a defining role.

Essentially Mead considers the act, the unit of our existence, as having a perceptual, a manipulatory and a consummatory phase. As we act we look ahead into the future and perceive a world that is there. However, in the attitude of our perception, objects are never simply visual things, but are indications, given our initial moments, as to how we should respond. As we look ahead we reach with our hands, and with our hands we bring the future into the present: 'The reality of what we see is what we can handle' (Mead 1972, p. 105).

In the manipulatory phase the object that is now in our hands and in our present defines our responses. As we interpret self from the perspective of the other, so we also take the perspective of the object: 'The stone defines the hand', as surely as the hand defines itself (Mead 1972, p. 186). Similarly, as we interpret the group from the position of the generalized other, so too we define our acts from the perspective of objects generalized (one might say contextualized) into a setting. As generalized, the setting becomes a constellation of acts collapsed into symbols which, like the generalized other, inform our actions and give them their particular character.[2] Once so informed, our actions have already moved into the consummatory phase and have passed from the present, in which we are, to the past, in which we were.

The plaza

Ubiquitous gardens of flowers and fountains centred in the grid-pattern of Spanish American towns from the Rio Grande to Tierra del Fuego, plazas are especially suited for a Meadian analysis of artefacts as symbols, for by the very nature in which nature is arranged within it, the plaza encourages the participants who stroll its walkways to distance themselves from the alternative realities that constitute Spanish-American culture (Richardson 1982).

As anthropological, interpretive observers, we place ourselves at the shoulders of the participants as, through their actions, they shape into being the world of the plaza. We may separate their shaping into three components corresponding to the three phases of the Meadian act: the material component, which corresponds to the perceptual phase; the interaction component, which corresponds to the manipulatory phase; and the image component, which is similar to the consummatory phase.

As people approach the material setting of the plaza, they look ahead into its characteristics that separate it from other public places, such as the market, where nature is piled into stalls – vegetables here, fruits there and flowers near the entrance – ready to sell; or the church, where saints stare down from their niches, their eyes aglow in the candlelight, and see in the plaza's walkways as the walkways circle past roses, carefully tended, and hedges, carefully pruned, a structure whose response is distinct from both market and church.

As they enter into the plaza, and into the present, stroll by the fountain or sit on benches under the whitewashed trunks of palms, people watch other people, suitably dressed for the occasion, watching them. Among those on parade are a young couple with a new baby in arms and the older child running ahead, a cluster of teenaged girls with their hands over their mouths in a vain attempt to suppress an outburst of giggles, and an older pair, married so long as to be identical in size, in manner, and in the glasses through which they note the anthropologist, notepad in hand, making observations. In their exchanges in the present of the plaza, people assume a role considerably distinct from the one they play in the market, where they haggle with one another over the price of maize, shoes and even pictures of the Blessed Virgin; or in church, in whose gloom they cross themselves beneath a thorn-crowned Christ and partake of the Word that has become Flesh and assumed the shape of a thin wafer. The role they play in the plaza, with all of its variations, is that of an appropriately costumed, self-conscious actor who presents to the others a structured, on-stage front.

In the present of the plaza, where in its now, nature is turned not into a commodity as in the market nor into a sacred object as in the church, but into an ornament that decorates their leisured lives, people generalize both nature and behaviour into a plaza other. Composed of both a material setting of ornamental nature and of an interaction unhurried in its pace, the plaza comes to have an image that contrasts sharply with the image of the market, which is opportunistic exploitation, or *listo* (smart), or with the image of the church, which is the lesson of suffering, or *paciencia* (patience). The image of the plaza is that of *cultura*, which is culture, not the anthropologist's culture, but the culture of the Enlightenment in which man seeks perfection, not in spiritual ecstasy, but in rational order. The plaza, located in the centre of grid-pattern towns from the Rio Grande to Tierra del Fuego, is the triumphal image of urbane, civilized man bringing nature – raw, brutal and unorganized – under control. In the present of the plaza world, ephemeral though it may be, we celebrate that triumph, as short-lived as it surely is (Richardson 1982).

Meadian archaeology

In Spanish-America, as people approach the plaza they see ahead a material setting forming itself to, even as it shapes, the attitude they are assuming. Once in the plaza, in response to the gestures of one another, they take on a role relevant to the setting. From that position they generalize the setting into an image of the reality in which they are. In their construction they have not imposed an interior, cognitive structure upon a formless future, nor have they discovered an existing, preformed reality, rather through reciprocal gesturing they have sought the 'creation of a structure to which the world that is there *answers*' (Miller 1973a, p. 107).

This Meadian philosophy of the act, which avoids the phenomenalist's fallacy of an antecedent self and the behaviourist's fallacy of meaningless stimuli, appears eminently suitable to the task of post-processual archaeology (Hodder 1985) to replace behaviour with action, reaction with construction and passive recipient with active participant; that is, to make archaeology a human rather than an Earth science. It suggests that as the archaeologist, deep into an excavation, reaches with his own hand to grasp the labour of another, has not in that grasping simply collected another residue discarded from a past that is no more, but that he has encountered a world that is there, a world that awaits him to create the appropriate structure so that it may speak once again of the human struggle.

Notes

1 Given the obvious sympathy between the Meadian perspective and anthropology, the scant use of his thought in the field is distressing. Leslie White's justifiably famous 'The symbol: the origin and basis of behaviour' (1949) closely parallels Mead's own discussion of the 'significant symbol', but if the lack of citation to Mead's writings in his work is an accurate indication, White apparently developed this key concept without influence from Mead. Among the major figures in contemporary anthropology, Clifford Geertz (1973, p. 45, see also Goodenough's 1979 review) acknowledges a debt to Mead in his argument that mind is a public trafficking in symbols, and Barkow (1978) has suggested how Mead's concept of the self, combined intriguingly with sociobiology, might illuminate the record of human evolution. These two men aside, the wealth of Mead's thought remains unmined (see Richardson 1987).

2 'As a symbol an object stands for certain consequences in activity' and it 'may be defined as a "collapsed act"; the sign of what would happen if the act were carried to completion' (Troyer 1978, Mead 1972, pp. 368–70).

References

Barkow, J. H. 1978. Social norms, the self, and sociobiology: building on the ideas of A. I. Hallowell. *Current Anthropology* **19**, 99–118.

Geertz, C. 1973. *The interpretation of culture*. New York: Basic Books.
Goodenough, W. 1974. Review of *The interpretation of culture*. *Science* **186**, 435–6.
Hodder, I. 1985. Postprocessual archaeology. *Advances in Archaeological Method and Theory* **8**, 1–26.
Lewis, D. G. 1981. Mead's contact theory of reality: the manipulatory phase of the act in the constitution of mundane, scientific, aesthetic, and evaluative objects. *Symbolic Interaction* **4**, 129–42.
Mead, G. H. 1972. *The philosophy of the act*, C. W. Morris (ed.). Chicago: University of Chicago Press.
Miller, D. L. 1973a. *George Herbert Mead: self, language, and the world*. Austin: University of Texas Press.
Miller, D. L. 1973b. Mead's theory of universals. In *The philosophy of George Herbert Mead*, W. R. Corti (ed.), 89–107 Winterthur, Switzerland: Armriswiler Bücherei.
Richardson, M. 1982. Being-in-the-market versus Being-in-the-plaza: material culture and the construction of social reality in spanish america. *American Ethnologist* **9**, 421–36.
Richardson, M. 1987. A social (ideational–behavioral) interpretation of material culture and its application to archaeology. In *Mirror and metaphor: material and social constructions of reality*, D. W. Ingersoll, Jr & G. Bronitsky (eds). Lanham, Maryland: University Press of America.
Strauss, A. (ed.) 1964 *George Herbert Mead on social psychology*. Chicago: University of Chicago Press.
Troyer, W. L. 1978. Mead's social and functional theory of mind. In *Symbolic interaction*, J. G. Manis & B. N. Meltzer (eds), 3rd edn, 247–51. Boston: Allyn & Bacon.
White, L. 1949. The symbol: the origin and basis of human behavior. *The science of culture*. New York: Farrar, Straus & Cudahy.

12 *The material symbols of the Winnebago sky and Earth moieties*

ROBERT L. HALL

The Winnebago are a Siouan-speaking American Indian group in the USA, encountered by Europeans west of Lake Michigan in what is today the state of Wisconsin. Winnebago social organization was based on patrilineal clans belonging to one or another of two major exogamous tribal divisions or moieties. The warriors of the Earth division of the Winnebago ('those who are on Earth') used a flat, angled or curved club (see Fig. 12.1) of a well-known kind sometimes called a 'gunstock warclub' because of its shape. The sky division ('those who are above') used the equally familiar ball-headed warclub. Here was an interesting use of items of material culture to symbolize a major social dichotomy within the Winnebago tribe (Radin 1970, pp. 133–42, 154–5, 162, pls 43, 45). Neither Radin, their principal ethnographer, nor the Winnebago themselves attempted to explain how the nature of the clubs could have related in any way to the social divisions involved.

It is nevertheless understandable why the sky division might have used the ball-headed club. The leading clan of this division was that of the thunderers, the Thunderbird Clan. Some tribes neighbouring the Winnebago are known to have believed that lightning bolts manifested themselves in the form of stone balls, so it is likely that the Winnebago themselves held the same belief. The Winnebago also referred to the ball-headed club as a 'bald' -headed club, a designation which must reflect the Winnebago image of thunderbirds, which were said always to appear to people as 'bald-headed individuals wearing a wreath made of the branches of the arbor vitae' (Radin 1970, p. 391). There was no equally obvious rationale for the use of the angled club by the Earth division. Some warclubs of the angled form were easily recognizable copies of the wooden stocks of European firearms, even to the detail of the trigger guard, but I have argued that this resemblance to a gunstock was a modern enhancement due to the originally coincidental similarity of the musket stock to the shape of a club which already had considerable antiquity and a wide distribution (Hall 1982).

The clan and moiety associations of the angled or 'gunstock' warclub cannot be easily studied through its distribution in the USA because the social context is rarely stated explicitly (Radin is the exception), and even Radin presents some conflicting data. One club he illustrates as belonging to a war bundle of the Thunderbird Clan is of the angled type and not of the ball – or bald-headed type at all (Radin 1970, pl. 57). Radin (1970, pp. 154–5) does note that this kind

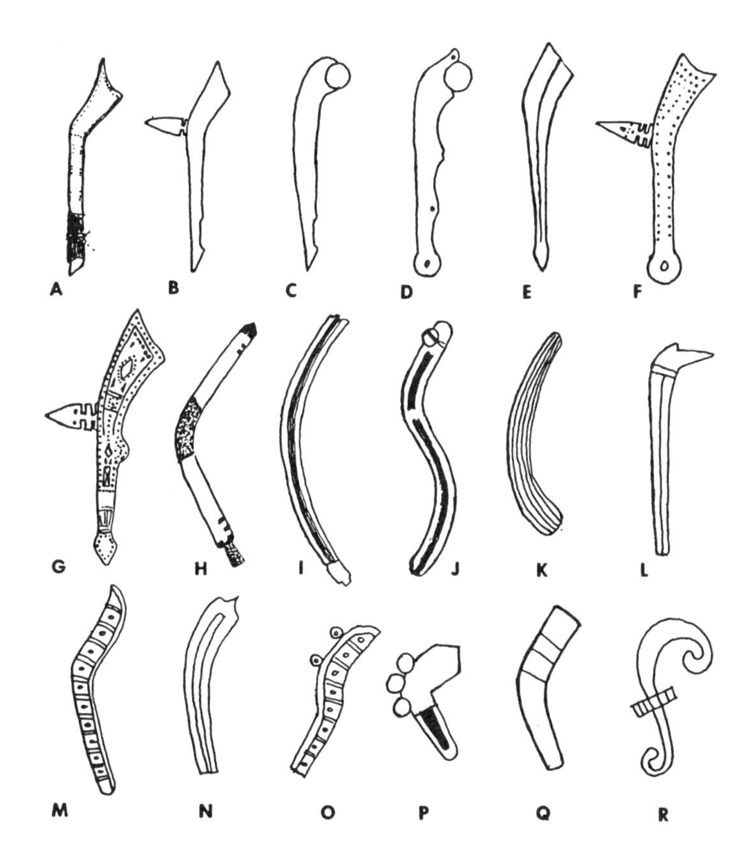

Figure 12.1 Curved clubs from the eastern USA and Mexico. A, B, from the Winnebago Earth moiety; C, D, from the Winnebago sky moiety; E, from the Ioway tribe; F, from the Omaha tribe; G, warclub consciously modelled after a European gun stock; H–J, throwing sticks from the southwestern USA; K, N, from bas-reliefs at Chichén Itzá, Yucatan, Mexico; L, from a Huastecan shell engraving, Mexico; M, from the *Codex Borgia*, Mexico; O–R, from representations of the god Quetzalcóatl, Mexico. A–C, after Radin 1970, pl. 45; D, after Radin 1970, pl. 43a; E, after Hall 1982, fig. 1d; F, after Fletcher 1972, Vol. 1, pl. 31; G, after Catlin 1973, pl. 99c; H, after Dietschy 1939, pl. 11–14a; I, after Parsons 1918, fig. 39; J, from a display in Mesa Verde National Park, Colorado; K, after and Maudslay 1895–1902, Vol. II, pl. 38; L, after Beyer 1933, figs 50–1; M, after Seler 1963, 66; N, after Beyer 1933, fig. 62; O, from *Codex Borgia* after Beyer 1933, fig. 56; P, from *Codex Vienna* after Beyer 1933, fig. 63; Q, from a carved stone box, after Covarrubias 1957, fig. 117a; R, from *Codex Ramírez* after Alvarado Tezozomoc 1878, pl. 26.

of ritual bundle was a gift of both the thunderbird spirit and the night spirit, and some night associations can be demonstrated for the angled club.

Krickeberg has noted several customs which appeared to him to be Mesoamerican traits echoed in the aboriginal eastern USA (see Fig. 12.2). Among these traits was the use of a flat, curved wooden club and the division of tribal powers between war and civil or religious leaders, associated in the USA with exogamous dual tribal divisions or moieties related to war and peace or sky and Earth (Krickeberg 1961, pp. 78, 81, 399–400, fig. 218). Krickeberg relates this particular kind of warclub in the eastern USA to the *xonecuilli*, an enigmatic curved symbolic form with which a variety of Mexican clubs or staffs had become identified (Hall 1982, fig. 1, Krickeberg 1961, p. 400).

The Náhuatl name *xonecuilli* has been given to several objects of S or reverse-S form, among them certain breads of this shape and a constellation called in Náhuatl *Citlalxonecuilli*, i.e. Star Xonecuilli (Sahagún 1953, pp. 36, 66–7). The shape was supposed also to represent the trace of lightning crossing the sky, but the word *xonecuilli* literally meant 'bent foot' or 'twisted foot', suggesting a form more like that of a simple bent or angled club, and the word was used to refer to these simpler clubs as well. The fact that such a club had a lightning association in Mexico in Sahagún's day provides an intriguing parallel to the lightning association of the Winnebago ball-headed club, but does little to explain why a club of the angled form would have come to have an Earth association among the Winnebago.

One variety of the curved club is represented in the hands of Toltec warriors sculptured in bas relief at the Post-classic Maya city of Chichén Itzá in Yucatán. Fragments of actual physical specimens of such curved clubs have been dredged from the mud in the sacred well of Chichén Itzá, recognizable because of a pattern of multiple parallel lines cut into the surface of the wood, a pattern replicated in the bas-reliefs (Coggins & Shane 1984, p. 49). Flat, curved, wooden clubs with similar grooves are also known from the southwestern USA, where they were in use almost 2000 years ago. These objects resemble the throwing sticks historically used in the southwestern USA to hunt rabbits, a kind of non-returning boomerang. Driver & Massey (1957, p. 359) look favourably on the proposition that the curved, grooved clubs found in the southwestern USA are historically related to those in Mexico.

At Chichén Itzá such curved sticks, referred to by archaeologists as 'fending sticks', were carried in both hands simultaneously or replaced the shield in the left hand of a Toltec warrior (Maudslay 1889–1902, vol. III, pl. 38). In the southwestern USA similar curved sticks have sometimes been found with spearthrowers, and it is believed that the sticks might have been effective in warfare as clubs to fend off the relatively slow-moving spears hurled with the aid of a spearthrower, hence the name 'fending sticks' sometimes used to describe them.

Beyer also saw the similarity of the simpler (non-S-shaped) *xonecuilli* club of Mexico to the angled warclubs of the eastern USA, saw this kind of club as a weapon typical of the Huastecs of northeastern Mesoamerica, and said that ancient Mexican scribes 'most probably' regarded it as a Huastec weapon (Beyer

1933, p. 188, cf. 1969, p. 506). This Huastec club lacked grooves, as did those of the eastern USA. The Huasteca is that part of Mesoamerica closest to the eastern USA. The southwestern clubs occurred both in a simple bent form and in an S-form, as did the *xonecuilli* club. For instance, Quetzalcóatl, a Mesoamerican god said to be of Huastec derivation, carried as his characteristic weapon a *xonecuilli* sometimes as a bent club, sometimes as a crook-shaped club and sometimes as a weapon of S-form (Brundage 1982, pp. 84–7 *et passim*).

Among the Winnebago certain staffs of crook shape were specific properties of the Bear Clan, the principal clan of the Earth moiety. Among the related Omaha the crook staff was known as a *washábe*, a word cognate with the Osage circumlocution for black bear, *wathábe*. The Sioux (Lakota and Dakota) word for this class of staff or standard was *wápaha*, a word cognate with Osage and Omaha *wábaha*, which glosses as Ursa Major, the Great Bear constellation.

Repeating Radin's information, the angled club of the Winnebago was used by the Earth rather than by the sky moiety. The Earth was regarded by American aborigines as a feminine aspect of nature which received fertilizing bolts of lightning and shafts of sunlight. Day was a masculine aspect of nature; night was feminine. The night sky was feminine and was equated with the underworld. Grieder (1982, pp. 116, 122) sees the S-form in America as having a primary association with female gender and a secondary association with the Earth. He sees the S-form basically as a symbol of the female sex organ, noting, for instance, that the S-element substitutes for the vulva of the female of a pair of cosmic crocodilians carved on the Tello obelisk at the Chavín type site in Peru (Grieder 1982, pp. 117–8). If the southwestern USA and Mexican clubs of S-form can legitimately be related to female sexuality by virtue of their shape, following Grieder, then the simpler form could also have some female or Earth fertility associations, which would help to account for the association of this form with the Winnebago Earth moiety.

Sahagún (1953, pp. 66–7) indicates that in central Mexico the Ursa Major constellation was conceived to be a scorpion. In Anderson & Biddle's translation of Sahagún, Sahagún (1953, pp. 66–7) is said to have identified Ursa Minor as the *Citlalxonecuilli*. The Ursa Major identification is hard to dispute because Sahagún specifically equates Citlalcólotl, the Star Scorpion, with *el carro*, 'the cart', a common European reference to the seven principal stars in Ursa Major. Anderson & Dibble's Ursa Minor identification is questionable because what Sahagún actually said was that the seven stars of *Citlalxonecuilli* formed a reverse-S located *in the mouth* of the *bozina* [*bocina* or 'horn'], which is the Spanish name for Ursa Minor, not simply *in* the constellation as the translators put it. Ursa Minor does have seven stars, but only four in the mouth of the horn.

The axis of rotation of the northern night sky today almost coincides with Polaris, the North Star, in Ursa Minor. In Preclassic times *ca.* 2500 BC the pole star was Thuban, in Draco, a reverse-S-shaped constellation sandwiched betwen Ursa Major and Ursa Minor. Draco was then central to a vortex composed of spiralling stars. Whirlpools, spirals and whorls were associated with underworld entrances in Mesoamerica, and in the southwestern USA with centrality and soul passages (cf. Furst 1978, p. 240, Reichard 1974, p. 36, 149).

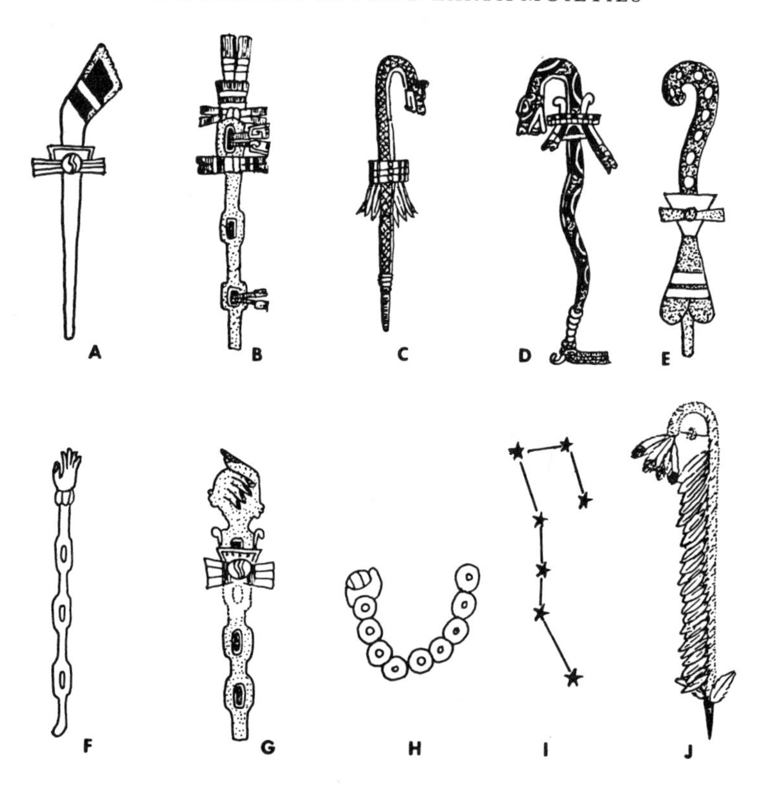

Figure 12.2 Clubs, staffs, and related forms from the eastern USA and Mexico. A–E, from representations of the god Quetzalcóatl, Mexico; B, F, G, scorpion tail staffs, Mexico; H, stylized scorpion tail, Mayan; I, constellation Ursa Major; J, *washábe* or crook staff, Omaha tribe. A, from *Codex Borgia* after Seler 1963, 56; B, from *Codex Borgia* after Seler 1963, 73; C, D, from *Vaticanus 3773*, 45, 76; E, from *Codex Magliabecchiano* after Carrasco 1982, fig. 14; F, from *Dresden Codex* after Thompson 1965, fig. 13; G, from *Codex Borgia* after Seler 1963, 56; H, from *Madrid Codex* after Thompson 1971, fig. 13, no. 24; I, from observation; J, after Fletcher 1972, Vol. 1, 155.

The image is that of the reverse-S-shaped Draco as a symbol of the sexual organ of a cosmic goddess represented by the night sky, such as the Aztec Citlalincue.

It makes sense to see Draco as the original inspiration of the S-form club or staff, an association which was transferred in more-recent centuries to the S-shaped Ursa Minor as the Earth's axis shifted relative to the stars because of the Earth's gyroscopic precession. Since Ursa Minor can be seen as cane-shaped as well as S-shaped, the symbolic equivalence of these two forms of club or staff can also be understood.

The angled *xonecuilli* was the shape of the tail of the Aztec scorpion constellation (Ursa Major) and appears to have been equivalent in the *Codex Borgia*

(Seler 1963) to the scorpion tail staff. This might be enough to conjecture an explanation of the tie between the flat, angled warclub of the Winnebago and the Winnebago Earth moiety, because the principal clan of the Earth moiety was the Bear Clan, one of whose symbols was the crook which we have related to Ursa Major. The quadrangle in Ursa Major was seen as a bear by a number of tribes in the aboriginal northeastern USA. However, the angled or bent warclub was also the shape of part of the Hand constellation seen in Orion by the Crow and Hidatsa, which had no explicit connection with bears. What both Orion and Ursa Major (as Citlalcólotl) did share was an association with a human hand (and possibly also with the scorpion as well, cf. Kelley 1979–80, p. 412).

Summary

The material symbols of the sky and Earth moieties of the Winnebago are found to have related logically to natural objects or phenomena relevant to the principal clans of these moieties, the Thunderbird and Bear Clans. The ball-headed warclub had a symbolic association with thunderbolts, believed to have been produced by the thunderbird, the eponymic animal of the Thunderbird Clan. Referrents can be found for the angled, flat warclub of the Earth moiety in the polar constellations Ursa Major and Ursa Minor, an inference supported by the clear relationship of the crook staffs of the Winnebago Bear Clan to Ursa Major and the implicit relationship of the *xonecuilli* club in Mexico to Ursa Minor as the *xonecuilli* constellation.

References

Alvarado Tezozomoc, H. 1878. *Crónica Mexicana . . . procedida del Códice Ramírez. . . ,* J. M. Vigil (ed.). Mexico City: Imprenta & Litografia de Ireno Paz.

Beyer, H. 1933. Shell ornament sets from the Huasteca, Mexico. *Middle American pamphlets*, No. 4, of Publication No. 5 in the *Middle American research series*. New Orleans: Department of Middle American Research, Tulane University of Louisiana.

Beyer, H. 1969. Conchas ornamentadas, en juegos, de la Huasteca, México. *El México antiguo*, Vol. XI, 471–526. Mexico City: Sociedad Alemana Mexicanista.

Brundage, B. C. 1982. *The phoenix of the Western world: Quetzalcoatl and the sky religion.* Norman: University of Oklahoma Press.

Carrasco, D. 1982. *Quetzalcoatl and the irony of empire: myths and prophecies in the Aztec tradition*. Chicago: University of Chicago Press.

Catlin, G. 1973. *Letters and notes on the manners, customs and conditions of the North American Indians*. New York: Dover.

Coggins, C. C. & O. C. Shane III 1984. *Cenote of sacrifice: Maya treasures from the sacred well at Chichén Itzá*. Austin: University of Texas Press.

Covarrubias, M. 1957. *Indian art of Mexico and Central America*. New York: Alfred A. Knopf.

Dietschy, H. 1939. Die Amerikanischen Keulen und Holzschwerter in ihrer

Beziehungen zur Kulturgeschichte der Neuen Welt. *Internationales Archiv für Ethnographie*, Vol. 37, 87–205. Leiden: E. J. Brill.

Driver, H. E. & W. C. Massey 1957. Comparative studies of North American Indians. *Transactions of the American Philosophical Society (New Series)* **47**(2).

Fletcher, A. C. 1972. *The Omaha tribe*, 2 Vols. Lincoln: University of Nebraska Press. (Originally published as part of the 27th Annual Report of the Bureau of American Ethnology, Smithsonian Institution, 1911.)

Furst, J. 1978. *Codex Vindobonensis Mexicanus I: a commentary*. Publication No. 4 of the Institute for Mesoamerican Studies, State University of New York at Albany.

Grieder, T. 1982. *Origins of pre-Columbian art*. Austin: University of Texas Press.

Hall, R. L. 1982. A second look at gunstock warclubs. *The Wisconsin Archaeologist* **63**, 246–53.

Kelley, D. H. 1979–80. Quetzalcoatl and his coyote origins. In *Mythes et rites des virgtaines du Méxique central préhispanique*, Vol. 3, M. Graulich (ed.), 397–416. Université de Bruxelles, Belgique.

Krickeberg, W. 1961. *Las culturas antiguas mexicanas*. Mexico City: Fondo de Cultura Económica. (Spanish transl. of the author's 1956. *Altmexikanischen Kulturen*. Berlin: Safari Verlag.

Maudslay, A. P. 1889–1902. *Archaeology: biologia Centrali-Americana*, 5 Vols. London: Dulan.

Parsons, E. C. 1918. War god shrines of Laguna and Zuñi. *American Anthropologist (New Series)* **20**, 381–405.

Radin, P. 1970. *The Winnebago tribe*. Lincoln: University of Nebraska Press. (Originally published as part of 37th Annual report of the Bureau of American Ethnology, Smithonian Institution, Washington, DC, 1923.)

Reichard, G. A. 1974. *Navajo religion: a study of symbolism*. Princeton & London: Princeton University Press.

Sahagún, F. B. de 1953. *General history of the things of New Spain*. Book 7: *The Sun, Moon, and stars, and the binding of the years* (transl. from the Aztec into English, with notes and illustrations, by A. J. O. Anderson & C. E. Dibble, under the title *Florentine Codex*. *Monographs of the School of American Research* **14**, Part VIII. Sante Fé, New Mexico.

Seler, E. 1963. *Comentarios al Códice Borgia*. Apéndice de láminas explicativas. Mexico City: Fondo del Cultura Económica.

Thompson, J. E. S. 1965. Mayan hieroglyphic writing. In *Handbook of Middle American Indians*, Vol. 3, Pt 2, 632–58. Austin: University of Texas Press.

Thompson, J. E. S. 1971. *Maya hieroglyphic writing: an introduction*. Norman: University of Oklahoma Press.

Vaticanus 3773 1972. *Codex Vaticanus 3773 (Codex Vaticanus B)*. Einleitung, Summary und Resumen [by] F. Anders. Graz, Austria: Akademische Druck- & Verlagsanstalt.

14 *Interpreting material culture*

CHRISTOPHER TILLEY

If one wishes to talk about paradigms in archaeology, where the term 'paradigm shift' means a fundamental change in the way in which archaeologists actually see the world of material culture, the decisive break occurs not in 1962 with the substitution of one form of empiricism for another (Binford 1962), but in 1982 with the appearance of *Symbolic and structural archaeology* (Hodder 1982a). This break involves, primarily, the conception of material culture as a signifying system in which the external physical attributes of artefacts and their relationships are not regarded as exhausting their meaning. This chapter briefly looks back at some of the assumptions involved in the 'structuralist' encounter in archaeology, then charts a course leading from structuralism to the post-structuralism of Derrida, Barthes and Foucault.[1] The change now occurring in archaeology is a move away from attempts to establish what basically amounted to the search for a methodology for assigning meaning to artefact patterning to a more fully self-reflexive position involving consideration of what is involved in the act of *writing the past*.

Saussure and the diacritical sign

Saussure, the father of contemporary linguistics, drew a fundamental distinction between *langue* and *parole*. *Langue* constitutes the system of codes, rules and norms structuring any particular language, whereas *parole* refers to the situated act of utilization of this system by an individual speaker (Saussure 1960). The object of linguistics was, according to Saussure, the *synchronic* analysis of *langue* as opposed to the diachronic analysis of specific changes in elements of languages through time. The essential building-block of *langue* on which linguistic analysis was to work was the diacritical linguistic sign consisting of a union of two facets or components, the 'signifier' and the 'signified'. The signifier is an audible utterance or a sound 'image' referring to a particular concept, the signified:

SIGN:	signifier (acoustic image)	:	signified (concept)

A number of points may be noted about this conception of the linguistic sign. It exists in no direct relationship with reality, because the relationship between the signifier and the signified is entirely arbitrary, a matter of convention. The arbitrariness involved here is directly analogous to that existing between words and things. In English we use the utterance 'dog' to refer to a class of creatures with four legs, whereas in other languages an equally arbitrary sound image (e.g. *chien, Hund*) may be used. The sign only gains meaning diacritically because the meaning is derived from the system in which it is constituted as different from other signs. In other words, 'dog' is only meaningful because it is *not* cat, rope or axe, and vice versa. Meaning therefore resides in a system of *relationships between signs* and not in the signs themselves. A sign considered in isolation would be meaningless. Furthermore, the meaning of a sign is not predetermined, but is a matter of cultural and historical convention. Consequently, it does not matter how a signifier appears, so long as it preserves its difference from other signifiers.

Saussure was not interested in actual speech or the social utilization of signs in encounters between individuals or groups, or both, but with the objective structures making such *parole* possible. This position had a number of consequences:

(a) the study of linguistics moves from concrete manifestations of speech to unconscious rules and grammars;
(b) an emphasis on relations between signs rather than the signs themselves;
(c) a conception of signs forming part of an overarching system; and
(d) an aim of determining principles underlying different linguistic systems.

From language to culture

Saussure regarded the study of linguistic systems as eventually forming part of a general science of signs – semiology. Language might then be regarded as one sign system among many which would have relative degrees of autonomy from each other. By the 1960s semiology or semiotics had, indeed, developed as a major intellectual field. It is difficult, and perhaps undesirable, to draw any clear distinction between structuralism and semiology, other than to say that the former constitutes a general method of enquiry, whereas the latter forms a field of study of particular sign systems, e.g. advertising, fashion and facial gestures. What both have in common is to use, modify or build on aspects of the linguistic theory outlined above in order to study areas of human culture other than language.

Language becomes the paradigm for understanding all other aspects of social life. If language is an exchange of messages constituted in their difference, governed by an underlying system of codes and grammatical rules, then the move made by Lévi-Strauss is quite understandable. Marriage practices are analysed in terms of systems of underlying rules, such systems being variant realizations of a limited number of structural oppositions defined in their relational difference. Totemism is explained as a way of structuring the relationship between social groups (Lévi-Strauss 1969). If clan A traces descent from the iguana and clan B from the kangaroo, then this is merely a way of stating that the relation of clan A to clan B is analogous to that between the two species. So iguana and kangaroo are logical operators, concrete signs. Hence, one can deduce the canonical formula, archetypal of any structural analysis:

iguana : kangaroo :: clan A : clan B

To understand the meaning of 'iguana' and 'kangaroo' they must be situated within an overall structured system of signs. Lévi-Strauss' most ambitious project is the study of myth (1970, 1973), in which he aims to show that the seeming arbitrariness of myths is in fact only tenable in terms of a superficial surface reading of the narratives. Instead myths can be understood in terms of fundamental principles or laws operating at a deeper level. The consequence is that if the human mind can be shown to be determined even in its creation of myths, then *a fortiori* it will also be determined in other spheres. He isolates a number of fundamental oppositions such as male–female, culture–nature, day–night, raw–cooked, and others of a less obvious nature. In doing so Lévi-Strauss is analysing codes and the manner in which categories drawn from one area of experience can be related to those in other areas and used as logical tools for expressing relations. He does not ask so much what the codes are that account for the meaning that myths have in a particular culture, since he is interested in constructing a transcultural logic of myth. This means that myths are always, and primarily, signs of the logic of myth itself. Myths can be broken down into 'mythemes' which, like phonemes (the basic sound units of language), acquire meaning only when combined in particular ways. The rules governing the combinations constitute the true meaning of myth residing beneath the surface narrative, and ultimately to be related to universal mental operations. People do not so much make up myths, but rather myths think themselves through people.

Material culture and structure

Barthes, in *Mythologies* (1973), is not concerned with general structures, but with particular cultural practices. All such practices are endowed with signification, and this is a fundamental feature running throughout the entire gamut of social life from a wrestling match to eating steak and chips to hairstyles – the list is endless. There is no 'innocent' or transparent fact or event. All facts and events 'speak' to their culturally conditioned observers and participants. Culture is a kind of speech embodying messages coded in various forms and requiring decoding. Furthermore, the meaning of signification may be analogous for those who 'produce' and those who 'consume' the signs. At other times signs act asymmetrically, becoming ideological, linked to the maintenance of power.

Given the intellectual force and power of the general perspectives outlined above, it seems, in retrospect, almost inevitable that archaeologists would come to reframe an understanding of their basic data – material culture – as constituting a meaningful significative system, the analysis of which should go far beyond a reductionist conception of it as merely constituting an extrasomatic means of adaptation, or as vaguely functioning in utilitarian or social terms. Such frameworks have no way of coping with variability or specific form. All that a functional argument can ever be expected to do is to rule on conditions of existence or non-existence. For example, ritual may exist because it performs the function of asserting social solidarity – but why any particular ritual? Such a question remains unanswered. Similarly, a consideration of economic practices must go far beyond simplistic accounts of how food resources might be obtained efficiently or inefficiently. The economy has a style, is part of a cultural and symbolic scheme. Of course, people eat to survive, but eating is a cultural practice. It involves a way of thinking and provides a medium for thought. This symbolic dimension is part of that which is to be explained. It might be said that the primary significance of material culture is not its pragmatic use-value, but its significative exchange value.

In archaeology the particular use of a structuralist or semiological perspective has not been concerned to analyse material culture in terms of the transcultural perspective of Lévi-Strauss. Rather, there has been a concern with historical and social specificity and context: particular rather than universal structures. Much of this work has been indelibly linked with Marxism, involving consideration, in particular, of ideology and power and dynamic processes of structuration or structural change. Here it is not the intention either to review or to analyse the strengths or shortcomings of this work, but rather to focus in a more abstract manner on archaeology as being a pursuit of sign systems.

If archaeology is anything, it is the study of material culture as a manifestation of structured symbolic practices meaningfully constituted and situated in relation to the social. This relationship is active, and not one of simple reflection. Material culture does not provide a mirror to society or a window through which we can see it. Rather, there are multiple transformations and relationships between different aspects of material culture and between material culture and society of, for example, parallelism, opposition, inversion, linearity and equivalence. In order to understand material culture we have to think in terms that go entirely beyond it, to go beneath the surface appearances to an underlying reality. This means that we are thinking in terms of relationships between things, rather than simply in terms of the things themselves. The meaning of the archaeological record is always irreducible to the elements which go to make up and compose that record, conceived as a system of points or units. Such a study involves a search for the structures, and the principles composing those structures, underlying the visible and the tangible. The principles governing the form, nature and content of material culture patterning are to be found at both the level of microrelations (e.g. a set of designs on a pot) and macrorelations (e.g. relations between settlement space and burial space). Such relations may be held to be irreducibly linked, each forming a part of the other. So each individual act of material culture production and use has to be regarded as a contextualized social act involving the relocation of signs along axes defining the relationship between signs and other signs which reach out beyond themselves and towards others becoming amplified or subdued in specific contexts.

Such an analysis is undeniably difficult, but it does at least have the merit of trying to capture the sheer complexity of what we are trying to understand. Several points require emphasis.

(a) Material culture is a framing and communicative medium involved in social practice. It can be used for transforming, storing or preserving social information. It also forms a symbolic medium for social practice, acting dialectically in relation to that practice. It can be regarded as a kind of text, a silent form of writing and discourse; quite literally, a channel of reified and objectified expression.

(b) Although material culture may be produced by individuals, it is always a social production. This is because it does not seem to be at all fruitful to pursue a view of the human subject as endowed with unique capacities and attributes, as the source of social relations, font of meaning, knowledge and action. As Foucault (1974) pointed out, this 'liberal' humanist view of humanity is largely an 18th century creation. In regarding material culture as socially produced, an emphasis is being placed on the constructedness of human meaning as a product of shared systems of signification. The individual does not so much construct material culture or language, but is rather constructed through them.

Structure and archaeological analysis

An underlying assumption of much structuralist work in archaeology has been that such studies either have discovered the real structures generating the observed variability in the archaeological record, or at the very least, are working painfully towards this end. The questions become: what are the signs at work? How can we recognize them? How do they differ? How did they operate in a past life-world? This involves a search for recurrent associated elements in relation to their contextual patterning. The meaning of the past is something that the archaeologist does not have but wants to work towards by means of an analysis going 'beneath' the materials to reveal the underlying principles at work, principles which may be held to be not only structuring the observed archaeological materials, but also implicated in the overall structuration of the social order.

The problem has always been the precise assignation of meaning. For example, a formal analysis of pottery decoration (e.g. Hodder 1982b, Tilley 1984) is not concerned with the actual perceived designs, whether a triangle or a zig-zag line, but with the differences between these designs, which may then be recoded in various ways – for example, in terms of horizontal and vertical distinctions, or alphabetically. How far does such an analysis take us? The structure so arrived at remains a simulacrum (almost Platonic!) of the design sequence, something previously invisible. A paradox is involved here. On the one hand, analysis becomes a form of repetititon. We are not told anything about the pot design which is not already there in it. On the other hand, the implication of the analysis is that something new has indeed been produced. The archaeologist has discovered the inner essence residing in the object, in this case the pot design, but what is the meaning of this 'recovery'?

Several strategies may be utilized. Meaning may be established by linking the pot design structure to other structures in the overall material culture patterning, e.g. refuse disposal and burial practices, such that these different structural aspects of the material culture can be regarded as being transformations of each other. The same basic structure may then be held to 'generate' how people are buried, how they design their pots, organize their disposal of refuse and the use of space in settlements. Ultimately, general overarching structuring principles (principles which structure structures) may be recognized. In the case of Hodder's (1982c) study of the Nuba these are:

pure–impure: cattle–pig: male–female: clean–dirty: life–death

So pure is to impure as cattle is to pig, and so on – all very neat.

Another way of assigning meaning, this time in a 'purely' archaeological study, involves a more abstract double-edged conceptual strategy. First, again, different types of material culture are analysed in terms of structural oppositions (usually entirely abstract), e.g. left–right and bounded–unbounded, in different contexts such as settlement and burial. So pot designs may be analysed in terms of boundedness and the treatment of human body parts (Tilley 1984). Secondly, a conceptual link is then drawn between boundedness in body parts and boundedness in pot designs and, through time, the archaeological record can be examined to see whether such an 'expression' of boundedness intensifies or decreases. The abstracted reconceptualized 'data' may then have its assigned meaning further mobilized by the introduction of social concepts such as contradiction, power and ideology.

In both these and other studies, a notion of 'context' and 'wholeness' is invoked, into which the material culture fitted as meaningful code. This whole may, or may not, be conceived as a fissured or contradictory totality. The archaeologist stands outside this whole, his or her gaze directed towards its internal structuring. A commentary is then produced, bringing order to the superficial chaos of the external appearances and forms of the artefacts. What is happening is the enclosure of the enigmatic (interpreted) object within the interpretative theory's pre-existent system, which then further comments on it.

The metacritical sign and polysemy

More comments on these commentaries are now required. First, is the notion of the diacritical sign one which can be sustained? If the meaning of a sign is just a matter of difference from other signs, then this conception can be pressed further until it breaches Saussure's notion of language forming a closed and stable synchronic system. This is because if a sign is what it is by virtue of its differences from all other signs, then each sign must be made up of a vast and never-ending network of differences from other signs. The outcome of such a line of reasoning is that there can be no clear symmetrical unity between one signifier and one signified. Meaning is then to be related to a potentially endless play of signifiers, and signifiers keep on changing into signifieds, and vice versa. So, the signifier and the signified become conceptually split (Derrida 1976, 1978). We arrive at what might be termed the metacritical sign. The meaning of the metacritical sign is never transparently present in it, but is a matter of what the sign is not. So meaning is both present and absent – to state this more simply, meaning is dispersed along chains of signifiers. Another piece of willed and deliberate obfuscation? Perhaps, but no more so than to mention a minimax satisficer strategy, ringing a dulcet tone of clarity in the attuned economistic archaeological ear. The corollary to the position just taken is quite simple – the meaning of material culture can never be objectified or exactly pinned down. Its meaning always, to some extent, evades the analyst.

Considering the concept of polysemy may clarify this further. An object, any object, has no ultimate or unitary meaning that can be held to exhaust it. Rather, any object has multiple and sometimes contradictory meanings. The meanings depend on a whole host of factors. One appropriate example is the safety-pin in contemporary Britain (Hodder 1985: 14) which, according to who wears it – an infant, a grandmother or a 'punk', changes its meaning. However, this is only part of the story. The meaning also changes according to the context in which the interpretation takes place (a kitchen or an underground station), who is carrying out the interpretation (to various people the safety pin may mean aggression, pity, children or bondage); and why they are bothering to interpret it in the first place. This last point is an appropriate cue to draw the archaeologist into the text.

From reading the past to writing the past

The previous section left the intrepid archaeologist grappling with the notion of meaning not being so much present in the artefact but absent, and being faced with a situation in which the notion of any unitary meaning residing in the past to which our analyses might strive to reach – whether by producing a structural simulacrum or by any other means – as a dangerous chimera. Meaning therefore becomes indeterminate and problematic. What is to be done, if anything? On one point we can at least be certain, the archaeological pursuit of signs is no easy business.

One possible escape route might be to renounce linguistic imperialism and develop a theory of the meaning of material culture not based on linguistic analogies. We might strongly assert that what material culture communicates is totally different from language. For example, it would require a vast number of material objects to 'say', in a material form, even the simplest sentence. If someone makes a statement and you do not understand what they mean, there is the possibility that a Socratic dialogue may bring illumination. Such dialogue is not possible with a pot! On the other hand, a stress can be made on the fact that material culture acts in multidimensional channels as a non-verbal mode of communication. In this respect its meanings could be held to be more complicated than those conveyed in speech. We could say that material culture is a material language with its own meaning product tied to production and consumption. Endless permutations of such arguments could be produced, but none of them can escape language. Thinking about material culture inevitably involves its transformation into linguistic concepts. However much we might try to escape from language, we are trapped in its prison house. So, although it might appear a laudable aim to escape a linguistic frame, this is an impossibility. There can be no meaningfully constituted non-linguistic semiological system.

The detour of attempting to embrace a radically non-linguistic analogy for the interpretation of material culture has apparently failed, leading us back once more to the archaeologist. Undecidability then, ambivalence: a free play of meaning? The 'structuralist', 'contextualist' or 'dialectical-structuralist' encounter as it has appeared in archaeology seems to be too important to be abandoned. In favour of what? The fact that such an enterprise leads inexorably towards its own critique and extension may be a sign of its vitality. A notion of metacritical and polysemous signs leads us to the margins of such an approach and our better understanding of it as an active interpretative exercise creating a past in a present which must renounce either finality or the notion that in the future we will be producing better, truer or more-precise accommodations to the truth of the past – whatever that might be.

The interpretation of the meaning and significance of material culture is a contemporary activity. The meaning of the past does not reside in the past, but belongs in the present. Similarly, the primary event of archaeology is the event of excavation or writing, not the event of the past. Consequently, the archaeologist is not so much reading the signs of the past as writing these signs into the present: constructing discourses which should be both meaningful to the present and playing an active role in shaping the present's future. Here an irony crops up. Archaeologists write, but many do not feel they should be writing! At best such textual production may be regarded as a transparent resource, a mere medium for expression. However, writing always transforms. The process of writing the past in the present needs to become part of that which is to be understood in archaeology. The ultimate aim of much contemporary archaeological discourse is to put an end to writing, to get the story right. Empiricism inexorably encourages such a futile goal. To the contrary, there will be no correct stories of the past that are not themselves a product of a politics of truth. There can only be better or worse re-presentations of history: his [*sic*] story.

What is important is the development of a truly self-reflexive archaeological discourse, aware of itself as discourse and systematically refusing the usual imperative of producing yet another methodology for grasping the past's meaning. Archaeological discourses are, by and large, framed in specific institutional settings and transmitted and disseminated through definite forms of media in which archaeological knowledge is located. Such discourses have their bases in forms of pedagogy imposing 'a will to truth'. As yet there is no true alternative discourse in archaeology. A crucial act in creating one will be the disruption of the discursive authority of the texts we have to hand at present. This will involve an awareness of the politics of discourse and the power structures in which it is embedded. This requires consideration of what kind of past we want in the present and why we produce the past in one manner rather than another.[2]

The general position being taken in this chapter suggests that material culture can be regarded as providing a multidimensional 'text' from which the archaeologist can construct his or her texts: not, therefore, an entirely free process. The text that the archaeologist writes will consist, in part, of a tissue of 'quotations' drawn from the material record and meaningfully activated in fresh constellations in relation to a particular argumentative frame of reference. The assignation of the meaning of the quotations drawn from the archaeological record requires a self-reflexive problematic.

We might set up a chain of signifiers to help us to understand the process of writing the past. First we might put interest. We are interested in interpreting some aspect of the archaeological record, making it meaningful for ourselves and others. However, this interest is at the outset dependent on our values (why we are carrying out this activity in the first place). These values are, in turn, dependent on our politics and our morality, which relate more generally to the sociopolitical context in which we find ourselves situated and positioned as agents. The chain we actually end up with is: positioned subject – politics, morality – values – interests – meanings – text.

The meaning of the past has to be inserted into the present through the medium of the text. So there is no meaning outside the text (conceived broadly to include film, etc.). This *meaning* has to be argued for and against. The act of writing always presupposes a politics of the present, and such writing is a form of power. It cannot escape power. Any kind of writing about the past is inevitably simultaneously a domestication of the difference of the past, an imposition of order. Writing the past is not an innocent and disinterested reading of an autonomous past produced as image. Writing the past is drawing it into the present, re-inscribing it into the face of the present.

This text is a pastiche or montage, a material production built on other texts, an extended footnote which, if anything interesting has been said, may become incorporated into another text. A formal conclusion is out of keeping with the spirit in which it is written. It will suffice to mention that in ending this contribution I wonder whether I should be saying what I have said. I would like to be looking over your shoulder and saying 'No, no – I didn't exactly mean it to be interpreted like *that*!'.

Notes

1 These authors are names for problems rather than formalized doctrines, and this is precisely their interest. Both Foucault and Barthes, in their early work, have been labelled structuralists. Both have renounced the structuralist enterprise. Post-

structuralism is characteristically a term not amenable to any rigid definition. It is simply a term applied to work without any unitary core that is temporally removed from a structuralist position. Those interested might look at Barthes (1974, 1977), Foucault (1972, 1984), Derrida (1976, 1981) and Sturrock (1979).

2 Aspects of post-structuralism, discourse, textuality, power, ideology and politics in relation to archaeology are discussed in detail in *Re-constructing archaeology* and *Social theory and archaeology* (Shanks & Tilley 1987a,b).

References

Barthes, R. 1973. *Mythologies*. London: Paladin.

Barthes, R. 1974. *S/Z*. New York: Hill & Wang.

Barthes, R. 1977. *Image, music, text*. New York: Hill & Wang.

Binford, L. 1962. Archaeology as anthropology. *American Antiquity* **28**(2).

Derrida, J. 1976. *Of grammatology*. Baltimore: Johns Hopkins University Press.

Derrida, J. 1978. *Writing and difference*. London: Routledge & Kegan Paul.

Derrida, J. 1981. *Dissemination*. London: Athlone Press.

Foucault, M. 1972. *The archaeology of knowledge*. London: Tavistock.

Foucault, M. 1974. *The order of things*. London: Tavistock.

Foucault, M. 1984. *The Foucault reader*, P. Rabinow (ed.). Harmondsworth: Penguin.

Hodder, I. (ed.) 1982a. *Symbolic and structural archaeology*. Cambridge: Cambridge University Press.

Hodder, I. 1982b. Sequences of structural change in the Dutch neolithic. In *Symbolic and structural archaeology*, I. Hodder (ed.), 162–78. Cambridge: Cambridge University Press.

Hodder, I. 1982c. *Symbols in action*. Cambridge: Cambridge University Press.

Hodder, I. 1985. Postprocessual archaeology. *Advances in archaeological theory and method*, Vol. 8, M. Schiffer (ed.). New York: Academic Press.

Lévi-Strauss, C. 1969. *Totemism*. Harmondsworth: Penguin.

Lévi-Strauss, C. 1970. *The raw and the cooked*. London: Cape.

Lévi-Strauss, C. 1973. *From honey to ashes*. London: Cape.

Saussure, F. de 1960. *Course in general linguistics*. London: Peter Owen.

Shanks, M. & C. Tilley 1987a. *Re-constructing archaeology*. Cambridge: Cambridge University Press.

Shanks, M. & C. Tilley 1987b. *Social theory and archaeology*. Cambridge: Polity Press.

Sturrock, J. (ed.) 1979. *Structuralism and since*. Oxford: Oxford University Press.

Tilley, C. 1984. Ideology and the legitimation of power in the middle neolithic of southern Sweden. *Ideology, power and prehistory*, D. Miller & C. Tilley (eds). Cambridge: Cambridge University Press.

4 *Divine kingdoms in northern Africa: material manifestations of social institutions*

ELSE JOHANSEN KLEPPE

Scope

The author supports the view that a relationship exists between the spread of iron use and of divine kingdoms. Attempts are made at identifying the presence of this specific centralized political system through material culture remains which are diagnostic of divine kingdoms as a political system. Certain objects or ornaments are shown to be worn, or possessed, by certain members of society throughout their lifetime or during certain stages in life. Such patterning may apply to members of society organized through kinship or through social position. The function is to maintain social order and cultural continuity. The result is that divine kingdoms can be traced archaeologically; however, the archaeologist may find it difficult to sort out the empirical material. Context should be made use of in the analytical approach, since material expressions of this order tend to be culture-specific. For example, a particular string of beads worn around the neck by certain members of one specific divine kingdom may carry the same social message as another particular string of beads worn around the waist, or perhaps a particular ivory bracelet worn above the right elbow by certain members of another divine kingdom. Social meaning can only be detected through contextual studies. Age, sex and other patterned associations including spatial distribution must be taken into consideration.

Three propositions can be put forward (see Kleppe 1986a, b):

> Certain symbols are used within a shared culture to represent a specific protection or affiliation; these will be used by any member of society in order to help him or her through fundamental stages in life.
>
> The use of symbols within a society may express political or administrative authority or other official positions recognized by society.
>
> Certain symbols may be used within a society to indicate group identity, or perhaps ethnic affiliation.

I will now compare two ethnographic case studies with archaeological material from my own fieldwork in the Upper White Nile area. However, first I shall look closer at divine kingdoms as a political and social system.

Divine kingdoms as political systems

Typical features in divine kingdoms are references to important events in the past, often in the form of myths. Myths form the background for the strong social organization based on kinship and on other social groupings which cross kinship ties, the most important of these being age-groups. Age-groups are male societies, and they function as the military organization serving to maintain law and order. Vansina (1961, p. 25) has defined African kingdoms as 'sovereign political groups, headed by a single leader who delegates authority to representatives in charge of the territorial units into which the country is divided'. In a divine kingdom the king is thought of as a supernatural being whose power is unlimited, at least in theory. His doings and his views and ideas express, confirm and maintain the religious foundation of his kingdom. The king prays not only to the spirits of his fathers, but also to his own spirit (Frazer 1932, p. 48). In African divine kingdoms there is believed to be a mystical connection between the physical and moral well-being of the king and the prosperity and success of the people of the kingdom (Gluckman 1965, p. 38). The time of election of a new king is a time when the kingdom is threatened. A divine king is an incarnation of the legendary founder of the kingdom, and the death of a king means disorder in society: it is of vital importance to re-establish social order. This is only done when a new divine king is installed. The death of a village chief also means social chaos, and also within this level of social organization it is important to bring back social order as soon as possible.

Myth, ritual and social organization

In the present context myth and ritual are discussed as sociocultural systems of communication underlining, reinforcing or perhaps even determining social organization within a society. Divine kingdoms are associated with a political power where the sanctions for maintaining law and order are beyond this world, but in the myths it is explained that people central in the mythical tradition had a former life in this world a long time ago. This applies, for example, to the founder of a particular royal lineage. How many generations ago a particular event took place is manifested in the genealogy. For most African kingdoms the royal genealogies are generally taken back in time to about AD 1500 (Vansina 1966, p. 32). The verbal tradition generally associated with a divine kingdom consists of a list of kings – in the case of the Shilluk of the Sudan also including a queen – which provides a relative chronology, and one or more myths about the origin of the kingdom. A myth is a tale about gods and god-like creatures and their connections with human beings; a myth is at least partly without foundation in events which really took place. In other words, all myths have a supernatural aspect which often serves to explain origin and sociocultural affiliation of central aspects in society. Myths are generally visually expressed in rituals; that is, in sets of rites which are formal religious acts and sacred practices carried out by the followers of a specific religion. Rituals function as a reminder and a guideline leading followers through fundamental stages in life. In the present context it is relevant to add that material expressions are linked with ritual performances, and that different ritual stages have different material expressions. Rites serve indirectly to maintain social institutions and social order and control in society; this implies that religion tends to have an adaptive function. Throughout history religion only changes if, or when, there is a radical change in the social system, in particular with regard to economy and politics. Such change also implies radical shifts in the balance of power between leading societies, and these may be ethnic units or they may be states.

Sociocultural contexts and material expressions

Objects and ornaments as isolated phenomena cannot bring forth general aspects of symbolic meanings. Information of this kind can only be achieved through contextual observation, including spatial distribution. Objects and ornaments found in different contexts, but within the same cultural setting, may carry different social meanings. Propositions which attempt to verify relationships between sociocultural features and material culture can only be verified through inductive reasoning. In any study based on material culture, classification is an important tool in the analytical process. Classification is useful in providing an unambiguous scientific language; but clear and unambiguous categories serve no purpose if they have not been established through a careful evaluation of the source material. This implies that the point-of-departure for classification ought to be in theory construction aiming at sorting out relationships between the social and the material.

In the context of divine kingdoms, myths and rituals express the uniqueness of a particular kingdom, and any member of society will acknowledge their importance, and communicate this through their participation in rituals and through their knowledge and use of traditional songs and tales, which have been passed on from one generation to another, and so have become a part of the cultural identity. Most songs and tales include mythical aspects. As an example illustrating this, I comment on one of the folktales of the Oromo Booran, also known as the Galla people (Kassam & Megersa 1986). It is about two boys standing at a lake; boy A has a particular necklace called *'dok'*. The name refers both to beads used in the necklace, and to the actual necklace. Boy B has no necklace. So boy B took the necklace from boy A and threw it into the lake. Boy A asked boy B to bring him back his necklace, but boy B refused. Boy A then went to boy B's father to ask him to persuade his son to bring back the necklace. The father told boy A that he was not able to do anything about it. Boy A then approached various beings – one after another – within a cosmos representing the fundamentals in life, the chain of being. Action is finally taken by the one instance whose role in society is that of taking over the leftovers after others. In this folktale it is the hyaena that agrees to help when approached by boy A. The hyaena initiates a whole chain of attacks, and boy B is finally beaten by his own father and forced to dive into the lake and return the necklace.

There is a universal aspect to the folktale from the Oromo Booran (see also Ch. 13), and similar tales are also found in contexts totally isolated from this one. My interpretation of the tale is that when an important event takes place – in this case the loss of that particular necklace – all aspects of the cosmos need to be involved in getting things in order again. The necklace in question was not a mere ornament worn by boy A for decorative purposes, it was the material manifestation of a ritual act. In Kassam & Megersa's interpretation of the folktale, the importance of the element water is pointed out. In the traditional Oromo Booran society boys had to go through water and back to water as an important aspect of a rite, perhaps one marking the admission of new membership into an age group; the necklace – the *dok* – would then be the material expression of having won that membership.

Myths and rituals which concern the foundation and maintenance of a society will always produce material expressions of the basic institutions, since this is the obvious way of communicating social order and commitment. This is of particular importance in oral societies.

Ethnographic case studies

As a further verification of the three propositions put forward, two ethnographic case studies of divine kingdoms are now compared. One of these is the divine kingdom of the Shilluk in the Upper White Nile area in southern Sudan, which I have recently studied. The Shilluk kingdom forms an ethnic group with its own language. The other case study is the divine kingdom of the Bafut, one of the Grassfield kingdoms of Cameroon (Mbunwe-Samba 1986). The Bafut kingdom is located in the Bamenda Grassfield on the hillside towards the highland, and the people belong to an ethnic group called the Tikar.

There are striking similarities between the two divine kingdoms of the Shilluk and the Bafut, not because they are both products of direct cultural contact, but rather because both are expressions of the presence of diagnostic features associated with divine kingdom as a specific political organization maintained through affiliated social institutions and their material expressions. Only material-culture items of a non-perishable nature have been included in the comparison, since the aim of this chapter is to verify its relevance to archaeology.

The structure and organization of Shilluk society is well known through the important contributions of Seligman (1931), Howell (1941), Evans-Pritchard (1948) and Lienhardt (1954), and the relationship between the social and the material has been revealed through my own fieldwork. Bafut society is known to me through Mbunwe-Samba (1986) and the important monograph by Ritzenthaler & Ritzenthaler (1962).

Both the Bafut kingdom and the Shilluk kingdom are 'class' societies, and in both cases kings can only be chosen from the royal aristocracy. The Shilluk aristocracy is made up of the descendants of any king (Kleppe 1986a, p. 83). The choice of a new king is always between two competing territorial units, the northern one and the southern one. The age-grade system functions as a military organization; it is the important social control mechanism, as it is the only organization which cuts across kinship ties. Members are recruited within the local group or within a settlement.

An aristocratic class is also found in the Bafut kingdom, but membership alone is not sufficient to claim the royal throne. Only a king's children who were born while their father was in power have a right to succession. In both societies the objects and ornaments which are the overt signals of the king in office are only to be used by him while he is actually reigning. On the death of a king, all objects and ornaments associated with his role and function as a divine king are removed and kept by a special group of the king's men until his successor is to be installed on the throne. In the Bafut society a king-elect wears only a loincloth and carries a staff with two small red feathers on top (Ritzenthaler & Ritzenthaler 1962, p. 73), an object which signals that he has killed a leopard, an animal with which the king is identified. The coronation ceremony is led by a group of elders, whose leader wears a necklace of plaited grass and a rope. It is interesting to note that the necklace indicating his role in this important event is made of perishable material. It is probably only meant to last as long as the event itself. Mbunwe-Samba (1986) has mentioned a series of objects and ornaments which are associated with the king. However, most of these will be difficult if not impossible to detect archaeologically. The only ones which will be present in the archaeological record are the royal beads and traces of the fly-whisk and of the country bag. The country bag among other things contains the medicine which is used for turning a person into a divine king. The fly-whisk is decorated with special beads or perhaps with cowrie shells, and the country bag may also be decorated with cowrie shells. In the Bafut society royal affiliation is shown through distinct bead use according to the information given by Ritzenthaler & Ritzenthaler (1962). A king's wife wears a cowrie shell necklace, a king's daughter a necklace of polychrome glass beads, and a king's son – a prince – wears chevron beads. Membership in the initial stage of Bafut secret societies is indicated by wearing a bead necklace, which the king has taken from his own neck and given to the new member.

In Shilluk society beads are also important markers of social identity. A string of small white glass beads worn as an anklet has one social meaning when worn on the left foot, and another one when worn on the right foot. In the former case it indicates membership in the royal aristocracy, and in the latter case it indicates a person holding the office of chief. A necklace of ostrich eggshell beads is also a chief's ornament, but it is also the ornament of a wife of any king in Shilluk society. Membership in the age-grade system is indicated by wearing a waistband, also of ostrich eggshell beads. An example of the use of a certain symbol within a shared culture to represent a specific protection or affiliation needed by all members of society is the specific power of the green bead, which in Shilluk society is believed to give special protection to newborn children and babies. These examples of material expressions of sociocultural institutions confirm the three propositions put forward above, and they are a useful instrument in identifying divine kingdoms through the archaeological record.

Divine kingdoms and the spread of iron

The divine kingdom is an ancient political institution in African cultural history. Haycock (1971, p. 27) has iterated the idea originally suggested by Arkell that there was a relationship between divine kingdoms and the spread of iron-working, and recently this view has been further developed with reference to ethnographic and archaeological data from Central Africa (de Maret 1985).

In the African context the divine kingdom is at least 4500 years old, since it existed from the beginning of the Old Kingdom in Ancient Egypt (Trigger *et al.* 1983, p. 56), and the earliest use of iron on the African continent is also known from this context. The kingdom of Kush flourished in northern Sudan, known as Napata in 806–295 BC (Adams 1977). By that time the capital was moved southwards to the island of Meroe, where it continued to exist until AD 320. Its decline and fall may be explained with reference to overexploitation of the environment – deforestation – due to the extensive iron-working there (Haaland 1985). The spread of iron-working into western Africa has generally been considered to be a product of contacts with ancient Meroe. In order to gain new insight into the problem of the spread of iron use, a reinvestigation into the context of the spread of divine kingdoms is suggested.

My own archaeological excavations in the Upper White Nile area have revealed a collection of small iron objects. Three radiocarbon datings carried out on associated organic material support a dating to about 1000 BC (Kleppe 1983), a dating which is remarkably early in the African context. It is perhaps less surprising that it has been obtained in this geographical area when seen in the light of the existence of an early divine kingdom.

References

Adams, W. Y. 1977. *Nubia. Corridor to Africa*. Princeton: Princeton University Press.

Evans-Pritchard, E. E. 1948. *The divine kingship of the Shilluk of the Nilotic Sudan*. Cambridge: The Frazer Lecture.

Frazer, J. G. 1932. *The golden bough. A study in magic and religion*. Part 1: *The magic art and the evolution of kings*, Vol. 1. London: Macmillan.

Gluckman, M. 1965. *Custom and conflict in Africa*. Oxford: Basil Blackwell.

Haaland, R. 1985. Iron production, its socio-cultural context and ecological implications. In *African iron working, ancient and traditional*, R. Haaland & P. Shinnie (eds), 50–72. Oslo: Norwegian University Press.

Haycock, B. G. 1971. The place of the Napatan–Meroitic culture in the history of the

Sudan and Africa. In *Sudan in Africa*, Y. F. Hasan (ed.), 26–41. Khartoum: Khartoum University Press.

Howell, P. P. 1941. The Shilluk settlement. *Sudan Notes and Records* **24**, 47–67.

Kassam, A. & G. Megersa 1986. Iron and beads: male and female symbols of creation. A study of ornament among the Oromo Booran. In *Archaeological 'objectivity' in interpretation*. World Archaeological Congress, vol. 2 (mimeo).

Kleppe, E. J. 1983. Towards a prehistory of the riverain Nilotic Sudan. Archaeological excavations in the Er Renk district. *Nubian Letters* **1**, 14–20.

Kleppe, E. J. 1986a. Religion expressed through bead use: an ethno-archaeological study of Shilluk, southern Sudan. In *Words and objects. Towards a dialogue between archaeology and history*, G. Steinsland (ed.), 78–90. Oslo: Norwegian University Press.

Kleppe, E. J. 1986b. Ritual use of beads: a case study of Shilluk traditions related to archaeological observations. In *Archaeological 'objectivity' in interpretation*. World Archaeological Congress, vol. 2 (mimeo).

Lienhardt, G. 1954. The Shilluk of the Upper Nile. In *African worlds*, D. Forde (ed.), 138–163. London: Oxford University Press.

de Maret, P. 1985. The smith's myth and the origin of leadership in Central Africa. In *African iron working, ancient and traditional*, R. Haaland & P. Shinnie (eds), 73–87. Oslo: Norwegian University Press.

Mbunwe-Samba, P. 1986. Traditional art and artifacts in Bamenda Grassfield: symbolism and meaning. In *Archaeological 'objectivity' in interpretation*. World Archaeological Congress, vol. 2 (mimeo).

Ritzenthaler, R. & P. Ritzenthaler 1962. Cameroons village. An ethnography of the Bafut. *Milwaukee: Public Museum. Publications in Anthropology* **8**.

Seligman, C. G. 1931. The religion of the pagan tribes of the White Nile. *Africa* **4**, 1–21.

Trigger, B. G., B. J. Kemp, D. O'Connor & A. B. Lloyd 1983. *Ancient Egypt*. Cambridge: Cambridge University Press.

Vansina, J. 1962. A comparison of African kingdoms. *Journal of African History* **32**, 324–35.

Vansina, J. 1966. *Kingdoms of the savanna*. Madison: University of Wisconsin Press.

16 *Towards an archaeology of thought*

WHITNEY DAVIS

The human mind can be regarded metaphorically as a complex disambiguation machine characterized in some moments by intentionality. Its 'output' in action and expression depends on conditions of operation, 'programs' and 'input'. Many of the conditions of operation and much of the 'output' leave traces in the archaeological record. However, the programs and aspects of the input are much less directly observable. They constitute a 'black box' problem for archaeology.

Some archaeologists ignore the black box altogether. They link external stimuli and external responses – that is, what turns up in the 'material' record – directly, without considering the mental 'processing' of either. This behaviourist approach is certainly inadequate. Others seem to feel that processing can be taken for granted, perhaps because it is always the same – 'rational', 'optimizing', 100 per cent error-free. Such idealizations are suspicious. A great deal goes on inside the black box of the mind, but how do we get a look inside?

Although in itself the product of hundreds of millennia of homin(o)id evolution, for our purposes the programs in *Homo sapiens sapiens* – perception (for example, Marr 1982), mental processing (for example, Block 1983), and language acquisition (for example, Fodor 1973, Chomsky 1980) – can be regarded as 'fixed'. A thought-experiment: plucked from its Aurignacian birthplace, an infant learns to speak modern Bostonian English or to use my word-processor.

In contrast with the 'fixed' programs, input is variable. Our infant could learn to speak Attic Greek just (and only) because she grows up in Periclean Athens. However, like the programs, the 'processing' of input is archaeologically inaccessible. We cannot be sure just how input was received and mentally transformed by our time-traveller: we cannot see her mind working. Processing is part of the black box.

Nevertheless, we are not utterly ignorant. The necessary condition of processing is that input is ordered. Input that is naturally structured (for example, Gibson 1979) can be archaeologically recovered: we can describe the world impinging on human perceptual systems. This world usually includes the output of other people. In social systems output becomes input. When input–output is ordered by human beings, let us say it is 'coded' in symbolic structures, structures or knowledge, or (as they will be called here) modes of representation (MRs) – language, images, gesture, and so on.

For lack of space, as used here the term 'MR' is loose and general. It refers both to extrasomatic symbol-systems like costume or musical notation and to the 'internal' representation of knowledge in 'propositions' or 'mental imagery' (leaving aside the question whether these may be different systems or reducible to more-basic systems: see Block 1983). For precise archaeological and experimental purposes it is critical to distinguish between types of MRs according to logical, functional or other criteria (for example, Goodman 1971, Block 1983). Elsewhere (Davis 1986) I have tried to apply a rigorous definition of images in considering the emergence of graphic figurations, at least in part as an example of the need for the precise logical, functional or other characterization of MRs.

An MR usually cannot be dug up and examined as a whole. Still, it can be reconstructed as a logical artefact or, perhaps more precisely, as the logic of artefacts.

In practice a field-worker retrieves only the partially degraded remains of output; that is, structured or coded input processed according to the programs – remains like 'texts', manufactured objects and traces of activities. The contents of the black box must be inferred from the characteristics and distribution of these remains.

Art history, literary criticism, cultural anthropology and other humanistic disciplines traditionally (if controversially) claim to be able to make these inferences. Four claims are stated here as greatly oversimplified hypotheses.

(a) The frequency and distribution of a feature of output are evidence for its derivation from a program ('universal'), an MR ('cultural'?) or processing ('individual').

(b) The morphological characteristics of a feature of output are evidence for its particular position and use in a program, MR or processing. Because the ordering of input depends on the variation of morphologies (light intensities, colour, sound frequency, texture, shape, and so forth), any particular variation will have a determinable place in the order.

Investigation of hypotheses (a) and (b) depends on comparative formal and structural analysis of various kinds (for example, Barthes 1983, Lévi-Strauss 1982, Wobst 1977).

(c) The 'form' (versus morphology) of output is always evidence of decision or reflection, and is to be perceived as such by others; output has been regarded as having intentional and aesthetic qualities. (For a development of the distinction between morphology and form, see Davis n.d.; for worries about the intentionalist element in the account, see Davis 1986, 1987).

(d) Many of the characteristics of output can be attributed to actual men and women of the past. Precisely because not all possible permutations of a program, MR or processing can be put to use by people living under particular environmental, technological and other conditions, those permutations which do appear are evidence for what those (or that) people could do (or did) under those particular conditions.

Investigating hypotheses (c) and (d) depends on detailed stylistic and historical investigation, including many of the analytic projects undertaken in stylistic taxonomy or connoisseurship (for example, Carpenter 1960), iconological analysis (for example, Panofsky 1939), and the 'social history' of production and interpretation (for example, Baxandall 1972).

Many of the descriptive and interpretative procedures of the humanities have a long ancestry in Greek philosophy, Latin rhetoric, medieval scholasticism and modern thought. Itself ultimately sprung from the scholarship of the renaissance and the enlightenment, why has modern 'analytic' archaeology made so little use of these means of reconstituting the operations of minds in history? Why has there been so little emphasis on how it is that one goes about determining meanings or identifying intentions in utterance (defined by Grice 1969, p. 177, to include 'any human institution the function of which is to provide artificial substitutes for natural signs'), when massive research programs in art history (for example, Baxandall 1986), philosophy (for example, Grice 1957, Searle 1979), cognitive psychology and anthropology (for example, Sperber & Wilson 1986) have devoted themselves to these issues?

Let us distinguish between the practical and the theoretical difficulties of the project from an archaeologist's point of view.

To be considered by an archaeologist in practice, the degraded remains of mental life must be sufficiently substantial. Language supposedly does not directly fossilize; certainly the 'meanings' or 'intentions' of which it is supposedly a physical expression or communication are not directly accessible to observation. It is not clear whether the archaeologist's problem here is any different from or any more interesting than anyone's day-to-day problem in interpreting the utterances of others – in decoding output. It is therefore not clear whether there is in fact any special archaeological problem to be faced, that is, beyond the 'archaeological' problem of the day-to-day inference from physical morphologies to 'meanings' or 'intentions' in speech, image making, and so on.

Furthermore, despite the difficulties of 'direct' access, whatever these are thought to be, inferences are still made about the evolution of language (for example, Lieberman 1984, White 1985). Classicists, Egyptologists, Sinologists and others have something to say about the role and history of language in culture (for example, Havelock 1963, Baines 1983, 1988). The study of images and other mark- and form-making in two or three dimensions ('art') promises intriguing results with better-fossilized media (for example, Lewis-Williams 1982, Marshack 1984, Davis 1982, 1986, 1987). Finally, tools, buildings and other classes of 'material culture' provide evidence about spatial and other programs, MRs and processing (for example, Hodder 1982, Wynn 1985).

In sum, approached imaginatively, the minimal testimony of often highly degraded output can be used to test the various hypotheses, like (a)–(d) above, of an 'archaeology of thought'. Not all archaeological remains are remains of mental life, but all mental life has remains. Except perhaps in its own self-description, the mind is not sealed off.

Theoretical objections are always more interesting than practical problems. Three broad worries deserve to be noted, with a sketch of a possible response.

An archaeology of thought seems crippled: (a) by the material unavailability of its object; (b) by its recurrent need to assume mind to explain mind; and (c) by the 'subjective' nature of many of its claims. It is worth noting that these problems beset any and all interpretation of output, whether it is conducted by an 'archaeologist' acting as an archaeologist or by that same 'archaeologist' acting as a competent member of her own society: there seems to me to be no essential difference between these situations. I take the problems up in turn.

(a) Archaeologists have been suspicious of talk about the 'ideas', 'values', 'beliefs' and 'intentions' of individuals in past societies, although such talk is deeply entrenched in all of the humanities, in mainstream history, and in cultural anthropology (what Shakespeare meant, what Hitler intended, what the Nuer believe). Why are archaeologists suspicious of integrating this talk into their argument? Apparently their suspicion in part derives pragmatically from the simple lack of remains of some (but not all) major media of representation; imaginative new analysis may yet wring blood from the stones. However, let us beware of the archaeologist's 'theoretical' assertion that he or she works with the 'material' or 'behavioural' and that other historians – of art, politics or religion – at least in part with the 'ideal' (ideational and ideological). Here, the suspicion actually rests on the fallacious assumption that MRs in themselves merely 'reflect' or 'express' ideas and intentions, still hidden, unobserved or unknowable. Paradoxically, in accepting this assumption modern archaeology encumbers itself with a rather orthodox idealism, legislating a separation of World and Idea.

Observe the simple consequences of eliminating the idealist assumption in 'material' archaeology. An MR does not merely reflect or express ideas, which exist somewhere else; an MR is in itself a set of 'ideas' or 'values'. What is represented *is* a culture's knowledge and the extent or extendability of its material life. 'Ideas' are *in* an MR, and an MR is *in* a medium: look at the locus, frequency, distribution, form, structure, uses and history of the medium, and you are necessarily already and always looking at the 'ideas'.

Now to some extent this reformulation amounts to little more than a play with words. The redefinition does not solve any problems, but simply makes them available for real study and possible solution.

For instance, it is a necessary feature of an MR that its elements do 're-present'; that is, refer or symbolize. Although we may be able to describe the symbol-system morphologically or even syntactically, referents and the pragmatic dimension may still elude us. The knowledge symbolized is not 'inaccessible', but is another sequence of symbols, perhaps in another medium. Symbols refer endlessly to symbols (Sperber 1975); a vast network of interpretations binds together the innumerable representations experienced consciously as a single, seamless knowing awareness. At the limit, our access to some of the internal symbolic media of perception and cognition becomes attentuated. We are better off with the more overt, conscious, world-attached links and levels.

If all thought is symbolic, then to say anything interesting, of course, we want to distinguish between types of symbols and their modes of referring to, translating into or montaging with one another. Sample problems are not hard to find. Why should palaeolithic 'notations' for information about celestial phenomena apparently use digital, 'sequential' MRs (Marshack 1972, 1984) rather than other logically conceivable but analogical, iconic MRs (for surely the uneducated organism's internal experience – and mental representation – of geophysical cycles, weather, its proximate milieu, and so on, is an experience of continuous variation), and how was this 'translation' – the cultural digitalization of sensory continua – effected in the first place? The 'primary expressional significance' (Panofsky 1939) of lines, of colours and even of figures may be universal, perhaps because mental processing prefers the *Gestalt* primitives (Arnheim 1954), but how then are the 'secondary conventional connotations' persuasively or coercively assigned and accepted? That is, what social forces must operate in particular conditions for certain conventions to emerge?

(b) It is easy to think of the machine running programs using various MRs, our metaphor for 'the Human Mind', as just simply there in history, a fixed structure of capacities or functions – *Kultur*, *Geist* or *la pensée* (*sauvage* or *rationalisé*) playing out its preordained role – which we study by examining its expression in or interaction with the world. A more idealist, even Hegelian, enterprise would be hard to imagine, but again seems to be characteristic of modern archaeology at a deep level. Assuming rather than explaining mind, archaeology merely records an actor's performances – the scenery, the glittering costumes, the changing props – without discovering who or what he or she is and why he or she plays his parts the way he or she does. Cleaving close to our anti-idealist intuition, let us acknowledge that there is nothing essentially the case about human minds (certainly not 'language' or communication, nor even intentionality or 'symboling'): the brain has evolved, and all aspects of the MRs, programs and processing necessarily have a history. This recognition justifies archaeology's very attempt to supplement the introspection of philosophers, the experiments of psychologists, or the portraits of painters and poets – always and everywhere bound to a mind somewhere particular in history.

This history can be variously conceived. For instance, despite the efforts of structuralists and some others, questions about origins cannot be waved away simply. The perceptual and cognitive representations of today evolved in some yesterday and have continuously emerged throughout human and homin(o)id history.

Accounting for the evolution of thought non-tautologously and non-reductively – without assuming the very capacities that we are trying to explain (see Biro 1979) or retreating to behaviourism (see Searle 1979) or adaptationalism (see Gould & Lewontin 1979) – is to my mind the most pressing problem of palaeo-archaeology (Davis 1986, 1987, 1989, n.d.).

Of course, capacities of mind are not actual acts or expressions. Throughout history, human beings with particular interests in particular social situations use only some elements of available representational systems. How and why aspects of a program or MR are used in a particular time and place is again an historical question, the question of 'style' broadly defined – that is, of the specific arbitrariness of representation – the traditional province of art history, sociolinguistics and literary study, and other critical disciplines in the humanities (for example, Lang 1979, Philipson & Gudel 1980; for some efforts in archaeology, see Conkey & Hastorf 1989).

(c) The overall project of studying style is not hopelessly subjective. In assessing the arbitrariness of thought and its outputs, our controls are objective, often experimental understandings of perception and cognition (for example, Marr 1982) and of the general logical character of MRs (for example, Goodman 1971). In archaeology and art history, style has been defined as a description of a polythetic set of similar but varying attributes in a group of artefacts, the presence of which can only be explained by the history of the artefacts, namely common descent from an archaeologically identifiable production system (Davis 1989). This definition calls for empirical examination of morphologies, and statistical examination of relations among them.

In the preceding paragraphs I have very briefly sketched some possible responses to the principal objections to an 'archaeology of thought'. I have not presented any detailed case examples, nor have I examined the particular advantages or disadvantages of any specific vocabularies or approaches.

Furthermore, some readers will regard my responses as conveniently naive. The relativizing demonstrations of recent hermeneutics, 'critical theory' and 'deconstruction' (statements in Philipson & Gudel 1980, surveys in Skinner 1985) undermine the more comfortable objectivities of science, history and interpretation. They can be regarded, as Skinner (1985) puts it, as 'the return of grand theory in the human sciences'; that is, as the revivification of the humanities in the more global project of understanding humanity. The effect of a powerful critical tradition in the humanities on the social sciences has yet to be measured. It is puzzling that the humanities themselves actually lack a truly 'archaeological' perspective, which necessarily relativizes human-ness (symbol–convention–language–meaning–ideology–society–history) to particular times and places in the material record of homin(o)id life. I think it is deeply misleading to consider symbolic life and exchange as the basic condition of human-ness and the necessary starting point for anthropological analysis; rather, I am convinced that a naturalistic investigation and understanding of this life still holds out the best hope for grasping it in its symbolic moments.

In producing an 'archaeology of thought', two distinctive contributions of archaeology have been and will be: (a) to focus on inferring the past work of human minds from the present degraded state of their output; and (b) to dramatize the evolutionary, historical, contingent nature of MRs, programs and processing, to the extent, even, of asking how and why they came into being.

Mind as we know it is a living artefact, an evolving network of representations which have a history, reconstructed from fragments or leaving decipherable traces. It has been the work of all archaeologies in all disciplines to peer into black boxes, on the principle that nothing in the universe is sealed off from all the rest. An archaeology of human thought in history is no exception.

References

Arnheim, R. 1954. *Art and visual perception*, 1st edn. Berkeley: University of California Press.

Baines, J. R. 1983. Literacy and ancient Egyptian society. *Man* **18**, 572–99.

Baines, J. R. 1988. Literacy, social organization and the archaeological record: the case of early Egypt. In *State and society: the emergence and development of social hierarchy and political centralization*, J. Gledhill, B. Bender & M. T. Larsen (eds), ch. 12. London: Unwin Hyman.

Barthes, R. 1983. *The fashion system* (transl. M. Ward & R. Howard). New York: Hill & Wang.

Baxandall, M. 1972. *Painting and experience in fifteenth century Italy*. Oxford: Oxford University Press.

Baxandall, M. 1986. *Patterns of intention*. New Haven: Yale University Press.

Biro, J. 1979. Intentionalism in the theory of meaning. *The Monist* **62**, 238–58.

Block, N. (ed.) 1983. *Imagery*. Cambridge, Massachusetts: MIT Press/Bradford Books.

Carpenter, R. 1960. *Greek sculpture: a critical review*, 1st edn. Chicago: University of Chicago Press.

Chomsky, N. 1980. *Rules and representations*. New York: Columbia University Press.

Conkey, M. W. & C. Hastorf (eds) 1989. *The uses of style in archaeology*. Cambridge: Cambridge University Press.

Davis, W. 1982. Canonical representation in ancient Egyptian art. *Res: Anthropology and Aesthetics* **4**, 20–46.

Davis, W. 1986. The origins of image making. *Current Anthropology* **27**, 193–215.

Davis, W. 1987. Replication and depiction in paleolithic art. *Representations* (forthcoming).

Davis, W. 1989. Style and history in art history. In *The uses of style in archaeology*, M. W. Conkey & C. Hastorf (eds) (forthcoming). Cambridge: Cambridge University Press.

Davis, W. n.d. *Seeing through culture: the possibility of a history of representation* (forthcoming).

Fodor, J. 1973. *The language of thought*. Cambridge, Massachusetts: Harvard University Press.

Gibson, J. J. 1979. *The ecological approach to visual perception*. Boston: Houghton Mifflin.

Goodman, N. 1971. *The languages of art: an approach to a theory of symbols*, 2nd edn. Indianapolis: Bobbs-Merrill.

Gould, S. J. & R. C. Lewontin. 1979. The spandrels of San Marco and the Panglossian paradigm: a critique of the adaptationist programme. *Proceedings of the Royal Society of London* **B205**, 581–98.

Grice, H. P. 1957. Meaning. *Philosophical Review* **66**, 377–88.

Grice, H. P. 1969. Utterer's meaning and intentions. *Philosophical Review* **78**, 147–77.

Havelock, E. A. 1963. *Preface to Plato*. Oxford: Oxford University Press.

Hodder, I. 1982. *Symbols in action*. Cambridge: Cambridge University Press.

Lang, B. (ed.) 1979. *Style*. Philadelphia: University of Pennsylvania Press.

Lévi-Strauss, C. 1982. *The way of the masks* (transl. S. Modelski). Vancouver: Douglas & McIntyre.

Lewis-Williams, J. D. 1982. The economic and social context of southern San rock art. *Current Anthropology* **23**, 429–49.

Lieberman, P. 1984. *The biology and evolution of language*. Cambridge, Massachusetts: Harvard University Press.

Marr, D. 1982. *Vision: a computational investigation*. San Francisco: Freeman.
Marshack, A. 1972. *The roots of civilization: the beginnings of man's first art, symbol, and notation*. New York: McGraw-Hill.
Marshack, A. 1984. The ecology and brain of two-handed bipedalism: an analytic, cognitive, and evolutionary assessment. In *Animal cognition*, H. L. Roitblat, T. G. Bever & H. S. Terrace (eds), 491–511. Hillsdale, New Jersey: Lawrence Erlbaum.
Panofsky, E. 1939. *Studies in iconology*. Oxford: Oxford University Press.
Philipson, M. & P. J. Gudel (eds) 1980. *Aesthetics today*, 2nd edn. New York: New American Library.
Searle, J. R. 1979. *Intentionality*. Cambridge: Cambridge University Press.
Skinner, Q. (ed.) 1985. *The return of grand theory in the human sciences*. Cambridge: Cambridge University Press.
Sperber, D. 1975. *Rethinking symbolism* (transl. A. L. Morton). Cambridge: Cambridge University Press.
Sperber, D. & D. Wilson 1986. *Relevance: communication and cognition*. Cambridge, Massachusetts: Harvard University Press.
White, R. 1985. Thoughts on social relationships and language in hominid evolution. *Journal of Personal and Social Relationships* **2**, 95–115.
Wobst, H. M. 1977. Stylistic behavior and information exchange. In *For the director: research essays in honor of James B. Griffin*, C. E. Cleland (ed.), 317–42. University of Michigan Anthropological Papers 61. Ann Arbor: University of Michigan Press.
Wynn, T. 1985. Piaget, stone tools and the evolution of human intelligence. *World Archaeology* **17**, 32–42.

23 *Tusona ideographs – a lesson in interpretive objectivity*

GERHARD KUBIK

Introduction

Tusona (as they are called in Lucazi, a language classed among the 'Ngangela' group of Bantu languages in eastern Angola and northwestern Zambia), or *sona* (as they are called in Cokwe), constitute a tradition of ideographic writing found in an area of West-Central Africa approximately as large as France (Fig. 23.1). It consists of almost all of eastern Angola, parts of Northwestern Province, Zambia, and southernmost Zaire, especially the Kasai River area. *Tusona* or *sona* may be considered as one of the most important graphic traditions in the Bantu languages zones of West-Central Africa.

The -Lucazi people, among whom I have researched this tradition since 1973, use the term *tusona* (in the singular *kasona*) for ideographs which are sized anywhere between half a metre square and two flat palms of the human hand joined together. These are drawn usually by adult men and elders, with a certain performance technique, using the fingers in the sand. They are drawn in the course of leisure time social gatherings in the *ndzango*, the assembly pavilion in the middle of a Lucazi village. Here men sit together and discuss issues, work, rest or play games. The person who knows *tusona* so well that he can captivate his audience is often offered free millet beer (*vwalwa vwa masangu*) by the others. Women are officially excluded from the *tusona* tradition, as indeed they are excluded from the *ndzango* gatherings. However, in reality, they know quite a lot about this tradition.

More rarely *tusona* may also appear on house walls as paintings (murals). Dos Santos (1961, p. 17) claims that among the -Cokwe they may also be drawn on objects such as calabashes. I have never seen this, and 'Je n'ai jamais relevé de *sona*, du type écrit sur le sable, dans la décoration des objets Tshokwe, comme le suggère Eduardo dos Santos' (Bastin, pers. comm. 1981). As sand-drawings, *tusona* are strictly ephemeral, because soon after production they are wiped off by the *mukakusona* (the drawer of a *kasona*) to obtain blank space on the ground for the next one. It is therefore difficult to assess how old the tradition is in absolute terms. Even those which may occasionally be seen on house walls are soon washed away by rain, or disappear when the houses in deserted villages (*zingundu*) disintegrate and break down.

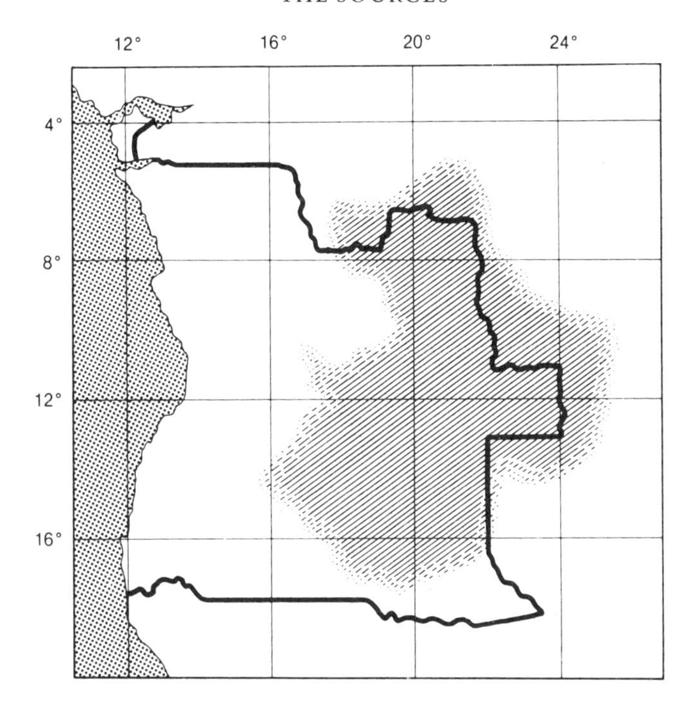

Figure 23.1 The eastern Angolan culture area where the *tusona/sona* tradition is found.

The sources

The first foreign observer who reported *sona* among the -Cokwe was Baumann (1935), who briefly discusses four such ideographs under the title *Sandzeichnungen* (sand drawings). He also contributed a photograph of enormous historical importance taken during his field expedition to northeastern Angola in 1930: a wall-painting in the traditional colours *mukundu* (red ochre) and *mphemba* (white kaolin), showing the *kasona* called *Vamphulu* (the gnus) in a shape absolutely identical with the one I documented from the late Chief Kalunga Ntsamba Chiwaya among another people, the -Lucazi, and in another place, Chikenge in Kabompo District, northwestern Zambia, in 1973 (see Fig. 23.2).

Numerous other accounts of *sona* or *tusona* have appeared since Baumann's, beginning with Hamelberger's (1951, 1952) pioneering studies. However, most collections contain material from -Cokwe informants in a relatively small area in Lunda Province, Angola, namely in the vicinity of the Museu do Dundo (see dos Santos 1961). Among these Fontinha's (1983) recently published book, based on material collected between 1945 and 1955, is the most comprehensive and the most analytical.

An independent collection of *tusona* from southeastern Angola by the Swedish

Figure 23.2 Baumann (1935) photograph of the *kasona* of *Vamphulu* (the gnus) painted in the traditional Cokwe colours of red ochre and white kaolin on the wall of a *ntsenge* (store, kitchen and women's fire-place). Why it was painted in the 'female area' of the village is a riddle still to be solved.

Missionary Emil Pearson, and dating back to the year 1927, testifies how widespread this tradition once was (Pearson 1977, 1984). It was in no way limited to the -Cokwe, but was shared by all of the eastern Angolan peoples of the so-called Ngangela-cluster (the -Lucazi, -Mbwela, -Nkhangala, -Mbunda, -Lwimbi, etc.). This has received further confirmation from my own studies among the -Lucazi in northwestern Zambia, Kabompo District, people who, as early 20th century migrants to this area, brought this graphic tradition with them.

My own fieldwork on *tusona* began in 1973 in Kabompo District, northwestern Zambia and continued in 1977/8 and 1979 in Zambia and in 1982 in Angola (Kubik 1986).

Structure, meaning and content of the *tusona*

Tusona/sona constitute a depository of graphic structures carrying social, educational, literary and metaphysical messages. The content and meaning of the *tusona* are often philosophical, serving the community as a form of entertainment as well as a written code for expressing abstract ideas on some of the people's most central issues and institutions.

The graphic components of the *tusona* that are worked into elaborate configurations can be reduced to relatively few graphemes whose meanings are variable. Their meanings also derive from their relationships in space, and from the overall content of a particular *kasona*. For example, a single dot, or a series of dots, produced in the characteristic technique of a *mukakusona* (writer of *tusona*) with the first and third fingers of his right hand, impressing the dots into the sand, can represent completely different things or ideas, according to context: tree(s), person(s), animal(s), eye(s) and mouth(s), beer vessel(s), etc. A line, drawn with the right index finger, can symbolize a path, a river, a fence, a wall, contours of the human body, and so on. Directional concepts are also prominent in the structures; for example, a series of dots is generally drawn away from the body or in a movement from the right to the left; a circular line is drawn counter-clockwise.

Some *tusona* are geometrically so complex that it takes considerable time to learn them and reproduce them from memory, whereas others require only a minimum of drawing action. In an ideograph which I collected from a -Lucazi expert in 1978, the late Livingstone Sanjeni Matemba, a thin curved line is first drawn with the tip of the index finger, starting at the top of the figure. The line is then crossed with a thicker, straight line, drawn by the first two fingers in the same direction as the original one. This ideograph (Fig. 23.3) represents the Lucazi proverb: *Cikuta cangendzi kucihonowa kucizitula, cakuzitula lyavene, weka kalikucihasa* (The bundle of a stranger – it is impossible to untie it, it must be untied by the owner himself, someone else is unable to do that). This proverb may be applied in daily life in a situation such as the following: if a person has done something that is considered to be wrong, then someone else cannot be expected to say 'Myself, I pay for it'. Only the person who has committed the offence is responsible. The message is that everybody has to disentangle his own guilt. *Cikuta* (the bundle, package, one's personal luggage), stands for *mulonga* (crime, offence, one's personal guilt). *Ngendzi* (a stranger, visitor, traveller) stands for the one who has disassociated himself from society by his wrongdoings.

There are *tusona* which are abstract in concept, and others which are pictographic, depicting concrete objects such as a crocodile (*ngandu*), and using a

Figure 23.3 *Cikuta cangendzi.*

specific drawing technique. The majority of *tusona* among the -Lucazi are based on a dot-and-line geometry, which can be quite difficult to interpret. Examples of these ideographs include: *Kambava wamulivwe* (the hyrax in the rock), *Kalolo-muzike na kalolo-wambata* (the bachelor rat and the married rat), *Tunwenu vwala vwetu* (let us drink our beer), and others. Here a single line circumscribes a given series of dots in a manner that follows the strict rule that it must return into itself. The most basic of these *tusona* is the *Katuva vufwati* or *Kangano kanthyengu* structure, in which only six dots are circumscribed by a single line.

Examples of *tusona* based on a dot-and-line geometry

The following examples were collected from various elders in Kabompo District, Northwestern Province, Zambia in 1973, 1977/8 and 1979.

Kangano kanthyengu (the footprint of a roan antelope), also called *Katuva vufwati* (the one who pierces into intestines); collected from Sachiteta Kakoma, born 1914; Kanguya village, Katuva River, 5 July 1979 (Fig. 23.4).

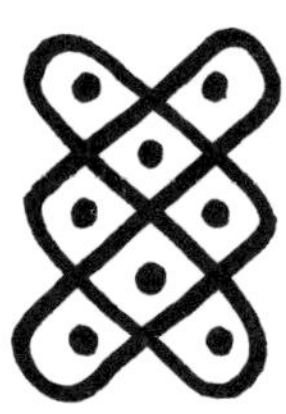

Figure 23.4 *Kangano kanthyengu.*

Associated text in Lucazi

Uze kasona uze, mwomu wakele kumphako, kaha lizina lyeni ikeye Katuva-vufwati. Wakele kumphako muze. Kaha vuno muvakumbata kaha kumbata luswango kaha kuhakaho muze. Kaha vunoni vuze vufwati vweni vunatwika, kaha kutalako ngecize: Nana! Oku kumphako kuli vufwati! Oku kumphako kuli vufwati! Oku kumphako kuli vufwati! Kaha ngwavo: Kal'iya? Kutotaho haze, kaha kutalako ngwavo: Kali katuva-vufwati, lizina lyeni.

Translation

This ideograph here, its name is *Katuva-vufwati*, because that animal named so, was found in a tree-hole. It was in the tree-hole just like that. Then the people took a long stick poking again and again there at the hole until [they pierced the animal through its abdomen] and the content of its stomach burst out. They looked at this and wondered: 'Hey! There in the tree hole there is the content of a stomach!' And they asked: 'Who is this small animal?'. When they cut the body out and looked at it, they found: 'It is *Katuva-vufwati*, that is its name!'.

The texts explaining a *kasona* are usually told after the drawing actions – undertaken in complete silence – have finished. The anecdote attached to this ideograph relates how hunters found a small mammal 'which can kill goats in the pen' in a tree hole and killed it.

An alternative meaning of this ideograph, provided by an informant in the same village, Benson Muzaza, born 1930, was that it represents the little footprint of a roan antelope (*kangano kanthyengu*), as seen by hunters in the sand.

Liswa lyavandzili (the nest of the *vandzili*-birds); collected from the late Livingstone Sanjeni Matemba, Chindzombo village, 3 January 1978 (Fig. 23.5).

Figure 23.5 *Liswa lyavandzili.*

Associated text in Lucazi	Translation
Njasoneka liswa lyavandzili, liswa lyavandzili. Eli liswa lyavandzili vaze tuzila tuze twatundende, tuzila twatundende. Liswa muvekukosa nakusemenamo vana vavo.	I have drawn the nest of the *vandzili*-birds. This is the nest of the *vandzili*-birds, those very small birds, the nest in which they sleep and in which they give birth to their children.

This ideograph was begun by impressing the two horizontal dots in the middle of the figure into the sand, using the pads of the tautly held first and third fingers of the right hand. Matemba then continued by marking the two dots above and below in the same manner. Finally, he impressed the two interlocking points, seen in the middle of the figure, in vertical movement, using his second finger. Then he drew the line circulocating the dots with the pad of his first finger, again tautly held, and continuing without interruption until the line reached its own starting point. Finally, he explained the meaning of this *kasona* as recorded.

Kambava wamulivwe (the hyrax in the rock); collected from the late Chief Kalunga Ntsamba Chiwaya (1898–1981) at Chikenge, July 1973; explained by the elder Kapokola Chimbau, Chikenge, 20 July 1979 (Fig. 23.6).

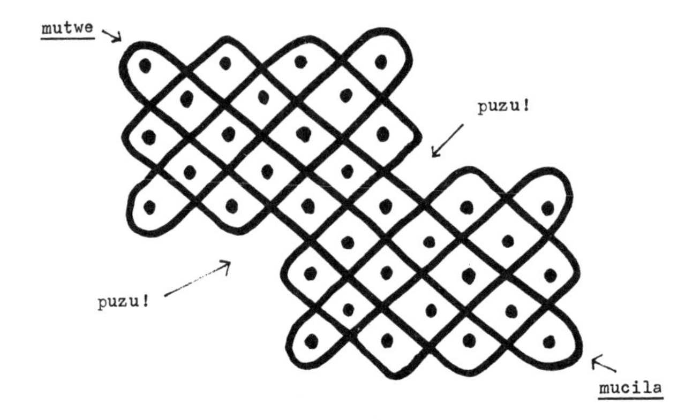

Figure 23.6 *Kambava wamulivwe.*

This ideograph was explained as follows. *Kambava* is a small mammal living in the wilderness. Its head and tail taste very nice. It once entered a rock. A hunter hacked at its body, *puzu*! with an axe, and a large piece was chipped off! Then the corpse decayed in the rock, until another hunter found it.

Puzu is an ideophone, conveying the idea of breaking up, disintegrating, crumbling. Although totally abstract, the structure implies that there is a head (*mutwe*) and a tail (*mucila*), and an abnormally narrow waist, where parts of the body of the hyrax were chipped off. In construction this is a most ingenious *kasona*. The 34 dots which form the basic screen must be circumscribed non-stop with a single line returning into itself. The path to be taken by this line is predetermined by unstated but implicit mathematical rules which operate in this type of *tusona*. The basic rule is that a line must always continue along a row of dots up to its end, or if it passes between two rows of dots, up to the end of the longer one. There it has to change direction by taking the course of the next row of dots 'within reach'. In practice this means, if the layout of dots forms a 'corner' to the right, that the line will take that corner, changing direction by describing a gentle curve of 90°. It will then follow the new row until that one is also finished, or, if the path leads between two parallel rows, until the longer one is finished. On the other hand, if there is no 'corner', i.e. if the end of a row of dots sticks out of the pattern of surrounding dots, then the line describes a half circle round the projecting dot, returning along the other side of the same row.

Vamphulu (the gnus); collected from the late Chief Kalunga Ntsamba Chiwaya (1898–1981) at Chikenge village, July 1973, explained by himself on 30 June 1979 (Fig. 23.7).

Associated text in Lucazi	Translation
Ndzita yezile mucifuti. Kaha ngwavo ineza mukutsiha vantu. Kaha vatinine kumusenge. Kaha muvevwa: Mbi!	War came into the country. So they (the gnus) said, it has come to kill people. And they ran away into the

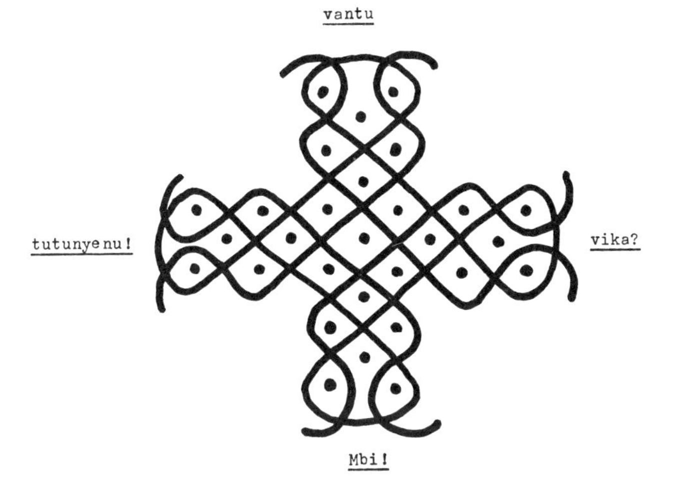

Figure 23.7 *Vamphulu.*

Ngwavo vuta vene ovwo. Kaha ndzo, ou ngweni: 'Vika?' Ngweni: 'Njinevu mbi!' – 'Ove unevu mbi?' – 'Ee.' – Ngweni: 'Angeco njinevu, iii! ngweha vantu.' – Ou ngweni: 'Vantu?' – 'Ngweny': 'Ee.' – 'He! Tutinyenu vovo vene vakwana-kutsiha vantu.' Kaha vatinina mumusenge, vakayoya.

forest. When they heard the sound *mbi*, they said, that is surely a gun! So then one of them said: 'What is that?'. The other one replied: 'I have heard *mbi*.' – 'You have heard *mbi*?' – 'Yes.' – The third one said: 'Me too, I have heard it, terrible! It is like people.' – And this one here said: 'People?' – The other one replied: 'Yes'. – 'Hey! Let us run away, over there they are really going on to kill people.' Then off they went, scattered, and in a moment they had run away. So they fled into the forest and survived.

This *kasona* may induce a meditative mood in the viewer. It has an oscillating quality in which its components may 'shift' in visual perception, i.e. like in a picture puzzle one may begin to see changing images, by associating the lines and dots in this or that manner.

Chief Kalunga used the standard technique for making this *kasona*. With his first and third fingers he impressed the basic pairs of dots into the ground. He began with the two vertical columns, working away from the body. Then he proceeded by extending the rows of dots horizontally. Only with one of the two fingers spanned apart did he impress a new dot, working gradually at first towards the right, then towards the left. Then the Chief imprinted the in-between dots with his first finger alone, thus forming the innermost cross-rows of this *kasona*. Here again, he worked from bottom to top, i.e. away from his body,

Figure 23.8 The Lucazi paramount chief Mwangana Kalunga (1898–1981) drawing a *kasona* at Chikenge, chief's enclosure (*lilapa*), Kabompo District, Northwestern Province, Zambia, 22 July 1973.

and then at first towards the right, then towards the left. He then began to draw the four hooked lines whose ends represent the horns (*zintsiva*) of the four gnus gazing out of the structure. He started at the bottom left (*Mbi!*) and eventually drew the single line completing the whole structure (Figs 23.8–12).

With the last line completed by the *mukakusona*, the spectator can see the four faces of the gnus, each with a 'mouth', two 'eyes' and two 'horns' emerging from the total structure. Chief Kalunga himself pointed immediately to the four heads of the gnus and then explained what each of them says in the story, starting at the bottom and moving counterclockwise. The first one says: '*Mbi!*' (sound of a gun). The second one asks: '*Vika?*' (what?), to which the third one replies: '*Vantu*' (people), and the fourth concludes: '*Tutinyenu!*' (let us run away!).

Tunwenu vwala vwetu! (Let us drink our beer!); collected from Jeremiah Makondo, *ca*. 70 years old, at Chikenge village, 30 June 1979, explained by Kapokola Chimbau of the same village (Fig. 23.13).

This *kasona* was explained as follows. People say to each other: *Tunwenu vwala vwetu!* (let us drink our millet-beer). This drawing represents two people, one on the left and one on the right, with their hands seemingly merged into each other. They seem to be bound together by something, or passing something between them, or perhaps they are united by a table between them. Such a situation characterizes the bonds between men during a beer-drinking party. The dots in the structure allude to 'eyes' and 'mouths' of the two human figures, but in the middle of the structure they rather represent vessels, calabashes or glasses containing millet-beer.

Drinking the mild millet-beer (*vwala vwa masangu*) is a most important social activity among VaLucazi men, it brings people together and promotes discussion. It is almost symbolic of the *ndzango* community as such. *Vwala* is, therefore, the first subject that occurs to a -Lucazi when looking at this figure.

Tunwenu vwala vwetu is one of those *tusona* with an intrinsic mathematical content. Jaritz (1983) has attempted to explain mathematically why a single line, after passing or circumscribing dozens of dots, must return to its starting point. On the basis of a sample of *tusona* from my own research material and a set of mathematical questions, he arrived at a Western mathematical explanation of the phenomenon by comparing the geometry of this genre of *tusona* (and its rules for directional changes of the single line) with the path of a billiard ball. The analogy is appropriate, because one can inscribe imaginary rectangles similar to billiard tables into most of these figures. After discussing permutations and a reduction algorithm for simply connected 'tables', Jaritz tackles the difficult question of several intersected 'tables', such as in *Tunwenu vwala vwetu* which can be reduced by cutting off some sections diagonally.

The results of such enquiries have confirmed that *tusona*, besides transmitting wisdom and abstract ideas are, in a sense, also mathematical puzzles. The forefathers of the Eastern Angolan peoples discovered higher mathematics and a non-Euclidian geometry on an empirical basis, and applied their insights to the invention of these unique configurations.

Figures 23.9–12 Four salient stages in the drawing of the *kasona* of *Vamphulu.*

Mukanda (the boys' circumcision school); collected from Mose Chindumba, *ca.* 30 years old, at village Chindzombo, 4 January 1978 (Figs 23.14 & 15).

Mukanda is the term in Lucazi and related languages for the circumcision school for boys. This is a central institution in the culture of the peoples of eastern Angola, northwestern Zambia and southern Zaire. The *mukanda* lodge is constructed outside the village and the newly circumcised boys, who are called *tundanda* (singular *kandanda*) in Lucazi, but *tundanji* (singular *kandanji*) in Cokwe and Luvale, are kept there in seclusion for several months in order to be instructed.

Mukanda among the -Lucazi starts at the beginning of the dry season, usually in April, May or June, and is closed in October, November or December. The age of the boys to be initiated is usually between 6 and 10 years. It is a pre-puberty school, intended to make the young boys self-reliant, group-conscious and independent of their mothers, in anticipation of their future tasks and roles as members of the society of men. During his prolonged stay in the lodge each *kandanda* has a personal guardian (*cilombola*, plural *vilombola*) who is responsible for

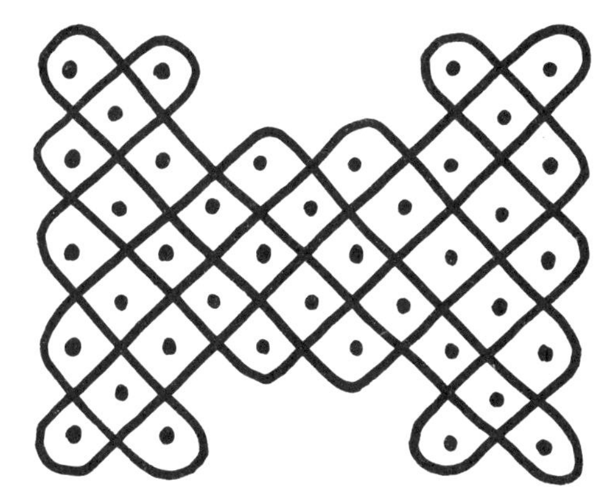

Figure 23.13 *Tunwenu vivala vwetu!*

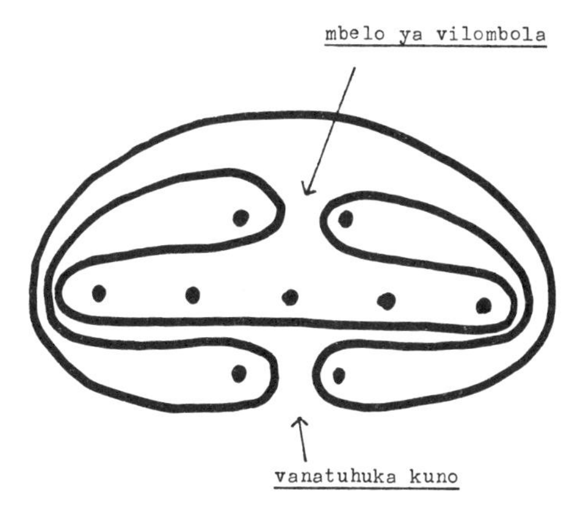

Figure 23.14 *Mukanda.*

his well-being and education. In addition, there are assistant guardians, usually adolescents, who perform minor tasks. These are called *tulombola-tito* (singular *kalombola-tito*). An uncircumcised male, i.e. someone who has not been to the *mukanda* is called *cilima* (plural *vilima*). This is a depreciatory term, implying that such a person lacks the education which is provided by Lucazi society for young males.

The five points in the middle of the drawing represent five *tundanda* who are inside the lodge in seclusion. The two points at the bottom represent two publicly acknowledged *vilombola*, whose task among other obligations is to bring the food which is cooked by the boys' mothers in the village to the boys in the *mukanda*.

The true *vilombola* know where to enter, because they are initiated, and went themselves to *mukanda* when they were young. In the ideograph this is expressed in such a way that the paths of the two acknowledged *vilombola* inevitably lead to the narrow entrance of the *mukanda*, seen at the top of the figure, the *mbelo ya*

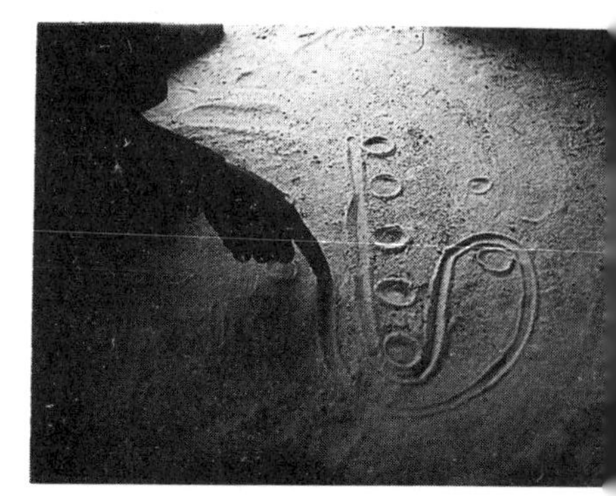

Figure 23.15 Stages in the drawings of the *kasona* called *Mukanda*. The performer in these photographs is Mose Chindumba, who learned to draw such ideographs from his father at Zambezi. Village Chindumbo, north of Kabompo District, Northwestern Province, Zambia, 4 January 1978.

vilombola (gate of the guardians). Everyone can comprehend – and this is explained by the 'owner' of the *kasona* – that the two dots, if they were movable, could move between the lines encircling the enclosure and reach the entrance without encountering any obstacle on their path.

However, there are also two false *vilombola*, who have never passed through a *mukanda* school – *vilima* (uncircumcised) – represented by the two dots in the upper section of the figure. They also want to carry food to the *tundanda* and are beginning their walk but, since they are uninitiated, they simply cannot recognize the entrance, they cannot see it. Their path leads out of the area. In the ideograph this is expressed in such a way that the paths which could be pursued by the two top dots do not lead to the five points in the middle, but out of the structure: *vanatuhuka kuno* (here they came out).

In the *kasona* of *mukanda* the main audience satisfaction derives from the fact that an axiomatic law of the *mukanda* institution is expressed so perfectly: namely that only someone who has previously graduated from this traditional school can ever freely enter it and assume functions, such as for example that of a *cilombola* or *kalombola-tito*. This is convincingly demonstrated by graphic logic: there is no path in the ideographic figure that would allow the uninitiated would-be guardians to reach the entrance to the enclosure. All attempts by them to penetrate *mukanda* are bound to fail, and the would-be guardians following the only path reserved for them, land outside (*hambandza*).

A precondition to an understanding of this *kasona*, and to the appreciation of its ideographic message, lies in the knowledge shared by the *mukakusona* and his male audience about this central Lucazi institution, which every young male has to pass through. The satisfaction arises from the perception of a 'written proof' that those false guardians who have never been to *mukanda*, and therefore do not even deserve their title – because they are *vilima* – cannot *a priori* discover the secrets of the circumcision school. The written sand figure corroborates by its structure the 'natural' order of things. As if blinded by magic, the false guardians are unable even to recognize the entrance to the enclosure.

Kalolo-muzike na kalolo-wambata (the bachelor rat and the married rat); collected from Jeremiah Makondo Musunya, *ca.* 70 years old, at Chikenge village, 1 July 1979 (Fig. 23.16).

A long story is associated with this *kasona*. The story is about two rats, one of whom was a bachelor (*kalolo-muzike*), whereas the other had married (*kalolo-wambata*). Each lives in his own village, the former in solitude, the latter with his wife. However, they are unaware of the fact that their villages, represented by the two dots in the middle of this ideograph, are very close to each other. The curved lines which separate the two dots from each other are 'like the borders' between the lands of each (*ize inapu ngwe ndzindza*). Each of the two rats owns two forest estates (*misenge* or *mahumbu*), which are represented by the four individual figures, each consisting of ten dots and the circumscribing line. *Kalolo*-the-bachelor owns the forest to the right and at the bottom of the drawing, *kalolo*-the-married those to the left and at the top of the structure. *Kalolo* is the Lucazi name for a very small species of rat described as 'jerboa, species of jumping-rat'

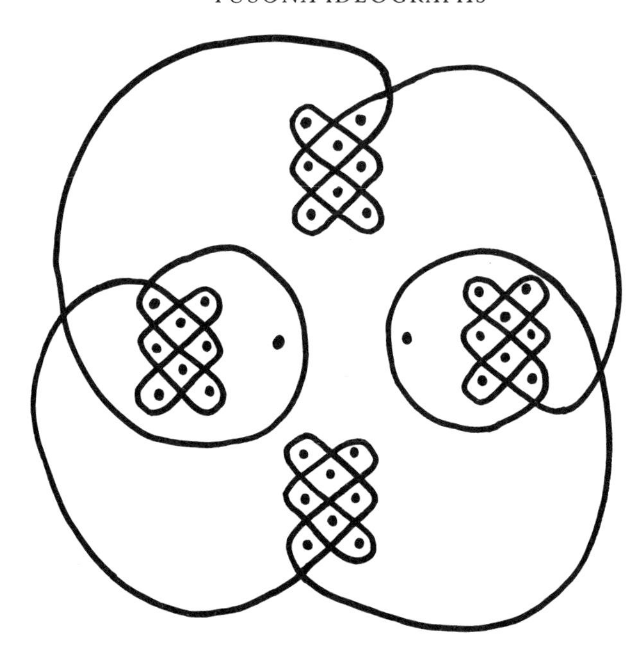

Figure 23.16 *Kalolo-muzike na kalolo-wambata.*

(Pearson 1970), but people in our research villages did not confirm that it jumps.

Since the two rats in the story do not know that their villages are situated next to each other, *kalolo*-the-bachelor always describes a long path leading him through his two forests in order to reach the village of *kalolo*-the-married. Arriving secretly, the wife of *kalolo*-the-married always gives food to *kalolo*-the-bachelor in the absence of her husband. Their affair continues for many months, and *kalolo*-the-married, who always comes home from work very late, never receives any food from his wife. In the end this relationship leads to the killing of the husband, because the two rats look so similar that the wife can no longer distinguish between them. *Kalolo*-the-bachelor, discovering that the two villages are just next to each other, cuts open a path to connect them in a straight line, and he marries the wife of the one whom he has killed.

Formally, it is noteworthy that this *kasona* is based on the *Katuva-vufwati* or *Kangano kanthyengu* structure (see above). Here four such structures are connected by roving lines creating a totally symmetric figure. This *kasona* is also an example of the close links between 'written' (ideographic) and 'oral' literature in Lucazi culture. Whereas some *tusona* have very short explanatory texts, some others have full stories of the *cisimo*-type attached to them.

Who invented *tusona*?

From all the evidence available, it seems that these discoveries were made by individuals in solitude during long journeys through uninhabited areas. Oral tradition confirms that in the past *tusona* were often drawn by hunters, when they sat down to rest and wished to pass time. The hunting connection is visible in the titles and the content projected into many of the *tusona*, e.g. *kambava wamulivwe* (the hyrax in the rock) alluding to an episode when a decayed hyrax was found by a hunter.

Footprints of animals in the sand, including those of birds, may have been a primary inspiration to the beginning of this tradition. In the white sands (*musekeseke*) of eastern Angola and northwestern Zambia, such footprints often appear with unusual clarity of design. In some *tusona* this reference is testified in titles such as *Kangano kanthyengu* (the footprint of the roan antelope), in others in some graphic motifs. An example for the latter is the *kasona* called *Kambilinginja kaNtumba* (a name) (Fig. 23.17) which is based on a famous Lucazi proverb: *Kambilinginja kaNtumba twatungu vunoni mazina katulizi* (Kambilinginja of Ntumba, as concerns building we have built our villages together, and yet we do not know each other's names).

In this *kasona* a drawing technique was employed which seems to represent a different tradition from the dot-and-line geometry discussed above. The clusters of three points which constitute a basic grapheme in this figure were formed by holding the first three fingers of the right hand tightly knit together and impressing the pads of the three fingers simultaneously into the sand. The clusters of dots produced in this manner resemble the traces of a bird in the sand or the footprint of a small mammal.

The story attached to this particular *kasona* and told by the *mukakusona* after completing his drawing, tells of a man called Kambilinginja, Son of Ntumba (his mother), who did not want to associate with his relatives, but preferred to live in splendid isolation. The two dots at the bottom of the ideograph represent the villages of Kambilinginja and his wife, which were extremely close to each other, only separated by a swamp (the thick cross in the ideograph). Kambilinginja never revealed to his wife the secret of the close proximity of his village to hers. Instead, after marriage he set out with his wife on a journey of several years during which she gave birth to several children, allegedly to reach his village. The paths of their journey are represented by the slung, curved lines, whereas the clusters of three dots represent villages or settlements which they passed on their way. One day, however, in her husband's village the wife suddenly recognized her mother pounding maize in a mortar on the other side of the swamp. With this, she realized the secret her husband had been withholding.

Although I do not have independent confirmation from present-day informants, there are hints that in the remote past some *tusona* may have served as a graphic means of communication between hunters. In the lonely, scarcely populated areas of eastern Angola, hunters would have left signs behind for their comrades to point out itineraries, directions where the game had moved, what kind of game could be found, as well as startling discoveries. Some *tusona* have survived which are maps drawn in the sand, showing rivers, villages and paths, from a bird's perspective. From the drawing of traces of game in the sand – sometimes even for deceptive purposes – more-elaborate ideographic structures could have evolved gradually, until the *tusona* became common practice among males and

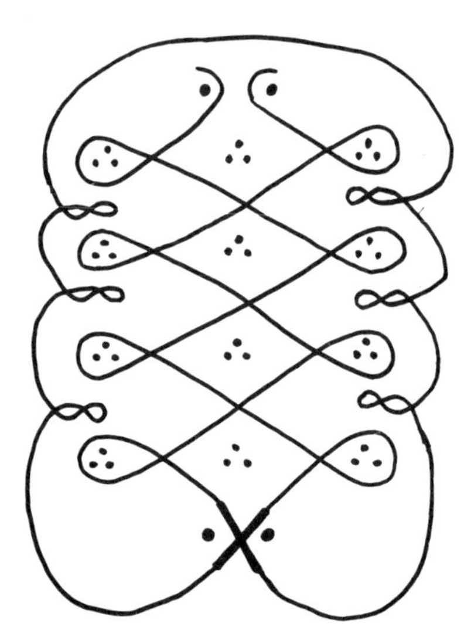

Figure 23.17 *Kambilinginja kaNtumba.*

knowledge began to be passed on during leisure time gatherings in the assembly pavilion (*ndzango*).

With this possibility in mind it would be good to have a fresh look at some of the 'rock art' in the Angolan culture area and elsewhere – especially at the more abstract geometric styles of this art. It is very possible that some of this 'rock art' did not serve mysterious 'magico-religious' purposes, as is so often suggested in the literature, but rather was used as a means of communication, i.e. communicating messages among prehistoric hunters. 'Rock art' might become legible to the investigator.

A *kasona* such as *Kambava wamulivwe* (see above) seems to have the rather thin story-line attached to it telling that a hunter went into the bush suddenly finding a hyrax that had decayed in the niche of a rock. However, the drawing also communicates a greater message, namely that its sides had been hacked out with a man-made tool: an axe. From this it follows that another hunter had passed there, killed the hyrax and for some reason – perhaps to mark an itinerary – left it behind. With regard to the message transmitted by this ideograph, the story may not be as thin as it first appears to be, since it served an important communication objective.

Today nearly every realm of social behaviour, and every important institution in -Lucazi culture, is represented in an abstract manner by a *kasona*. There are *tusona* about men's secret associations such as *mungongi*, about the evil deeds of wizards, and there is one, shown to me by Mrs Likumbi Kapyololo (the not unusual case of a woman being knowledgeable in *tusona*) about the founding tree of a new village: *muti wamundzango* (Fig. 23.18). Many women know the ideographs but keep their knowledge to themselves, since they are excluded from the *ndzango* (men's assembly place). Long ago, when a new village was founded,

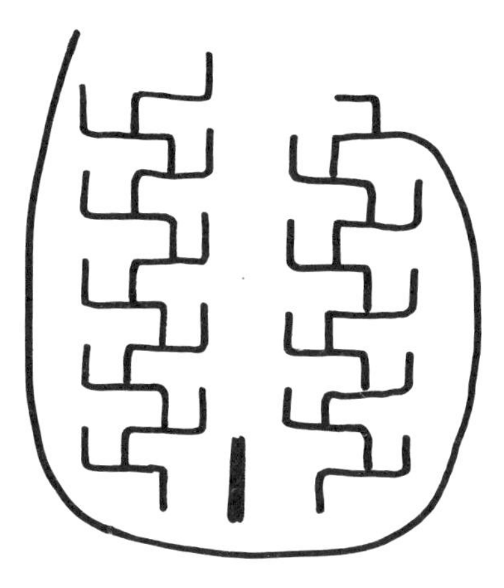

Figure 23.18 *Muti wamundzango.*

the leader of the group was expected first to select a tree, bind *vikakavizi*, a type of grass used in ancestor worship, around it, and declare the tree as the new assembly place. It then stood symbolically for the village.

Tusona in history

A comparison of *tusona* collected by observers independently over a large area reveals that the same ideographs occur today with little, and sometimes no, variation at distances of hundreds of kilometres among people who have lived separately for generations. Such observations, plus the structural evidence, suggest that the *tusona* tradition is old, certainly precolonial, although we do not know how old it is. Outside the Eastern Angolan population cluster, sand ideographs are also drawn, for example, by Kimbundu- (-Mbondo) speaking children in Malanji Province, Angola. Ideographs showing close structural parallels with the *tusona/sona* have also been found among the Bakuba of Zaïre (cf. Torday 1925; Zaslavsky 1979, pp. 106–9). It cannot be merely coincidental that the most basic *kasona* among the geometrical ones, known in Lucazi as *Kangano kanthyengu* (the footprint of the roan antelope) or *Katuva vufwati* (the one who pierces into intestines) is also known in Kuba culture. Even the most complex *tusona* configurations among the geometrical types are, in fact, merely proliferations of this embryonic type. It is thus important that this structure may be seen on raffia cloth of the -Kuba of Zaïre far off the main present-day distribution of *tusona*. This particular embroidered raffia cloth (now in the British Museum) is said to date back to the 18th century (Zaslavsky 1979, p. 108).

Although such evidence gives historical depth to the existence of a central motif in the *tusona* genre constructed upon a dot-and-line geometry, a probe into the remote history of this tradition would really only be possible if similar structures are discovered in rock paintings or petroglyphs (rock engravings). So far this is not the case, although some rock engravings discovered by José Redinha and others in the Upper Zambezi region (Angola) show stylistic affinities with *tusona* and other motifs of regional 'decorative' art. For example, two interlaced loops (*zinkhata* in Lucazi) which provide fascinating evidence of a spatial conception in this rock art (Bastin 1961, p. 148), often appear as platted grass rings at the entrance of a *mukanda* (boys' circumcision school) to 'chase away men-lions' (*kutinisa vandumba zyavantu*).

Another motif known in Cokwe as *cingelyengelye* (see Bastin 1961, pp. 147–9) is also found in rock engravings of the Upper Zambezi.

Here it is interesting to note that both in *tusona* as drawn in the sand and in the rock engravings of the Upper Zambezi, as well as in Kuba carvings on drums which are comparable structurally to the *tusona*, we find a *spatial concept* of drawing which gets lost when the *tusona* are reproduced with a pen on paper. Drawing a *kasona* in the sand – when two lines cross – is like highways crossing one on top of the other. Thus the *kasona* of *Katuva vufwati* (see above) is better depicted as in Figure 23.19.

Intracultural conceptualization of the *tusona* is therefore in a sense three-dimensional, as is the conceptualization of the rock engravings of the Upper Zambezi, a notable link between a prehistoric tradition on the one hand and a present-day tradition on the other, which has been transmitted for an unknown period.

The *tusona* or *sona* tradition occurs in a culture area which is extremely rich in graphic traditions of various kinds. Bastin (1961), who attempted to investigate the meaning of graphic symbols among the -Cokwe of Lunda Province, Angola, summarized her findings in the form of a table (Bastin 1961, p. 62). The symbols occur on utensils, wood carvings, calabashes, etc, representing a graphic genre different from the ideographs drawn in the sand, although they are also referred to as *sona*. The differences are historical, but also a consequence of the use of different tools. Sand ideographs are produced by pressing one's fingers on to a flat sand plain or 'impressing' a brush on a house wall. Hence the typical dots and lines. Carved decorations produced with a knife are carried out by a quite different technique. Therefore, referring back to dos Santos (1961, p. 17), the sand drawings could hardly be expected to be in the form of engravings on calabashes.

Tusona and extra-African parallels

Outside Africa there is one culture area in which a surprisingly analogous tradition to *tusona* occurs with configurations sometimes even identical in concept and approach. In South India *kolam* (Aditi 1985) figures are traced on the floor at the threshold of a house, often in a dot-and-line geometry very reminiscent of the *tusona* (Fig. 23.24).

In the above example, as in the *tusona* of the geometrical type, there is a screen of basic and interlocking dots spread equidistantly over the floor (Figs 23.20 & 21) and circumscribed by lines returning into themselves. In this figure

Figure 23.19 *Katuva vufwati.*

there are three lines (Figs 23.22–24); however, their order of movement does not follow *tusona* rules for the straight line (cf. Kubik 1986, p.249ff.) and this, no doubt is an important difference. Baumann (1935) was the first cultural anthropologist to point to the striking parallels between the two traditions, but the diffusionist explanations which were readily accepted in Baumann's days sound precipitate and a bit simplistic today. There are only a limited number of possibilities to explain such parallels.

(a) The *tusona* and *kolam* traditions are completely unrelated; the two different culture areas invented these similar structures independently.
(b) The two traditions are to be compared in terms of Jung's (1950, 1974) analytical psychology as manifestations of the collective unconscious. The collective unconscious would therefore produce and reproduce such archetypal structures in any culture under certain psychological conditions.
(c) The two traditions are related by diffusion (i) involving some kind of maritime contact or (ii) by slaves from inner Angola being settled in southern India and introducing the tradition there.
(d) *Tusona* and *kolam* are the remains of an identical graphic tradition which was once widespread in Asia and Africa, but which was subsequently lost in most of Asia.

This is an area of investigation where interpretive objectivity is very difficult to maintain. We can 'objectively' determine the intracultural meanings of ideographs like the *tusona* with the aid of informants; we may also project our knowledge into the past and arrive at a tentative content interpretation of 'prehistoric' petroglyphs if these are similar and found in the same culture area. However, interpretive objectivity greatly diminishes when it comes to cross-cultural, and even cross-continental, comparisons of apparently analogous traditions. At this point contemporary material alone is a fragile basis for comparison and the latter may be dangerously speculative, if not inconclusive. Here progress can only be achieved if archaeology and prehistory are able to make a contribution in the form of datable graphic configurations, comparable with those found today, discovered in an archaeological context. So far, perhaps the most important discovery is a small copper tablet excavated by Sir John Marshall at Mohenjo-daro between 1922 and 1927. This tablet shows a figure which is identical with the *kasona* of *Liswa lyzvandzili* which I have described above (Fig. 23.5), except that the dots are missing.

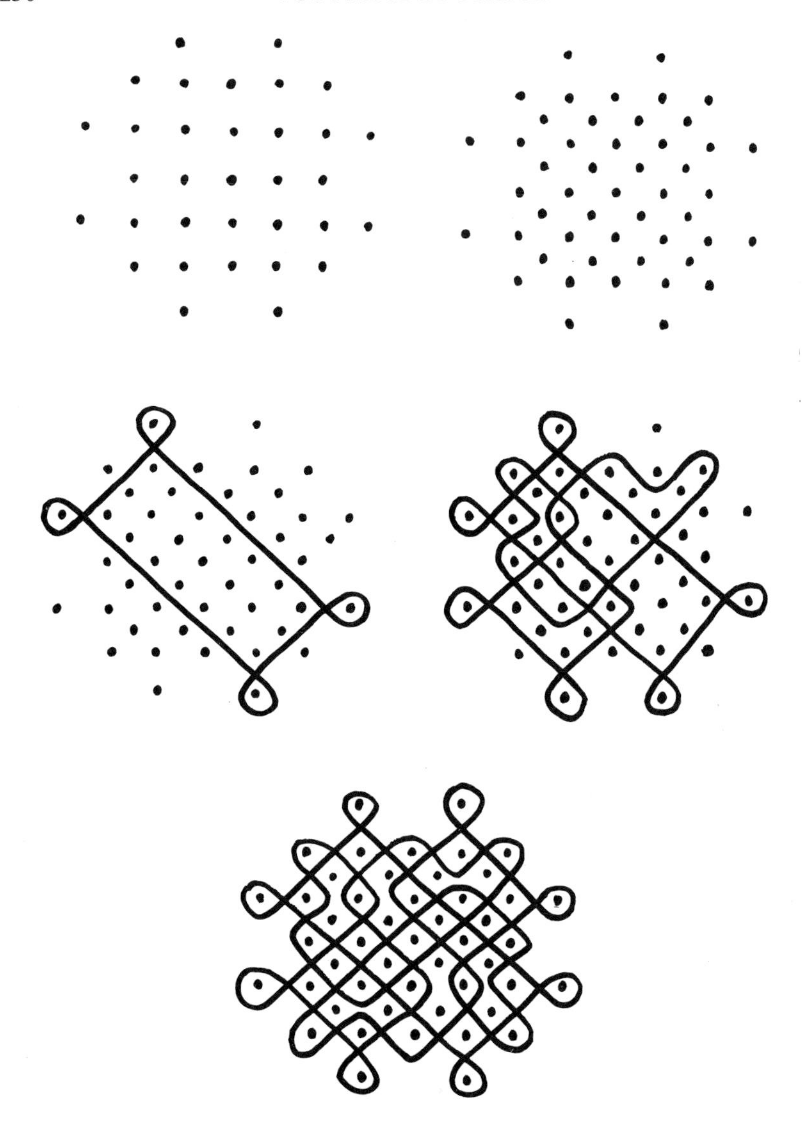

Figures 23.20–24 Tracing of the *kolam*.

Obviously we cannot come to any conclusions on the basis of one isolated find. Nevertheless, this example does serve to raise the fundamental question, where is the threshold, the border, between figures simple enough to be re-invented at any point of history, and those complex enough to exclude the possibility they might have been invented twice?

References

Aditi, A. 1985. *The living arts of India*. Washington, DC: Smithsonian Institution.
Bastin, M.L. 1961. *Art decoratif Tshokwe*. Lisbon: Diamang (Companhia de Diamantes de Angola).
Baumann, H. 1935. *Lunda*. Berlin: Museums für Völkerkunde.
Fontinha, M. 1983. *Desenhos na areia dos Quiocos do Nordeste de Angola*. Lisbon: Instituto de Investigação Cientifica Tropical.
Hamelberger, E. 1951. Ecrit sur le sable. *Annales Spiritaines* **61**, 14–23.
Hamelberger, E. 1952. A escrita na areia. *Portugal em Africa* **9**.
Jaritz, W. 1983. *Über Bahnen auf Billardtischen – oder: eine mathematische Untersuchung von Ideogrammen angolanischer Herkunft*. Graz: Mathematisch-statistische Sektion.
Jung, C. 1950. *Gestaltungen des Unbewussten*. Zürich: Rascher Verlag.
Jung, C. 1974. *Man and his symbols*. London: Aldus Books.
Kubik, G. 1981. *Mukanda na makisi – Circumcision school and masks*. Double album with commentary. Berlin: Museum collection.
Kubik, G. 1986. *Tusona – Luchazi ideographs. A graphic tradition practised by a people of West-Central Africa*. Wien: Stiglmayr.
Pearson, E. 1970. *Ngangela–English dictionary*. Morelos: Cuernavaca.
Pearson, E. 1977. *People of the aurora*. San Diego: Beta Books.
Pearson, E. 1984. *Tales of the aurora*, Seal Beach, California: El Dorado.
Santos, E. dos 1961. *Contribuição para o estudo das pictografias e ideogramas dos Quiocos*. Lisbon: Estudos sobre a Etnologia do Ultramar Português.
Torday, E. 1925. *On the trail of the Bushongo*. Philadelphia: Lippincott.
Zaslavsky, C. 1979. *Africa counts*. Westport, Connecticut: Lawrence Hill.

19 *Organizational constraints on tattoo images: a sociological analysis of artistic style*

CLINTON R. SANDERS

Introduction

Analyses of art works have traditionally focused on their form and content and on the sources of change within artistic style. The 'production of culture perspective' (see Peterson 1976, Sanders 1982, Tuchman 1983, Jensen 1984) approaches these issues by emphasizing the social organization of art and media production systems as the central factor shaping the style of cultural items. This perspective directs attention to the activities of social actors working together within production organizations ('collective action') to conceive, create and distribute artistic materials (Becker 1974). Interaction is importantly constrained by structural features such as the division of labour, available resources, technological developments and distribution channels.

'Product conventions' (Sanders 1982) – shared understandings regarding the commonly encountered form and content of art products – are key determinants of style. Conventions specify appropriate materials, suitable dimensions, acceptable abstractions and other stylistic features (Rosenblum 1978a, p. 424, Gombrich 1969, p. 291, Becker 1982, p. 29); they are known and expected not only by producer–artists, but also by critics, collectors, and other members of the art 'public'.

The response of the larger art audience and the commercial success of the artistic product are directly related to the producer's compliance with or violation of conventional expectations. Conventions imply an aesthetic and artists who alter or ignore established aesthetic expectations must pay the price. Leaders of stylistic revolutions affront the political *status quo* of the art world in which they operate. They commonly find it necessary to increase the efforts needed to produce their work and encounter limitations on the acceptance and saleability of the artistic commodity.

Violation of convention (typically referred to as 'innovation' within some art-world segments) may gain some measure of acceptance. In turn, stylistic deviations come to be employed by other artistic workers. This acceptance of innovation is principally impelled by an allegiance to 'creativity' which is a typical feature of the expressed ideology within many contemporary art worlds. Deviations from stylistic expectations become routinized conventions in their own right; changes in artistic style derive from the dialectic relationship between the traditional ease of convention and the innovative pressures of creativity (Becker 1982, p. 303, Hauser 1982, p. 409).

The following discussion[1] focuses on major structural features of contemporary tattooing as they affect the stability and change of stylistic conventions. Style within this minor decorative art form is constrained primarily by available technologies and material resources (cf. Lyon 1974, Kealy 1979), the perspectives and experience of the artists and their clientele (cf. Faulkner 1982) and the stigmatized social definition of tattooing within both the art world and the surrounding society. Stylistic change, in turn, is impelled by alterations in this structure over time as well as the incursion of new images and techniques drawn from the body art traditions of both non-Western cultures and insular Western subcultures.

Tattooing as an art form

As a form of cultural production, tattooing has deep roots in folk art tradition. Until fairly recently Western tattooing was practised entirely outside the institutional constraints of a professional art world. Tattoo images tended to be relatively crude and highly conventionalized, with death symbols (skulls, grim reapers and so forth), certain animals (especially panthers, eagles and snakes), pin-up styled women and military designs predominant. The traditional clientele consisted of young men from working-class backgrounds who tended to acquire a number of small, unrelated, badge-like designs with little thought to continuity of body placement (Rubin 1983, Fried & Fried 1978, pp. 158–69). Practitioners were commonly from the same social background as their clients, unassociated with the larger art world and motivated primarily by desire for economic gain. The basic skills involved in the tattoo craft were typically acquired through apprenticeship with established tattooists. The dominant occupational values emphasized technical skill rather than aesthetic qualities (see Sanders 1985).

Although this commercially oriented craft structure continues to dominate contemporary tattooing, significant changes have been occurring since the early 1960s. Younger tattooists, frequently having university or art school backgrounds and experience in traditional artistic media, have begun to explore tattooing as a form of expression. Congruent with their background and aesthetic orientations, the new tattoo artists draw images from diverse artistic sources. Fantasy and science fiction illustration, traditional Japanese styles, tribal designs, portraiture and abstract expressionism are major influences on contemporary, fine art tattooing (see Tucker 1981, Rubin 1983, Wroblewski 1981). The new tattooists are also involved in technical innovation, experimenting with an expanded colour spectrum, moving away from the traditional hard-edged black outline and employing single-needle techniques which produce highly detailed and fragile images.

In line with the movement into tattooing of practitioners who define themselves as 'artists' and present their products as 'art', the larger art world has begun to take notice of the medium. Tattooing is increasingly legitimated as the work is shown in museums and gallery shows, subjected to critical discussion by academics and critic–agents of the traditional art world. As a consequence the tattooists profit as their work comes to look like art, is displayed like art, is discussed like art, and is bought and sold as art. Their social and occupational status is enhanced, they enjoy greater control over their work lives, and they encounter a new client pool of individuals with more-sophisticated aesthetic tastes and sufficient disposable income to purchase extensive custom-designed art products (cf. Manfredi 1982, Christopherson 1974, Rosenblum 1978b, pp. 122-9).

Organizational structure, producer perspectives and style

Systems of commercial cultural production typically display a 'craft' organization; the structure centres around the activities of a body of 'creative professionals' who produce materials which are, in turn, evaluated by members of an administrative group who choose which products will be marketed, on the basis of their assumed commercial potential. Decision-makers at the managerial and administrative level are continually uncertain about those features which will assure success in the marketplace. This problem of 'commercial uncertainty' is dealt with, in part, through a reliance on formulae. Products which have proven to be commercially successful in the past are reproduced with only minor variation (Hirsch 1972, cf. Gitlin 1983). Production systems which display centralized and oligopolistic organization are minimally inconvenienced by competition and tend to market materials characterized by stylistic homogeneity. In contrast, less-centralized and bureaucratically organized production entails more competition and increased reliance upon the decisions made at the creative level. Creator autonomy generates innovation and product diversity (see Peterson & Berger 1975, DiMaggio 1977).

Given the apparent decentralized organizational structure of tattoo production, one would expect considerable stylistic heterogeneity. Tattooing is characterized by entrepreneurship, decentralization, competition and minimal interaction among primary creators. The relatively simple materials necessary to do tattooing are available to anyone who gains access to equipment suppliers, and the basic techniques are easily acquired. Why has this highly decentralized and competitive system not generated stylistic diversity rather than the homogeneous, formulaic and tradition-bound corpus of work which has, until fairly recently, typified contemporary tattooing?

Most professional tattooists emphasize a commercial, rather than creative, occupational orientation. The desire to maximize profit requires the tattooist to cede considerable control over his or her work life and to respond primarily to the typically highly formulaic requests of the customer (cf. Sinha 1979, Faulkner 1982, pp. 148–67). The tattooist is, in other words, subject to limited market demands and feels little commercial pressure to engage in innovative or educational interactions with the client.[2]

Tattooing is also highly formulaic, because a few tattoo supply firms are structurally central and exercise considerable power. Commonly run by ex-tattooists, these organizations provide most tattooists with the equipment and materials they need to do business. They are also at the centre of the organizational communications structure. Supply firms publish tattoo newsletters and organize annual conventions which are attended by tattooists and tattoo enthusiasts. Although of widely varying technical quality, the work displayed in the newsletters and at the conventions is overwhelmingly formulaic. Most tattooists and tattooees are therefore rarely exposed to stylistic diversity, and evaluations of tattoo quality are made on the basis of apparent technical skill rather than design innovations.

These dominant perspectives and organizational features have had a significant restraining effect on stylistic innovation in tattooing. The changes in style which have occurred in the past two decades have been due primarily to the incursion of a new breed of tattooist with a markedly different perspective and the concurrent expansion of the client pool by 'collectors' from diverse social backgrounds. The new clients have tastes and views of the functions met by the tattoo–product which are very much unlike those of the traditional tattoo consumer.

As mentioned in the previous section, the new 'fine-art' tattooists value control, innovation and aesthetic quality over commercial success, and tend to view the larger art world as their primary reference group. Most tattoo 'artists' focus their energies on the creation of large-scale, custom-designed pieces; they typically refuse requests to inscribe traditional images.[3]

The fine-art tattooist commonly is motivated to pursue tattooing by dissatisfaction with the constraints and occupational limitations encountered in the traditional art world. Although they usually bring new aesthetic orientations and modes of evaluation to tattooing, artistic practitioners consistently express appreciation for and connection to the history and tradition of Western tattooing. At the same time they find much of the symbolic content of American folk-style tattooing to be boring, repetitious or, in some cases, morally or politically repugnant (Sanders 1985, Rubin 1983).

Diffusion, innovation and style

As is the case in stylistic change within other media, 'new' approaches to tattoo form and content derive from the process of cultural diffusion (cf. Bell 1976, p. 96, Rosenblum 1978b, p. 112). The rich tradition of Japanese tattooing has had a major impact on contemporary fine art style. The use of stylized background elements (e.g. wind, fire and wave designs) to frame and tie together foreground images in a form of tattoo mural and traditional images (e.g. dragons, chrysanthemums and carp) are major consequences of this diffusion.

Similarly, the borrowing from and adaptation of tribal or pre-technological tattoo design have had some impact in the past five years. Drawn from the tattoo tradition of Hawaiian, Maori, Samoan and other Pacific Island cultures, this stylistic form consists of solid black, commonly abstract, designs which closely follow body contours.

Innovative designs and techniques have also entered contemporary tattooing through the diffusion of approaches developed in marginal subcultures. The recent advent of the 'single-needle' tattoo style is an example of this process. American tattooing has traditionally been characterized by strong black outlines made with groups of from three to seven needles. Influenced by a style which evolved in American penal institutions, in the late 1970s California tattooists began experimenting with a single-needle outlining style which allowed the artist to produce extremely detailed, almost photo-realistic designs. This innovative style – sometimes referred to as 'institution' or 'positive–negative' style – typically involves the sole use of black ink to produce, when handled with technical and artistic skill, startlingly realistic tattoo portraits. This innovation was greeted initially with considerable scepticism by some practitioners who maintained that multiple-needle groups were necessary in order to produce the capillary action which drew ink into the liner, that the single needle would only cut the skin surface rather than infuse pigment, and that the fine-line tattoo would quickly fade and become illegible over time. Despite this resistance to innovation, younger artists began to experiment with the technique, and detailed monochromatic tattoos similar to those commonly worn by prison inmates were increasingly displayed as exemplary work in the major tattoo publications and at conventions sponsored by tattoo organizations. Having gained some degree of acceptance among both tattooists and collectors, the innovative approach became institutionalized and conventionalized as the initiators began to market design sheets ('flash') incorporating the new style.

Clientele, market and style

In all commercial art worlds the clientele is a central element of the production process. The client pool is, in essence, a 'market' which is identified, defined and targeted by system actors whose interests are primarily financial (Peterson 1982, p. 146, DiMaggio 1977).

The growth and changing character of the tattoo consumer pool in the past two decades has had a considerable impact on both the form and content of the product. The traditional client had narrow experience with tattooing, and defined the indelible images as having limited functional utility (principally decoration or symbolization of personal association or self-identification, or both). These customers most commonly chose to purchase images which were similar to those carried by friends, family members or other primary associates (Sanders 1984).

Coming from a higher socio-economic background than the traditional tattooee, the new client commonly has more disposable income; emphasizes the aesthetic, rather than the affiliational, function of the tattoo; and shares the tattoo artist's interest in the production of a creative and innovative custom-designed image. The previously homogeneous tattoo 'taste culture' (Gans 1974) has given way to an enlarged and more diverse market which has, in turn, led to a correspondingly more heterogeneous repertoire of available styles (Rubin 1983, Tucker 1981).

This relationship between a changing market and stylistic innovation in tattooing is a specific example of what has come to be a general understanding within the sociology of art. Art product consumers are not passive recipients, but act both individually and collectively to shape and constrain the style of art works (see Watson 1968, Rosenberg & Fliegel 1970).

Technology, materials and style

The resources available and routinely used in the creation of cultural products are key determinants of stylistic conventions. The equipment employed in the production process embodies these conventions; they are learned as practitioners gain experience with the technology and materials (cf. Fine 1985).

The tattoo machine is the primary technological resource. The development of this electric instrument in the late 19th century (see Eldridge 1982) allowed for more-rapid, cheaper and less-painful tattooing. The relative ease with which tattoos could be produced increased the number of practitioners and the availability of tattooing. Electric instruments also allowed the creation of more-detailed and more-enduring designs than was previously possible with simple hand implements.

Pigment is the second essential resource. Tattooists have adapted inks developed for other graphic purposes and, during the past 20 years, the available palette has expanded from three to more than 30 distinct colours. The tattoos produced have, in turn, become significantly more colourful.

Human skin is the third major resource the tattooist requires. The availability and physical characteristics of this material place significant constraints on tattoo style. The novice tattooist usually encounters problems in finding available 'canvas' upon which to practise (Sanders 1985, pp. 24–7). Most commonly the novice learns by working on his or her own skin, that of accommodating friends and associates, and various 'skin substitutes' such as melons, potatoes or chicken carcases (Sanders 1985, pp. 24–7).

The physical characteristics of human skin and musculature limit both the form and the content of tattooing. Skin is highly elastic, and its texture varies considerably from individual to individual. Tattooists, who often adopt the perspective of amateur dermatologists, tend to judge clients by the quality of their skin. The 'ideal' subject is of medium build with light, finely textured skin. Customers who bleed profusely, display negative physical reactions to the pigments or evidence severe discomfort while being tattooed present technical problems and are disvalued by tattooists. The prototypical tattoo – a small, badge-like, minimally detailed image located on the tattooee's arm – is largely a consequence of the technical problems inherent in working on the surface of the human body.[4]

Social stigma, legal restriction and style

All art worlds exist within a larger sociolegal environment which constrains production activity and the related style of artistic products. Legal authorities often act to restrict artistic content which is seen as threatening the moral or political *status quo*, and to regulate production processes or cultural products which, in their view, may negatively affect the public health.

The stigmatized social definition of tattooing derives largely from its traditional use by members of deviant or marginal groups as a symbolic boundary-maintaining mechanism. Professional criminals, outlaw motorcyclists, users of illegal drugs, prostitutes, those that identify with 'punk' culture and other members of counter-conventional subcultures commonly acquire tattoos which symbolize their membership and demonstrate their commitment to the group.

Few modes of cultural production are as extensively regulated as tattooing is. Although the legal restriction of tattooing derives primarily from its association with social deviants, the most common official rationale emphasizes the protection of public health. Anecdotal evidence linking the tattooing process with the spread of communicable diseases is typically presented to justify official regulation or outright prohibition. Recent attempts in the USA to define tattooing legally as an art form protected by Constitutional guarantees of free speech have, at the time of writing, proved to be unsuccessful.[5]

The association of tattooing with stigmatized groups and communicable disease, and the danger implied in its regulation by official agents of social control, significantly affect tattoo style. The movement of innovative practitioners and new consumers into tattooing is restricted, with the consequence that a limited stylistic repertoire continues to predominate.

Fine-art tattooists chafe under the continuing public distaste for the medium. In response they consistently refer to themselves as 'tattoo artists' and their establishments as 'studios'. They take great pains to disassociate themselves from 'scratchers' who are technically unskilled and 'stencil men' who are incapable of doing creative custom work. They actively seek the media attention which allows them to define tattooing publicly as an art form with an honourable history and an extensive cross-cultural tradition. They attempt to associate themselves with 'legitimate' institutions such as museums and universities, through participation in shows and academic discussions. In short, fine-art tattooists are engaged in a process of collective legitimation. Like a wide variety of disvalued social actors (e.g. homosexuals and ex-mental patients), tattoo artists are attempting to redefine themselves and their activities as non-threatening, unproblematic and even admirable (cf. Spector & Kitsuse 1977). To the extent that they are successful in this endeavour, tattooing will continue to expand as it comes to be more broadly defined as a legitimate (if somewhat minor) art form, as it continues to be taken up by skilled practitioners who value creativity and stylistic innovation, and as the pool of collectors and enthusiasts becomes more heterogeneous and requests art products which are unique, aesthetically exciting and socially relevant.

Conclusion

Constrained by a strong folk tradition and a history of symbolic association with marginal social groups, contemporary tattooing is striving for legitimacy as a reputable art form. The base reputation of tattooing severely limits the opportunity for serious creators to produce 'significant' works within the medium. The new tattooists, with the perspectives and objectives of fine artists, must develop their technical skills and explore innovative styles at the same time as they, like other commercial artists, tend to the practical concerns of carrying on a business. They are also involved in public-relations activities directed at building the social consensus within both the larger art world and the general society upon which legitimacy is based (Becker 1982, pp. 358–65).

In addition to the perspective and skill of the individual practitioner, the organizational structure of the production world, the limitations imposed by essential equipment and the availability of materials, the characteristics and requirements of the market and the sociolegal context within which the production activity proceeds are key variables which shape style and direct the process of stylistic change. The analyst interested in understanding this aspect of cultural products must attend to the organization of the social world surrounding the production process. The structural context both shapes and is the result of the complex web of collective action – real people interacting together to achieve both personal and collective ends – which is the essence of cultural creation.

Notes

1 This presentation is based on data collected between 1981 and 1985 during participant observation in a variety of the settings in which tattoo production takes place. Additional information drawn from the lengthy interviews with 14 working tattooists provided much of the foundation for this analysis.
2 See Sanders (1983, 1985) for more-detailed discussions of the tattooist's career and occupational experience.
3 The tattooist interviewees all stated that they refused to inscribe swastikas and overtly racist slogans, because of the potential impact of these designs on the public's image of tattooing and the practitioners' personal dislike for the connotations of these symbols.
4 Kealy's (1982) discussion of the rise of the rock-music aesthetic as it relates to the development of recording technology provides an excellent example of this important relationship.
5 See, for example, Yurkew versus Sinclair, 495 F. Supp. 1248, 1255–56 (D. Minn. 1980); Golden versus McCarty, 337 So. 2d 388, 390 (Fla. 1976); Grossman versus Baumgartner, 218 N.E. 2d 259, 261 (N.Y. 1966).

References

Becker, H. 1974. Art as collective action. *American Sociological Review* **39**, 767–76.
Becker, H. 1982. *Art worlds*. Berkeley: University of California Press.

Bell, Q. 1976. *On human finery*. New York: Schocken.
Christopherson, R. 1974. From folk art to fine art: a transformation in the meaning of photographic work. *Urban Life and Culture* **3**, 179–204.
DiMaggio, P. 1977. Market structure, the creative process, and popular culture: toward an organizational reinterpretation of mass-culture theory. *Journal of Popular Culture* **11**, 436–52.
Eldridge, C. 1982. *The history of the tattoo machine*. Berkeley, California: Tattoo Archive.
Faulkner, R. 1982. *Music on demand*. New Brunswick: Transaction.
Fine, G. 1985. Occupational aesthetics: how trade school students learn to cook. *Urban Life* **14**, 3–32.
Fried, F. & M. Fried 1978. *America's forgotten folk arts*. New York: Pantheon.
Gans, H. 1974. *Popular culture and high culture*. New York: Basic Books.
Gitlin, T. 1983. *Inside prime time*. New York: Pantheon.
Gombrich, E. 1969. *Art and illusion*. Princeton, New Jersey: Princeton University Press.
Hauser, A. 1982. *The sociology of art*. Chicago: University of Chicago Press.
Hirsch, P. 1972. Processing fads and fashions: an organization-set analysis of cultural industry systems. *American Journal of Sociology* **77**, 639–59.
Jensen, J. 1984. An interpretive approach to culture production. In *Interpreting television: current research perspectives*, W. Rowland, Jr & B. Watkins (eds), 98–118. Beverly Hills: Sage.
Kealy, E. 1979. From craft to art: the case of sound mixers and popular music. *Sociology of Work and Occupations* **6**, 3–29.
Kealy, E. 1982. Conventions and the production of the popular music aesthetic. *Journal of Popular Culture* **16**, 100–15.
Lyon, E. 1974. Work and play: resource constraints in a small theater. *Urban Life* **3**, 71–97.
Manfredi, J. 1982. *The social limits of art*. Amherst, Massachusetts: University of Massachusetts Press.
Peterson, R. 1976. The production of culture: a prolegomenon. *American Behavioral Scientist* **19**, 669–84.
Peterson, R. 1982. Five constraints on the production of culture: law, technology, market, organizational structure and occupational careers. *Journal of Popular Culture* **16**, 143–53.
Peterson, R. & D. Berger 1975. Cycles in symbolic production: the case of popular music. *American Sociological Review* **40**, 158–73.
Rosenberg, B. & N. Fliegel 1970. The artist and his publics: the ambiguity of success. In *The sociology of art and literature* M. Albrecht (ed.), 499–517, New York: Praeger.
Rosenblum, B. 1978a. Style as social process. *American Sociological Review* **43**, 422–38.
Rosenblum, B. 1978b. *Photographers at work*. New York: Holmes & Meier.
Rubin, A. 1983. Prologue to a history of the tattoo renaissance. Paper presented at the Art of the Body Symposium, University of California at Los Angeles, January.
Sanders, C. 1982. Structural and interactional features of popular culture production: an introduction to the production of culture perspective. *Journal of Popular Culture* **16**, 66–74.
Sanders, C. 1983. Drill and fill: client choice, client typologies and interactional control in commercial tattoo settings. Paper presented at the Art of the Body Symposium, University of California at Los Angeles, January.
Sanders, C. 1984. Tattoo consumption: risk and regret in the purchase of a socially marginal service. In *Advances in consumer research*, Vol. XII, E. Hirschman & M.

Holbrook (eds), 12–7. New York: Association for Consumer Research.
Sanders, C. 1985. Selling deviant pictures: the tattooist's career and occupational experience. Paper presented at the Conference on Social Theory, Politics and the Arts, Adelphi University, Garden City, New York, October.
Sinha, A. 1979. Control in craft work: the case of production potters. *Qualitative Sociology* **2**, 3–25.
Spector, M. & J. Kitsuse 1977. *Constructing social problems.* Menlo Park, California: Cummings.
Tuchman, G. 1983. Consciousness industries and the production of culture. *Journal of Communication* **33**, 330–41.
Tucker, M. 1981. Tattoo: the state of the art. *Artforum* (May), 42–7.
Watson, B. 1968. On the nature of art publics. *International Social Science Journal* **20**, 667–80.
Wroblewski, C. 1981. *Skin show: the art and craft of tattoo*. New York: Dragon's Dream.

10 *A semiotic approach in rock-art analysis*

ANA MARIA LLAMAZARES

Introduction

After several years of studying rock-art evidence according to traditional methods, the shortcomings became clear, and the analysis of those limitations has suggested the need for a new approach.[1]

When we face the problem of analysing rock art, the risk of interpreting its meaning and function in a subjective way is very high. Every rock-art expression is a semantic phenomenon. Those shapes and signs certainly had meaning for their authors. No human act is banal, not even those which seem to be so. However, that former function and meaning have disappeared, together with the authors. If we expect to carry on our work along scientific lines, then this initial shortcoming must be accepted. We only have the signifier; that will be our empirical basis.[2] (For further consideration of this limit see below.)

What are we to do then with this signifier? Although we cannot reconstruct its original meaning, it is too valuable a trace to be abandoned because of the above drawback, since it is one of the few remains which allow us to go into the superstructure, a dimension of prehistoric life which has been almost completely lost.

Why do we consider semiotics as a science which can help us in our effort to overcome these limitations? In the first place some general assumptions drew us to such a field. We think that in societies without phonetic writing, other forms of graphic representations become particularly important for the transmission and preservation of certain ideas. Should this be the case, then these ways of representation can be considered semiotic in so far as they are systems of signs structured according to certain rules of internal coherence which ensured their communicability.

The main hypothesis which holds that rock art may be structured as a language, i.e. as a communication system, is based on its undoubtedly cultural nature. As such, its existence relies on the existence of a human group, a society which embodied and used it. Its sociocultural character implies that the phenomenon was shared and understood by the group. Also, even if we presume it to be the result of an individual or solitary act of creation – which could be laid aside by its amazing recurrence – the person who produced it would be expressing him or herself through structures which already existed in the community to which he or she belonged.

We have designed our theoretical frame foraging into the fields of linguistics and semiotics. Much attention must be paid when actually applying it to the data, so as to preserve the anthropological scope. We therefore assume that semiotics is the appropriate field to deal with rock art viewed as a communication system. Semiotics, incidentally, has proved to be most fruitful in interdisciplinary co-operation.

Theoretical foundations

The issue can be considered on three different levels.

(a) That of semiotics in general, or systems of signs which produce communicable meaning effects.
(b) That of specific fields of semiosis, determined by different expression-substances. This means that not all the rules which belong to the linguistic field, for example, can be applied to graphic, gestural, musical or other semiotic fields (semiosis). This level could itself be divided into more-specific subfields. Such would be the case of rock art, within the iconic or graphic fields.
(c) That of particular languages identifiable within those fields of semiotic expression, usually determined by their cultural belonging and their correlation with a particular social group.

Each of these levels would have its corresponding level of grammar, understood as the formation and transformation rules underlying every order.[3] Our approach will proceed from (a) to (c), i.e. from the most general to the most specific. We believe that it is essential to take advantage of the experience which has tried to overcome the obstacles set by inductive procedures in other fields, and which in our discipline is quite clearly shown in the limited results achieved by the construction of taxonomies and typologies based on observation and association of formal elements.

Level (b) of specific fields of semiosis is determined by the demands of the expression-substance (Hjelmslev 1943), which set the limits of each peculiar field. Just as language expresses itself through sounds and writing, rock art does it through graphic or iconic forms, whose substances are given by the techniques used.

Hjelmslev contends that the linguistic theory he tries to formulate must be general enough to account not only for the texts of one particular language, but for any manifestation of language (Hjelmslev 1943). This shows the exact degree of generality needed in the level mentioned above as (b).

If we admit that reconstructing a particular grammar in order to explain the iconic – and rock art in particular – would in this field be synonymous with the construction of a linguistic theory, we should consider the need to work out for prehistoric art an explanatory theory which could account for the mechanisms of articulation and generation of any kind of rock-art expression. Having a theory of such a scope, we could overcome a drawback in stylistic typologies – the sole explanatory tool which has been tried so far in this field of events. The drawback lies in the fact that their explanatory power is restricted to a given geographical area, and is useless for between-area comparisons.

Level (c) will allow us to build up the particular grammar of a semiotic system restricted in time and space, and allotted to a certain sociocultural group. We expect that, were it possible to find this new entity called 'grammar' within the field of rock art, we would be touching upon a stronger tool than 'style' to determine prehistoric cultural belonging.

Before coming to this point, we must find out whether the rock-art phenomenon can be included in level (a); that is, whether it can be classed as a communication system, as a sign system or semiosis. In order to discover this, we must begin by accepting an explicit definition of semiosis. In other words, we must organize a set of traits which would operate as generative conditions for all languages, thus placing the analysis in level (a). (For a deeper treatment of this point, see Llamazares 1988.)

For the time being we will only advance certain methodological considerations which we believe to be useful for reflection and analysis of the actual issue.

Methodological problems: some guidelines

The inductivistic obstacle

Overcoming the limitations of traditional approaches implies dodging the inductivistic obstacle which leads us to start work by recognizing and ordering rock-art motives according to a particular classification system. Besides the objections one can raise against taxonomies *per se*, or the scarce rigour with which classification categories are often built, such proceedings bear a basic epistemological fault. The outline of the first unit of analysis is taken for granted, and this is usually an evident choice, a perceptual identification modelled to our own standards of whatever is 'naturalistic', 'geometrical', 'straight' or 'curved', etc.

The fact of posing something evident as the starting point leads to a dangerous situation in science, which has seen a continuous struggle against the evident, against what is obvious, the phenomenical. We expect to discover cognitive structures which we take to have been real when rock art appeared. We must be careful not to turn our research into a beautiful kaleidoscope whose multiplying reflections are none other than our own cognitive structures.

If we mean to follow a different way of thinking, then we must change our stand. Having a theoretical model – which in our case is related to the concepts of language and semiosis, and to the traits which can be transferred from them to a visual semiosis – provides the evaluation criteria that will guide the actual work on the recorded designs. At times this inevitably becomes a sort of inductive quest, but this quest will not be more or less hazardous, nor will it be implicitly guided by some underlying theoretical corpus. It will be followed according to a model of semiosis and language requisites based on results which have proved fertile in other fields.

We will work inductively in so far as we expect to generalize, from the analysis of the particular 'groups'[4] of designs which we take as our texts, the laws of their organization. However, we will work deductively, as long as we are guided by a theoretical method.

Changing the aim of the search: looking for relationships instead of elements

The semiotic status of rock art would only be proven if we can determine in it the presence of some organizational regularities which follow a certain rule. Although we may not be able to discover what the rule is, we may think out how to find it. We expect to detect regularities which, when recurrent, may show that certain structuring and generating mechanisms are working, and can be included in a system of cognitive rules. The starting point must not be the recognition of elements, but of the relationships which connect those elements.

The graphic character of rock art leads us to gear relationships around the physical location of the elements on a two-dimensional plane. We will be able to ask, for example, whether a particular shape always appears in a certain place or never does so. If its presence is accidental it would prove either the absence of a rule, or the existence of a loose relationship.

It is important to view the elements as crossroads of relationships. There is no point in stopping to describe their shapes. It is not so essential to check whether it is a circle or a dot, as to study its combinatorial possibilities. The elements must be defined not according to their morphological shape, but noting their possible relationships with other elements. Operations are constant relationships among elements which, on their part, are nothing but sets of other less extended relationships.

Seeking regularities does not mean searching simultaneous presences or merely repeated associations. It means looking for the law which relates those groupings. We do not intend to organize presences, but to rebuild the cores of possibilities which were in the author's mind before he or she actually created the designs. In the remains we will only find clues, signs of the network of cognitive options which we expect to rescue as previous to their emergence.

Our aim is to formulate the laws of that grammar; that is, of that system of operations and rules which the community had at its cognitive disposal.

Restriction to the 'signifier'

The initial circumscription to the signifier field, admitting the loss of the semantic component, means limiting the possibilities of reconstruction, at least at a first stage, to what Hjelmslev would call the 'expression-plane', in its two orders: 'form' and 'substance'; or to what Chomsky would call the 'phonological component' (or its equivalent in rock art) and the 'syntactic component'.

Nevertheless, it must be noticed that what appears as a major limitation is not so strong after all. If we accept Hjelmslev's suggestion about the correspondence between 'expression-plane' and 'content-plane' (near to Saussure's 'signifier–signified'), then it would be reasonable to presume that there should be a series of categories in the content-plane which should correspond to a division seen in the expression-plane, although we may be ignorant of them at any one time. If the semiotic function is seen as a dependence in which the 'expression-form' organizes the 'content-form', then any change in the first plane implies a change in the second.

The organization of all possible forms of such sequences would result in the total number of entities which could have been said with that system. We would not be able to assign specific content to each of them, but we do know that each had a meaning in the world.

More-recent developments in linguistics (Chomsky 1965, 1982) show that the semantic component is strongly conditioned by the syntactic component. Knowledge of the latter would lead into the world of semantics. It would seem that the syntactical structure is the one that holds the cue for explaining the generation of sense for a given language.

If we carry the statement into our field, we will realize that although we may not come to know the specific significant correspondence of each element, we may catch a glimpse of the way in which its users assigned a meaning to them.

The search for the 'signified' level

Although we have established as a necessary methodological assumption, the initial restriction to the signifier plane, we consider it possible, by means of this kind of analysis, to come closer to the point where the attribution of a semantic content would be more likely to start, within the growing complexity in which signifiers are becoming gradually organized.

As we see it, this is related to the possibility of testing whether in rock art, as well as in language, there is a 'double articulation' (cf. Martinet 1949); that is, that rock art consists of meaningful units ('first articulation') composed by other smaller meaningless ones ('second articulation'). We suggest as a way of detecting this feature the identification of units of different hierarchies by analysing the contextualization of the elements.

The same element associated in different contexts implies an autonomous way of articulation and, consequently, we can suppose that it is meaningful by itself. On the contrary, whenever an element appears in a regular and constant way associated with others, and never isolated, then it is quite possible to infer that it becomes integrated to others in order to form larger units, and consequently, that it bears no meaning.

This analytical procedure also relies on the idea that a greater variability is more closely related to the semantic field. Thus, if the elements and their relationships with other elements are constant, rather than variable, then we could assume that they are meaningless. It would be necessary at this point to investigate whether these stable elements gather themselves into other not-variable clusters which do appear associated in different contexts, that is to say, to identify at what level of organization variability starts, because there the signified plane would become more apparent.

Reconstruction of the system[5]

Discrimination between two dichotomous complementary fields in every linguistic phenomenon seems sufficiently established. 'Language–speech', 'system–process' and 'competence–performance' are pairs of concepts which – in spite of the slight variations attributed to each other by their authors – refer to the sign system which makes up language as a social product, on the one hand, and the particular use or actualization of that system brought about by each speaker or text, on the other hand (cf. Saussure 1916, Hjelmslev 1943, Chomsky 1965).

Should we accept, at least temporarily, the hypothesis of the semiotic structure of rock art, then our aim will be to reconstruct whatever corresponds approximately to the first term of the dichotomy mentioned above, viz. the system of shared rules, the social element, the common code which generates and gives meaning to each sign of that language.

We search the explanation of the phenomenon through the description of the system which produces it. However, that is not all. We also aim at explaining why a system is transformed, not merely through the description of the different steps of that system, but also by going into the processes and mechanisms of that change, into that which makes a system assume a new order.

We may go even further and presume that each group shared the same code, or at least an important part of it, substantial enough to bring about cultural identity. Different kinds of changes in the code, and not merely a change in style or a technical variation would become a determinant marker of cultural change.

Even though we would like to place these steps in their historical development, we believe it is impossible to reach explanatory levels in the social sciences through an exclusively diachronic initial approach. Every change is a more or less thorough transformation of a function or of a system, and its understanding demands a previous knowledge of its synchronic articulation.

Acknowledgement

I owe a special debt of gratitude to Juan Angel Magariños de Morentin who, as co-director of this research project, is a constant stimulus and guide. Many of the ideas which are expressed in this chapter derive from discussions with him.

Notes

1 The theoretical and methodological approach that we propose in this paper is only the first stage of a research project, started in 1985 and sponsored by the CONICET (National Council of Scientific and Technological Research), Argentina, which also

includes its application to the study of rock art in northern Patagonia. It is related to another project which plans to achieve a broader archaeological reconstruction of the Pilcaniyeu area, in the province of Rio Negro, Argentina (cf. Boschin 1984).

2 Although this approach could be used in any kind of prehistoric art, we must point out that it was conceived when working with almost exclusively geometrical designs. Its abstraction enables this restriction. Nevertheless, if this methodology proves to be useful, we will try its application on naturalistic designs.

3 We use the term 'order' in the sense given to it by Foucault (1966).

4 We use the 'group' as the starting point for our data analysis. The 'group' is seen as the set of designs topographically bounded. This implies considering the author's limiting intention *ab initio*. Although we may ignore why he or she chose that particular space to place the designs, the fact is that it is not an arbitrary delimitation forced on the data by the researcher. On the contrary, it respects the limits imposed upon it by the author, which probably answered to semantic reasons, although they remain veiled to us.

5 We use the term 'system' in the strict sense given to it by Hjelmslev (1943).

References

Boschin, M. T. 1984. Plan de investigaciones arqueológicas. Paraje Paso de los Molles, area Pilcaniyeu, provincia de Rio Negro. Unpublished research plan, CONICET, Buenos Aires, Argentina.

Chomsky, N. 1965. *Aspects of the theory of syntax*. Cambridge, Massachusetts: MIT Press.

Chomsky, N. 1975. *Reflections on language*. New York: Pantheon.

Chomsky, N. 1982. *Lectures on government and binding. The Pisa Lectures*. Dordrecht: Cinnaminson.

Foucault, M. 1966. *Les mots et les choses. Une archéologie des sciences humaines*. Paris: Gallimard.

Hjelmslev, L. 1953. *Prolegomena to a theory of language* (transl. from the Danish, 1943). Bloomington: Indiana University Press.

Llamazares, A. 1986. Hacia una definición de semiosis. Reflecciones sobre su applicabilidad para la interpretación del arte rupestre. Cuadernos, Il Instituto Nacional de Antropologia, Buenos Aires, Argentina.

Martinet, A. 1949. La double articulation linguistique. *Travaux du Cercle Linguistique de Copenhague* **5**, 30–7.

Saussure, F. de 1916. *Cours de linguistique générale*. Paris: Payot.

20 *Habitus and social space: some suggestions about meaning in the Saami (Lapp) tent ca. 1700–1900*

TIMOTHY YATES

Introduction

This chapter discusses the tents (*kåhte*) of the mountain Saami (Lapps) over the period *ca.* 1700–1900. These dates are arbitrary, defined respectively by Scheffer's *History of Lapland* published in 1704 (but drawing upon 17th century sources) and the memoirs of Johan Turi, a Saami from Kautokeino, Norway, originally published in 1910. Over this period continuity in the form and structure of the *kåhte* space is demonstrable, and analysis will concentrate on defining the fundamental structures (Habitus) that account for this continuity.

In this chapter I discuss the evidence of a few key-texts in order to demonstrate a possible direction for analysis – the first few tentative steps towards a 'structuralist' approach to the meaning invested in the Saami domestic context in the past. The approach is generalized, in a manner perhaps similar to that used by Ränk (1949), but it is the contention here that through a structuralist problematic it is possible to move towards a more powerful explanation of the Saami *kåhte*. I am seeking a new direction in this contribution – a structuralist re-analysis of the kind of material dealt with by Rånk. Like Rånk's essay, this chapter should be regarded only as 'an attempt to trace some general lines of approach' (Rånk 1949, p. 87).

Theoretical basis

> In a social formation in which the absence of the symbolic-product-conserving techniques associated with literacy retards the objectification of symbolic and particularly cultural capital, inhabited space – and above all the house – is the principal locus of the generative schemes; and, through the divisions and hierarchies it sets up between things, persons and practices, this tangible classifying system continuously inculcates and reinforces the taxonomic principles underlying all the arbitrary provisions of this culture.
>
> (Bourdieu 1977, p. 89)

The house is an important focus of structures in society. Through the distinction set up between public and private, the house and its walls create a fragmentary picture of society that denies both the totality and the continuity of meaning in which these units are themselves articulated. The structures within the household walls are divorced from the wider cultural principles in which they belong – totality is dissolved through the private.

These structures are culturally specific rather than the universals proposed by classic structuralism. The problem with such deep structures was that they were, like Freud's unconscious, ahistorical because of their universality. To reconstitute structures as historical, it was necessary to dissolve the distinction between surfaces and depths. In the work of Bourdieu (1977, 1979), deep-structure consists of the principle of binary opposition, rather than its content. It ceases to be the object of analysis, and becomes the theoretical given: analysis seeks the content of these oppositions as a totality of cultural structures, called by him 'habitus'.

Structures in this sense can only be reached by analytical abstraction from the real, but they are themselves concrete, not abstract. They are present in the real through practice, constituted as meaningful within practical consciousness – a set of cultural principles that are conscious to their agents but which lie beyond their capacity to describe them. They are historical through a conception of structural duality, where structures are both medium and outcome of human action (Giddens 1982, pp. 36–9). Thus, there can no longer be a distinction between what is deep and what is superficial – if structures are reciprocally influenced by practices, then the two must be continuous, rather than separate. This relation is best conceived as a dialectical one, where deep and visible structures are both part of the same system and yet different and opposed to each other.

This totality of structures is 'a system of durable, transposable dispositions which function as the generative basis of structured, objectively unified practices' (Bourdieu, 1979, p. vii, n. 2). Although these are not reducible to habit (Bourdieu 1977, p. 218, n. 47), the similarity of terms emphasizes their location within the practical rather than discursive consciousness. Space is particularly important, as all actions performed within it are 'so many structural exercises by which is built up practical mastery of the fundamental schemes' (Bourdieu 1977, p. 91). Structural analysis must seek the oppositions as they are related within a cultural totality.

The divisions of household space

The divisions of the internal space of the *kåhte* have been studied by Rånk, who concluded that there 'must have been quite a general pattern in these areas [northern Lapland]' (1949, p. 92). This pattern consisted of three general areas, which are then subdivided to produce nine separate social zones. Each area had a specific name and, although these names vary, the divisions themselves are pervasive.

In the centre was the hearth, *arran*. The area between the door and the hearth was known as the *uksa*, and that beyond the hearth as *påssjo*. The areas to either side of the hearth, from front to back, were known as the *luoito* (or variants). These areas were then further divided – the area to either side of the hearth was the *arran-luoito* or *kaske-kåhte*, and those to either side were given the suffix *-gaecce*. (Fig. 20.1). These areas received varying amounts of physical representation: in the illustrations provided by Scheffer & Leem (Figs. 20.2 & 3) each is bounded by logs. There is some change of layout observable between the two, but the continuity in spatial terminology, meaning and social positions argues that this was a change of form alone. The structure was continuous from Scheffer into the 19th century and up to the 1900s. Indeed, even today, where the *kåhte* is to be found in use in the Saami summer villages, the basic divisions of space, terminology and people are still evident.

Household space: boundaries and gender

> The traditional pattern lived on in the Saami milieu and created a complex of customs and purely ritualistic behaviour in everyday life. Above all, these evaluations centred around the woman's behaviour patterns around the *påssjo* the holy place.
>
> (Fjellström 1985, p. 246)

The divisions of the Saami *kåhte* articulated the system of values and authority upon which Saami society was based. Inherent in these was the opposition of male and female, and of men's power over women, for although there was an emphasis in Saami society upon equality between the sexes, in the rules of bilaterality, property and inheritance (Pehrson 1957), women were distinguished from men both conceptually and in practice. Gender differentiation is marked and pervasive in Saami society – there are even separate verbs for male and female urination (Pehrson 1957: 32) – and this differentiation can be shown to structure the internal space of the *kåhte*.

Scheffer, in his *History of Lapland* (1704), provides an early account of the internal layout of the Saami *kåhte*:

> Things are so ordered that every tent has two doors, one a fore-door, the other a backward; the former bigger and more ordinarily used, the latter less, through which they bring in their provisions, especially the prey that they took in hunting, which it was unlawful to bring in at the fore-door.
>
> (Scheffer 1971, p. 84)

He provides a sketch of the floor of the *kåhte* to show the social divisions of the internal space (Scheffer 1971, p. 85, fig. 1). At the back was the *påssjo*, marked by logs, where only men were permitted to pass, 'and it is unlawful for any woman to pass these logs and go into it'. The woman's position was by the fore-door, in the *kitta*, but men were permitted to pass through this zone. The area between

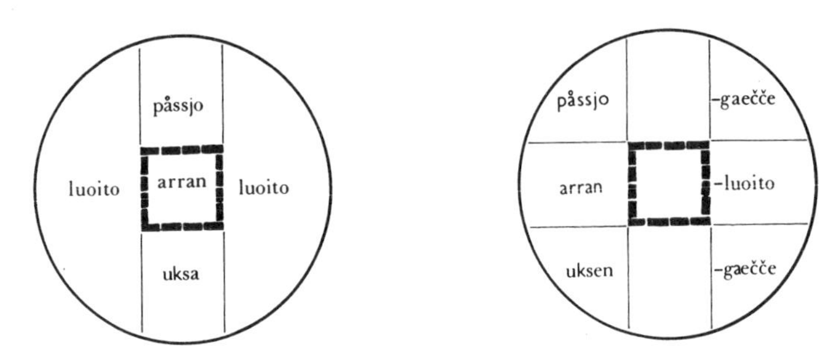

Figure 20.1 Saami names for areas of the *kåhte*.

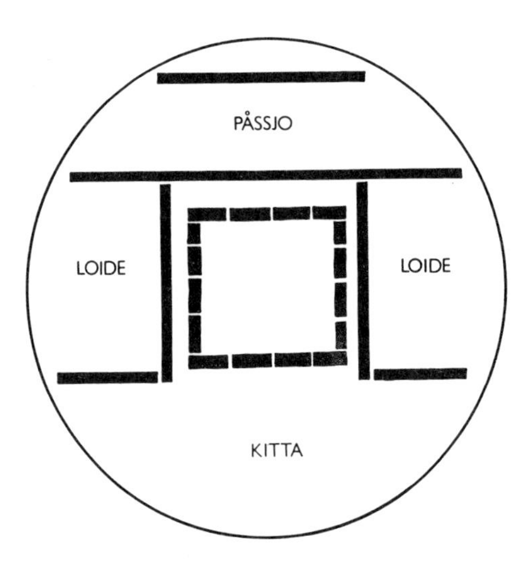

Figure 20.2 Floor plan of the *kåhte* according to Scheffer (1704 (1971: 84)).

was the *loide*, the common zone, but even there men and women were separated. Nensén, writing later in the 18th century, records that the woman was not allowed to reach across her husband to fetch pans and other items from the *boassju*. She was required to circle the *kåhte* and come to the *påssjo* from the other side. In the Lule Saami area the positions of husband and wife were physically separated, by the *akka-kerrke*, the housewife's stone (Fjellström 1985, p. 247).

There is a marked continuity in these social divisions. Scheffer (1971, p. 85) writes that in the *loide* (*luoito*) the parents sit on one side and their children on the other. This was still the case at the time Joseph Acerbi visited Lapland in 1798–9 (Acerbi 1802). The general pattern throughout the 18th and 19th centuries would appear to locate the 'master of the house' in the division furthest from the door on the right beside the *påssjo*; his wife sat next to him, in the area from the hearth to the door. The children's side was opposite that of the parents, along with the servants who resided by the door. Strict rules governed the movement of people around the *kåhte*. Von Buch, writing in 1813, notes:

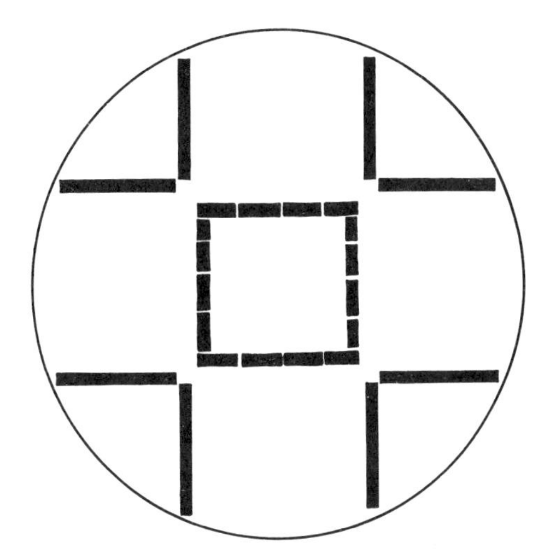

Figure 20.3 Floor plan of the *kåhte* according to Leem (1767).

> The daughters do not come over to the more distinguished side of the mother, nor the mother, except accidentally, to that of the daughters. The fire and the small hearth in the middle separates the herile and servile sides.
>
> (Von Buch 1813, p. 290)

It is thus possible to distinguish a lateral and a vertical system of oppositions running through the *kåhte*. Predominant was the gender opposition, running laterally through the *kåhte*, with men sitting and sleeping at the back, females at the front, the focus of the separation being the hearth (Rånk 1949, p. 111). Yet the fire was also the fulcrum of the vertical division between generations – on one side parents and small children, on the other side the older children (Rånk 1949, p. 98, 111, Erixon 1937, p. 137, fig. 11). Although the precise nature of these divisions varied, with the parents on the left in the southern parts of Lapland, the integrity of the opposition male : female and parents : children seems pervasive (Vorren 1962, pp. 45–6). Figure 20.3 represents the floorplan of the *kåhte* according to Leem (1808, p. 388).

This order within the household is underlined by Von Buch's (1813, p. 315) description of the arrival of a visitor who, if allowed admittance, 'then becomes a member of the family and a place in the house is allotted to him'. The house and the family were mutual orders, and thus *kåhte* means both the structure and the social unit occupying it (Whitaker 1955, p. 37). The *kåhte* was a physical representation of the structure of relations of the Saami household.

Guests were expected to reside on the children's side of the *kåhte*, in the area adjacent to the door. This was normally occupied by the servants who, like the guests, were outsiders not generally related to the family for whom they worked (Whitaker 1955, p. 85) and whose duties were herding (male) and domestic (female). Servants, like the main family, were sometimes separated by gender (Rånk 1949, p. 107). Only the missionary, or later the pastor, was allowed to reside elsewhere than in the servants' area, and then would be given the area adjacent to the *påssjo*, and the master and his wife would leave the *kåhte* rather than move to a lower-status area (Acerbi 1802, p. 173).

However, it was also often the case that more than one family would occupy the same *kåhte*. Pehrson observes that in Könkämä village it was only during the summer and autumn that the household was so clearly based on the elementary family, and at other times, during the migrations, households join together under one roof (Pehrson 1957, p. 95). In such a situation each family would take one side of the *kåhte* and its three divisions – the *påssjo-kiaeshie*, where the parents sat, the *arran-luoito*, the children's place, and the *uksa-kiaeshie*, the servants' place (Acerbi 1802, p. 173, Leem 1808, p. 389).

The conceptual meaning of space

The *kåhte* mediated a system of oppositions, based on gender, which were repeated conceptually in the ordering of the heavens. The gods were conceived on five levels – the higher, the lower, the terrestrial, the subterranean and those 'in the very bowels of the earth' (Leem 1808, pp. 457–8). At the apex of the Cosmos resided *Peive*, the Sun-god, who supported all other gods on his rays (Manker 1962, p. 119). *Peive* chased away the cold and the dark, and rendered the ground snow-free and fertile for the reindeer – 'the author of generation', as Sheffer (1971, p. 38) calls him. With *Peive* resided *Tiermes* (perhaps identifiable as Thor), the god of thunder, who 'drove away the demons which are prejudicial to their hunting, fowling and fishing' (*ibid.*, p. 37). Although conceived as elements of the same god, *Pieve* and *Tiermes* opposed each other in space: offerings to *Peive* were placed over the main doorway (Collinder 1949, p. 144), those to *Tiermes* in the *påssjo* and behind the back door (Scheffer 1971, p. 38). During sacrifice a doe was offered to *Pieve*, a bull-reindeer to *Tiermes* (*ibid.*, pp. 43–4). The *kåhte* always faced the south (Regnard 1808, p. 177, Scheffer 1971, p. 85), and it was in the south that the Sun was visible during the winter. *Påssjo* originally meant north (Ränk 1949, p. 93).

In the absence of the Sun, which above the Arctic Circle is for up to 3 months, the fire was venerated, 'which they believe to be a living representation of the sun, and which produces on the earth the same effects which the other does in the heavens' (Regnard 1808, p. 179).

Beneath *Peive* resided *Radien-Attje*, the ruling father, and *Radien-Akka*, the ruling mother (Manker 1962, p. 120). The former was responsible for the well-being of the herd, the latter perhaps for the prosperity of the household (Leem 1808, p. 458).

The space within the *kåhte* therefore represented the order of the Cosmos. The hearth was the centre of the *kåhte* as *Peive* was the centre of the heavens, the fire connecting the two. As *Peive* brought life to the land, filling it with light and fertility, so did the fire within the *kåhte*, the enclosed space appropriated from the outer domain of *Peive*. Under the hearth resided the goddess *Sarakka*, responsible for the birth of reindeer and children (Leem 1808, p. 459). *Sarakka* was a terrestrial being who spanned Heaven and Earth by receiving the souls of the dead from *Radien-Akke* to be born anew. The *kåhte* was thus the focus of the worlds of the living and the dead, the front, southerly and the back, northerly, which met in the hearth. Other terrestrial beings inhabited the *kåhte*. Under the fore-door dwelt *Uks-Akka*, the door goddess, who protected the newborn and attended to 'the monthly ills of the [feminine] sex' (Leem 1808, p. 459). Under the back-door dwelt *Påssjo-Akka*, the goddess of the hunt (Manker 1962, p. 120).

Ritual worship of the gods could be carried out only by the men, and the spatial and social implications of this emerge from the accounts of the festival attendant upon the killing of a bear. Women were considered to be ritually impure, and the bear had to be kept separate from them, as women were believed to contaminate the hunter and his prey (Scheffer 1971, p. 84). For this purpose all ritual took place within a separate *kåhte*, to which only the men were admitted (Leem 1808, p. 485). The reindeer that had carried the bear back to the *kåhte* could not be used by a woman for a year (Leem 1808, Collinder 1949, p. 161, Scheffer 1971, p. 96).

Blood was at the centre of all ritual (Regnard 1808, p. 179, Scheffer 1971, p. 43). The Saami word for bear's blood, *laeibe*, also meant the ruddy sap of alder bark and women's menstrual blood (Collinder 1949, p. 56). Bear blood was associated with the hunt, and thus the *påssjo*, where the goddess of the hunt resided. Thus, among the Kola and Skolt Saami, the back, *påssjo*, door was also known as *varr-lips*, the bloody-door. Here the hunting equipment was stored, smeared with blood as a protection against pollution by women (Ränk 1949, pp. 101, 103). Thus, the *påssjo* and *påssjo*-door were reserved for the access of men alone, 'the reason for which I think partly this, because in that place they kept Thor [*Tiermes*, the shaman's drum] and partly this, because it was esteemed an ill-omen for a hunter to meet a woman' (Scheffer 1971, p. 84). The shaman was also known as 'the man of blood' (Acerbi 1802, p. 305). The opposite side of the *kåhte* was associated with women's menstrual blood, the goddess *Uks-Akka*, who resided beneath the main doorway. When a woman was menstruating or in labour, it was beside the *uksa* that she was expected to reside (Ränk 1949, p. 106).

The blood of the prey and menstrual blood therefore represented conceptual oppositions that were bound up with the opposites in space, the two opposing doorways. The goddess of the hunt and the goddess who presided over menstruation were opposed on separate sides of the *kåhte*, as death was opposed to life and ritual purity was opposed to ritual impurity. The two worlds could not be mixed – women who stray into male ritual space 'must expect many misfortunes to befall them, perhaps even death itself' (Scheffer 1971, p. 40). Before a hunter could return to his own *kåhte* after a kill, he had to remain three nights apart from his wife (Regnard 1808, p. 194, Scheffer 1971, p. 96, Thomson 1796, p. 461) and a special cleansing ceremony had to be performed upon his return, involving the juice of alder bark – a substance which might be said to mediate between life and death, between the blood of the hunt and that of menstruation. It was with alder

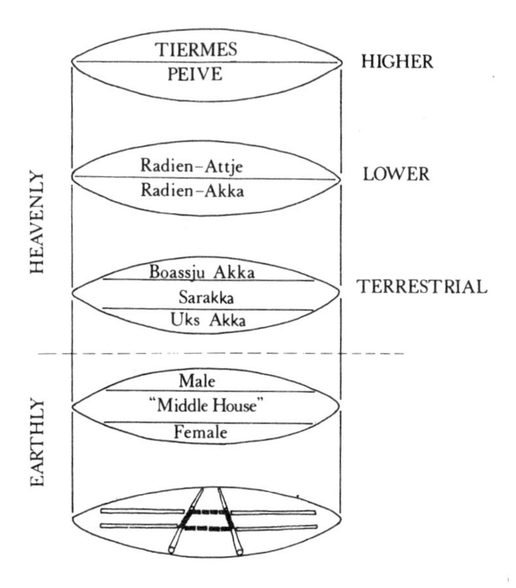

Figure 20.4 The mutuality of ritual and social maps of the *kåhte*.

bark juice that the young were baptized (Leem 1808, p. 483), the *rite-de-passage* between this world and the other.

The meaning of the social division of space can thus be regarded as a transformation of the ritual divisions of the heavens (Fig. 20.4). The *uksa*, the main doorway through which women could pass, was juxtaposed with the *påssjo*, the back door through which they could not, as menstrual blood and ritual impurity were opposed to the pure blood of the hunt and the sacrifice. At the back dwelt death, the place of *Tiermes* and *Radien-Attje*, the ruling father who received the souls of the dead. Here was kept the magic drum of the *noide*, the shaman, with which he was able to enter the world of the dead to recover the 'lost souls' of the sick. At the front dwelt *Peive* and *Radien-Akka*, the ruling mother who presided over the prosperity of the household. Over the *uksa* were placed offerings to *Peive*, the god of fertility in the land (Collinder 1949, p. 144), and the goddess of menstruation resided under that door.

The *kåhte* thus consisted of two opposed worlds – that of life and that of death. Thus, Turi records that a corpse could not be taken through the *uksa*, but had to be passed underneath the tent cloth, 'and that is a sign that the living and the dead shall not tread the same trail' (Turi 1931, p. 90). The products of the two worlds, flesh and milk, had to pass through separate doorways, outside which were carried out the separate activities by which they were produced – slaughter at the back, milking in the *sjaljo* at the front. The two worlds met in the hearth, where the passage between the living and the dead was mediated within the terrestrial realm by *Sarakka*. The area to either side of the hearth, *kaske-kåhte* or the 'middle-house' (Ränk 1949, p. 111), was the transitional zone, where male and female met in neutral space, the liminal area belonging to both worlds.

Hunting and the cooking of (some species of) prey were activities reserved for men (Leem 1808, p. 399, Regnard 1808, p. 186, Thomson 1796, p. 466). In the past there were minute precepts as to which part of the prey could or could not be eaten by women – the hind-parts and the head meat were forbidden, the head and neck being eaten by the men as part of the ritual (Scheffer 1971, p. 44). It was only the fore-parts that women could eat, and they had to be cooked separately from that of the men (Collinder 1949, p. 160, Leem 1808, p. 485, Regnard 1808, p. 194, Scheffer 1971, p. 96). Only men were allowed to handle meat and fish, and women were permitted to prepare only milk and its products (Ränk 1949, p. 111). Men were responsible for the butchering of the reindeer (Linnë 1971, p. 50, Whitaker 1955, p. 85), which was always carried out on the *påssjo* side of the tent (Scheffer 1971, p. 38, Turi 1931, p. 69). Behind the tent was also the place of sacrifice to both *Tiermes* and *Peive* (Collinder 1949, p. 143, Scheffer 1971, pp. 38, 44). Milking was the task of the women (Leem 1808, p. 405, Regnard 1808, p. 186, Whitaker 1955, pp. 77, 85), carried out in front of the *kåhte* in the *sjaljo*, or 'milking place' (Beach 1981, p. 88). This opposition of milking–front and slaughter–back can be linked to the further associations of the *kåhte* space – south–north, summer–winter and front–back. Milking was carried out during the period from late spring to early autumn, and rarely in the winter, which was the main slaughter period (Beach 1981, pp. 84–93). The main period of sacrifices was the late autumn (Acerbi 1802, p. 304, Scheffer 1971, p. 43).

The opposition of male and female thus finds itself repeated in several different concepts, transposed through the same basic series of oppositions which can be seen to structure all aspects of Saami life:

male–female
sacred–profane
clean–unclean
death–life
back–front
hunting–milking
hunting blood–menstrual blood
north–south
winter–summer

Figure 20.5 represents the principal conceptual and spatial oppositions within the *kåhte*. The male world was forbidden to women, whereas men were permitted to pass through the women's world.

All material items followed these oppositions. Women had to keep their objects, such as footwear and clothing, in their area of the *kåhte*, the *uksen-bele*, and men kept their hunting and fishing equipment within the *påssjo*. Many of these positions were very precise – Linne (1971, p. 15) records that 'behind the first reindeer skin is the place of the harness' – that is, within the woman's area, and she was responsible for the draught reindeer.

Personal belongings were imbued with the gender of their owner, and simultaneously with the conceptual schemes associated with it. Thus, women's items were spiritually unclean – during ritual, 'it was subjoined that they [men]

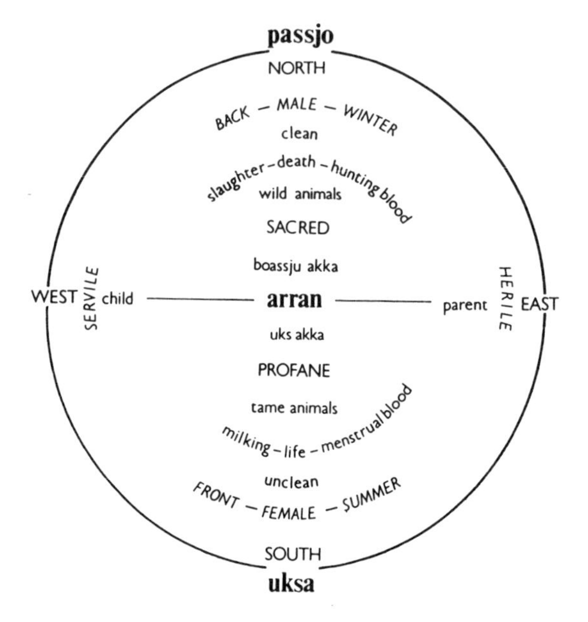

Figure 20.5 The principal oppositions of the *kåhte*.

should not wear the shoes that were made up together with the woman's' (Leem 1808, p. 468). Moreover, they were regarded as a danger to men – when ill, a man was not allowed to sleep with his wife or touch her belongings, nor she his (*ibid*, p. 483). Space, material items, the division of labour and ritual were thus all part of the same structure which appear to be transformations and elaborations of a basic scheme based on gender differentiation. The structure of the heavens as conceived in Saami religion was a definite metaphor for the relationships between men and women on the terrestrial plane, and a justification or *legitimation* for them. Both schemes thus focus upon the *kåhte*. Household space can thus be argued to be the locus for the gender ideology, created and controlled on the behalf of men, that pervades all aspects of Saami life.

One further point can be advanced. The architectural attributes of the *kåhte* also have a role to play in this process of structuration. Hansegård (1978, p. 118) notes that when the Jukkasjarvi Saami became sedentary, the social divisions of the *kåhte* were never applied in roofed dwellings with wooden floors, although the names for general parts, such as the walls and ceiling, were continuous. This is partly to be explained by the different spatial context, but Ränk (1949, pp. 88, 111) has noted that there is a direct relationship between the fundamental divisions of the *kåhte* and the positions of the poles that support the tent. The vertical divisions, *uksa–arran–påssjo*, are directly reflected in the construction of the *paellje*, the four bow-poles that constitute the frame. The secondary beams, *påssjo-cagge* and *uksa-cagge* similarly reflect the lateral divisions of the *kåhte*, *påssjo-* and *uksen-gaecce* (Fig. 20.6).

The architectural structure of the *kåhte* therefore serves as a further structuring

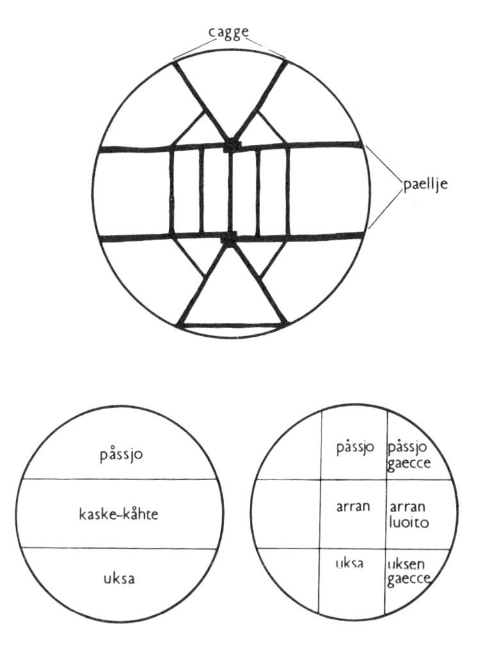

Figure 20.6 The relationship between architecture and social space.

device in the definition of concepts in space and in the mind. This emphasizes the need to understand space as a three-dimensional entity – as a structured totality created through the constitution of boundaries through the mental and the material.

Opposition and mediation: a model for the habitus of Saami domestic space, *ca.* 1700–1900

> In the majority of cultural cases . . . the differences between men and women are conceptualised in terms of sets of metaphorically associated binary oppositions.
>
> (Ortner & Whitehead 1981, p. 7)

Mediation is the process of the naturalization of structural oppositions, and the contradictions that these necessarily involve. Gender relations, created through structural practice, are legitimated and thus reproduced through a transposable system of structures which act together metaphorically. In this sense it is possible to speak of a structural totality, called here the domestic habitus.

The critical concept within this is *praxis*, which 'mediates between consciousness and activity' (Tilley 1982, p. 32). It is the dialectical constitution of structural meaning and practice. The totality of structures, the domestic habitus, is a particular orientation of *praxis* in which structural practices are related to each other in terms of metaphorical association. Totality does not stand in opposition to other structuring principles, therefore, but as a contextual system of interdependence or relevance within the wider cultural habitus.

Practices (the production and reproduction of structures through action) cannot but be embodied under temporally variable conditions – the killing of a bear, for example, which usually took place in winter (Collinder 1949, p. 156), or sacrifices in the late autumn (Acerbi 1802, p. 304, Scheffer 1971, p. 43). It is the articulation of their meaning within a total series that makes them compatible and interchangeable (Bourdieu 1977, p. 107). This series is defined in relation to ideology – in this case the ideology of gender. Through structured practice, differences between the sexes are asserted within certain structural categories and resolved through the integration of these in a series. This emerges most clearly with blood-categorization. As Testart has argued, blood is of critical importance in hunter–gatherer societies in the creation of gender relations, and is used to structure and legitimate a host of other practices, such as the male domination of (forms of) hunting. Blood is the '*–motif idéologique pertinent*' (Testart 1986, p. 1197).

However, totality is only known to the social actors within practical consciousness, in which the mutuality of diverse practices is possible. The reconstruction of totality is therefore an analytical construct, or 'privilege' (Bourdieu 1977, p. 106). It need not be supposed that all the relevant structures have been identified, and in this sense the series is open-ended. However, totality is intended to refer to a configuration or disposition in the ideological constitution and legitimation of meaning through *praxis*. It is ideology that closes the series and relates structures meaningfully to each other. The essentialism that may seem to underlie the presentation of meaning here is not inherent within structures, but is the product of their ideological context. Domestic structures produce gender relations, but are not themselves reducible to those relations alone.

It follows from this that it should not be assumed that structures relate to only one scheme. Strathern (1981) has shown that among the Hagen of Papua New Guinea the categories that structure gender relations also simultaneously order relations among men and among women. We should thus not exclude the possibility that the same set of oppositions structure several different ideological schemes. Domestic totality is a situational orientation through ideology of structures within the cultural habitus, towards a specific context of social relations, made possible by the location of temporally diverse structural practices within a simultaneous space – the tent.

Conclusions

This chapter has explored the system of oppositions that structure the domestic context of the Saami cultural habitus, through an analysis of the major texts of the period 1700–1900. At this level of analysis it has been necessary to stress the similarities, rather than the differences, within what is a complex context. The result is therefore a composite picture of Saami domestic space.

Acknowledgements

I am grateful to Ian Hodder, Knut Odner, Bjørnar Olsen and Chris Tilley for reading and commenting upon earlier drafts of this paper.

References

Acerbi, J. 1802. *Travels through Norway, Sweden and Lapland, to the North Cape, in the years 1798 and 1799*, 2 Vols. London: Joseph Mawman.

Beach, H. 1981. Reindeer herd management in transition: the case of Tuorpon Saameby in northern Sweden. *Uppsala Studies in Cultural Anthropology*, **3**.

Bourdieu, P. 1977. *Outline of a theory of practice.* Cambridge Studies in Social Anthropology, 16. Cambridge: Cambridge University Press.

Buch, L. Von 1813. *Travels through Norway during the years 1806, 1807 and 1808*, transl. from the German by J. Black. London: Henry Colburn.

Collinder, B. 1949. *The Lapps.* New York: American Scandinavian Foundation.

Erixon, S. 1937. Some primitive constructions and types of layout, with their relation to European rural building practice. *Folkliv* **2**, 124–55.

Fjellström, P. 1985. *Samernas Samhalle: I Tradition och Nutid.* Umeå, Sweden.

Giddens, A. 1982. *Profiles and critiques in social theory.* London: Macmillan.

Hansegard, N.E. 1978. The transition of the Jukkasjarvi Lapps from nomadism to settled life and farming. *Studia Ethnographica Upsaliensia* **39.**

Leem, K. 1808. An account of the Laplanders of Finnmark, their language, manners and customs. (1767) In *A general collection of the best and most interesting voyages and travels in all parts of the world*, 17 Vols, J. Pinkerton (ed.). Vol. 1, 376–490. London: Longman.

Linnë, C. 1971. *A tour in Lapland* (1811) (transl. R.M. Goldwyn). New York: Arno Press and The New York Times.

Manker, E. 1962. 'Intellectual culture'. In *Lapp life and customs: a survey* by Ø. Vorren and E. Manker (trans. K. McFarlane) London: Oxford University Press.

Ortner, S.B. & Whitehead, H. 1981. Introduction: accounting for sexual meanings. In *Sexual meanings: the cultural construction of gender and sexuality*, S.B. Ortner & H. Whitehead (eds) 1–27. Cambridge: Cambridge University Press.

Pehrson, R. 1957. *The bilateral network of social relations in Könkämä Lapp District*. Publication 3, Bloomington: Indiana Research Centre in Anthropology, Folklore and Linguistics.

Ränk, G. 1949. Grundprinciper för disponeringen av utrymmet i de Lapska kåtorna och gammerna. *Folkliv* **12–13**, 87–111.

Regnard, M. 1808. A journey through Flanders, Holland, etc (1801). In *A general collection of the best and most interesting voyages and travels in all parts of the world*, 17 Vols, J. Pinkerton (ed.). Vol. 1, 131–230. London: Longman.

Scheffer, J. 1971. *The history of Lapland, wherein are shewed the original, manners, habits, marriages, conjurations, etc, of that people* (1704). Facsimile edn. (transl. G. Ahlström). Stockholm: Rediviva.

Strathern, M. 1981. Self-interest and the social good: some implications of Hagen gender imagery. In *Sexual meanings: the cultural construction of gender and sexuality*, S.B. Ortner & H. Whitehead (eds.), 166–91. Cambridge: Cambridge University Press.

Testart, A. 1986. La femme et la chasse. *La Recherche* **181**, 1194–201.
Thomson, W. 1796. *Letters from Scandinavia on the present and past state of the northern nations of Europe*, 2 Vols. London: G.G. & J. Robinson.
Tilley, C. 1982. Social formation, social structures and social change. In *Symbolic and structural archaeology*, I. Hodder (ed.), 26–38. Cambridge: Cambridge University Press.
Turi, J. 1931. *Turi's book of Lapland* (*Muittalus Samid Birra*) (transl. E. Gee Nash). London: Jonathan Cape.
Vorren, Ø. 1962. Material culture. In *Lapp life and customs: a survey*, by Ø. Vorren & E. Manker (transl. K. McFarlane). London: Oxford University Press.
Whitaker, I. 1955. *The social relations in a nomadic Lappish community*, Vol. 2. Oslo: Samiske Samlinger.

Index